21ˢᵗ Century Leisure: Current Issues

Second Edition

21st Century Leisure: Current Issues
Second Edition

Valeria J. Freysinger
Miami University of Ohio

John R. Kelly
University of Illinois

 Venture Publishing, Inc. • State College, Pennsylvania

Production Manager: Richard Yocum
Manuscript Editing: Michele L. Barbin, Valerie Fowler
Cover by Echelon Design

Library of Congress Catalogue Card Number 2004108369
ISBN 1-892132-53-2

Table of Contents

Part IV
Forms of Leisure

Preface

The study of leisure has gone through two generations reflected in textbooks. The first period was one of exploration and affirmation. A variety of sources was employed to develop a rationale or "philosophy" to justify the significance of leisure and recreation. The founders of the field developed their sets of ideas from theories of education, development, and even psychiatry. The focus was almost entirely on public recreation. The second generation replaced such theorizing with a research base from the social and behavioral sciences. A substantial body of knowledge expanded from sociology and economics to social psychology and other disciplines. The texts published in leisure studies were largely based on research informed by mainstream disciplinary approaches. Further, these texts presented the material as agreed-on "facts" rather than as problematic issues. The view of leisure was more inclusive with some attention given to market-sector provisions and resources.

The authors of this book believe the time has come for a third-generation approach. This text reflects on many of the current issues that emerged in contemporary study. In general, the social sciences have moved away from an uncritical consensus to a variety of critical perspectives. There is less agreement on just what is encompassed by the term *leisure*, its separation from other aspects of human life and society, and its meanings and outcomes. Leisure is seen to be constructed from a wide diversity of cultural elements. One example of a central critical perspective is that of gender as differences in power and life conditions—as constraint and opportunity. Other divisions in societies and cultures are brought to bear on understanding leisure resources, opportunities, orientations, and ethics. Again, what was taken for granted as a largely positive factor in human life is now viewed more critically. Several dimensions of this new critical perspective brought to the fore a number of issues previously kept in the background or ignored. This book features the debates around which the study of leisure will be focused as we enter the 21st century. It is, then, the first third-generation text.

Contemporary Issues

The purpose of this book is to engage instructors and students in a common enterprise of exploring and debating contemporary issues. There may be, of course, disagreement as to which are the most significant issues as well as how to approach them. This book introduces a wide spectrum of issues from which some may be selected for primary attention. The mode of instruction should be something other than the presentation and memorization of "facts." Rather, the authors suggest there may be no uncontested facts in the study of leisure… or probably anything else. Education from this perspective involves critical analysis, assessment of evidence, and marshaling arguments. It is always a two-way rather than a one-way presentation. Education is not securing information, but developing the ability to think, analyze, and communicate. These skills, of course, are valuable in any productive enterprise.

In the study of leisure, it is no longer adequate to present material as though there were no differing perspectives, disagreements, and conflicts. Just as society is recognized to have divisions, conflicting interests and vastly different resources, so has leisure. It is not a separate and transcendent realm; it is part of ordinary life. It is day-to-day at least as much as special. It is integrated with the roles, relationships, institutions, and cultures of the society. It is also a construction, reconstruction, and sometimes, a transformation of society. Further, any society is increasingly part of a world in which cultures as well as economies are in complex relationships. The old walls of isolation and segregation are collapsing. The resulting world is one of variety and conflict as much as functional integration. The paramount issues in this world are not resolved. Rather, there is no final authoritative resolution to any of the debates opened in this book. This is not an argument for relativism but for a conscious acknowledgement of the social construction of "facts," "truths," and "reality."

The Debates

The format of this text revolves more around the issues rather than the results of research and theory building. There is, of course, a lot of beliefs about leisure and recreation that are not rendered obsolete by any new perspectives. Such knowledge is a foundation for developing contemporary understanding if such knowledge is reflected on critically. Some of what was formerly taken-for-granted has turned out to be inadequate or even wrong. Current "knowledge" may also prove to be wrong. Further, the world of leisure is changing along with everything else. Nothing is final for Century 21 or any other time period.

This book is an invitation to enter the debates that invade and surround leisure…and life. In critical analysis, constructing arguments, marshaling evidence and organizing presentations, the students will have an opportunity to learn rather than simply to absorb. We believe that learning is an interactive process in which the student must take an active part.

Is this different from an ordinary text? Yes. However, we believe that it is consistent with how people learn best and with developing those skills that will be valuable throughout life. The facts will change. Even the issues will change. Learning, from this perspective, is lifelong. We hope we can make a contribution to that process.

Valeria J. Freysinger, Associate Professor, Miami University, Oxford, Ohio
John R. Kelly, Professor Emeritus, University of Illinois, Champaign, Illinois

Introduction to Teaching Styles

The authors believe teaching styles that actively involve the students in a common enterprise *with* the instructor are both most effective and most enjoyable. It makes the classroom a place for dialogue rather than monologue totally centered on the instructor. Teaching in this way is not always easy or comfortable. Opening issues up for discussion as opposed to presenting them as uncontested facts means the direction of the discussion and the emotional engagement of the participants is less controlled or predictable. In asking students to debate an issue, instructors and students have to be ready to hear things they disagree with as well as things they find agreeable. They also have to be prepared for confusion, anger, defensiveness, excitement, uncertainty, and passion. The issues, and many of the debates, presented in this book will center both instructors' and students' values instead of asking them to leave these issues outside the classroom door. For example

- What is the good society?

- Who is advantaged and who disadvantaged by the existing order of things and by changing the order?

- What is the "nature" of human beings?

- Whose voices are and are not heard?

- Why should we care about access to leisure?

These debates are often disturbing to individuals, because while we all like to think of ourselves as "good people," where we stand on these issues may start to make us feel otherwise. Instructors and students bring various biases into the classroom and discussions—based on religious beliefs, upbringing, ignorance, past experiences—that shape perspectives and constrain their willingness to consider alternative points of view.

However, it is precisely because of the uncertain or controversial nature of the material that teaching about leisure in this format can be invigorating (as well as draining). Most students can "connect" to at least one of the issues presented in this book. This is because most of these issues are contemporary—examples can be found on the nightly news, in newspapers, on MTV, in *Time* and *Newsweek*, and in popular music. Hence, it is useful to supplement the introductory information presented in this book with materials from the media as well as research journals and other scholarly texts. Suggestions for additional references are provided at the end of each chapter. However, current material can be found in television specials, periodicals, and newspapers. Students should be encouraged to identify and bring in such materials through various assignments. For example, "media reports" which require each student to bring a recent newspaper or magazine article or television news clip to class and make a five-minute report on it in relation to class material facilitate application of course information to the "real world"—and it encourages students to read a newspaper and stay up with the news!

The Debate Format

Each chapter in this book contains at least one debate. The style is simple and based on classic debate format. A statement, intended to be clear and unambiguous, is offered. An introductory list of arguments, both for and against the statement, are presented to initiate thinking about the issue. Some arguments are supported by strong evidence; some are not. These arguments are to be analyzed critically, not read off as some kind of final statements of support or opposition. That is, students should find further evidence in support or refutation of each of the arguments. The hope (and experience) of the authors is the arguments will be used to inaugurate debate on the issues inside and outside of class.

The debates presented are not all the possible debates on each chapter subject. Other critical questions are raised in the text that merit analysis and argument. A class that gets engaged with the spirit of the book will tend to debate almost everything. We believe that is central to learning. It is also imperative that the instructor be prepared to push students on their thinking—encouraging them to develop their arguments and analyze the direction their thinking is taking them and asking them to be clear about what is "informed opinion" and what is "their opinion." Other students will need support when openly disagreeing or "arguing" with the instructor or classmates if they are not comfortable or the topic considered appropriate.

How Can the Debates Be Used in the Classroom?

The simplest format, useful in smaller classes, is just to present the debate statement, discuss questions of clarification, and allow each student to select a side and defend it in an open discussion—either with others or independently. It can be interesting to find out how many students change sides during the discussion.

In larger classes, the instructor may want to organize some of the debates more formally. That is, the instructor may form two teams based on the students' preferences, require students to research the debate topic ahead of time and find additional sources of evidence for their position, write a paper clearly articulating their position, and present it in teams (i.e., pro and con with opportunity for rebuttal) in class. The other students can be asked to evaluate the debate from a variety of standpoints. They can select a "winner" based on the quality or effectiveness of the debate itself. Or, they can respond as people who are affected by the debate's focus. Students can also be asked to serve as moderators or the instructor can play this role. More informally, students can just choose sides, present their arguments, and evaluate the evidence based on the information presented in the book.

In deciding which approach to use, factors such as the size of the class, preparation of the students, and the "personality" of the class are important. Again, several possible formats are possible:

- A schedule of debates for the term may be established. Students then sign up for the "Yes" or "No" side for one or more of the debates. Students can work individually or as a team. If as a team, a coordinator should be responsible for scheduling meetings to formulate arguments and to gather evidence. Each team presents their side of the debate to at least initiate class discussion. They should search for material and evidence outside the text. When working individually, students each would have five minutes to present their positions. If working as a team, each side should have 10–15 minutes to present their case, first Yes and then No, and five minutes for each team to offer a rebuttal. Questions and comments can then be received from the class. Or, when the teams have finished their presentations, the class can vote on the outcome, critique the arguments, and continue the discussion.

- For some of the debates students can be assigned roles to play. For example, in a debate on changing schools to be more fun (Chapter 9), the "audience" can each be assigned roles—teacher, school board member, taxpayer, parent, high school student—and asked for their reactions to the debate based on their assigned "identities." At the end, the instructor may want to reserve some time for comments and additions. The class as a whole may be asked to vote on a grade for each team.

- Written work for the class can be the formulation of an argument on a debate statement that includes evidence and materials from other sources and a reformulation of the introductory arguments in the text. A further step would be for students to critique their own arguments or reflect on who is advantaged and who is disadvantaged by both the Yes and No positions.

- Test material could involve a presentation of the strongest arguments on each side of one of the debates rather than a "right-and-wrong" set of questions and answers. Such an examination

procedure is a sampling process rather than an attempt to be comprehensive. Again, the stress is on critical thinking and clear written
presentation—skills that are useful throughout life.

There are many resources for the students. Some books and journal
references are presented in the text. There are also some other resources
suggested. Television specials that are oriented toward issues can also be taped
and used in class (e.g., *Frontline*, *60 Minutes*, *Dateline*, and PBS specials
often address many of the topics in this text). Students themselves are wonderful sources of relevant popular culture—music, videos, television programs,
commercials and advertisements—and should be asked for their ideas. Again,
any of these sources should be selected for how they raise issues, however
controversial, rather than as final statements of what is right. No authority should
be above criticism, including the authors of this text.

Part I

Introduction

Chapter 1

21st Century Leisure

What is leisure? There are many approaches to defining leisure as will be outlined in Chapter 2. Many languages, such as German, Spanish, and Japanese, have no equivalent term. Most languages have some concept of "free time." Many have a word that connotes laziness or doing nothing. In North America we don't use the word a lot. When we do, we usually mean something like this: "Leisure is what we do for fun." A slightly more sophisticated version would be that leisure is activity we do primarily for the experience. And that may be enough—at least for a beginning.

After all, we are also not that precise about most other terms that are basic to human life. What is work? It is more than the employment for which we are paid. Work includes such unpaid activity as caring for and nurturing children, providing for the maintenance of a household, preparing ourselves for economic roles through study, and all sorts of activity that supports life and community. What is love? We mean so much and so many things by the term that a clear definition would seem impossible.

However, while one perspective on leisure is that it is "activity that is primarily for the experience itself," another is that leisure is "legitimated pleasure" or where we learn and are allowed to find enjoyment, fun, or pleasure. These two very different and conflicting notions of leisure characterize a tension that exists in the study of leisure and recreation today. Is leisure freedom of the individual or is it also what the individual is "allowed" to do? This tension between leisure as freedom and opportunity and leisure as constraint and control frames many of the discussions in this book. The conclusion you reach may be that leisure is *both*.

The Variety of Leisure

One thing that is clear about leisure is that it is incredibly varied:

What is done as leisure? Leisure may be a challenging and exciting game of skill such as basketball. It may also be dreamlike contemplation alone alongside a stream. It may be intense physical exertion or relaxed day-dreaming. It may involve significant interaction with the people most important to us or it may be solitary. It may be carefully organized or quite spontaneous. It may be almost anything.

Studies in several North American and European communities have found most people list the following as ordinary activities: informal conversation in person and on the telephone, watching television, walking and talking with friends and family, playing with children, intimate affection, shopping, and reading. Less common activities include: sports and hobbies, gardening, electronic communications and games, entertaining, eating out, watching videos and movies, and outdoor activities. But that is only the beginning. For leisure, relatively small numbers of people climb cliffs, train horses, soar and fly light planes, engage in martial arts and yoga, find and polish rocks, collect tea cups and guns, and even round up rattlesnakes. They gamble, drink, do drugs, and buy sex. In fact, almost anything could be leisure for someone living down the street or across town.

When is leisure? There are the designated times, such as vacations and weekends for those with traditional work schedules. Yet there are also the moments found in the midst of daily life. There is the joking conversation in the hall on the way to class. There is the moment of lightness in the midst of serious planning and even in the math class. We are not on task all the time. The mind wanders far from the work task. The coffeemaker provides an excuse for meeting, kidding, and even flirting in the office. In fact, it may be that some playful behavior, even silliness, is needed to get us through the day. Some would even argue that breaks add to productivity. Some leisure is set apart and scheduled, but some just happens.

Where is leisure? Again, almost anywhere. The gym may be deadly serious and the office full of play. Even factory workers have been found to play with their machines. Perhaps most leisure takes place at home, especially with television and electronic entertainment centers. Some is at special destinations such as Disney World and Las Vegas. Some occur in special environments of forest, mountain, and shore. More is in the ordinary places where we spend most of our lives.

The Variety of People

Activity, time, and place are only the beginning of the variety. There is also a variety of people.

Economic status makes a difference. The wealthy travel further and more often, flying to Aspen for a weekend of skiing (and shopping) and to London for a pair of plays. They purchase privacy in exclusive country clubs, high-priced restaurants, and upscale resorts, They value time more than money and may even equate quality with price. The poor, on the other hand, facing the challenges of meeting the basic necessities of life, do what is free, inexpensive, and available. In between the wealthy and the poor are the middle mass, watching television, eating fast food, and planning a once-a-year trip on a budget. The contrasts are clear.

Cultures differ as well. There is the high culture of the educated, the pop culture of the masses, and the special cultures of youth. There are the cultural traditions of ethnic and racial identity. The cultural traditions brought by those enslaved as well as immigrants may persist for generations. Food, entertainment, family roles, religions, and practices vary. In one California town there are fourth generation Anglos, first generation Latinos, eighth generation Mexican Americans, first generation Cambodians, and fourth generation Japanese Americans. They have different games, customs, symbols, resources, and traditions.

Gender remains significant. This culture still has rather different expectations for women and men as for little girls and boys. Even when the same activities are encouraged, gender differentiates styles of behavior. As will be discussed in Chapter 13, women may even be defined as ornaments for the leisure of men, as demonstrated in almost every televised athletic contest.

Skill differentiates other activities. Most adults experience sport only as entertainment. A minority focus on the development and exercise of skill. Some find excitement and involvement in doing activities while others are entertained by watching. There is even Las Vegas "sport" which promises excitement without skill.

People are unique in their leisure as well as in the rest of their lives. Some are relatively conventional and even predictable; others combine themes and activities in their own ways. The point, however, is clear. Leisure is varied in terms of the human actors who both develop and are given their leisure and their conditions, as well as in the things they do.

The Scope of Leisure

At first glance, leisure may seem relatively unimportant and secondary in comparison to work, family, or education. There seems to be a cultural bias against the significance of play. Without going into detail, a few counterarguments may alter the perspective. First, as already introduced, leisure is much more than a few set-apart activities done in leftover time.

Second, there is the economic scope of leisure. As will be detailed in Chapters 11 and 23, leisure is a major and growing segment of modern economies. Wander through your local discount store and count how many products are leisure-based. Electronics, sports equipment and apparel, toys, shoes and shirts, and even leisure chairs are only the beginning. Wall Street firms and Sunday newspapers have leisure departments. Tourism is growing rapidly. Estimates vary by what is included, but $300 billion a year is a conservative estimate of the leisure segment of the American economy.

Third, there are the resources designated for leisure and recreation. The federal government alone manages at least 400 million acres for recreation and combined uses. Local governments preserve and develop extremely valuable land for parks and recreation. States hold scarce lake, river, and seashores. The market sector now far exceeds public programs in building and operating indoor facilities for sport, cultural, and fitness activity.

Fourth, there is time. The old designation of the labor movement was eight hours for work, eight hours for rest, and eight hours "for what we will." That may be oversimplified, but suggests the potential scope of time that may be allocated to leisure. Nor does this include days without employment, often weekends, vacations for some of two weeks to over a month, and the lengthening years of retirement.

Fifth, there is the personal significance of leisure. This theme will be developed throughout the book. At this point, let it suffice to suggest that teens tend to center their lives and much that is most important to them in their leisure, many adults work primarily for the income that supports the rest of life, and much of the development of our most important relationships takes place in leisure. Many people define themselves more by their leisure than their work as they seem to identify with their favorite television show, fishing skill, summer softball team, music, church office, craftwork or motorcycle.

What seems clear is that leisure is a major part of life on every level. It is significant to the day-to-day living of young and old, to families and friendships, to the economy, and even to the expression and preservation of cultures. This is just a beginning in exploring leisure in our lives.

The First Issue: Social Change

One aim of this book is to look not only at the past and the present but also to the future. We live in a society that is changing in almost every way.

Amidst this change, leisure has undergone considerable transformation and will change more in the future. Leisure, like life, in the 21st century will not escape the impacts of social change. First, then, we need to summarize some central elements of that change. What is clear in the beginning, however, is that the world in which today's students live out their life journeys will not be the same as that of their parents.

Longer-Term Social Change

1. **Urbanization:** In the 1800s, the United States was beginning to change from a rural and agricultural society to an industrial and urban society. The Civil War was won by the industrial power of the North. The factory brought together a work force with raw materials where the rivers, seaports, and railroads met. Since World War II, the "metropolitan sprawl" has spread out along the rails and highways to form linked towns and incremental suburban development. Not only manufacturing but also finance, culture, and recreation, are found in the megalopolis. Now there is a decentering of the city into the malls and strips of retailing and entertainment dependent on private transportation.

2. **World economic integration:** A visit to any discounter demonstrates the global nature of economic activity. Ordinary goods are manufactured almost anywhere in the world, especially where labor costs are low. What is an "American" car when parts are shipped from Europe and the Pacific Rim to be assembled in Mexico or Canada? Almost all major corporations are global in finance as well as production and distribution. American movies dominate the theaters of every country with the international market counted on for cost recovery and profits. Even agriculture depends on markets in Europe, Asia, and Africa. In turn, the supermarket produce department features fresh fruit and vegetables from the southern hemisphere in the dead of winter, and Midwest factories close when labor-intensive manufacturing is moved to Latin or Asian countries.

3. **Racial identification:** In the United States, the long taken-for-granted forces of segregation and discrimination began to be shattered in the 1960s. Civil rights, however, have been only the beginning of change that has penetrated every institution of the society. People of color insist on defining their own identities and lives. Ethnic and racial diversity also means a self-identification with accompanying assertion of rights of recognition, opportunity, and justice in every

aspect of life. This long-term process is coupled with a world perspective that recognizes the numerical minority status of those who are "White" despite their disproportionate control of power and resources.

4. **Gender:** The women's movement in North America and Europe dates back to the 19th century. The limitations placed on women's political and economic participation have fallen at an increasing rate although real and subtle barriers persist. The focus on women with an insistence on a full set of opportunities for social and personal development is now central to changes in every social institution.

5. **Geographical expansion:** A century ago, most people never left their communities or regions except in time of war or in response to opening frontiers. Now the jet airplane, interstate highways combined with comfortable and reliable cars, and the development of a massive travel industry have widened the horizons of those of middle and higher incomes. At the same time, the media, especially television, have brought an awareness of the larger world into every home. Globalization is more than an economic development; it is also cultural and social.

6. **Sexual "revolution:"** Beginning in the 1890s, sexual customs and behaviors began to change drastically. Aided by contraceptive technologies, the norms of sexual behavior have changed on every level of modern society. Today's parental generation accepts behavior in their children that would have been a social disgrace only a few decades ago. No social change has been as pervasive as the general acceptance of sexuality in a variety of forms and practices.

7. **Family:** Family size on average has decreased so that now many families have fewer children in a shorter period of time. One consequence is that more of adult life is "nonparental" in the sense of having no children living with their parents, despite the increased though still small number of "adult children" returning home to live with parents due to unemployment, divorce, or other life changes. With 50–60% of mothers of preschool and school-age children now in the paid work force, entire new patterns of childrearing are being attempted. Divorce rates seem to have leveled off at about 50%, but most children will experience some such disruption in parenting.

8. **Education:** Rates of high school and college completion have been rising for decades although there are still large differences

among economic and racial groups in education. The result is that the required educational credentials for entry into most occupations have escalated. At the same time, the cultural background of each generation tends to be greater than the one before.

These and other changes have been under way for long periods, some since World War II and others for over two centuries. Some are so gradual that they pass almost unnoticed, yet they affect every life in their continued impacts on the social and economic contexts in which we work out our lives. At the same time, a number of more current changes will make a difference in how we live in the next century. Among them are the following:

Current Social Change

1. **The "postindustrial" economy:** Any economy has to produce some goods and services that command markets somewhere in the world economy. No economy is postindustrial and no longer needs to produce steel, plastics, chemicals, medicines, and even cars and airplanes. Nevertheless, almost all the job increases in the last two decades in North America have been in the "service" sector. Retailing, human services, healthcare, hospitality, entertainment, and even recreation have produced almost all the new jobs in North America. There have been shifts in production, new products, and many product-oriented small businesses; however, more and more employment has come to mean direct or indirect service of some clientele. It may be in hotels or nursing homes, in the mega-mall or the resort boutique, but the service economy is growing. Among the implications are the large number of entry-level, direct-service jobs, seven-day-a-week and 24-hour-day varied work schedules, and an increase in jobs designated for women.

2. **Communications:** As late as the 1950s, households in some rural areas were just being connected with telephones. Now the telephone connects households with electronic communications in a worldwide network. The information age is rapidly making communications faster, cheaper, wider, and more pervasive. Hookups to fiberoptic cable systems that transmit and receive are being challenged by satellite dishes and other wireless networks. There may be an information overload and a proliferation of choices, but the rate of change seems to be escalating—from radio and telephone to television and video recorders and now cable, computers, wireless, fiberoptics, and

satellites. The scope and immediacy of communications may be on the edge of even more dramatic change.

3. **Capitalism:** The global economy no longer is divided between market and planned economies. The market system, often in partially regulated forms, has encompassed the world economy although not without resistance. There are central and peripheral national economies, concentrations of power and investment capital, and great inequalities of resources and opportunities both within and among nations. Nevertheless, despite concerns about the problems of moving overnight from a planned to a market system, there seems to be no alternative to participation in global capitalism with its costs and benefits. Problems of great disparities in resources remain in distribution of income and opportunities and in conditions of work. There is a clear dominance of a few nations with most of the investment capital, technological competence, and military might. Nevertheless, despite some pockets of backlash and many distortions, the market system has become dominant with no viable alternatives in sight.

4. **Conflict:** Despite such global communications and increasing integration, there remain conflicts on many levels. Some are localized in particular cities and regions as between inner cities and suburbs. Some are racial, ethnic, or religious. Some have long histories, and some are current and contemporary. Nevertheless, the end of the Cold War did not end conflict. In fact, increasing political freedom and communication links can lead to a renewed awareness of differing interests and conflicts held in check by now defunct authorities. Some recognition of such conflict may lead to greater freedom and autonomy in the long run for formerly oppressed people. In the short term, however, such conflict is destructive for both individuals and their communities. It may even be an instrument of economic power.

5. **Leisure:** Amid such change, leisure is changing as well. The issue is whether such change is gradual and evolutionary or dramatic and fundamental. Looking back, it is clear the automobile and television radically changed leisure patterns. It may be less clear that such technological impacts are now under way. Nor are the impacts of societal changes on leisure as clear, especially if leisure is largely a private matter. That is the issue for debate in the remainder of this chapter. The format will summarize arguments on both sides of the question for use and consideration as suggested in the Preface to the book.

Debate: Leisure in the 21ˢᵗ century will be new and different.

YES

A number of arguments support the idea that leisure will be quite different in the future rather than largely "more of the same." Of course, the question is embedded in a larger question of social change. Leisure produces and reproduces its social and economic contexts. How will the 21ˢᵗ century be really different from the 20ᵗʰ? Will the changes of the past hundred years be only the prelude for even more rapid and drastic change in the future?

- **New technologies:** The geography of leisure was radically changed by the automobile and to a lesser extent by commercial airlines. Time use, especially in the home, was transformed by television (see Chapter 16). Is it likely that new electronic developments will bring about the same kind of change in leisure? As home computers become more common and the software for communications, information and games proliferates, will leisure styles become more focused on communications? Those now in school will take the computer for granted and erase much of the fear of older generations. Also, in-home electronic entertainment centers will offer an incredible range of entertainment through fiberoptic and satellite technologies. Large-screen, surround sound, digital high-resolution pictures, DVDs, interactive systems with on-demand sports, movies, and other programs on a fee basis, and increasingly diverse offerings on the World Wide Web make the home an all-purpose work, play, and education center. Will such technologies only increase the programmatic offerings to fit into current lifestyles, or will they transform current patterns? And what of other technologies related to travel, communications, and new forms of games and entertainment? Will ordinary television and DVDs look as quaint as Big Band concerts and the Model T in a decade or two?

- **Market expansion:** Chapter 23 will suggest how the market sector of the economy is expanding more into leisure. New technological developments expand markets for products, services, and activities themselves. Examine the yellow pages for examples of leisure-based businesses that did not exist a decade ago. Will the expansion increase? Does supply create demand? There is little doubt there are more local leisure-based businesses. At the same time, more destinations are developed that promote themselves as centers of fun. Orlando and Las Vegas compete with domestic and international destinations. On television, from soap operas to sitcoms, life is centered around glamorous travel, eating out at expensive restaurants, and going to a variety of shows. The images of the "good life" are those of leisure that are cost-intensive and promise an enhanced social and sexual status for those willing and able to be extravagant leisure consumers.

• **Consumption values:** Advertising features glamour, excitement, and pleasure. Is there a new "leisure ethic" emerging that no longer requires that leisure be positive and productive? Is consumption presumed to be pleasure enough of a rationale for leisure spending? With gambling legalized in most states, sexually explicit entertainment found in most communities, and leisure symbols displayed everywhere, leisure consumption patterns seem to signal a new acceptance of leisure as self-justifying and of mass entertainment as leisure. Leisure is at least an OK reward for less-than-stimulating work. Leisure consumption seems more central to value systems as measured by how so many spend their money and their time.

• **Individual and developmental values:** Along with consumption values, leisure seems less tied to other people. Leisure is identified with the self. More than just pleasure, leisure is the primary social space for the development of the self. Both the body and the spirit become foci of leisure investments. In the past, for example, women were expected to make their leisure, if any, revolve around their family roles. They often were encouraged to feel guilty if they devoted time or money to anything that was just for themselves. Now the reverse is true. Women are encouraged to have time, space, and activities of their own. There is a general cultural acceptance of orientations toward the self: self-expression and self-development. Perhaps as those who have always been expected to put others first finally begin to engage in such leisure, there are concerns that such a focus on the self is not good—it is self-absorption. Still, the self is "in" in leisure for both men and women—even if it is not equally accessible.

• **A "leisure society:"** As we will see, former predictions of vastly increased time for leisure have not proven accurate. In a more profound way, however, society may become more leisure-centered rather than work-centered. One aspect is changes in work. As will be discussed in Chapter 11, work careers are becoming more variable and uncertain, work timetables more diverse and changing in the service sector, and work commitments weakened by continual layoffs and "downsizing." What will take the place of work as a central commitment? For some, may leisure not be the reward for work? The signs are everywhere. People wear leisure gear around town rather than work outfits. They make friends in recreation more than at work. They organize their children's after-school and summer lives around recreation programs. They use their credit cards to take trips they can't afford and buy toys that symbolize a life that is more than survival. If work becomes more instrumental and inconsistent, will leisure become the center of who we are and of our social identities? If so, this would be a change more profound than can be produced by any technology.

NO

The argument against radical change in leisure takes quite a different perspective. It begins by suggesting the previous "pro" points operate on the periphery of real leisure as people live it day to day. After all, fewer than 5% go to Las Vegas even yearly, most never can afford much international travel, and a lot of the new leisure toys are soon stuffed in the back of closets. People don't change just because there is all that stuff out there. Further, there is the cost factor. Many of the new technologies are prohibitively expensive for most people. Old-fashioned television sets have gone down in price, but the leading-edge technologies are always sold at a premium.

- **The household base of leisure:** Most consumer leisure items are designed to get people out of the house and into more expensive locales and activities. The truth, however, is that measured by time, most leisure is in and around the home. That seems unlikely to change. Teens want to get out of the home, but things change when they move into their own residences. They have protection and privacy. Further, presumably they are living with others whom they have chosen as companions. A lot of leisure is just interacting with those co-residents, whether there is a committed relationship or not. At some times, the residence offers privacy and an opportunity for rest and relaxation. All the glitz and glamour out there may not be attractive as an everyday opportunity. The home is inexpensive with almost-free television, conversation, reading, and just goofing off. For those rearing children, the home and family are the center of leisure. That seems unlikely to change just because of marketed goods and services.

• **The leisure "core:"** What do people really do in the ordinary days of their lives? Research has demonstrated that there is a core of activities that is central to day-to-day living through most of life. That core includes informal interaction and conversation with co-residents, watching television, often some reading for pleasure, and other home-based activity. Parents play with their children. Many walk, garden, fix up the house, and even do some special cooking. Outside the home, most do some shopping as leisure. These are the informal, accessible, low-cost kinds of activity that children, teens, adults, and the aging continue most of their lives. Teens hang out with their friends and take Walkmans and MP3 players everywhere. There are no indications that this core is changing to any measurable extent. New technologies such as DVDs and high-definition television (HDTV) may increase variety and enhance opportunities, but the basic patterns do not change much. Special events are more market responsive. The core is really what the majority do most of the time they are not on the job, commuting, sleeping, or engaged in maintenance activities. Pretty much everyone wants some undemanding and easy engagement. Most engage in some communication and even affection with family and friends. New technologies and market offerings don't affect this core much.

• **Television:** As will be outlined in Chapter 16, there are variations in the amounts of time devoted to television. And there are some who resist the tube almost entirely. Most, however, watch more than two hours a day and more on weekends. It may be a residual activity of low investment and intensity. But it is there, paid for, and generally somewhat entertaining. Cable and satellites have increased the choices available and given some control over the medium. Other technologies will yield variety, higher quality, more selection, and other changes in the technology. But the patterns of easy access and popular entertainment are unlikely to change people's habits to any great extent. There are fads in programming. There will be promotion of new goods and services. Most will go back to what is easy and available.

• **Lack of change:** There are many social and economic changes of significance going on now. There will be more. Nonetheless, there are many things that are not changing much. Our society still has the wealthy, the poor, and the middle mass. The economy still requires employment to have more than survival economic resources. School is still required of children. Most adults marry and have children, even if the percentage is down 10% or so. Mass entertainment still captures more time than novel and different leisure. Markets for everything are still segmented according to income. Aging still leads toward death. We are still gendered beings in all we do despite new opportunities and roles for women and men. We are still the thinking and self-conscious beings who are also animals who eat, drink, move, and have sex. Leisure is still a part of all these dimensions of life that are relatively stable. Adding some new and fancy frills will not change the basics of human existence.

- **The "work society:"** Leisure may be changing in many of its marketed technologies and programs. Those with discretionary incomes may be spending a marginally higher proportion of their household income on leisure (see Chapter 11). However, any economy that does not produce the goods and services required to maintain the society is condemned to decline and failure. The social timetable is still structured around factory and office schedules. Financial resources for living, including leisure, still depend on being paid for employment as well as for investment. Every study of employed women and men demonstrates some time scarcities and pressures related to work. We still tend to identify ourselves in terms of our economic roles. Our personal schedules give priority to work requirements. We may value our jobs as primarily instrumental and look forward to retirement, but we don't want to be laid off or fired. Even leisure is often supported in terms of its contribution to productivity, health, and other work factors. Work may be changing as it becomes less stable, less secure, and less predictable, but it is still central to our lives. Leisure gives way to work more often than work to leisure. Perhaps that will change some day, but it hasn't yet.

How can this debate be resolved? It is probably more important to engage in the examination of our lives than to reach a final verdict on this debate. Both stability and change are real. To some extent it is a matter of focus. What do we include in our argument, and how do we rate the relative importance of different elements? It should be clear that looking into the future is not as simple as we might have thought at first.

Discussion Questions

1. Is there anything that can never be leisure? Is there anything that is always leisure?

2. What are examples of the impacts of the world economy on every-day life?

3. How is popular culture global in scope? Give examples.

4. What is the most important new leisure technology?

5. Identify new leisure-based businesses. Are they successful?

6. Looking ahead to your lives in ten years, what will be more important—work or leisure? Why?

7. Measured by time, where is most of your leisure located?

Resources

Butsch, R. (1990). *For fun and profit: The transformation of leisure into consumption*. Philadelphia, PA: Temple University Press.

Erikson, K., and Vallas, S. (Eds.). (1990). *The nature of work: Sociological perspectives*. New Haven, CT: Yale University Press.

Godbey, G. (2003). *Leisure in your life: An exploration* (6th ed.). State College, PA: Venture Publishing, Inc.

Jackson, E. and Burton, T. (Eds.). (1999). *Leisure studies: Prospects for the 21st century*. State College, PA: Venture Publishing, Inc.

Kelly, J. (1996). *Leisure* (3rd ed.). Boston, MA: Allyn and Bacon.

Kraus, R. (1994). *Leisure in a changing America: Multicultural perspectives*. New York, NY: MacMillan.

Robinson, J. and Godbey, G. (1997). *Time for life: The surprising ways Americans use their time*. University Park, PA: Pennsylvania State Press.

Rojek, C. (1996). *Decentring leisure: Rethinking leisure theory*. Thousand Oaks, CA: Sage.

Schor, J. (1992). *The overworked American: The unexpected decline of leisure*. New York, NY: Basic Books.

Chapter 2
Leisure, Recreation, and Play

In the first chapter, one way leisure was defined generally was as activity chosen primarily for the experience. It is assumed some satisfaction, even "fun," is anticipated. That is adequate as a beginning, but there is much more. The concept of leisure, after all, has a long history. It was important to the classic Greek philosophers and has commanded considerable attention ever since. As a consequence, there have been a variety of conceptual approaches which often appear to be in conflict.

Defining Leisure

Definitions are always partly a matter of perspective. That perspective may be based on certain philosophical presuppositions, cultural biases, or personal preference. Some definitions are useful for particular purposes. Leisure, never a very specific concept, has been defined in a number of ways.

Leisure as Time

Leisure is approached as time beyond that required for subsistence, maintenance, rest, and other necessities of living. When international research employed daily diaries of time use (Szalai et al., 1972), it was assumed that labeling activities permitted them to be designated as work, maintenance, or leisure. However, walking could be for many purposes, cooking for pleasure, and reading required for work preparation. The term *discretionary* was then included in many definitions (Brightbill, 1960, p. 4). Leisure was seen as "free time" that was more than residual or left over; it was a matter of choice. The problem with this was obvious: How do you know? Does the seemingly simple measure of time require knowing what is going on in the mind of the actor? In what sense is anyone ever really free? This complication led to other approaches. The concept of free time, however, remains important because it allows for simple comparisons. Studies using this "objective" measure indicate teens have more free time than young adults, single men than married, the retired than those in midcareer, and employed single mothers least of all. The leisure-as-remaining-time approach is limited by the fact that all obligations are seldom completed. The leisure-as-discretionary-time model is limited by the problem of constraints that must be overcome to engage in most leisure. Further, such an approach assumes that it is possible to separate the individual from society and society from the individual. Nevertheless, for comparison purposes the concept remains useful.

Leisure as Activity

Leisure is commonly assumed to be defined by the form of the activity. This, too, is useful for such purposes as survey research. Checklists of activities— for example, going to concerts, basketball, watching television—are combined with some measure of frequency to obtain a profile of a person's leisure. Like time, the results can be quantified and compared: For example, males engage in more team sports than females, or women are more involved in the arts than men. The problems are also similar. Is a pickup basketball game leisure after school but not leisure in a required physical education class? Is swimming leisure at the beach but not as a health assignment after a heart attack? Is a cocktail party leisure on weekends but not at a sales conference? Is shopping leisure sometimes but not when filling the weekly grocery list? Is leisure always activity?

It is true that leisure is usually doing something that has a recognized form. Further, some forms are leisure more often than not. But there is nothing, except perhaps daydreaming, that is always leisure. The activity approach, like time, is useful but not an adequate definition. Meaning is more important than the form. Joffre Dumazedier proposed an activity definition based on meaning:

> Leisure is activity—apart from the obligations of work, family, and society—to which the individual turns at will, for either relaxation, diversion, or broadening his [sic] knowledge and his spontaneous social participation, the free exercise of his creative capacity. (1967, pp. 16–17)

Such a definition, however, includes the social context and the meaning to the actor, a far cry from just listing the name of the activity. Such definitions have led to attention to meaning as well as form.

Leisure as a State-of-Mind

The most extreme response was to assert the form of the activity is irrelevant; only the meaning counts. Leisure is defined by attitude or the state of consciousness—not form, time, or place. Leisure is defined by meaning to the actor. In the classic book, *Of Time, Work, and Leisure*, de Grazia refers to leisure as a rare condition, a "state of being, a condition of man [*sic*], which few desire and fewer achieve" (de Grazia, 1964, p. 5). This is more than feeling good. It is a condition that connotes freedom and self-fulfillment. Psychologists tend to take a more attitudinal approach. Leisure is activity in which the actor perceives freedom, intrinsic motivation, and non-instrumentality (Neulinger, 1974). An activity is leisure when the actor feels it has been chosen primarily for its own sake—for the experience itself. From this experiential perspective, then, leisure is located in the consciousness of the individual, not the social context or form of the activity. It can occur any place and any time. Anything that produces this feeling, the use of drugs for example, may be leisure regardless of longer-term meanings or outcomes.

Leisure as a Quality of Action

This approach begins by asserting that leisure is more than a state of mind; it is doing something. That something may be mental and imaginative as well as physical. It may be solitary or socially involved. But it involves doing something in a real time and place. It may focus on the experience, but is in a context that includes the self-taking action in a defined environment. It is not just feeling free; it involves real choice, even in the midst of all kinds of limits and constraints. The quality of the activity—its "playfulness"— makes it leisure. It may take place anywhere and any time, but it has a quality of self-contained meaning. It is related to work, family, education, the economy, government, religion, personal development, sexuality, and almost everything else. Yet it has distinguishing dimensions of action with its primary meaning in the experience.

Leisure as a Social Construction

This perspective challenges the notion that leisure is a primarily a psychological experience of the individual. It maintains that what individuals come to identify and experience as leisure is learned in ways both conscious and unconscious. Leisure is not an experience of freedom or choice of the individual. Rather, it is legitimated pleasure (Rojek, 1985). Individuals' interest in, and time, skills and money for leisure are shaped by opportunity and access. These, however, are not equally distributed across society. Rather, opportunity and access are constructed by gender, race and ethnicity, sexual orientation, social class, age, able-bodiedness, and other markers of social stratification.

Leisure as Political

Another approach is that leisure is political in the sense that leisure is a context like work and education where relationships of power and privilege are both reproduced and contested. That is, in leisure those with more power and privilege seek to maintain their power and privilege and control those with less power and privilege. At the same time for those without (or with less) power and privilege, leisure is a context within which to challenge or resist those with power and privilege and transform the existing social order. Leisure from this perspective is not some ephemeral state-of-mind or psychological experience. Rather, leisure is a political act where the distribution of advantage or power in society is perpetuated and challenged.

Leisure as a Dimension of Life

It would seem evident at this point that it is difficult, if not impossible, to draw clear and consistent boundaries around anything people do and call it leisure. It is experience, but in context. It has form, but is not defined by the form. It takes place in time, but defines the time rather than being defined by it. One possibility is that leisure is not a clearly defined domain of activity or consciousness at all. Rather, it is a dimension of life. It is an adjective more than a noun, a quality more than a thing. Some research has found just this: a dimension of being done primarily for the experience in the midst of all kinds of activity including family responsibilities and work (Kelly & Kelly, 1994). Leisure is the expressive dimension of life that may occur or be constructed in any context.

Themes of Leisure

It seems evident there may be no one "best" definition of leisure. Rather each has some values and some limitations. It is usually best, then, to refer to "leisure time," "the experience of leisure," "activity," or even "play" as a quality of action. There are, however, certain themes that are persistent. The first is as old as Aristotle who referred in Book I of the *Politics* to "time *free* from the necessities of work." Some understanding of freedom runs through most definitional approaches. This does not, however, mean freedom from all limits, regularities, and constraints. Leisure is *in* contexts that are integral parts of its meaning. It is freedom *to* act, not freedom *from* form and context. It is freedom within constraint.

The other persistent theme of defining leisure is its focus on the meaning or quality of the experience. Leisure has a "playful" quality in that its meaning is primarily in the experience. The general agreement begins to break down, however, when those qualities are to be identified. What does it mean to have "choice" in a scheduled sports contest with boundaries, rules, officials, priced tickets, and performance expectations? What does it mean to be "free" when males and females of all ages work out in an attempt to construct the "ideal" masculine or feminine body or when girls spend hours with their girlfriends looking at fashion magazines and talking about the latest hairstyles, clothing, and makeup? What does "play" mean for the mother at a picnic for which she has spent hours in preparation and has to watch out for the safety of four children? What does it mean to be "intrinsically motivated" when we are practicing skills for a later event or performance? The focus may be on the experience, but leisure experiences are more complex in their meanings than any simple slogan can encompass.

What is clear is that leisure may be almost anything at any time and any place. This means that leisure is not always positive and constructive. There is a dark side to anything including leisure. Leisure may be wasteful, destructive, and dangerous. It is gambling as well as religious contemplation. It may involve the sexual use of other persons or fully committed and caring communion. It may be cruel as well as compassionate. And as already proposed, it may take place at the workplace as well as the playing field and in family time as well as vacation time. As such it may well be time, activity, experience, a quality of action, a social construction, a political act, or a dimension of life. Or it may be all this, and more.

Defining Play

"Play" is usually used to refer to the activity of children. Children play and adults have leisure. Of course, we know that animals play as well. Historically and philosophically, however, the term *play* is far more encompassing. Yet, we do speak of being "playful" as a quality of our activity. Play connotes spontaneity, openness, action, and intrinsic satisfaction. Play is said to be developmental for children for whom play is their central activity—the primary context of learning. Play, however, seems to drop out of adult reference.

Like leisure, play may be seen as a quality of action. Johan Huizinga argues play is a fundamental human activity. He stresses the enjoyment of play as well as its intrinsic motivation. He adds that play is "out of the ordinary" (1955, p. 4)—a sphere of action that creates a temporary reality. It may have order and beauty but is not for any preset external purpose. Just because of its openness, play is fundamental for creativity. It is in play that the innovative ideas are produced that become the basis of social, cultural, and even economic development. In its own created order, play is the context for exploration of the "not yet." This is true for the person as well as for the society.

Play may be spontaneous or structured. It may incorporate both freedom and order. In fact, in a context of order we are most likely to experience what

Csikszentmihalyi (1990) calls "flow." Flow is a heightened state of consciousness in which there is total involvement and immersion in the current activity. When skill and the challenge meet, externals disappear in the highly satisfying experience. Flow may take place anywhere and is the quality that draws us back to challenging and creative activity. Other thinkers identified play as the context of all sorts of deeply satisfying, personally developmental, and socially significant action.

One approach would be that play is the quality of action in creative, fulfilling leisure. Another would be that any activity, creative or destructive, that is open in its outcomes and focused on the immediate experience would be called "play." In any case, play is not confined to childhood. Rather, play is activity with a childlike "lightness" of style, is expressive, done primarily for its own sake, and creates its own world of meaning. We may be playful at work, with others, in rule-bound games or projects, and for brief moments as well as for longer events. Play, then, becomes a quality of action or even a dimension of life. It is fundamental to human nature.

Defining Recreation

Recreation may be defined in much the same way as leisure—inclusive and multifaceted. Its Latin root, *recreātiō,* refers to restoration. Re-creation connotes a preparation for something else, usually work, family tasks, or civic responsibilities. Recreation, then, becomes a social issue. It is organized for social purposes, a means to the economic end of productivity, the personal goal of health, the social aim of building relationships, or some kind of growth or learning. As such, recreation may be required activity in a school program or sponsored by a corporation concerned about the physical and mental health of its employees.

Recreation, then, is organized activity with the purposes of the restoration of the wholeness of mind, body, and spirit. It presupposes some other activity that tires, depletes, or deteriorates that wholeness. *Leisure* has the language roots signifying freedom and *recreation* connotes restoration. As such, recreation becomes a social institution. It is intended to benefit the society through the health or wholeness of its citizens. It may be rest from demanding work or preparation for those demands. It may be mental, physical, or spiritual. It may be routinized or unique. It may be highly organized, even as a drill, or relaxed and unstructured. But it has external purpose, measurable or immeasurable benefits. Recreation is defined as "voluntary nonwork activity that is organized for the attainment of personal and social benefits including restoration and social cohesion" (Kelly, 1996, p. 27).

Mini-Debate: Leisure is a human universal.

Is there any society and culture without leisure? It may depend on how leisure is defined. If leisure is clearly set-apart and demarcated time, then there have been relatively simple societies without such organization and social boundaries. In some societies, leisure is woven throughout the day in ways that do not draw clear lines between work and leisure. If leisure is defined as a quality of action or even a dimension of life, then it seems unlikely it would be absent from any human life or culture.

YES

- Leisure is really another way of referring to a fundamental quality of human, and even animal, existence. To be human is to play. Leisure is inclusively viewed as this quality of action or life. As such, it is impossible to conceive of life without it.

- Leisure and play are such basic dimensions of life that they are found throughout the life course. Infants play simple response games before they speak or walk. Children play in more complex ways and learn how to be social actors in the process. There is no age that abandons leisure as irrelevant or unimportant. From an individual perspective, play and leisure are deeply expressive of our natures.

- From a social perspective, leisure is universal in its bonding function. It is in leisure that we develop, strengthen, and extend many of our most important relationships. What is a friendship or a family without leisure/play as the context of exploring new facets of relationships and expressing enduring ones.

- We are not automatons or robots. Rather, it is human to be expressive and free. We concentrate on the experience of an action so that we may truly be ourselves. We cannot go through life always taking orders, obeying rules, and conforming to every little social expectation. We need to be able to be novel, different, and be ourselves. We need to immerse ourselves in what we do, even experience flow, to be more than totally scripted beings.

- Any culture has to be open to what is new, creative, and different. In work, there are predetermined outcomes. In leisure, we can attempt the different and see what results. We may play anywhere— at the computer and in the wilderness. In any case, we are trying out, testing, and realizing possibilities we cannot attempt in the routinized and prescribed world. In leisure, we create the culture, play with ideas, and test seeming inconsistencies in ways that re-create the future.

NO

- A society must have an economic surplus to have leisure. If both children and adults are at a level of economic scarcity so severe time is completely devoted to survival, then there is no time or energy for leisure. Pacific Island cultures may have leisure woven throughout the day in their relative abundance and simplicity. But the Sahil desert in Africa is quite another matter. Even families may compete for scarce food in a famine. In extreme privation, there is no time or place for leisure.

- Leisure as we know it in North America is a product of the industrial revolution. Factories, the efficient division of labor, and economic surpluses produce the designated times that make leisure possible. Productivity growth has now led to a society that devotes more and more time to the consumption of leisure goods and services. Leisure as the legitimate reward for productivity is part of an economic/social system that separates work and leisure. Further, postindustrial economic expansion identifies leisure as an economic sector in which consumption must be expanded. Leisure, then, is very much a product of a particular set of organizations and even ideologies.

- No matter how widespread play or leisure is, it is not basic. Most fundamental to human life are primary commitments, such as work, and primary relationships, such as family. Businesses run efficiently with nothing arranged for leisure. Social bonding can take place as families perform their necessary tasks of maintenance and nurturing. Leisure is secondary to what is necessary and, therefore, not a human universal.

- As suggested by the multiplicity of definitions of leisure in this chapter, there is no consensus as to what leisure is. Anything that vague and uncertain can hardly be a human universal. Play may be a human dimension, but leisure requires time and place. It takes particular forms in any culture. It is, thus, a construction of a particular time rather than a basic dimension of life. Further, the forms of leisure differ so widely among different cultures that finding the common elements that would make it a universal would seem an impossible task. As will be demonstrated in the next debate, even "freedom" is problematic. Leisure is a social construction of its specific culture rather than a human universal.

This debate illustrates how important definitions are for an exchange of ideas. Just how leisure is defined sets the terms of argument. Opponents who agree on terms may no longer be in opposition.

Debate: Leisure is free choice.

The common definitions of leisure in North America all make some reference to freedom, free choice, or at least discretionary time. How realistic is this assumption of freedom?

YES

- The classic definitions of leisure from Aristotle on refer to freedom. To be realistic, this does not mean a total freedom *from* all constraints or limitations. Rather, it means that there is a real element of choice. It is freedom *to* engage in the activity or not. Leisure is distinct from necessity. That is its distinguishing characteristic. Leisure is chosen because of anticipated satisfaction in the experience—not because of social or economic requirement.

- Leisure is personal. Although leisure may involve other people, the culture, and forms of activity, its meanings to the individual are primarily personal. Its meanings are for the person. As such, there is a fundamental freedom. Over time, individuals develop leisure styles and commitments that fit them. Even longer-term meanings are developmental. We engage in activities because we are becoming something more in the process. If the activity is a social requirement, it is not leisure.

- Leisure is separate from our work, family, and community roles. It is never required by those roles. Dumazedier's definition is a standard for such separation. Leisure is "apart from" the necessities of our social roles.

- Leisure is a special world. As in Huizinga's approach to play, leisure creates its own separate world of activity. The playing field, the stage, and other leisure venues are special for that activity. They have their own boundaries that make free and creative activity possible.

- From one perspective, leisure is a state of mind. It is a special consciousness that includes a sense of freedom. Without that sense, there is no leisure, only an extension of all the obligations of life. For example, a picnic is just another chore for the mother/caregiver/manager unless she or he feels that it is an experience of freedom. That's what makes it leisure.

- When we define leisure as time, it is the "free" element that makes it leisure. It is "discretionary" time in that we have multiple options for its use. When there is only one possibility, that is not leisure. Leisure is "freedom to" do it or not.

- Further, leisure is experience for its own sake. It is what goes on in the process that is defining. For example, we may experience leisure with almost anyone. There is "family leisure," but it is not all nonwork activity when other family members are present. When caregiving and nurturing expectations allow for no choice, then even a family vacation or picnic may not be leisure at all.

It is, then, a matter of definition. Leisure from this perspective is defined by freedom. The term *existential* refers to selfhood created by decision and action. It is the existential element in human activity that creates leisure— and it is that element that makes it profoundly human.

NO

- It may be a matter of definition. Modern definitions are of two types. One argues that leisure is the product of modern society with its surpluses and division of labor. As such, leisure is not free but has to be earned. It is a reward of the system—not a human quality. The second type of definition argues that leisure is a product of a particular culture. (See the previous mini-debate.) It is a social construction that incorporates the elements of that culture. Greek leisure was based on a slave system. Contemporary leisure takes place in a market economic system. Even the language we use to think about leisure is from a particular history of a particular culture. "Freedom" is what we call it; not a condition of life.

- Leisure is learned. We not only develop interests and learn skills in our particular communities, families, environments, and schools but we also learn from our friends and companions. We are not free in the sense of being independent and autonomous. We are both producers and products of our histories with all their limitations.

Especially if we have been subject to some deprivation due to discrimination, we carry that lack of freedom with us all our lives. We learn in directed and limited ways.

- Leisure is contextual. How can we really be free when gender, race, economic class, sexual orientation, culture, and everything else has shaped what we are able to learn and do? We do not magically become separate from the rest of our lives in our leisure. Rather, we are shaped by social conditions that impact everything we are and do. The separate world of leisure and play is an illusion—not a reality of life. Certainly not life in the real, crowded, segregated, and separated city.

- Leisure is role-related. We do most of our leisure with those who are related to us in other roles. We are still family members, workers, and community figures in our leisure. There are all kinds of expectations that limit and direct what we do in leisure, how we do it, and with whom we do it. Studies of the "leisure" of employed mothers demonstrates what a struggle it is to secure a little time separate from those work and family roles. Often employed mothers can gain separation from such roles only in some act of dramatic abandonment. Certainly, with most leisure activity taking place in the residence, these mothers are not free of their roles among those whose expectations for them never go away.

- Considerable leisure is highly structured. Sports and games have rules, admission controls, spatial lines, and position expectations. How we play is anything but free. We either do it consistent with the rules or we are out of the game. To a lesser degree, almost all activity has structures. We cannot act freely or any way we please. Perhaps only the imagination is really free, and even that is subject to all the "rights and wrongs" we have learned throughout life and what is seen as possible by the cultures in which we live.

- What is "free time" when our obligations are never entirely completed? We always have some maintenance undone—the laundry or the dishes. We always have some things others would like us to do. The obligations of life are endless. We may be able to manufacture some time for play, but it is never free. There is always a price to pay in what we leave undone. If free time were really what is left over after all else is completed, we would surely have no leisure at all.

- Even leisure as escape presupposes obligations and expectations remain in our consciousness. There has to be something to escape from—something that is still there. Leisure is mixed into life, into the realities of life that makes demands on us. Further, in our leisure there are all the timetables, clothing requirements, and elements of acceptability that we must meet in order to participate. We are never free in the sense of separation from everyone and everything else.

- Leisure has commitments. Some are commitments to ourselves. We promise ourselves to practice the piano an hour a day, not drink so much, exercise three times a week, watch less television or spend more time with our children. Some commitments are to others. We make dates, join teams, and accept responsibilities. Once we make those commitments, we are not free to do whatever we like unless we are willing to pay some price. We break commitments at a cost to ourselves and often to others. Insofar as leisure is social, it is hardly free.

Is it all a matter of definition? Or are there realities of life that place so many limitations on our actions that the very idea of "freedom" is a deception? If so, then what do we mean by leisure? We will explore various aspects of that question in other chapters.

Discussion Questions

1. Which definition of leisure seems best for you personally? Why?

2. Which is best for research purposes? Why?

3. What are the most important limits to freedom in leisure?

4. How do we develop our ideas of leisure and play?

5. Can leisure ever take priority over life's obligations? How?

6. Do we have to "get away" to have leisure?

7. How much of our leisure is recreation?

8. Are play and leisure essentially the same?

9. Is there "good leisure" and "bad leisure?"

References and Resources

Brightbill, C. (1960). *The challenge of leisure*. Englewood Cliffs, NJ: Prentice Hall.

Callois, R. (1961). *Man, play, and games* (Meyer Barash, Trans.). London, UK: Thames and Hudson.

Cheek, N. and Burch, W. (1976). *The social organization of leisure in human society*. New York, NY: Harper and Row.

Clarke, J. and Critcher, C. (1985). *The devil makes work: Leisure in capitalist Britain*. Urbana, IL: University of Illinois Press.

Csikszentmihalyi, M. (1990). *Flow: The psychology of optimal experience*. New York, NY: Harper and Row.

de Grazia, S. (1962). *Of time, work, and leisure* (Stewart E. McClure, Trans.). Garden City, NY: Doubleday.

Dumazedier, J. (1967). *Toward a society of leisure*. New York, NY: Free Press.

Goodale, T. and Godbey, G. (1988). *The evolution of leisure: Historical and philosophical perspectives*. State College, PA: Venture Publishing, Inc.

Hemingway, J., and Kelly, J. (1995). History and philosophy of leisure: Past present, and future research. In L. Barnett (Ed.), *Research about leisure: Past, present, and future*. Champaign, IL: Sagamore.

Huizinga, J. (1955). *Homo ludens: A study of the play-element in culture*. Boston, MA: Beacon Press.

Kelly, J.R. (1996). *Leisure* (3rd ed.). Boston, MA: Allyn and Bacon.

Kelly, J.R. and Kelly, J. (1994). Multiple dimensions of meaning in the domains of work, family, and leisure. *Journal of Leisure Research, 26*(3), 250–274.

Murphy, J. (Ed.). (1974). *Concepts of leisure: Philosophical implications*. Englewood Cliffs, NJ: Prentice Hall.

Neulinger, J. (1974). *The psychology of leisure: Research approaches to the study of leisure*. Springfield, IL: C.C. Thomas.

Pieper, J. (1964). *Leisure: The basis of culture* (Alexander Dru, Trans.). New York, NY: New American Library.

Rojek, C. (1985). *Capitalism and leisure theory*. New York, NY: Tavistock.

Szalai, A. et al. (Eds.). (1972). *The uses of time: Daily activities of urban and suburban populations in twelve countries*. The Hague, Netherlands: Mouton.

Veblen, T. (1953). *The theory of the leisure class*. New York, NY: MacMillan. (Original work published in 1899)

Wearing, B. (1998). *Leisure and feminist theory*. Thousand Oaks, CA: Sage.

Part II
Historical Perspectives

Chapter 3
The Classics

Leisure is not a new concept. Rather, themes of leisure have come down through the centuries and across languages and cultures. It would seem that there may be two fundamental approaches to leisure:

1. The first separates leisure from other domains of life. Leisure is seen as something different from ordinary life. The classic philosophers of Greece set this theme into Western culture. Some argue modern leisure is a product of the temporal and spatial separations of industrial society. Leisure is clearly identifiable as quite different from work and the obligations of social relationships. The usual distinguishing mark of leisure, from this perspective, is its relative freedom.

2. The second, in many relatively simple cultures, tends to weave play into the daily round and rhythm of life. In contemporary Eastern cultures, leisure is also understood as more of a theme or integral element of ongoing life. Some Buddhist and Hindu scholars find leisure to be more of a state of being than a social realm. Leisure is found in the way of life of the human being.

In some cultures, the distinction may not be so clear. Leisure may be a dimension of both life and the social system. Freedom may be both individual orientation and institutionalized time and space. For example, according to the Dutch historian, Johan Huizinga (1955), play is both an orientation of life that makes possible creative activity and a set-apart time and space with its own forms and rules. In the analysis that follows, we will find both approaches. Historical study, however, tends to approach leisure as a social, economic, and political domain of a social system, while philosophy tends to see leisure more as an element of life or even a set of values.

Greek Ideals and Realities

The Philosophical Ideal

There is no one "Greek" philosophy of leisure. Each of the two great philosophers of Greece, Plato and Aristotle, had a significant place for leisure in his scheme of thought. They agreed on its importance for the development and governing of the society. Further, they agreed that, however necessary, leisure is an end in itself and essential to being a free person.

In Plato's philosophy of culture, being free meant not being a slave. Leisure is the time free for self-development and expression. More than freedom *from* necessity; it is freedom *for* engagement with the culture and especially the arts of music, poetry, and philosophy. In such engagement, the free person come closer to sensing the meaning of the eternal "Ideas" or forms of meaning. True happiness comes in coming closer to what we are meant to be. Also in such activity, qualities of leadership for the state are enhanced (*The Republic*, Book 2).

Aristotle's approach to leisure (*schole*) in Book 1 of the *Politics* begins by defining leisure as freedom from necessity. He proposes there should be an elite leisure class supported to assure a wise and just government. Leisure is an end in itself, intrinsically good and the highest end of human activity. It is contrasted with work (*ascholia*), the play of children, and the restoration of recreation. Rather, leisure is a state of being—always desirable and never for the sake of anything else. It is in "a class by itself" (de Grazia, 1962, p. 13).

Nevertheless, the use of such freedom has social and political meaning. Leisure is not self-centered or self-absorbed. Rather, it involves governing and preparing to govern. The personal development of leisure, coming closer to the fulfillment of one's nature, has an element of responsibility. Contemplation yields wisdom. Leisure is not just intrinsic pleasure; it involves putting rational principles in a middle ground of virtue and character that is the basis of being a good citizen (*Nichomachean Ethics*, Book 2). Philosophy, the arts, and physical discipline are forms of activity that lead toward fulfillment and civil responsibility. Leisure has both a personal and a social ethic.

The Social Reality

The social context of such an ideal, then, may seem contradictory. The relatively small cities (even Athens did not exceed a population of 200,000) were planned for leisure with parks, baths, theatres, sports arenas, gymnasiums, and exercise grounds. There were academies of music, the arts, and philosophy. Lifelong learning was expected of those free citizens. People met in public forums and discussed the issues of the day. The city was planned for fulfilling and civic activity.

The other side, of course, is Greek elitism. It was for free males only. Slaves, women, and the poor were excluded. Leisure was for the relatively few free males of property. Slaves, as many as four for each free male, did most of the necessary work. The poor were occupied with survival. Women were almost all confined to work in the home and "the only slave a poor man had was his wife." The majority did all the work, especially the routine drudgery, so the minority could exercise the freedom of leisure. Leisure, then, was more than a philosophical ideal; it was an economic, political, and social system. The society was deeply divided between the leisure class of privilege and the majority of slaves and servants. Wealth and gender separated the leisure class.

We tend to applaud the philosophy, urban planning, support of the arts, and social ethic of justice and principle. It is convenient to forget the human cost and the inequity. What is the reality of freedom that is so limited? What is the value of sexual openness when women and the young are relatively powerless? Or, is Greek society just a dramatic example of the way things have to be? Does "freedom from necessity" require a division of labor? Does personal freedom for some require the servitude of others? At least it would seem that ideas of leisure are expressive of and ever perpetuate the social system and put in question the concept of leisure as a separate domain of life.

Debate: Leisure requires an exploited class of workers.

YES

- Greece is not the only historical example of a servant class producing leisure for elites. In fact, almost every complex culture—Ming and Ching China, Victorian Britain, Colonial and Pre-colonial India, and so on—has had a leisure class and a servant class. In some cases, such as the antebellum South in the United States, that class were chattel slaves. In others, they were just the poor and powerless. Nonetheless, historically high degrees of leisure have usually been associated with slavery or near-slavery. Servants designated by ethnicity, race, gender, or just poverty have done the "necessities" so that others might exercise their so-called "freedom." The "theory of the leisure class" applies to more than American capitalism (Veblen, 1899/1955).

- In contemporary societies, the servants of the leisure classes are seldom actual slaves. They are, however, the relatively poor and powerless. Motel beds are made by undocumented workers who cannot protest low wages. All kinds of "service" occupations are paid at or near minimum wages. Servers in restaurants survive on tips, not hourly wages. The very nature of most tourism implies being cared for by others. Destination areas employ workers at such low wages that they have to be bussed in from low-cost housing enclaves. Someone has to make the beds and pick up the garbage. So tourism is priced to exploit local workers who have lost both their land resources and their traditional economies. Just list all the low-wage and entry-level workers who supported your last leisure trip or outing. Modern market leisure implies being taken care of by others who exist on low wages and tips.

- One classic leisure study, *Of Time, Work, and Leisure* by Sebastian de Grazia (1962), goes so far as to propose that few will ever experience the sublime state of being called leisure. Writing from his Italian villa, he offers a vision of elite leisure that is separated from the ordinary pleasures of the masses. Claiming to be based on Aristotle, de Grazia seems to buy into the entire Greek social framework. Leisure is for the privileged few who can really appreciate it. However, this requires others do the chores to make it possible. Of course, de Grazia argues that culture and civilization call for such special freedom from necessity.

- Leisure is nonproductive. It is for its own sake. To be truly so separated from obligations, others must take care of what has to be done. After all, even leisure requires "infrastructure"—power, transportation, sewage, for example—as a context for doing anything. Someone has to be productive so that others may be nonproductive. In a capitalist economy, this is made possible by rewarding investment first and labor second. The system itself requires servants—however labeled—who do the daily work.

- Real leisure is not just time-outs from work. According to the classical theorists, leisure is a state of being, a quality of life. It transcends the daily obligations of life. Therefore, others must fulfill those requirements. Ordinary workers may have bits of time to strive for "fun," but leisure lifts the human spirit above such negotiation and struggle. It is a style or condition of life. Ordinary workers may be so worn down by toil that they lack the motivation or personal resources for real leisure.

- The Greek philosophers agree leisure is best expressed in the arts: the contemplation of philosophy, the forms of poetry, the grace of music. To be skilled in the arts calls for practice and discipline. Even excellence in sport requires regular time and training. Such time and disciplined learning is supported by others who never have the opportunities to develop such skills themselves. Fine art and physical ability are supported by the commonplace—the servants of excellence. Most people can only struggle for minutes of escape and expression.

- The ideal, of course, is for mechanization and automation to become the nonhuman servants of the new age. Toil and drudgery will be assigned to machines, not people. That is a lovely dream, but is not supported by actuality. In fact, service occupations are growing. Nursing homes, restaurants, and hotels are hiring the new servant class, while factories and offices become electronically automated—even there someone punches in the credit card data and task specifications. Servants remain in even more interchangeable roles, but are increasingly invisible to those who are served.

NO

- There are some examples of societies of relative abundance that do not have any distinct servant class. Rather, leisure is a part of the rhythm of daily life in an inclusive way. Such societies are rather different from modern mass society. They are simple, small, and based on easy access to natural resources. They are integrated and inclusive. They may be rare, but they are possible.

- Contemporary societies, of course, are far more complex. Nevertheless, there are provisions for ordinary people. Life for the masses, too, has a kind of rhythm. There are times and places for productive work, whether in the factory, office, or home. There are also times and places for play. The week has its rhythms of weekends. The year has periods of disengagement of seasons and vacations. The benefits of an economy may not be equally distributed, but neither are they totally denied to many. A worker may well be a servant for eight hours and at play in off times.

- Further, modern societies provide leisure opportunities for the masses. There are public programs and facilities in most communities. National parks and forests are open to those who can afford to get there. The market sector offers more and more diverse leisure opportunities. Las Vegas and Disney World are hardly elitist or exclusive. Television is everywhere at little cost. Leisure opportunities are there, even for the new service class who spend their working hours taking care of the needs and wants of others.

- Most leisure does not require anything special. It is day-to-day interaction with friends and family, activities around the residence, and available electronic entertainment. It may be ordinary, but it is inclusive. It is not special or specialized.

- Almost everyone has the modest resources to engage in such ordinary leisure as well as in occasional special events. The average 40-hour workweek provides the time. The 80% with above-poverty incomes have some financial resources. Leisure doesn't have to be expensive. Some may envy the elites who spend $2,000 on a single night of luxury lodging, but they still do many of the same things in a different styles as do the masses. Leisure has been made a viable reward for those who contribute to the economy at all levels.

- The average household spends about 8% of its income directly on leisure (see Chapter 11). Surely that is enough to support a variety of activities and possibilities. Such household spending patterns are not exclusive, but instead are a taken-for-granted part of life for all but the poor.

- Exclusive models are just wrong. Writers such as de Grazia just do not understand that fixing up an old car may be as creative as poetry or the ballet. Gardening may be as deeply satisfying as sculpture or painting. Riding a motorcycle may be as exciting as downhill skiing at Aspen. "Leisure class" arguments are more than a little snobbish.

- The automated factory and office are here. It is true that we have not solved the problem of an equitable distribution of work and leisure. The possibility is there, however, to diminish the dominance of work and extend the possibilities of leisure. Even if we grant that the potential of leisure is currently restricted, the economic resources are available to lift more and more lives above routine and necessity to new potentials of self-determination and freedom. It will require a redistribution of work, income, and household responsibilities. It will call for giving up privilege by some and a sharing with others. There will have to be hard political choices, but societies do change.

Rome: The Politics of Leisure

Like the Greeks, the Romans built and planned for leisure. However, their stress on law and custom rather than learning and contemplation gave leisure quite a different cast. The social and political context was also quite different. Rome itself was a large city governing a vast empire. The governing class was concerned about the possible revolt of the military and the masses, especially when unemployment ran high. The result was that leisure came to be more consumption than creation, and a political instrument wielded by the aristocracy.

The Social Context of Leisure

Like Greece, Rome was a stratified society with elites of wealth and power, ordinary citizens, and slaves. As Rome grew, the population of small farmers driven off their land, workers displaced by slaves, and soldiers unneeded in peacetime grew. Like Greece, Rome built for leisure with baths, stadiums, gymnasiums, and forums. The wealthy built suburban villas with their own pools, gardens, hunting preserves, and libraries. There were facilities for soldiers to improve their fighting abilities. The elites tended to be separated from poor citizens except for the slaves who served them directly. As the empire grew in power, this separation from the masses increased.

Leisure as Control and Consumption

By the first century, Rome had become a city of a million beset by unemployment and underemployment. The political threat of a mass uprising was of great concern to the rulers. One answer was mass leisure. More than 150 holidays punctuated the calendar in the first century and grew to over 200 by the middle of the third century. These holidays were filled with mass entertainment to keep the plebeians distracted from political action. Entertainment was provided to dull dissatisfaction.

More than 800 baths were made available at nominal cost. Sport became mass spectacles with gladiators fighting to the death, violently contested chariot races, and circuses with simulated sea battles and wild animals imported to fight each other or political prisoners. The enormous Circus Maximus held 385,000 spectators.

Too much emphasis on the details of chariots, gladiators, and arenas may obscure their political purpose. Leisure in these mass entertainment forums was intended to preserve the political structure. The power of the ruling class and their economic privilege was not to be threatened—even by the masses with little power or privilege. Rather, they were distracted by spectacles that became more and more violent and colorful. Bloodshed and danger provided artificial excitement for those who packed the coliseums. Mass leisure was provided to those who had little political influence or satisfying economic engagement. The society was organized to preserve elite wealth and power—and for some centuries the system was successful in its aim.

Debate: Mass leisure is used to control the masses.

YES

- Rome is only the most dramatic example of the use of mass leisure to divert social protest with entertainment. The conditions, however, are significant. Rome was a great city with masses of people jammed together. There was unemployment and underemployment denying large numbers of citizens both the satisfaction of constructive work and its rewards. There was elite political control with only a pretense of mass political participation. These conditions were seen as explosive. One answer was that leisure that distracted the populace from such conditions.

- Fireworks and sports spectacles are not unique to Rome. In contemporary societies, there are still stadiums full of sports fans. Now there is also mass entertainment and most especially television is always there to entertain and distract. People identify with teams and stars rather than engaging in action of their own. Vast profits are made on media successes promoted as being something wonderful that "everyone must see." Sports organizations such as the National Football League are designed for mass consumption via television as well as for the fans in the stadium. The profit is in the media contract—the mass distribution. Popular culture promotes the star system, even when such figures come and go rapidly. All of this creates a mass leisure system which substitutes for any kind of significant action—especially anything that might threaten the system.

- Now a worldwide industry produces such entertainment. This entertainment is escapist, artificially exciting, and even violent. It utilizes sex, often with exploitation and violence, to attract viewers. It is a vicarious world that keeps imaginations occupied and time full without challenging anything fundamental. Further, mass entertainment is available at all price levels so no potentially disruptive segment of society is left out.

- Much work may be routine and boring. Much of the government with its bureaucracies seems out of reach and even out of control. Nevertheless, those who go along are rewarded with enough economic resources to join in the entertainment and enough security to accept the political system. The Romans called it "bread and circuses" (i.e., pānis et circēnsēs).

- There is an evident expansion of certain kinds of leisure. Most tend to provide artificial excitement of some sort. For example, is the appeal of gambling that it is exciting and involving without requiring any long-term investment in acquiring skill? Why are laws being changed to expand such possibilities when the economic benefits are questionable and uneven? Does society have to provide entertainment that is more exciting and distracting?

- The theme is that mass leisure provides for having fun without challenging the system. In fact, the entertainment industries are more than mass diversion. They are at the same time one more way for a few to amass profits on their investments. What could be more system-supporting than that?

NO

- The focus on mass entertainment is too narrow. There are also countless manifestations of folk culture integrated into the round of life. Do-it-yourself involves more than just getting the chores done. All kinds of crafts, hobbies, and skills are part of the full panoply of leisure in every society. Art is ordinary as well as fine. Music is made in the home as well as the concert hall. Even sport is more engagement than being a spectator for some. Woven into the daily and weekly round of life are so many things that people *do* because they find them satisfying.

- As already introduced, the daily round of leisure is profoundly social. The relationships are more important than the activities in many cases. Even going to the mass spectacle of professional football is done with friends with social interaction essential to the experience.

- The market provides variety. There is entertainment. There are also all kinds of experiences made possible in the for-profit sector of the leisure economy. Not only equipment but also the special places for physical activity, the arts, and social gathering are offered at a variety of price levels and styles. The market does respond to demand as well as create new interests. Too narrow a focus on mass entertainment misses that whole world of possibilities for doing things that are developmental, challenging, and creative. Note especially the provisions for children that enable activity rather than passivity.

- National parks are so crowded that some are being redesigned to minimize the impacts of crowds. There is clearly a desire to encounter the natural and the real. There are the forests, rivers, and mountains that attract so many, especially when they are accessible to population centers. There remains a desire for the real and authentic that is not extinguished by all the artificial entertainment and easy escape.

- Leisure is more than a reward for drudgery and compliance. Real productive work is not evil, even when it involves some efficient routines. The engagement-disengagement rhythm of life involves work and leisure, the productive and expressive, the individual and the social. The fact that there is escape and entertainment in the overall scheme does not mean that there is nothing else in life. Mass entertainment can be part of the balance rather than dominant.

- In a democratic political system, there is no need for such social control. Even though most citizens sometimes feel that they have little influence, in a representative democracy there are mechanisms of response and influence. Only a truly totalitarian system requires the kind of massive diversion of the Roman culture. After all, we can vote and no one has to watch the NFL (even if tax revenues help pay for stadiums). Further, leisure itself may be a context for resisting, challenging, and changing the social order. Rap music, women's involvement in sport, gays suing for entry into Boy Scouts—all are forms of challenges to the existing order. While quickly accommodated by the mainstream, or shut down by political directives, these forms of leisure are expressions of resistance and revolt that slowly transform society.

- What kinds of leisure do the majority of people value most? Research suggests interaction with those we truly care about and activity in which we have invested to gain skills are the kinds of activity most people would not want to give up. Entertainment is fine in its place, but it is not everything in leisure or life.

- There is no need to overthrow a system that changes and is responsive. It is no accident that totalitarian regimes are in retreat in most of the world. Those that remain will in time succumb to the forces of the global culture and economy. Of course, every society has problems that need to be addressed. Most change is gradual and evolutionary. Political change may be slow and uneven, but suppression of dissent is not so complete that systems of control need to eliminate critical thought or action within the system.

The Repression of Leisure

The opposite side of mass entertainment and the promotion of leisure is repression and regulation. In some cases, leisure is seen as a threat to the social order. Rather than provide entertainment, the society limits and regulates leisure. There are a number of historical examples. Probably the two most often cited and studied are Puritan New England and the Victorian era of the early industrial age.

The Judeo-Christian religious heritage has been ambivalent about leisure. On the one hand, there has been the glorification of meditation and contemplation as both religious devotion and leisure. On the other hand, the early Christian church adopted through the influence of the apostle Paul a Greek dualistic philosophy. In this dualism the "spirit" is considered to be good and the material to be evil. The body itself is a "tomb" and indulgence of the body and its pleasures is evil. Jewish ethics tend to be more holistic, affirming history as the arena of divine action and the whole of human life, body, and spirit.

The Puritan Social Ethic

The aim of the Puritan social ethic was to establish a theocracy—the city of God on Earth. Underlying the ethic of obedience was the ancient dualism that the body needed to be subdued and controlled. The "flesh" and its pleasures were to be held in check by personal discipline if possible and by community regulation if necessary. Further, in the Massachusetts Bay colonies only 4,000 of the 16,000 who migrated in the 1630s were church members and considered capable of participating in governing the colony.

Restrictions on merriment were especially rigid on the "Lord's Day" when all games and sports were forbidden and even walking limited to necessity. The "blue laws" of Sabbath observance and public conduct were imposed by the "saints" on the entire colony to create a godly commonwealth. Further, in an economic condition of privation and scarcity "no idle drone" was tolerated. All were to do their share of the work so that the colony would survive and prosper.

Some amusements were allowed. On days other than Sunday, there were festival games and sports enhanced by eating and drinking. However, public displays of affection were considered wanton and dancing lascivious.

For a time the theater and all sorts of gambling were banned. Wasting time was evil. Hunting and fishing combined replenishment of the community larder with pleasure. The militia gathered for drill and shooting matches and often adjourned to the tavern. The basic rule was that no one was allowed to break community solidarity with public offense to the moral codes. Private pleasures, such as those associated with courting, were permitted as long as they did not become publicly offensive.

Of course, in time the majority of "strangers" who were not regenerated church members rebelled against such restrictions and challenged the Puritan ethic. The theocracy was splintered by diversity and growth. The breakdown of the religious and moral consensus provoked an attempt to control deviant behavior with more extensive blue laws. As they were compromised and eroded, the attempts of the godly to regulate the life of the community were focused on the Sabbath and the control of leisure on that "holy day."

The Industrial Worker and Victorian Repression

In the early part of the 19th century's industrial revolution, the repression of leisure had a more pragmatic and less religious basis. When the workweek was six days of more than twelve hours a day, Sunday was the only time for rest and escape. Further, poverty limited opportunities for expression. As a consequence, drinking to excess was common among workers. Not only did this have impacts on the family but also it often rendered workers unfit to return on Monday. In fact, "Saint Monday" too often was an unholy holiday for those recovering from Sunday.

There were many attempts to deal with the problem. Working-class churches were supported by mill owners. "Sunday schools" were begun for children who spent the week in the mills and mines. Programs of education and "constructive" recreation were established by reformers. Settlement houses were opened to offer practical education to women and children in their hours away from the factory. And, of course, there were all kinds of laws regulating behavior. Taverns were licensed and hours limited. Even ethnic celebrations were regulated as to time, place, and behavior. Despite the moral pronouncements, however, the greatest concern was with drinking and its effect on productivity. Blue laws governing Sunday behavior had economic as well as religious purposes.

Asceticism versus Expression

The conflicts over leisure often seemed to be conflicts between religion and leisure. That conflict continues in societies in which there are close ties between the government and religion. In most societies, however, there has been accommodation, reconciliation, and even cooperation between religious and recreation institutions. Mainline churches now offer recreation programs as part of their efforts to recruit members and form communities of interaction. Other religious bodies remain that separate themselves from the mainstream culture and actively resist many aspects of leisure and expression.

The main conflict is more one between asceticism and expression than between religion and leisure. The debate can be put in philosophical terms: Is the chief aim of humankind to be productive (i.e., *Homo faber* in Latin) or to play and develop (i.e., *Homo ludens*)? In theological terms, is life to glorify God or to express what it means to be human? Those who stress work and worship tend to promote life that is disciplined and ascetic—a life focused on what is considered to be ultimately worthy. Those who stress expression and self-development tend to glorify the freedom and self-justifying activity of leisure. Value systems that exalt work and seriousness stress community and the basic institutions of the society: economic production, religious devotion, and family stability. Whatever distracts from them is condemned. Those who stress expression and creativity, on the other hand, tend to focus more on the development of the individual.

Discussion Questions

1. How can leisure be free when others are enslaved or forced to serve?

2. Does leisure require an economic base of surplus rather than scarcity?

3. How does leisure produce, reproduce, and transform the social system in North America?

4. How does the government support and promote mass entertainment through licensing and taxation policies?

5. Are there still government attempts to regulate leisure? Give examples.

6. How does religion still attempt to control leisure in the local community?

7. Does any community have to set limits on behavior that does not directly injure others? Why?

8. Is there something inherently dangerous about the relative freedom of leisure?

References and Resources

Dare, B., Welton, G. and Coe, W. (1987). *Concepts of leisure in Western thought: A critical and historical analysis*. Dubuque, IA: Kendall/Hunt.

Davies, W.D. (1962). *Christian origins and Judaism*. Philadelphia, PA: Westminster Press.

de Grazia, S. (1962). *Of time, work, and leisure*. Garden City, NY: Doubleday.

Goodale, T. and Godbey, G. (1988). *The evolution of leisure: Historical and philosophical perspectives*. State College, PA: Venture Publishing, Inc.

Hemingway, J.L. (1988). Leisure and civility: Reflections on a Greek ideal. *Leisure Sciences, 10*, 179–181.

Huizinga, J. (1950). *Homo ludens: A study of the play-element in culture*. Boston, MA: Beacon Press.

Kelly, J.R. (1996). *Leisure* (3rd ed.). Boston, MA: Allyn and Bacon.

Pieper, J. (1963). *Leisure: The basis of culture* (Alexander Dru, Trans.). New York, NY: New American Library.

Veblen, T. (1953). *The theory of the leisure class*. New York, NY: MacMillan. Originally published in 1899

Chapter 4

Work and the Industrial City

Industrialization created a different society. The acceleration of change in Western societies gathered such momentum by the middle of the 19th century that nothing was left quite the same. The spatial and social ordering of life, the security of tradition in the small town, the passing on of trades and land from generation to generation, and the agricultural cycle of seasons and harvests was pushed to the periphery of the society. Now it was the city, the railroad, the factory, and the machine that dominated.

There was conflict as well as change. Conflict between mill and mine owners and wage workers involved safety, hours, conditions, and wages. The drive for productivity led to programs to control the workers' leisure as well as their work. For decades, production was labor-intensive, employing women and children as well as men. Sixty hours or more was the normal workweek, and wages were a few dollars a week. It is no wonder that the city and the factory changed every aspect of home and family, as well as work itself.

Industrialization and the City

The Civil War in the United States spurred industrialization in the North and brought to an end the slave-based economy of the South. New citizens from Europe entered through the New York gateway and stayed in the cities of the Northeast. Electricity and the gasoline reciprocating engine began to revolutionize the home and transportation. The day of the gaslight, horse, and dispersed agricultural economy was almost over.

Cities had been centers of commerce and culture, government, and retailing. The new city surrounded the factory demanding power, raw materials, transportation by river and rail, and *people*. The factory replaced handwork and crafts with machines. The factory also required concentrations of capital as well as labor. The new world was one of iron, steel, and power. For workers it was also a world of crowding, danger, privation, and a life dominated by work.

In Britain there were the new textile factories and the flows of raw materials and manufactured goods throughout the empire. In the United States, change involved the steam engine in ships and railways, electric lights and power, radio, the mass-produced automobile, and the typewriter and calculating machine in the office. Between 1850 and 1900 everything was transformed.

It was the factory, however, that made the new city. Interchangeable parts and mass production were introduced into gun making, all kinds of metal products, electric motors, gasoline engines, and eventually the car. The sewing machine was introduced into the clothing factory by 1850. Steel production rose from less than 100,000 tons in 1870 to 25 million tons by 1910. Railroads increased their freight hauling from 10 billion ton-miles in 1870 to 150 billion 40 years later.

Change accelerated in the first half of the 20th century. The population of the United States doubled to 150 million, life expectancy increased from 50 to almost 70 years, per capita income went from $231 to $1,870, and the number of automobiles soared from 13,000 to 44 million. Society after 1850 became industrial and urban.

Life in the Industrial City

To bring in the raw materials, most cities in the United States grew at harbor sites or where rivers joined. Factories tended to be centralized. The workers at first were within walking distance of the factories and crowded into tenements lacking elementary sanitation or privacy. Workers came from the "old world," from poverty-ridden rural areas within the United States, and from the slavery of the post–Civil War South. They came to shacks and slums to fringe areas and tenements. In mining towns they were housed in company barracks and paid in script usable only in the company store. They came pushed by poverty and persecution because there was work, food, a roof, a bed, and the hope for a better tomorrow.

In the early 1900s child labor laws removed those under age 12 (and later 15) from the mine, mills, and factories. Women tended to be at the sewing machine and men in the fabricating mill. Wages of $5 a week required the entire household to work to survive. Workplaces were dangerous. Illness and accident ended a worker's income and increased the burden on the remainder of the family. To the mill owner, workers were replaceable and far less costly than machines.

Of course there were protests. There were over 2,000 strikes between 1880 and 1900. Some were so bitter that armed militia were used to crush the workers and "preserve public order." In the Homestead steel strike 20 workers were killed and 3,000 fired. Most of the millions who struck before 1900 were defeated by the united power of industrialists and the government.

By the turn of the century, industrialists had increased productivity by introducing more machines. Under union pressure, working conditions improved and hours were reduced. The workday was shortened to about ten hours and the workweek to six days with Sunday off. Urban transportation improved so that workers were dispersed more widely and crowding was somewhat alleviated, at least for those who were allowed and willing to assimilate into the dominant society. As children of European ancestry left the factories, they were gradually absorbed into schools that kept the same starting time as factories. After school there were delivery and cleaning jobs and the streets for play.

By 1960 city dwellers were more than 70% of the population occupying 1% of the land. The industrial city gradually spread out from its original tight rings to neighborhoods linked by transportation and communication. Racial and ethnic segregation characterized the city determined by waves of immigration, discrimination, and poverty. Many who could fled the city for the safety and space of the suburbs. In time the metropolis expanded cities to ten times their early industrial size.

The Work Schedule

Many significant changes have occurred since 1850. It required a century for the average workweek to be halved, from as high as 80 hours in the beginning of the factory era to 70 hours in 1850, 65 in 1870, 62 in 1890, 55 in 1910, 45 in 1930, and to about 40 in 1950. The decrease came at a decreasing rate. Factors in the reduction included union pressures, social reform efforts, and the greater efficiency of the mechanized assembly line. Manufacturers came to realize that long hours were less productive.

People gradually came to have more time. A common union slogan was "eight hours for work, eight hours for rest, and eight hours for what we will." There was even time for pleasure on Sundays, weekday off hours, and eventually a half or whole day off on Saturday (Rybczynski, 1991). There were paid holidays, both sacred and secular, factory "down times," and eventually the vacation (Aron, 1999).

The social timetables still revolved around work and the necessity to operate the factory and the office in a synchronized way. Yet, life could also be divided between work on the one hand and family/leisure on the other. Increasingly the geography of the city, together with the factory and office schedule, divided the domains of life. From one perspective, this division is the beginning of modern leisure. It can be seen as separate, at least from the times and places of work.

At first everyone within the laboring class was in the factory—men, women, and children. In time, however, children were barred from the workplace and women became less likely to stay in the mills once they married and bore children. The factory not only separated people from the land but also separated families from each other by gender as well as age. Employed women were in gender-segregated industries. More and more, men became the "provider" and women expected to focus on home and family. Women were in the paid work force mainly in conditions of economic necessity. Work at home was directed toward women, unpaid, and considered of marginal economic value. Paid employment was also segregated by race and ethnicity and discrimination stratified all of life—including leisure.

The Struggle for Leisure

There was concern about the leisure of workers. As outlined in the previous chapter, the focus was on the loss of productivity due to Sunday dissipation. Apprehension was expressed from church pulpits and in editorials about the inability of industrial workers to develop leisure that would contribute to work and family life. Of course, the work schedule kept the machines operating as long as was considered efficient and productive. Shorter hours and better working conditions developed slowly as mill owners found they led to increased productivity and fewer accidents. The so-called "work ethic" was hardly universal among workers who experienced the power of owners to shape their lives. The workplace was an area where access and opportunity, conditions, hours, and wages were contested.

At the same time, there was a struggle for leisure—for time and freedom of expression. Industrialists joined with social reformers, religious organizations, and political machines to offer to workers leisure alternatives that did not threaten the social order or reduce productivity. Control was exercised over ethnic celebrations imported from the "old country" and over bars, drinking, gambling, and disruptive "street" activity. Nonetheless, alcohol was common and gambling continued on boxing, cockfighting, cards, animal combat, and other contests. Most went underground as did the consumption of alcohol during Prohibition. Workers rebelled against such regulation and subverted the system of control by hiding places of such recreation and bribing the police. Women protested their legally limited economic, political, and leisure rights and opportunities. Unions began their long fight for better working conditions, fair wages, and time for leisure—at least for those of European-American ancestry.

During this period of struggle, there were the thousands of strikes and demonstrations of resistance in the workplace. There were also conflicts over leisure and resistance to attempts to control activity away from the workplace.

Alternatives to such self-organized leisure began to be offered by private institutions, public agencies, and the market.

The Recreation Movement

The recreation movement expressed in its inception a humanitarian response to the city, an economic concern over productivity, and a political attempt to socialize individuals into "their place" in an increasingly diverse society. Children were being arrested for swimming off piers in New York. The only playgrounds were the streets. Reformers such as Joseph Lee, Jacob Riis, Luther Gulick and Jane Addams worked to organize public concern and develop programs for the cities. In 1885 a little sand was placed in a Boston churchyard for neighborhood children. By 1900 a few small playgrounds and parks for recreation rather than just the strolling and carriages of the upper class were established. Just before and after World War I, provision of neighborhood recreation centers became part of public programs in many cities. The more than two million acres in city parks in the 1970s had taken over a century for development. Among the significant events were:

1820–1840: Some schools and colleges provide outdoor gyms and sports areas

1853: Land purchased for Central Park in New York although the design was for strolling more than games and sports

1885: Sand garden at Parmenter Street Chapel in Boston

1892: Model playground at Hull House in Chicago

1892: 100 cities had designated land for parks

1905: Opening of the South Parks in Chicago

1906: Playground Association of America organized with support of President Theodore Roosevelt

1924: President Calvin Coolidge calls the first Conference on Outdoor Recreation

1930: National Recreation Association formed. First national congress held in 1932

1945: North Carolina establishes first state recreation commission

The reformers in the recreation movement protested the indifference toward those working in the factories and their living conditions. Coming from schools and churches, they protested child labor, degrading working conditions, low wages, unemployment, the health threats of tenement living, and even the compliance of government officials in suppressing worker protests. Some were especially concerned with the lack of opportunities for children and youth to play, learn, and develop healthy bodies and minds. They saw children with no place to play and the consequent waste of human lives. They were also concerned that "healthy exercise" replaced activities that rendered workers unfit for their 60 hours a week in the factory.

Joseph Lee and others considered constructive leisure to be essential to rebuilding the industrial city to support life, health, human growth, and development. Play, while providing its own intrinsic motivation, was essential to the full development of human life from childhood on. It therefore was a public responsibility to provide opportunities for everyone to engage in constructive play and recreation. The public recreation movement was, from its beginning, reformist and political as well as humanistic and inclusive of those whose heritage was European. It was only later, when racism was recognized as a social problem, that those from other parts of the world—such as Africa and China—were included in public recreation provision.

The public sector was joined by numerous private organizations. Luther Gulick, for example, was director of physical education for the YMCAs in the United States. Jane Addams' Hull House on the near West Side of Chicago combined recreation programs with education, health, and political organization. The Ladies' Club of the Staten Island Cricket and Baseball Club offered opportunity for women to play tennis. However, many of these private organizations as well were segregated in their programs (Henderson, Bialeschki, Shaw & Freysinger, 1996). Still, marginalized racial groups had organizations of their own, including those that provided for recreational interests (Kraus, 1994). Urban churches joined in the provision of neighborhood opportunities. On the local level, countless women and men of all races worked for better conditions of education, housing, sanitation, and recreation. For the most part, the private organizations complemented public programs in their more age-focused and localized efforts. In some communities, the mill and mine owners also opened various institutes for the education and recreation of their workers.

Market Sector Recreation in the City

Some of the market sector provisions of recreation were precisely what the reformers decried: places for drinking, gambling, and fighting. There were dance halls where female textile workers met men from the factories to the despair of those who would protect the virtue of women (Piess, 1986). In the crowded city, it was difficult to find any place to gather for leisure of any kind. In the emerging ethnic and racial minority neighborhoods of the city, in warm weather the tenement doorways and porches became alternatives to the crowded flats. Men met in taverns and illegal shebeens.

In time, a variety of amusements dotted the city streets. The Bowery in New York combined melodramas and variety acts with the atmosphere of smoke, beer, and sweat. Theaters offered melodramas and such extravaganzas as Buffalo Bill's Wild West, Rocky Mountain, and Prairie Exhibition that played to over a million people in a five-month tour with cowboys, Indians, stagecoaches, and even Sitting Bull himself. P.T. Barnum's Circus was a national institution by the 1840s. Burlesque, vaudeville, and other entertainment shared the stage with drama. There were dance halls, shooting galleries, bowling alleys, pool halls, and beer gardens (Cross, 1990).

By the end of the 19th century, the electric trolley transported people to amusement parks on the outskirts of the cities. Coney Island in New York had bathhouses, minstrel bands, dance halls, shows, and a series of exciting rides. Chicago's Midway at the World's Fair of 1893 introduced the Ferris wheel, soon duplicated in hundreds of the trolley parks. Harlem in New York City, with its theaters, restaurants, nightclubs and burlesque shows, provided social life and entertainment for affluent African Americans. Over time the talent and entertainment Harlem offered also attracted wealthy Whites whose pleasure may have been enhanced by the excitement of crossing the "color line."

Attempts to ban various "unhealthy" activities and venues in time turned to regulation. Selling alcoholic beverages required licenses. All gathering places, such as theaters and dance halls, were required to have licenses and inspections. Hours of opening and closing were controlled. The churches continued in their efforts to control activities on the Sabbath. Ethnic holiday celebrations were policed and even shut down if they were considered a threat to public order. Yet, the range of market-sector recreation provisions continued to expand, especially as wage levels increased and factory hours were reduced.

At the same time, the scale of such amusements changed. Great movie palaces owned and developed by national syndicates replaced the neighborhood penny movies. The film industry became dominated by a few corporations that controlled both production and distribution. Sports became spectacles to be consumed as leagues were organized and franchises sold as profit-producing enterprises. In time, government and business combined to control the airwaves for radio, television, and electronic communications. The neighborhood scale of commercial entertainment became national and in the end global.

The Rise of Spectator Sports

Even before the Civil War, there were major sporting events for males. As many as 100,000 crossed the Hudson River from New York for horse races. Boxing was generally illegal, but drew crowds in the back rooms of saloons, warehouses, and outdoors where authorities could not enforce the prohibitions. By the 1860s, athletic clubs promoted track and field meets, gymnastics were sponsored by the YMCAs and YWCAs, and colleges began intercollegiate football.

For the upper classes there was lawn bowling, tennis, the foxhunt, polo, coaching, cycling, rowing, and other elite sports. In time, many filtered down to the working class as well. The peculiarly American sport was baseball. By 1845, some men had formed the Knickerbocker Club and adopted rules specifying nine men to a side, three outs to an inning, and 21 runs as the winning score. The first teams were composed of "gentlemen," but by 1855 the Eckford Club in Brooklyn was made up of mechanics and shipwrights. The sport moved West. By 1858, Chicago had four teams. The National Association of Base Ball Players was formed to organize the sport nationally. In 1869, the Cincinnati Red Stockings became the first professional team to tour. In 1871, the amateurs of the National Association lost a dispute with the professionals. Within a few years, the players lost control to the owners and the present economic basis for professional sport was established. African-American men organized their own teams and Rube Foster founded the Negro Baseball League in Chicago in the early 1920s.

In the "trickle-down" patterns elite sports were adopted by the middle and lower classes. The roller skating rinks for the wealthy in Newport led to popular arenas in cities across the country. The first recorded football game between Princeton and Rutgers in 1869 was revived by Harvard and Yale three years later. By 1888, 40,000 attended the Princeton-Yale contest and football as a mass spectator sport was under way. Again, such sports were primarily for upper-class Caucasian males at the time. In time, working-class men, not women, entered the playing fields, often with considerable opposition.

The trends were evident: elite inauguration leading to mass adoption, professionalization, and the growth of spectator sports. Sport became a major form of urban recreation in its marketed provisions of mass entertainment.

Did the Industrial Revolution Create Modern Leisure?

Certainly, the new industrial city was nothing like the agricultural small town. In size, crowded conditions, racial and ethnic diversity and living arrangements, the city was a new creation that changed every aspect of life. Working conditions in the mine and mill were nothing like the farm or home-based handcrafts. The family was divided by the age and gender divisions of labor. The home and the workplace were separated as well as segregated by class, ethnicity, and race. The entire social timetable became based on factory schedules rather than the rhythms and seasons of agriculture. Formerly separated ethnic and racial groups were jammed together in the same city, factory, and sometimes neighborhood. Space in and around the living quarters was reduced by the need to have masses of workers near the factory.

In the process of change, leisure was also transformed. It became time segregated from work rather than interwoven into the round of the day and week. It became more secularized and cut off from religious influence. It moved from the crowded tenement to places where workers, especially men, could gather. It was a break and an escape from the long hours and dangerous conditions of the factory. In time it became more a matter of being entertained in the commercial leisure places. Leisure was regulated and organized in the time and space scarcities of the industrial city.

Industrialization and the Work Ethic

From the preceding outline of change, it is evident the nature of industrial work had become quite different from former crafts—especially those associated with agriculture. It would be expected that meanings of work would be changed in the process. Yet, there was an old tradition that life should have work at its center. In fact, according to some traditions, work was a central value for life with leisure seen as peripheral or even a danger. This tradition of the Puritans was claimed to be a consequence of the European Protestant Reformation in the 1600s.

Religion, the Reformation, and the Work Ethic

One consequence of the Protestant Reformation that occurred in Europe in the 1600s was to shift the attention of the faithful from the heavenly world to the earthly. The Reformation is credited with focusing on the work of this world. Martin Luther's writings are full of the concept of the *secular calling*—the idea that God calls people to their work in commerce and agriculture as much as to prayer and holy orders. His stress on "salvation by faith alone" placed a new emphasis on work and the joys and responsibilities of family life.

In Geneva, Switzerland, John Calvin took up the same themes and intensified certain aspects of them. To develop a city government, he stressed the responsibilities of citizenship and the common life. He also added a religious motivation for engagement in the commerce of the world at a time that business and trade were developing. As commerce became more widespread and complex, the early modes of capitalism began to emerge. Money became a medium of both investment and exchange. It was also a standard of accomplishment that could be measured and compared. The feudal focus on titles, land, and inherited status was broken by adding the control of financial resources for investment as well as spending.

Max Weber: The Rise of Capitalism

Over three centuries after Luther and Calvin, Max Weber, a German sociologist, attempted to combat the Marxist argument that history was essentially determined by economic or "material" structures and forces. Weber (1958) tried to demonstrate that ideas, even religious ones, could be factors in shaping economic change. He noted capitalism was most developed in Protestant-dominated areas of Europe and especially those where Calvinist influence was strongest. His argument can be outlined as follows:

1. Capitalism requires the availability of capital. To attract capital, there must be an acceptance of the idea that money can make money and that investment should be rewarded.

2. The connection between capitalism and Protestantism is an ethic that stresses life in the secular world of work as a sphere of faithful activity.

3. Paradoxically, such a this-worldly ethic is based on a doctrine of the absolute sovereignty of God in which humans can do nothing to gain their own salvation. However, they can demonstrate the likelihood of their divine election in the manner of their earthly lives.

4. These qualities of earthly life include a devotion to work, sobriety, discipline, and consequent economic success. Such "this-worldly asceticism" means that the profits from business success cannot be spent on pleasures, but are available as investment capital. The work ethic combines with a lifestyle of carefulness and discipline to further the development of capitalism. This lifestyle, according to Weber, denies personal pleasure in order to invest one's life properly in the church, family, state, and economic enterprise.

Later analysis raised many questions about the accuracy of Weber's historical analysis, but the idea of the work ethic has taken on a life of its own. Further, the idea has been useful in understanding the expansion of this value system, especially in its Puritan form, to England and the New World. More recently a secular form of the work ethic has been separated from its religious origin. No one argues that there is anything peculiarly Protestant about a work ethic that glorifies a secular calling to productivity. Further, it is hardly surprising that a work ethic has been promulgated by those who benefit from it most—those who invest themselves and their capital in productive enterprise.

What is the current relevance of the work ethic? There is little question that a serious view of life and work has characterized many of those who gather capital and operate businesses on America's Main Streets or those whose financial interests have been improved by the hard work of others. There is evidence of the centrality of work to many who have a career orientation and the idea that hard work today will lead to a better economic future.

Evidence of the continued relevance of a negative aspect of the work ethic also exists. There is still a suspicion that leisure, especially in its pleasure-seeking forms, may be a danger to both the individual and the community. Recreation as a restoration for work is justified by its contribution to productivity and health. But leisure as activity done primarily for the experience, especially if that experience is one of pleasure rather than constructive development, is not accepted as a positive value by many with some residue of the work ethic and its this-worldly asceticism. There may even be vestiges of Puritanism hiding beneath layers of the culture.

Industrial Work and the Work Ethic

The history of work conditions in the mine and mill sketched earlier, the decades of conflict and strikes, and the excesses of Sunday leisure do not support the likelihood of a strong work ethic among those workers of the early Industrial Revolution. Theirs was more a struggle for survival, often against those whose investments built the factories of industrial capitalism. It seems unlikely a strong work ethic from a period of crafts, agriculture, and small business would have survived generations of life and death in early industrialization.

Nonetheless, the myth of the work ethic survived. It was reinforced by waves of immigration from Europe and later from Asia bringing workers who believed in the "American Dream" that hard work would yield a better life. Such an ethic was promoted as an ideology by those who believed that, in time, a growing economy would benefit all, or at least more, of its work force. Ethnic, racial, and gender barriers to rewarding work tended to be ignored by those who had gained access to some level of the system. At the same time, work conditions of safety and hours were improving for many—though not all as racism continued to shape everyday life and opportunities. Wages went up as hours went down. Eventually, the regularly employed American worker had a very different life from that of those earlier days of privation and danger.

But there was more going on in the workplace than an improvement in conditions, hours, and wages. The factory with its expensive machinery and the competitive marketplace placed a greater and greater emphasis on productivity. The changes now are referred to under the labels of "Taylorism" and "Fordism."

Friedrich Taylor applied the stopwatch to design time-and-motion studies of production processes. His "scientific management" divided tasks to their simplest components and reassembled them to maximize efficiency. Every sense of fabrication and relationship to the product was sacrificed to make the worker an efficient component of the mechanized process. In the Bethlehem Steel Works, Taylor's designs increased steel handling efficiency fourfold. In this scheme, the worker became a complex machine, to be routinized into maximum productivity. No consideration was given to making work fulfilling, challenging in complexity, or autonomous.

Henry Ford wanted to make automobile manufacturing a mass production rather than a craft operation. To make the Model T, he redesigned the factory and production line into standardized repetitive processes. The consequent productive efficiency produced a car that the masses could afford. At the same time, he paid his factory workers the unheard-of wage of $5 a day so that they might become consumers of the product they built. The key to this "Fordism" was absolute control of every motion of the production process. His aim was also to control the family and leisure lives of his workers. In their conformity to the factory and their application to productivity, they were to be rewarded by becoming consumers, not only of Model Ts but also of the myriad products of the growing economy. Fordism combined mass production and mass consumption. Ford's experiment was barely the beginning. The great American production economy, especially in hard goods such as steel and cars, was the strongest in the world. Only since the mid-20th century has globalization threatened American economic power.

There were, however, questions raised about the modern production process. One was the alienation from the process and the product created by dividing tasks into their simplest components. Working became repetition rather than actually "making" something. Further, the modern factory made social exchange among workers difficult because of the pressures of the assembly line.

More recently, other threats to the meaning of work emerged. The security of industrial employment has been eroded as labor-intensive manufacturing has been moved to low-wage parts of the world. The contract of security between ownership and labor has been broken as plants have closed. Also, the reduction in manufacturing jobs has been accompanied by the increase in service sector employment. In discount retailing, healthcare, and other such workplaces, lack of security has been joined with low wages. Households, as in the early industrial period, are often supported by several jobs, no one of which can pay the bills. The whole idea of a work career with anticipated progression in a single corporation or trade has been attacked by production and market globalization.

In such conditions, some proposed the "leisure solution to work." If work has become insecure, unfulfilling, and largely instrumental, then the answer may be in the nonwork domains of life. Of course, the job may support the household, and the family in its nurturing and supporting roles. It may also support leisure—activity in which an individual can find meaning and fulfillment. And there is also all the consumption related to both the household and leisure. The purchase of both durable goods—the refrigerator and second car—and of pleasure are made possible by work, however uncertain and routine. This is "Fordism" carried into what has been called a "postindustrial age."

Debate: The work ethic has been lost.

YES

- The work ethic was a good fit in a preindustrial capitalist economy. The results of disciplined hard work were immediate and evident. This connection, however, was a casualty of industrialization. The discipline of the factory was forced, not voluntary. Obedience to rules and routines is not an internalized ethic. The factory had its division of labor, detailed and synchronized tasks, and rigid articulation of worker and machine. The worker became just another means of production. No wonder a work ethic disappeared.

- The promoters of the work ethic in the 20th century were those who benefited from it—owners and managers in production and those in small businesses. They were usually those who used the labor of others or invested in its processes. Productivity is essential to competitive capitalism, especially now in a global economy. Those who lament the loss of the work ethic are often the same corporate executives who move their production to $2-a-day regions and "downsize" their own companies.

- The history of labor in the United States is one of resistance and conflict. The harsh and exploitative conditions of the mill and mine with long hours and low wages went a long way to kill the work ethic brought from the crafts of the old country.

- The value of work has become largely instrumental. Work is what we do to support a family, provide a home, buy a car, and finance a vacation. All kinds of research demonstrate that home, family, and even leisure are valued more than work by most of those who are employed. Now that more workers are in the insecure service sector rather than production, there is no indication of change. Of primary importance to most people are their relationships with those they share life most fully and intimately.

- The contemporary economic stress on cost has been accentuated by the global economy. Even small businesses are in competition with the discount chains and their worldwide supply sources. In global capitalism, investment is rewarded first and labor considered a cost of production. Why should workers be loyal to a company that is always ready and willing to eliminate their jobs to shave the cost of production 5%?

- Considerable employment now is temporary. Most of those in the paid work force have jobs, not careers. Further, those jobs come in no particular sequence of advancement. Especially in the service sector in which the skills of most jobs can be acquired in a few days (or even hours), people are interchangeable. The former connection between hard work and a secure position with a career of advancement is lost. Many work long hours out of fear of being replaced— not from positive motivation. The skills are now in the automated machine and the computer, not the worker. The remaining jobs mostly involve cleaning up. Entry-level wages at age 30 or 40 hardly stimulate a work ethic.

- Finally, the traditional work ethic involves "this-worldly asceticism" as well as a devotion to the job. What kind of sense does this make in contemporary society? Ours is a culture of possession, consumption, and expression. "Do it" and "flaunt it" are the current watchwords. Go with the style. Buy the latest status symbol. Leap into the fad. "Godly, righteous, and sober" hardly describe the lives of the middle masses today, not to mention celebrities and the wealthy. This is a culture of display, not restraint. In fact, both themes of the work ethic are gone—the devotion to hard work and the restrained lifestyle.

NO

- Work is still a central identity for most adults. We introduce ourselves by what we do in the economy. Men and women wear corporate labels. Many women are now embarrassed to admit they are "just housewives and mothers," and men cannot accept being primary parents or "househusbands." Work remains a major source of pride, a sign of ability, and a sign of worth. Even the retired claim the identity of their former work. Within the work context, there is still some pride in doing the job well. Work is a part of who we are and how we present ourselves to others.

- There are all kinds of new craft dimensions to many jobs. Computerization now requires new skills that have to be learned. Look at what is necessary in retailing to check out customers or to complete the quarterly inventory. The information processing of even the smallest business is computerized and demanding. The hard and dangerous physical labor of the old factory has been largely replaced by electronic controls that call for intelligent maintenance and supervision, not backbreaking toil. Such work can be a challenge as workers need to continually acquire new skills.

- The work ethic has been contained, not lost. Of course there are routine jobs. There always have been. But those who have some control over their work destinies are motivated by a drive to do well and succeed. The "new class" of workers who have gained costly skills and are expensive to replace are likely to work hard and long. They see a connection between what they do and their own futures. They can tie rewards of status and income to what they produce on the job—and they tend to be well-rewarded for their efforts. Granted, some jobs discourage a work ethic, but there are a significant number of those that do not.

- Work still gives us a sense of worth. We are rewarded with income and status because what we do is considered important. Nothing quite substitutes for that recognition. Further, most want to make some kind of contribution to their society. Work may not be the only possibility for this, but it remains a central one. Even those who are retired often want to do things that are recognized as being of value, even when they are not paid for it.

- It is possible we are slowly coming to redefine work. It is more than what we get paid to do. Rather, work is anything that is of value which contributes to our common life. What is more important than caring for and nurturing children (a task for which parents are not paid)? Work may be satisfying because of its challenges, its worth, and its recognition. In fact, some paid employment is hardly work by those criteria. In the more inclusive sense, it is activity of social as well as economic value. Fulfilling life always incorporates work. In such activity, there is a built-in work ethic that is part of its essential meaning.

- Any number of efforts are being made to enhance productive work by giving workers more control over the process and more of a relationship with the product itself. Workers may move down the line with a car as a team and then drive it off the end of the line themselves. Redesigning jobs may increase both productivity and satisfaction. Pride may be instilled in programs to increase quality. Insofar as a work ethic requires certain work conditions, an ethic may be redeveloped by redesign.

- In many of the services, there is considerable human interaction. Caring for frail elderly in a nursing home may be extremely underpaid, but there may also be some satisfaction in contributing to the comfort of those being cared for. Even conversation at the check-out counter can be enjoyable and yield a sense of relatedness and community. Such work is personal and direct with the meanings and satisfactions of human response and interaction.

- There is also the possibility of transferring the work ethic to other domains of life. For many, the development of healthy and happy children is the most important work of their lives. For others, the satisfactions of developing and exercising a skill, once limited to work, may be found in leisure. One theme of the work ethic, doing something well, may be moved to other parts of life. The work ethic may be transferred rather than lost for some people.

Discussion Questions

1. How have factories changed since the early days of the Industrial Revolution? Have computers really ended the drudgery of work?

2. How is work intrinsically rewarding? Can work involve play? How?

3. Who is working longer hours? shorter hours? Who is most likely to have more than one job?

4. Can leisure provide an adequate solution to the problems of work?

5. What are the current dimensions of conflict between management and labor?

6. How is work gendered, or different for men and women?

7. How do ethnicity and race differentiate work today?

8. Should we now learn to find most of satisfaction and meaning outside of work?

9. Can work hours be reduced further? Why or why not? How?

References and Resources

Andrew, E. (1981). *Closing the iron cage: The scientific management of work and leisure*. Montreal, PQ: Black Rose Books.

Aron, C. (1999). *Working at play: A history of vacations in the United States*. New York, NY: Oxford University Press.

Bettman, O. (1974). *The good old days—They were terrible*. New York, NY: Random House.

Boyer, P. (1978). *Urban masses and the moral order in America: 1820–1920*. New Haven, CT: Yale University Press.

Chinoy, E. (1955). *Automobile workers and the American dream*. New York, NY: Doubleday.

Cross, G. (1990). *A social history of leisure since 1600*. State College, PA: Venture Publishing, Inc.

Cumbler, J. (1979). *Working-class community in industrial America: Work, leisure, and struggle in two industrial cities, 1880–1930*. Westport, CT: Greenwood Press.

Cunningham, H. (1980). *Leisure and the industrial revolution*. London, UK: Croom Held.

Dulles, F. (1965). *A history of recreation—America learns to play* (2nd ed.). Englewood Cliffs, NJ: Prentice Hall.

Ehrenreich, B. (1991). *The worst years of our lives: Irreverent notes from a decade of greed* ("Good-bye to the Work Ethic"). New York, NY: Pantheon Books.

Eisen, G. and Wiggins, D. (Eds.). (1994). *Ethnicity in sport in North American history and culture.* Westport, CT: Greenwood Press.

Hardy, S. (1982). *How Boston played: Sport, recreation, and community, 1865–1915.* Boston, MA: Northeastern University Press.

Henderson, K.A., Bialeschki, M.D., Shaw, S.M., and Freysinger, V.J. (1996). *Both gains and gaps: Feminist perspectives on women's leisure.* State College, PA: Venture Publishing, Inc.

Hunnicutt, B. (1988). *Work without end: Abandoning shorter hours for the right work.* Philadelphia, PA: Temple University Press.

Kraus, R. (1994). *Leisure in a changing America: Multicultural perspectives.* New York, NY: MacMillan.

McPherson, T. (2003). *Reconstructing Dixie: Race, gender and nostalgia in the imagined South.* Durham, NC: Duke University Press.

Piess, K. (1986). *Cheap amusements: Working women and leisure in turn-of-the-century New York.* Philadelphia, PA: Temple University Press.

Rodgers, D.T. (1978). *The work ethic in industrial America, 1850–1920.* Chicago, IL: University of Chicago Press.

Rosenzweig, R. (1978). *Eight hours for what we will: Workers and leisure in the industrial city, 1870–1920.* New York, NY: Columbia University Press.

Rybczynski, W. (1991). *Waiting for the weekend.* New York, NY: Viking Penguin Press.

Terkel, S. (1974). *Working: Working people talk about what they do all day and how they feel about what they do.* New York, NY: Pantheon.

Weber, M. (1958). *The Protestant ethic and the spirit of capitalism.* (T. Parsons, Trans.). New York, NY: Scribner's.

Chapter 5
The Consumer Society

Change, however dramatic, does not stop. A glance at 50-year periods in the United States makes this clear. From 1850 to 1900 the Industrial Revolution transformed both the economy and its geography. Work, family, and leisure were all transformed. In the 50 years from 1900 to 1950, there were two World Wars, an economic boom in the 1920s followed by the Great Depression of the 1930s, and a continuation of industrialization and urbanization. The first 50 years of the century were an unsettling time—a time of disruption with each decade different from the one before.

The end of World War II was the beginning of another new era. Pent-up consumer demand from wartime led to remarkable economic growth. The cities expanded into the megalopolis with its suburban rings. Interstate highways and the jet airplane made travel more time-efficient. A higher proportion of the population went to college, led by the GI Bill classes returning from the war. Of course there were economic downturns, but they seemed largely contained by momentum and government action. There were challenges to the system, especially in the Civil Rights movement and opposition to the war in Vietnam. On the whole, however, the 1950s to 1970s was a period of growth and confidence in which each generation seemed to have a fuller material life than the one before. Science and technology were seen as the center of continual growth and expansion. The Cold War and nuclear threat were clouds on the horizon and then even those dissipated.

In their impacts on leisure, three changes appear to have been most significant in the second half of the 20th century: suburbanization, technological development, and consumerism.

Suburban Growth

The industrial city had its core of finance, retailing, and culture surrounded by rings of factories, warehouses, and housing. The wealthy lived in enclaves on hilltops or along the shorelines. Workers lived in more dense neighborhoods with the most recent immigrants crowded into older areas. Further, racial discrimination closed most of the city to Latino, African, and Asian Americans and concentrated them into segregated ghettos. Railroads spoked into the city carrying raw materials in and manufactured goods out.

In time suburbs grew along the rail lines that carried passengers commuting to central city offices. Most suburbs were populated by middle-class, white-collar workers. Working-class suburbs were the exception until late in the century. By then, many factories moved out of the city to be along the railways and expressways and drew their work force with them. The patterns were not geographically uniform. Some suburban communities were built for the wealthy with estates that provided ample space and privacy. Some of those have remained exclusive. Other suburbs ringed the city with the estates of the wealthy furthest out from the central city.

Where Are the People Now?

The ecology of the city changed during this 50-year period from the centralized industrial city to the decentralized metropolis. Suburbs were developed for all households with relatively stable incomes and employment (Jackson, 1985). Suburbs were initially populated by European Americans. The federal government guaranteed home loans with low interest and low down payments. Home ownership became a realized dream for a large proportion of the population. The suburb was seen as the ideal environment for raising children. The private home had indoor and outside space for family life. There were yards and parks for children's play. The schools were new and prepared students for further education. As cities became more and more racially diverse, "White flight" to the suburbs occurred. At the same time, suburbs also developed that were predominantly populated by racial minorities. Increasingly suburbs had their own retailing enterprises and became less dependent on the central city. Five days a week the suit-and-tie garbed businessmen (usually men) left for the city in the morning and returned in the evening. Work was separated from the family by distance and by schedule. The weekend was for the family. There were a number of elements in this new suburban lifestyle:

- The residence became the center of leisure. There was space in the home and yard for play, especially for children. Entertaining was also done at home. The housewife was the home and family manager—

a full-time if not an honored job. The husband was the provider who also engaged in "manly" tasks around the home on weekends.

- Work was in the city and leisure in the suburb. There might be occasional forays back into the city for special events, but ordinary leisure was separated from work. In fact, a neighbor's city-based work was often unknown. Home, car, children, and possibly some community activity constituted a segregated realm of leisure.

- As a consequence, public recreation also became suburbanized with the expansion of traditional sports programs into more comprehensive offerings, especially for children.

- Leisure also tended to be segregated by gender. Community organizations such as service clubs and fraternal organizations were for men, often with a separate auxiliary for wives. Sports were a male fortress. Even churches tended to divide their social programs by gender with the assumption that women were available on weekdays during school hours. Of course, women were also the support staff and chauffeurs for children's after-school activities. The ideology of motherhood and domesticity ruled the lives of suburban women. In one study of suburban leisure, the round of club meetings, visiting, parties, and child-centered roles became a complete round of obligatory activity in the new suburb (Lundberg, Komarovsky & McInerny, 1934).

- Leisure was also segregated by race and ethnicity. For example, community organizations were developed by Jewish and Polish Catholic groups, and suburban neighborhoods were often ethnically homogeneous. Race continued to distinguish the suburbs as well and today we still see affluent and more modest suburban neighborhoods surrounding the larger cities that lack racial diversity. This is a result of both preference and opportunity.

- The private car was the key. It enabled the individual and the household to go in any direction and considerable distance for almost anything. At elementary levels, there might still be the neighborhood school. Everything else required the car. It did not take village governments long to begin to require parking for most buildings in which people gathered. Detached homes and large yards took up a lot of space, but the car made it all possible.

This trend toward suburbanization impacted every aspect of life. Almost all urban growth has been suburban. Churches have become multifaceted leisure providers surrounded by large parking lots. Retailing has moved out of the central city and even out of the suburbs downtown to the malls and strips along the multilane highways. Interstate highways and limited-access motorways draw megamalls at their intersections. The neighborhood movie theater has given way to the multiplex and its acres of parking.

Not only the neighborhood but also the distinct town and suburb have become more and more marginal to life. Public schools are built on campuses outside the town. Shopping is in the magnet malls to which one must drive. Restaurants are franchises in the same malls. Even small shops have moved to the strip malls along the main streets and outside the downtown. The suburban complex is an entirely new geography of life. In this dramatic shift, the poor have been left behind in the areas of the city that have been abandoned by industry, retailing, and almost all kinds of development. With the population, economic opportunity has become suburbanized.

Suburban Life and Leisure

In this built ecology, leisure has two main locales. The first is in the private residence. The home is designed for more than eating and sleeping. It is the primary locale of leisure, augmented by the new technologies of entertainment. The second locale of leisure is the commercial development. Most often also in the mall, entertainment is united with retail business. Giant developments, such as the Mall of the Americas in Minneapolis, combine shopping and play under one massive roof.

Suburban life is a life of separation. Work and family are separated. Leisure in the home is privatized, separated from the larger community. Both public and market-sector leisure provisions tend to separate by age, income, and often by gender and race. The most common out-of-the-home leisure activity may be shopping in a combination of play and commerce. Stores are open seven days a week and sometimes all or most of the day and night. The multicar family in the suburb goes all directions at once in search of pleasure that can be purchased.

There are, however, new communities being formed. They are not the "natural" communities of the work group or the neighborhood. Rather, they are "intentional communities" formed around a particular activity or association. Groups are formed around common interests and activities, such as the studio, exercise center, or sports arena. Groups are constructed by life stage and its leisure, such as the retirement communities of the southeastern or southwestern United States. Regular associations are formed around all kinds of activity. The team, class, or group that travels together may become a primary group. Such intentional communities of leisure may also have quite limited commitment. One can drop out with little social cost. In a time when people move, associate and dissociate, everything, including friendship, seems temporary and transient.

Transforming Technologies

Photography was invented by 1839, the telephone by 1876, radio by 1902, television by 1934, the transistor by 1953, and the integrated circuit by 1961. Each technology has had significant leisure as well as industrial applications. A technology may transform patterns of social life. The same kinds of family groups that listened to radio comedies during the Depression 1930s and War news during the 1940s turned to television in the 1950s and 1960s.

Technologies have transformed activities. Fiberglass and epoxies have dominated the boat market. The same material technologies were applied to skiing, permitting revolutions in technique as well as greater safety and broadened participation. Fiberglass, graphite, and ceramics have permitted the redesign of racquets in tennis and other racquet sports. No sport or activity has been untouched by the development of related science and technology.

A few *transforming technologies* have changed more than activities. They have changed entire patterns of living. Their impacts have been so powerful and near universal that no element of common life was untouched. The two technologies that transformed leisure were, of course, the private car and television. However, there are other technologies that have had profound impacts. Now the electronics revolution promises to change patterns of everyday life. Probably some would argue that even microwave cooking had significant effects on leisure scheduling.

Early Leisure Technologies

The geography of leisure in the industrial city was changed by electricity. The electric trolley expanded leisure possibilities, as well as the environment, by replacing the horse-drawn trolley. Silent films in little neighborhood parlors were replaced by grand "movie palaces." Amusement parks required electricity for transportation, power, and light. The telephone not only permitted conversations across distances but also allowed people to make arrangements for leisure events and assemblies. Photography became a mass activity when Kodak took the unreliable glass plate and, in time, offered the box camera and the Brownie.

The "wireless" transmission of sound across distances was another revolution. Radio, first a means of communication, became a medium of mass entertainment in the home. The home had long been a center of family leisure and celebration as families ate, read, played games and music, and organized celebrations. For many, but not all, crowded tenements were replaced by homes with some space for activity. Then the radio brought entertainment into the home. It required no more than imaginative listening. There were programs for children as well as adults. Some questioned such "passive" leisure, but families scheduled their lives so as not to miss their favorite programs.

The Car and the Expanded Space of Leisure

At first the crafted car was only for the wealthy. Then in 1914 Henry Ford introduced the mass-produced Model T accompanied by the $5 wage for a eight-hour a day (six days a week) at his factories. The assembly line, standardization ("Any color as long as it's black." — Henry Ford), and simplicity of design were to bring the automobile within the reach of an enlarged market.

The results were astounding. By 1927, 85% of the world's cars were built in the United States. In the 1920s a new Model T cost $290 and by 1930 one household in five owned a car. The Depression and the Second World War slowed expansion of the market and production. After 1950 the car came to be taken for granted. Now households often have more than one so that family members can disperse to work and play. Most leisure outside the home requires a car to get there on time. The flexibility of private transportation has dispersed leisure and expanded its catchment areas.

As already suggested, the suburban sprawl of the modern city is one result of the car. The centralized city became decentralized along its superhighways. Private transportation came to dominate travel with over 85% of trips being made by car. The old urban/suburban electric trains were bought up and closed by the automotive industry. Residential dispersal, business location, and leisure provisions all presumed the car. In fact, not to have private transportation means being cut off from all kinds of opportunity.

The entire ecology of the economy developed around the car. Weekend and vacation trips were served by travel-support industries as downtown hotels outside the main cities were replaced by highway motels. "Service" stations lined the highways. Recreation businesses responded to the car. Drive-in movies were teen "passion pits." Drive-in restaurants launched the fast-food industry—and in 1923, the first shopping mall was opened in Kansas City.

Most vacations were taken by car. Just as important to leisure, however, was the ability to move around the community on demand rather than on the timetables of public transportation. The Sunday drive itself became important to family leisure. In the community walking distance became largely irrelevant to leisure except for the play of small children. The car widened leisure opportunity. Dirt roads were paved. Narrow highways were widened and in time became limited access. Travel times were halved and then halved again. National and state parks, scenic drives, public beaches and seashores, regional parks for picnics, camping, and just going out to eat, drink, and be entertained were all made possible by the car.

Far less transforming, but still significant has been the jet airplane. In the second half of the 20th century, air travel has been transformed from a rare and elite experience to an accepted part of ordinary life. The busiest flying period is traditionally Thanksgiving as masses go home for the holiday, but the distances of pleasure travel have also been multiplied by the jet. Cross-country trips are commonplace. Oceans are crossed in a few hours rather than days or weeks. The modern tourist industry is, to a large extent, the product of the jet plane and the complex network of travel it has made possible (see Chapter 22).

Television and the Privatization of Leisure

No study of leisure prior to television is of anything but historical interest. Television has changed everything—and almost everywhere. A recent multinational study of leisure found in every country that watching television and informal social interaction were the chief uses of leisure time. Television was introduced widely in the 1950s. By 1960, television was in 87% of American homes and by 1978 about 98%. Now most homes have VCRs and DVD players as well. No other technology has changed ordinary life so thoroughly and quickly.

The extent and intensity of television watching will be investigated more fully in Chapter 16. In general, those with the most free time watch the most television. In most households, the television is usually on when people are home. There are several leisure impacts:

- Television brought entertainment—easy, accessible, and inexpensive—into the home. The whole concept of the home entertainment center began with television.

- Television has presented new images of play with special locales, equipment, dress, and activities that were formerly strange and distant. The allure of the leisure market is offered in every home.

- Television has expanded horizons of the arts, sports, and travel. The star system is tied to the advertising basis of commercial television. Now cable and satellite offer 50 to 200 channels of entertainment of all kinds, any hour of the day and night.

- Television has reshaped leisure and household timetables with its prime time programming and special events at times once reserved for family interaction, religion, personal development, and education.

The progression from the original small-screen black-and-white sets to color, large screen, video and DVD players, cable, satellite, and pay-per-view programs has been smooth and seems inevitable. Each development has added to choices in both quality and quantity. The big change came with the introduction of television itself. Since then, the home has been the center of entertainment. Patterns of leisure were radically changed. Now there is more to fit into the revised personal and household timetables. The point is that television and its additions have changed everything. Leisure is now more than ever before confined to the home. It is "privatized" and personal in use—a mass consumption product in almost every home.

Other Leisure Technologies

Mass tourism, as already introduced, in its present form was made possible by the jet airplane. The industry, however, has added all sorts of destinations and experiences to the possibilities of travel. There are cruise ships, package tours to almost everywhere, and all sorts of travel-entertainment possibilities built around the airline industry.

The telephone, and now videophone, transformed communications and made it possible to make social and business arrangements without face-to-face contact. How much of life depends on such communication at a distance? But that is not the end. Several forms of electronic communications now allow for both delayed reception and immediacy. The cellular phone makes voice communication portable to car, beach, or any other venue. Electronic mail and digital cameras facilitate messages and allow high-quality images to go quickly to entire groups of people all over the world. Web sites are another form of multiple communication through electronics. Now broadband and digital connections increase speed and variety. We can be assured the industry will continue to develop and offer new communications technologies that may or may not actually make a significant difference in connecting people across physical distances.

A far-reaching technology in the world of finance has been the credit card. Now that technology, too, is global, electronic, and almost instantaneous. It is no longer necessary to carry cash either in one's home community or when traveling. Reservations for hotels, air travel, and rental cars are made with plastic. Meals, equipment, and recreation itself are paid for on credit with a card. Trips for which vacationers have not saved can be taken anyway. "Play now and pay later" fits the mood of pleasure-seekers consuming all kinds of leisure. The shopping mall and the night out are no longer limited by previously earned cash. Of course, one result is skyrocketing credit-card debt and increasing personal bankruptcies.

All this becomes part of a global leisure industry offering a wide variety of entertainment for most segments of the population. The proliferation of theme parks, theme restaurants, and theme malls blend leisure with marketing. And all of this is made alluring daily through the advertising of the great market medium—television. The new technologies continue to proliferate—always at a price. What is the future of leisure technologies? Are there any limits as products and possibilities come on the market at a faster and faster rate?

The Consumer Society

Leisure has changed significantly since World War II. Mass media, pleasure travel, outdoor recreation, local museums, gardens, parks, and libraries became more common and accessible to millions of Americans. Government became more involved in recreation at every level. The greatest expansion, however, was in the market sector.

The economic base of the United States was the era of relative affluence of the second half of the 20th century. There was still poverty. There were recessions and times of high unemployment. Overall, however, household incomes increased dramatically. Both purchasing power and expectations for consumption grew. For decades the proportion of household income spent directly on recreation remained stable at about 6%. Discretionary income increased and more went toward leisure in its various forms. Further, more spending on homes, clothing, travel, cars, and other goods had leisure dimensions. Homes were more than housing; they became entertainment centers. Cars were more than transportation; they symbolized affluence and style. In the 1920s, leisure was identified with consumption. The middle class began to spend as well as save—then the Depression and the War stopped the growth of consumption for most.

After World War II, incomes rose. At the same time, television brought images of consumption and entertainment into most homes. This advertising bombarded viewers with repeated images of what could be purchased. Many of the products and services were leisure-related. In other advertising, leisure settings and events were employed to sell clothes, cars, beer, cosmetics, and even toothpaste. There were also the indirect messages from the programs themselves in which images of pleasure were associated with marketed leisure places and events. The issue is the extent to which leisure came to be associated with spending money and with consumption.

New Markets and New Styles

The purpose of marketing style is to render still serviceable goods obsolete. Apparel is most subject to style, but style is a factor in almost everything else on the market. All change is not to improve function. Some just symbolizes that the product is new and up-to-date. In the 1950s, considerable consumption was catching up from wartime shortages. Housing, cars, appliances, and just about everything else needs to be replaced. Further, salaries and wages frozen during the war began to rise. A new cycle of consumption was under way.

A number of economic avenues were opened. There was all the new housing, especially in the suburban developments. The new homes had to be equipped and furnished. Delayed marriage and childbearing created other markets. The division of labor was intensified as women were bumped from factories to make way for the returning men. The ideology of the "family" idealized the nurturing, managing, and consuming mother at home. The ideology of leisure turned attention to all the wonders offered by the market and made accessible by the car and highway system. Acres of parking at malls welcome shoppers in cars with room for more purchases than those without cars.

Further, the metropolis offered a wide variety of leisure resources. The limitations of the small town were replaced by the great retail world of the city in which everything could be purchased. Women were still expected to construct their leisure around the home and community. They were also the center of household consumption. The poor, crowded into racial ghettoes and cut off from most opportunities, participated in the new leisure vicariously by viewing it on television. The images of the "good life," however, were saturated with the new leisure.

Even romance with all its appeal has become coupled with leisure consumption (Illouz, 1997). Leisure settings and commodities have become central to the symbolism of romance. In the mass media, especially soap operas and dramas, romantic dinners, costly toys (especially cars), stylish clothes, and exotic travel are the material context of romantic relationships. The ideal may be an enduring relationship, but the setting is marketed leisure. Romantic practices are those of the consumption of leisure goods. Food, entertainment, and travel are the rituals of romance. Research finds that adults connect romantic images more to the champagne and candlelight dinner than the canoe on a quiet lake. Advertising has reinforced the relationship with "Hallmark holidays" and romantic success always presented in the context of leisure consumption.

Mass Culture and Mass Leisure

Leisure, of course, is a matter of taste. The culture is divided into many "taste cultures" that respond to the offerings of popular culture. Every such culture is the product of a market that produces and promotes its differentiating leisure possibilities and products. Yet, there is also "mass leisure" marketed for most people most of the time. The wealthy are able to purchase privacy, access, and exclusive leisure that symbolize their social status. The poor struggle to survive in hostile environments with leisure that is a combination of low-cost entertainment and escape from oppressive conditions.

For the middle mass, however, there is mass leisure—the kinds of things that most people do most of the time. First, of course, is television. Second is shopping itself—trips to retailing centers to view, dream, and buy. Third are all the away-from-home entertainments that draw people to shows, places to eat and drink, and other venues designed for pleasure. Fourth, there is travel—an industry selling a variety of experiences for all ages and a variety of tastes.

Leisure, from this perspective, is seen as a reward for work that may be less than satisfying. It becomes a separate element of life with its own budgets, timetables, ascribed meanings, and symbol systems. The preindustrial connection between work and leisure is broken. Now leisure is tied to nonwork associations and home. Mass leisure is composed of market commodities rather than experiences integrated into the fabric of social life.

Has leisure become more consumption and less a dimension of life? Have the images of leisure become so commodified that the poor who lack market purchasing power are excluded? Is there a general dissatisfaction when television constantly presents pictures of glamorized leisure beyond economic possibility for most? Have many come to identify leisure with spending money rather than building deeply satisfying experiences? Is everything for sale—even people who can be used for one's pleasure? Has the market of mass leisure become so central to our perceived quality of life that we identify satisfaction with spending and freedom with discretionary income? Have our leisure desires become insatiable because the market always offers something more at a higher price?

What are the contemporary images of leisure? Are they the real: the forest path, the deep conversation, and the moment of shared lightness? Or are they the fake: Las Vegas and the easy excitement of gambling, Disney and the pretend trip around the world, "ethnic" theme restaurants that actually microwave their menu, and now the electronic "virtual reality" that makes its own images? Do we want more excitement with less investment of skill, discipline, and effort? Has leisure become the product of technology and the market?

After all, life in the city can be hard. Commuting is time-consuming. Families are less stable. Recreation resources are crowded—especially at prime times. Work careers are less secure and regular. Households juggle work schedules and multiple roles with most adults, women and men, in the paid work force. Even shopping involves standing in line to spend money. For the poor, life in rural or urban locales becomes a constant day-to-day struggle to survive. The appeal of mass leisure is plain. Home electronics make just sitting there so easy. The expanding "leisure industry" offers great variety in responding to all sorts of tastes. Households with multiple cars can split off in many directions in search of fun. For the majority, there is enough income above necessities to buy some leisure things and dream about even more. All the market requires in return is a profit—a regular return on investment capital. Belief in the market is, after all, a fundamental part of American culture—and increasingly of most of the world as well.

Debate: Technologies will transform leisure.

YES

- History demonstrates the power of new technologies to transform leisure. The car and television are only two of the most dramatic examples. In this age of technological innovation, there is no reason to think such a process has run out of steam.

- Leisure is activity, but often with some kind of implements. Fiberglass has transformed skiing. Plastic has replaced heavier and more dangerous equipment for many sports. The transistor and computer have made music portable. Electronic games come in all sizes and forms. GPS systems and ultrasound sensors on bass boats have altered the "sport" of fishing. There is always something new on the market that makes a difference in some activity. That is the nature of the market economy: to create demand for new goods and services. New leisure technologies are inevitable and inescapable.

- Some technologies create activities. Composition wheels improved rollerskating followed by skateboards and then inline skates. Each technology produced related activities and games. No activity seems unaffected by such development.

- Leisure travel—tourism—is growing into an enormous international business, by some measures the largest single segment of the world economy. Transportation technologies are constantly being improved to provide more travel more efficiently. With the credit card, even paying for services has become quick and easy. Cars are more reliable and comfortable, and highways faster and safer. Local businesses offer flying trips just for sightseeing. All kinds of travel are for sale to the masses as well as the elites.

- A "technological imperative" argues "If it can be done, it will be done." Technology has a power of its own to do what can be done. Racquets will be made more powerful and durable. Jet Skis will be faster and possibly cheaper. Computers will add features to their word processors and printers. Business will keep creating technologies to create markets. The process has no endpoint or boundary. Technology can even lower costs and create bigger markets.

- Style also creates demand. Advertising only increases the desire to "do it right" to be in style. Social acceptance and style go together— and style is always changing, by design.

- "Fads"—new things that catch a wave of demand and then fade away—respond to the desire to have and do the latest thing. They may be the product of promotion and publicity, but they still sell. There are temporary technologies that may affect leisure for only a short time. People move from one fad to another. Yet, for a short time, there is a new technology-based activity.

Technology is just one aspect of consumption as leisure. Consumption is always attractive and usually easy. Technology stimulates consumption. Marketing finances the development of technologies. It is part of the economic system and the culture. Why would it change?

NO

- Basic patterns of leisure change less than superficial observation indicates. Television was an exception. Most technologies are successful when they fit into habits and patterns. They find markets when they are consistent with the culture. Time-diary research demonstrates that change comes slowly. There may be new leisure resources, but for the most part they do not alter the regular round of life very much. For example, the video just enhanced the home entertainment patterns already firmly in place. What technology, for example, would get people out of the home more for leisure? There just aren't any more transforming technologies like the car or television on the horizon.

- Leisure is social in the sense that it is learned from others. The forms of leisure are incidental to its social meanings. We may do somewhat different things with friends and family, but the nature of the leisure remains the interaction. Who we are with is more important than what we do. Technologies will not change that.

• Most technologies replace older ones without transforming the meanings or satisfactions of the activity. The excitement of skiing has not changed much with ski and binding technologies. Tennis remains the same game despite all the new racquets. Graphite shafts have not made golf hooks and slices disappear. Technologies may enhance an activity, but seldom change it.

• Technologies are temporary. There is a succession of innovations and sometimes even cycles. Old activities come back and new ones recede. The meaning of sport competition has not changed despite the development of "sport science." Even gambling is an old excitement, despite all the new styles and locations. The basic forms of the activities continue.

• Styles are superficial. They are a matter of marketing—not meaning. For the most part, what are promoted as significant new technologies are just marketing hype. Change is artificial rather than fundamental to leisure.

• Look at the longer term results of leisure promotions. Most businesses go bankrupt partly because they really don't have anything new to offer. The businesses that tend to be most successful are those that build on continuities rather than fads. Marketing is powerful, but there are limits to the acceptance and incorporation of innovation.

• Finally, there are also cost limits to technological development and adoption. The mass markets cannot afford everything that becomes available. The amount of discretionary spending, especially on leisure, is always limited. New technologies will be purchased only at an acceptable price. The upscale markets are quite limited in size. When technological development lowers costs, it may enlarge markets. The demand for anything new or improved, however, is limited by its cost and the purchasing power of consumers. Most people are not driving a new Mercedes convertible or flying first-class.

Discussion Questions

1. Now that most married women are in the paid work force, what has happened to the former segregation of women into suburban enclaves?

2. How important is shopping as leisure?

3. Have malls become the new recreation centers? How?

4. Where are most friends made: at work, leisure, or in the community?

5. Has the car become an urban necessity for work? for leisure?

6. Can anything replace television in contemporary leisure?

7. What are the most successful electronic developments for leisure? Do they have wide appeal or rather narrow markets?

8. Would you invest in a new Las Vegas hotel? Why or why not?

9. Is most leisure consumption? as measured by time? as measured by importance?

References and Resources

Bellah, R., Madsen, R., Sullivan, W., Swidler, A., and Tipton, S. (1987). *Habits of the heart: Individualism and commitment in American life.* Berkeley, CA: University of California Press.

Butsch, R. (1990). *For fun and profit: The transformation of leisure into consumption.* Philadelphia, PA: Temple University Press.

Coontz, S. (1994). *The way we never were: American families and the nostalgia trap.* New York, NY: Basic Books.

Cross, G. (1990). *A social history of leisure since 1600.* State College, PA: Venture Publishing, Inc.

Illouz, E. (1997). *Consuming the romantic utopia: Love and the cultural contradiction of capitalism.* Berkeley, CA: University of California Press.

Jackson, K. (1985). *Crabgrass frontier: The suburbanization of the United* States. New York, NY: Oxford University Press.

Kelly, J. and Godbey, G. (1993). *The sociology of leisure.* State College, PA: Venture Publishing, Inc.

Kuttner, R. (1998). *Everything for sale: The virtues and limits of markets.* New York, NY: Alfred Knopf.

Larrabee, E. and Meyersohn. R. (1958). *Mass leisure.* Glencoe, IL: The Free Press.

Lundberg, G., Komarovsky, M., and McInerny, M. (1934). *Leisure: A suburban study.* New York, NY: Columbia University Press.

Lynd, R. and Lynd, H. (1937). *Middletown in transition: A study in cultural conflicts.* New York, NY: Harcourt Brace.

Marcuse, H. (1964). *One-dimensional man: Studies in the ideology of advanced industrial society.* Boston, MA: Beacon Press.

Rojek, C. (1995). *Decentring leisure: Rethinking leisure theory.* Thousand Oaks, CA: Sage Publications.

Veblen, T. (1953). *The theory of the leisure class.* New York, NY: New American Library. (Original work published in 1899)

Part III
Contexts of Leisure

Chapter 6
Leisure Styles and Lifestyles

Leisure is not all that special—at least not in the sense that leisure is perfect, absolutely free, separated from ordinary life, or a unique category of human activity. Leisure is not different from everything else. Rather, it is a part of life with characteristics that distinguish it. The dominant view in North America is that leisure is a focus on the experience rather than outcomes and some measure of choice. It is what we do primarily because we want to. Yet leisure is also enmeshed in all our relationships and roles.

One problem is that we often stereotype the leisure of other people. We associate the blue-collar factory worker with Pabst Blue Ribbon beer, television, football, and a gun rack in the pickup. We think all professors drink dry white wine, listen to string quartets, and read the *New York Times* on Sunday mornings. We seem surprised when mothers of preschool children read the *Wall Street Journal* instead of books on babies and go backpacking instead of wheeling the baby carriage. We stereotype other people—not ourselves—and assume that most people's leisure is quite one-sided. Jocks do sports and don't read. Eggheads are physical incompetents. We ignore the athlete who writes poetry and the professor who is a state tennis or motocross dirt-track champion.

The truth is that almost everyone watches some television, spends time with friends, goes shopping, and has some special hobby or interest. There is also amazing variety in what people do, not to mention the different styles of participation. In fact, no two people we know have leisure styles that are just alike—perhaps not even similar. Our leisure is as different as our lives.

Ordinary Life

Life is not made up of independent events. It is not just chunks of activity. Rather, there is a rhythm of the day, the week, the month, and even the year.

Ordinary life has its daily tasks and requirements. It includes bodily functions, preparing for whatever is coming next (i.e., work or play), communicating with others, getting things done, and just coping with life. Some of ordinary life is very routine and much the same from day to day. Other elements of the day vary from the daily—especially on weekends and holidays. For most, the day is structured around work or school schedules. However, there are other timing factors, such as the schedules of those we live with, daylight and nighttime, and even television timetables. We eat, talk, rest, relax, start and stop activities, and in general make it through the day.

One view of leisure is that it is set apart from all this. Leisure is just special reserved times and places in which we do special things. The list of activities that we identify as leisure supports this idea of separation. We work, study, take care of ourselves and others, and complete our routines. Then there is leisure in its purity. The problem is life just doesn't divide up so neatly.

For example, we may play on the job—kidding someone at the coffee-maker or when crossing paths in the hall. On the other hand, we may think about and even solve some work or study problem while taking a walk, reading the paper, or daydreaming. We fix breakfast for our children, plan transportation for the day, and engage in silly word games all at the same time. Further, a serious financial problem may impact what is supposed to be a leisure event. Life is not composed of chunks of time clearly identified as work, leisure, loving, or anything else. Life, rather, is a mixture of elements.

Further, life has both big and little rhythms. The big rhythms are referred to as the life course or the life cycle. Students are in a future-oriented period of preparation even though they have to make it through the days and weeks of that period. Young adults are trying to get their lives started and established. The retired and those forced out of their jobs have to rebuild their lives without the demands and associations of employment. As we will see, these big rhythms are one way of analyzing the life journey.

However, there are also the little rhythms. After a time hard at work on task, we usually want some sort of break. We may believe we deserve some light entertainment in the evening. On the other hand, we may become bored with work or one more television sitcom and seek the challenge of practicing the piano or playing volleyball. We may want to be with other people or alone. We may want relaxation or challenge. In the rhythms of the day or the week, we seek some variety in activities or *balance*.

In this process, ordinary life is partly just getting through the day with its demands and scheduled activities. It has its ups and downs, its peaks and valleys. If there is an adequate balance, it contains both times with high levels of involvement and excitement and times of disengagement and rest. If we are deeply involved with other people at work, we may want to be alone in the evening. If we have worked with words all day, we may want to play with machines on the weekend. Overall, daily life is made up of so many tasks, plans, exchanges, and playful experiences that we just go through the process taking its variety for granted.

What Is a Lifestyle?

Are there ways that we can characterize and distinguish the ways people live? A lifestyle consists of the bundles of activities and objects that make up our lives. Those bundles have a kind of shape that distinguish our lives from others and yet may be similar to some others. Further, these activities are based in the combinations of social roles that we take at work, school, home, and in the community. To understand our styles of play, you have to know something of the rest of our lives—that we are college students, sons and daughters, sisters and brothers, friends and lovers, employees and volunteers, and so on. All these roles together make up the social world in which we live, compose our identities, and live out our lives.

Yet, we do not live our lives in some fixed pattern that can be described or predicted just by knowing our roles. Rather, we play our roles in ways that are distinctively our own. Our relationships with family, friends, lovers, and teammates always have twists and turns that are changing and even unexpected. In the journeys of our lives, there is both stability and change. The elements that tend to characterize how we generally construct our lives we call *lifestyle.*

Most of the attempts to identify lifestyles combine a number of elements. One study of the loss of community in America referred to lifestyle *enclaves* (Bellah, Madsen, Sullivan, Swidler & Tipton, 1987). An enclave combines elements of culture, location, financial resources, value orientations, and customs into an overall lifestyle. The analysis, based primarily on studies in such affluent places as California's Silicon Valley, suggests that households are becoming increasingly privatized with styles not tied to the community and its connecting organizations. Instead of community engagement, the Silicon lifestyle is to amass electronic home entertainment and eat and drink at commercial establishments that require no commitment to other people.

A more inclusive lifestyle typology employed to identify categories of consumers is based on values as well as demographics, such as income and education. Dimensions of work, family, intimacy, community, leisure, lifecourse period, and values make up the inclusive dimensions of the types. According to Mitchell (1983) these types are

• The **Need-driven:** Old and poor survivors and marginal sustainers.

- The **Inner-directed:** Self-centered and self-preoccupied *I am me* youth and leisure-oriented *experiential* young adults.

- The **Outer-directed:** Middle-mass conventional *belongers,* ambitious *emulators* who use leisure for status, and success-oriented achievers under time pressures.

- They also locate a few **Integrators** who are relatively autonomous, flexible, mature, and balanced.

Note the elements that are included in the descriptions: income, education, family status, consumption patterns, and value orientations. Perhaps inadequate attention was given to ethnicity and gender because of the focus on households.

Another typology called *Claritas* is almost entirely based on consumption. Note that the aims of such lifestyles programs are to identify markets for a variety of goods and services. The Claritas scheme focuses on consumption, leisure, life course, and location. Their *lifestyle enclaves* include consumption of particular styles of cars, electronics, clothes, media, financial programs, and leisure. Among the types are

- suburban *kids and cul-de-sacs* who stress parenting,

- *pools and patios* with affluent elite tastes,

- *executive suites* in high-status cultural pursuits, and

- *upward-bound* younger individuals who are into aerobics and the latest electronics.

Further, they add the geographical dimension by placing the types into housing areas and developments designed for their lifestyles (Reardon, 1995).

The point of such lifestyle schemes is to bring together crucial elements that combine into overall patterns. The particular elements vary partly with the aims of the programs, especially those that are marketing-oriented. They raised the question as to whether we are really best characterized by our consumption in a market economy. There may be other factors at least as important. For example, what about the following?

- **Ethnicity:** To what extent do our cultural roots shape our lives? Does it make a difference that our families of origin are Irish Catholic, Cuban American, or rural southern African American?

- **Gender:** As will be discussed in Chapter 13, how do our always relevant gender identifications impact how we live in every context?

- **Sexual orientation:** What lifestyle elements vary according to our personal and social sexual identities?

- **Economic status:** In a market economy, does our control of financial resources shape everything we are able to do?

- **Life course:** Not only periods of work and family roles but also changes and transitions across age are basic to the social resources and expectations out of which we construct our lives.

What are the central elements in lifestyles? One possibility is that some are more contextual—where we live, our access to resources, and our cultures—and others are more personal—values, aims, friends, and families. In any case, there do seem to be combinations that, in general, together describe our lives—and leisure is very much a part of those lifestyles.

How Do Leisure Styles Differ?

Are there identifiable leisure styles? A number of possibilities come to mind. Are some, mostly young, so focused on sports as to be accurately identified as *jocks*? Are others such party animals that they are primarily *socials*? What about the members of symphony guilds and other community status organizations who are *joiners*? Are there really environmental *greens* or *tree huggers*? Adventurous *risk takers*? Conventional *family focused*? Possession-obsessed *materialists*? Can leisure be so one-sided that such labels give an accurate picture of any real people?

Individuals who like sports may also read. Socials also watch television. Joiners play with their children. Environmentalists entertain friends indoors in the winter. Risk-takers rest and relax. The family-focused want to be alone sometimes. Materialists enjoy sunsets. Is there a danger that we stereotype other people in ways that distort the combined and varied elements of their lives?

The next chapter describes leisure styles centered around a particular skill-based leisure commitment. Some persons are so devoted to being amateur musicians, surfers, bowlers, dancers, squash players, classic car restorers, or quarter-horse breeders that everything else in life, including work, must fit into that commitment. They are, however, in a minority. Most people have more varied leisure styles. They do many things with many levels of skill and commitment. Some activities are occasional or seasonal. Some things are done only with particular companions. Some activities extremely significant in one period are given up as the years pass. For example, summers organized around Little

League coaching usually change as children move out of that age bracket. The life course has its rhythms as does the day and week.

Perhaps even more important than the activities we do is how we do them. Style is much more than a list of activities ranked by time allocations. In fact, the activity labels may be quite deceptive. A midlife adult may swim regularly for health and fitness. A teen may swim as a member of a high school competitive team. Another teen may go swimming primarily for the social life on the beach or the deck. How we do the activities may be far more significant than the activities themselves. Fishing may be a solitary engagement with nature in the backcountry or a noisy competitive bass fishing tournament with special boats, big motors, and sophisticated sonar. When we describe leisure styles, the *how* may be more important than the *what*.

There have been a number of attempts to identify leisure styles through a statistical clustering of activities. No two attempts have produced the same style of typologies. Further, they have been based on activity labels rather than studies of styles of participation. Nevertheless, some of the styles have been found often enough to be suggestive. For example, among identified styles have been family-focused, fast-living, status-symbolizing, and aesthetic. Some may organize their leisure around home and children. Others try to live continually seeking excitement. The labels suggest there may be organizing themes around which many people build their leisure. Quite distinct from those addicted to gambling or some other such activity, there are many with a primary leisure engagement. It can be almost anything, from birdwatching to computer hacking. There are those so attached to running, fantasy games, religion, or softball as to seem quite one-sided and almost addicted. They make their friends among other committed participants, wear badges and uniforms almost everywhere, and schedule their lives around the timetables of the institutionalized activity.

There is a major problem with jumping on the single-theme, stylistic bandwagon too quickly, however. Almost everyone has a set of activities they prefer throughout most of their lives. This core of leisure patterns is so common as to be taken-for-granted. To begin with, there is television. Every study of how people use their time finds that other than work and sleeping, most people spend more time watching the tube than anything else (see Chapter 16). Older persons in their 70s and 80s may not engage very much in physically demanding activities, but instead they attempt to retain their informal and often formal social activities. In fact, the core of leisure is central to most lives from youth to later life. It consists of at-home media (especially television), informal socializing with family and friends, reading, other activity at home, walking, and shopping. There are variations in all such core activity patterns. There may be more television watching and less socializing by those who live alone. Some hate shopping. Others barely read the newspaper and get their news from television. Nonetheless, there is a core of accessible activity that tends to claim the bulk of everyday time through most of the life course.

On top of that core there is a *balance*. It is this balance that varies more from person to person and group to group. It may include more sports and partying for those in school. It tends to be more child-oriented and nurturing for parents of young children. It may stress travel in preretirement and early retirement years. More individualistically it may focus on an activity with a long history of participation. For example, one study found many mothers of young children hold fast to a special activity despite all the pressures of work and family. The balance may change through the life course or may have a more continuous history. It is by that balance that we tend to characterize leisure styles.

The balance also has another dimension. Few individuals want to be highly involved and engaged all the time. Leisure styles usually include both engagement and disengagement, demanding activity and relaxation. The balance may also involve social and solitary activity. Activity may have aims of personal development and learning at some times and pure pleasure at others. The balance metaphor suggests that the leisure styles of many persons tend to be varied with more than one theme or meaning.

Perhaps even more important is the matter of style—how we engage in activities. We may ski at exclusive resorts in Colorado or in jeans on a nearby hill. We may attend rock concerts in football stadiums or symphony concerts in the formal hall. We may fight for a tee time on a badly worn urban public golf course or ride a cart over the links of a carefully manicured, half-empty private club. We may swim in a crowded public pool or on the private beach at our lakefront condo.

Style includes mode of participation as well as place. We may play tennis very competitively or in a social and conversational mode. We may go to church for the worship experience or to see friends. We may go ballroom dancing to associate with social status peers or country-western dancing to exercise and meet new people.

All these elements come together in a leisure style. It seems evident that the variations are almost endless. Nevertheless, there may be themes that characterize leisure styles:

1. **Privatized:** One tendency in current leisure styles seems to be to concentrate more on immediate locales and associations. The traditional view of American community leisure included considerable involvement in the community—in organizations, the neighborhoods, and extended families. Now the residence is more and more

a self-enclosed entertainment center. For most males over 40, sport means Sunday afternoon and Monday evening games on television. Involvement with others is reduced to soap operas. Entertainment is less and less "just dropping in." Fences replace front porches. For the affluent, pools are locked behind guarded gates. The level of community integration has been reduced in urban environments with their anonymity and fear-driven seclusion and protection. There are those, of course, who respond to being cut off with new forms of community by rebuilding relationships in a recreational group or church.

2. **Technologized:** Major industries produce new technologies for leisure. They are so widespread that owning and using the technology may become central to doing the activity. Bass fishing involves electronics, special boats, and high-powered motors, and thousands of lures, new rods and reels. There is a new golf club design every year or so. Snowboards change in length and width as well as materials and bindings. Food processors, breadmakers, and espresso machines turn the home kitchen into an enclave for gourmet cooking. Every activity seems to have its latest style of equipment claimed to improve performance. The most obvious set of new leisure technologies is in electronics. Television and state-of-the-art sound reproduction and car equipment all offer new "improved" models every year. Now the personal computer is a leisure toy. New games and communication require more memory, more speed, and more computing capacity. Complex software games and entertainment challenge the level of hardware. Just keeping up with the changes could become a full-time leisure avocation—not only in what the technologies do but also the equipment itself may become the center of a leisure style.

3. **Commodified:** Leisure styles may become focused on buying and owning the things associated with the activity rather than doing it. Advertising directed at leisure markets stresses having the latest equipment, wearing the right clothes and shoes, and being in the right places. As discussed more fully in Chapters 5 and 23, the meanings of doing and becoming may be replaced by having and possessing. Owning the right things may become an end in itself rather than a means of participation. The things of leisure become status symbols. In a megalopolis, few symbols of work status can be brought home. Leisure toys, trips, clothes with the right labels and badges, and even shoes symbolize social status through and in leisure.

4. **Family-focused:** Several studies identified a significant proportion of adults whose leisure styles are almost entirely organized around family roles. In this day of loss in family stability and the likelihood of changes and transitions in intimate relationships, it would seem likely that such a pattern is less common. Nevertheless, at any given time, most adults are in some stable, committed relationships that yield an immediacy of social context. Further, those relationships tend to be highly valued and are a principle around which much of life, including leisure, is organized. As the forms of family change, the priority on "primary relationships" other than the "traditional" family may persist in leisure styles.

These are overall styles that we may tend to view in a somewhat negative way. They suggest we become one-sided, one-dimensional, and manipulated. There seems little doubt that these themes, at the very least, are present in contemporary leisure styles.

It may be more realistic, however, to see a balance in most leisure styles. As already suggested, most people have a core of accessible activity. Beyond this, we tend to seek a balance that makes sense in relation to everything else that is going on in our lives. Chapters 9 and 10 will suggest how this balance tends to shift as we make our way through the journey of life. There are also individual elements to our balances related to our histories and to the other conditions of our lives as suggested in these lists. Most of us are not totally one-sided in our leisure or our lives. We want some challenge and some rest, some involvement and some separation—and the balance changes as we and our circumstances change.

Is Leisure a Dimension of Life?

Life has many dimensions. The idea of balance applies not only in leisure but also in all of life. Our overall lifestyles include many dimensions. One formulation proposes at least four central life dimensions: productivity, bonding, learning, and expression (Kelly & Kelly, 1994). We need to be productive in the sense of doing something of worth to others, bonding to other persons in real community, learning, developing ourselves and our abilities, and expressing ourselves in experience-centered activity. All four are dimensions of being human. The balance changes through the life course. We concentrate on learning in school years and on productivity in the adult establishment period. Nonetheless, we work out some combination of all four throughout life.

This approach suggests leisure and play are not just times and places set apart from the rest of life. Rather, we may play almost anytime and anywhere. Play is a quality of dimension in life as is development, community, and work. It is a theme of meaning in activity rather than a list of activities. Almost anything from chopping wood to designing computer programs can be playful and expressive rather than product-oriented and required.

The trick, then, is to identify those dimensions in ordinary life. When do we play? Is there playful exchange walking to class and even in class? Do we work out productive plans and ideas while walking on the beach? Do we develop skills and a sense of competence in games as well as on the job? Do we relate to others when sharing communication and even affection almost anywhere? The answer, of course, is yes. Life has its rhythms within activities, even minute-by-minute. We are not on task all the time at work. We may care for and about others any time. Life does not divide up neatly and clearly. In fact, one approach to our lifestyle is how we combine those dimensions.

Is all this needlessly complicated? Don't most people just watch television and hang out with friends? Measured by time use, for many the answer seems to be *yes*. Yet, closer examination suggests there are styles of leisure that have some kind of fit into overall lifestyles. They include ordinary day-to-day activity—the *core*. They also include extraordinary activity, the special engagements that give a distinctive flavor to life patterns.

Some of the patterns reflect our conditions and access to resources. However, they may also reflect our values, what we think is most important in our lives. Out of our resources and in some relationship to our values, we construct a life. Ideally, that lifestyle includes significant dimensions of work, play, community, and development.

Then there are *leisure styles*. They may be complex and changing. All sorts of conditions and factors may be significant for their understanding. In fact, no single perspective would seem to be adequate for identifying lifestyles and leisure styles. There are, however, significant differences in both what people do and how they do it in their ordinary lives. These differences are one basis for understanding this complex phenomenon we call leisure.

Debate: Leisure has become a primary symbol of social status.

One view of leisure is that it is essentially personal and private. Almost 100 years ago, however, Thorstein Veblen (1899/1953) argued leisure had become the main way in which the affluent demonstrated their status. The issue remains pertinent: In a mass culture, has leisure become, for more than just the wealthy, the primary way in which we demonstrate to others who we are and how well we are doing?

YES

- Style is status. The main purpose of style is to distinguish oneself from others. We are not just part of the mass. We are ourselves, unique persons with our own identities. It has become almost impossible to maintain status in the ordinary world of jobs. Leisure is now how we signal we are special. As advertising portrays a distinguishing leisure style, we may buy the package.

- Status is association. With whom do we associate? With which social group do we identify? Youth wear caps and clothing that identify their social group or gang. They listen to the "right" music and even drive the "right" cars. Adults join the clubs and associations appropriate to their status—the symphony guild, Junior League, Rotary, or the American Legion. Churches are clearly divided according to social status. High status is Episcopalian, not Baptist. Our leisure associations are symbols of our status.

- Activities themselves also signify status. The poor do not engage in golf or skiing. Softball and bowling tend to be middle mass or working class. Symphony concerts are upper status and country-western music is not. Of course, some people venture outside the appropriate activities, but most do not. After all, leisure style is clear evidence of social level and identity. To attain this status, people use credit to purchase the toys that symbolize the activity.

- Leisure style is as much a matter of how as what. Tastes differentiate status levels. Trips to Copenhagen and Tivoli are high status. Trips to Disneyland are middle. Trips to the corner bar are low status. Golf at the exclusive club is high, on the public course middle, and no golf at all is low status. Some argue taste cultures are designed to symbolize status so we can quickly identify those who are "our kind of people." Leisure is central to the *cultural capital* by which we consolidate our access to social opportunities.

- Leisure symbols, then, are social identifications. With our designer labels and toys, we make clear statements as to our place in society. When we are young the stage tends to be the peer group. Adults may operate on the larger community stage. In any case, we are actors who use leisure to tell others just who we think we are. Barbara Ehrenreich (1989) argues a fear of losing middle-class status may lead to leisure that makes a cultural statement.

- Tourism, especially, is a status symbol. An inability to recount the international trip of the year clearly labels one as an outsider in some status groups. Of course, cost is a symbol. Little detail is required to label a high-price trip. On the other hand, lower income groups travel by car to visit relatives in Iowa or South Carolina. Destinations, mode of travel, and activities themselves symbolize the trip level. Our condo in Aspen is a far cry from the Motel 6 in Missouri.

NO

- Veblen's argument applied only to the "leisure class" who wanted to demonstrate that they did not have to work. They could live a life of leisure. Most people now have to work and even want to work. Leisure is not a symbol as much as it is what we have found to be personally satisfying. It is the realm of life in which we do what we really want to do, not what pleases or impresses others.

- Ordinary leisure is quite diverse. As illustrated in the discussion of leisure styles, we do many things for many different reasons. We seek a balance of meanings and activities. While that balance may include some activities that reflect status, it is mostly a matter of being with congenial people with common interests. Economic position is still central to social status. There are just too many kinds of leisure available to all but the poor to use it to make clear social status statements.

- As demonstrated by the diversity of leisure styles, leisure choices are personal and reflect our own unique histories. Of course, our friends and groups are part of our leisure styles, but they are chosen more for common aims and experiences than social status. The variety of leisure is evidence that we come to our activities more through our ordinary associations than any plan to symbolize status.

- Leisure styles are based primarily on satisfaction. We stay involved in sports, outdoor activity, or the arts because they have been satisfying. Styles are patterns of activity that together form a somewhat integrated set of satisfactions, for example, relaxation and excitement, or social involvement and being alone. Over time, we learn what is right for us.

- Considerable leisure is private, not display. We read, watch television, and garden. We do ordinary things that don't attract attention or impress anyone.

- Activities change with available resources. We may waterski when we live in Florida, downhill ski in Vermont, and cross-country ski in Wisconsin. We play bridge with friends who like that game and poker with others. We may travel more as our children become independent and our incomes rise. That is, however, resource-based, and not a matter of status.

- There are just too many exceptions to the status stereotypes to support the idea that leisure is primarily a matter of symbolic styles. High-status people ride motorcycles and backpack. Middle-mass people do all sorts of things that are available. Students find inexpensive ways to do almost everything, even international travel. By and large, people do what they like.

Discussion Questions

1. How do lifestyles incorporate leisure?

2. How is leisure a part of ordinary life?

3. Are there any accurate leisure stereotypes? Describe them.

4. What are the most important factors in shaping leisure style?

5. What themes of leisure style are becoming more important?

6. Is leisure more personal or social? How and why?

7. Are most adult leisure styles balanced and varied or singular and focused?

8. What is the place of special and extraordinary leisure?

9. What is the most important dimension of life: work, leisure, family, or other?

10. What are the status symbols of youth leisure?

11. How can we go about building a satisfying lifestyle?

Resources

Bellah, R., Madsen, R., Sullivan, W., Swidler, A., and Tipton, S. (1987). *Habits of the heart: Individualism and commitment in American life.* Berkeley, CA: University of California Press.

Ehrenreich, B. (1989). *Fear of falling: The inner life of the middle class.* New York, NY: Pantheon.

Howell, J. (1973). *Hard living on Clay Street: Portraits of blue-collar families.* Garden City, NY: Doubleday.

Kelly, J. (1987). *Peoria winter: Styles and resources in later life.* Lexington, MA: Lexington Books, Free Press.

Kelly, J. (1998). Leisure behaviors and styles: Social, economic, and cultural factors. In T. Burton and E. Jackson (Eds.), *Leisure studies: Prospects for the twenty-first century* (pp. 135–150). State College, PA: Venture Publishing, Inc.

Kelly, J. and Kelly, J.R. (1994). Dimensions of centrality and meaning in the domains of work, family, and leisure. *Journal of Leisure Research, 26*(9), 250–275.

Levine, L. W. (1998). *Highbrow, lowbrow: The emergence of cultural hierarchy in America.* Cambridge, MA: Harvard University Press.

Mitchell, A. (1983). *The nine American lifestyles: Who we are and where we're going.* New York, NY: Warner Books.

Putnam, R. (2000). *Bowling alone: The collapse and revival of American community.* New York, NY: Simon and Schuster.

Reardon, P.T. (1995, November 5). The new geography. *Chicago Tribune,* pp. D5–7.

Rojek, C. (1996). *Decentring leisure: Rethinking leisure theory.* Thousand Oaks, CA: Sage.

Veblen, T. (1953). *The theory of the leisure class.* New York, NY: New American Library. (Original work published in 1899)

Chapter 7

Experiences of Leisure

There is an apparent contradiction in terms when we refer to "leisure." On the one hand, when we say "leisurely," we usually mean an activity that is relaxed, undemanding, and even restful. Leisure, however, also includes physically demanding sport, disciplined arts, and other activity that is anything but relaxing. In fact, some leisure may be more strenuous than work. Some people even talk about going to work on Monday to rest up from the weekend.

There is even more than this contradiction. Certainly there is a relaxation dimension and even an escape dimension to some leisure. People do flop in front of the television in the evening to be entertained after a hard day at work. They do go into the forest to get away from the telephone. When asked to name the activities they would least want to give up, however, most adults will refer either to some kind of skill-based activity to which they have a commitment or to what they do with the people most important to them.

At the very least, there is a rhythm to leisure that includes both relaxation and challenge. There is the separation side in which we try to get away from the expectations and demands of our various roles as workers, family members, and community participants. We do need to relax and rest. That, however, is only one side of leisure. The other side is activity in which we commit ourselves to learning and practicing skills in which there is challenge. Such activity has been called *serious leisure*. This contrast illustrates that there is no single leisure experience. Rather, there are many kinds of experience found in the varieties of activity that may be leisure. Leisure is characterized by variety, and even by contrasts.

One approach to understanding leisure is to focus on the individual. The psychology of leisure investigates the nature of experiences and their internal conditions. This does not mean that external conditions and purposes are irrelevant. Rather, one important way of approaching the meanings of leisure is in individual experience.

What Is Experience?

Leisure has been defined as activity done primarily for its own sake. That is, the central meaning of the activity is the experience itself. The question is, what is experience? Is it simply emotion, how we feel? Or is it a more complex phenomenon?

A classic psychological approach to leisure is that of John Neulinger (1974) who defined leisure in terms of three attitudinal dimensions. Leisure consists of *perceived freedom*, an attitude of intrinsic motivation, and final rather than instrumental goals. More recently there have been a number of additions to this model along with various research methods of measuring such attitudes. In general, however, the perception or feeling of freedom along with a focus on the immediate experience have been agreed on as the defining characteristics of leisure from a psychological perspective. Note this definition is entirely in terms of the inner state of the individual. External conditions are said to be irrelevant. Leisure, then, becomes theoretically possible in any condition—poverty, prison, or with any other limitation. There is also no way of evaluating outcomes—anything that yields such attitudes becomes a valid leisure condition. For example, gambling on a sports contest is the same as playing if the experience of involvement and freedom is the same.

One problem this model presents is that of duration or persistence. Normally a leisure event occurs over a period of time—minutes or hours or days. What is the defining period of time? If there is any flash of perceived freedom and intrinsic motivation in the event, is it leisure? Or, conversely, if there is any drudgery or duty in the event, is it disqualified? Is leisure a matter of the moment so that the defining experience is a slice of the entire process, or is there some kind of summary evaluation after the event is completed? If the attitudes are relatively stable, this may not be a problem (Iso-Ahola, 1980). More often, however, emotions, moods, levels of engagement, and even evaluations change through the event. At a party or on a hike, we may alternate between being high and low depending on multiple factors. In a golf game, there may be a sequence of pleasure and disgust depending on the last shot. We may be angry or thrilled within minutes or even seconds. On a hike we may plan a business agenda during one period and thrill to the rich environment during another.

Experience, then, consists of a stimulus or environment, attitudes or mental states, and behaviors. Further, an experience consists of anticipation, perception, response, interpretation, evaluation, and recall. It is a process in which these steps occur quickly and continually. It is an interpretive activity, often going on largely without recognition unless we stop to evaluate. Further, as we interpret and evaluate, the immediate perception is already past. Any human experience, then, including leisure experience, is a complex process, not a simple unfiltered perception.

This process takes place in an environment. A number of contextual factors always influence the perception and interpretation including time, space, the form of the activity, the social context of whom else is involved, and a history of meaning for the activity. There are also all the factors that went into the decision to engage in the activity in that time and place. There is the culture of symbols, including language, by which we interpret the meanings of the activity. In short, experience is not just perception; it is also a construction of the individual in a particular context.

Properties of Leisure Experiences

There is no question the experiential dimensions of leisure are crucial, for both its definition and its meanings. Whatever else it is, leisure is experience in the full sense outlined above. It may be defined as action or activity, but it is activity focused on the experience. The temptation, then, is to try to identify *the* dimension, element, or meaning that makes an experience leisure. Is it perceived freedom? Then, what about meeting the expectations of other persons engaged in the joint activity? Is it being totally *autotelic*—without any extrinsic motivation? Then, what about longer-term health consequences of a game or the mental health gains from going fishing? Are there any activities that have only immediate meanings—nothing related to the future?

The argument here is research has demonstrated that leisure is multidimensional in its meanings. There are leisure experiences, not just one leisure experience. In fact, such variety may be part of the overall meaning and attraction of leisure. It may be more open, sometimes even spontaneous, rather than totally focused. Further, those multiple meanings are in part a result of giving priority to the experience rather than a predefined outcome.

This is nothing new. The study of adults in Kansas City conducted by Robert Havighurst and others in the 1950s identified several dimensions of leisure in the context of community roles and cultures. Among those dimensions were autonomy versus other-directedness, enjoyment versus time-killing, instrumentality versus expressivity, gregariousness versus solitariness, service versus pleasure, relaxation versus arousal, and ego-integration versus role diffusion (Havighurst, 1957). These multiple meanings were found to be related to social roles such as family and work, resources including income and education, and the class cultures of the community. A serious problem with this or any approach to such multiple meanings has been how to identify them. From 1972 to 1976, research in three communities found leisure activities were meaning-laden in the sense of being chosen because certain outcomes were anticipated (Kelly, 1978). Some such outcomes were closely tied to the nature of the activity, some to their social contexts and companions, and some to social roles such as parenting.

A number of psychological studies concentrated more on the mental states in various leisure contexts. As presented in Chapter 20 on outdoor recreation, B.L. Driver of the U.S. Forest Service engaged in a long line of research identifying personal outcomes of backcountry experiences. Other research identified a wide range of such meanings for other kinds of leisure and recreation. One compilation of such findings was produced at a University of Illinois conference that brought together a number of scholars working on this issue:

1. Enjoyment of nature/Escape from civilization

2. Escape from routine and responsibility

3. Physical exercise and health

4. Creativity

5. Relaxation

6. Social interaction

7. Meeting new people

8. Sexual contact

9. Family interaction

10. Recognition and status

11. Social power

12. Altruism and service

13. Stimulus seeking and excitement

14. Self-actualization, development, and feedback

15. Achievement, challenge, and competition

16. Killing time and avoiding boredom

17. Intellectual and aesthetic engagement (Crandall, 1980)

Such a listing is never final or complete. Rather, it suggests the variety of meanings that may be found in what people do primarily for the experience. There are immediate and long-term meanings, personal and social outcomes, high- and low-intensity activities. The instruments and scales developed to measure such meanings are now beyond listing or counting. Each has some particular perspective or bias. They vary according to their chosen population segment: teens or the retired; Californians or Chinese or Chinese Californians; urban, suburban, or rural. The results are consistent only in the myriad combinations of meanings people find in the infinite number of things they may do as leisure.

Some research approaches focus on perceived outcomes. Some attempt to enter the leisure experience to measure mental states at the time of engagement. Some direct attention to recalled motivations. In a useful pair of chapters, Iso-Ahola (1989) deals with motivations and Mannell (1989) with satisfactions. In the motivations chapter, the common distinction between intrinsic and extrinsic motivation is suggested as fundamental to leisure. A dialectic is proposed between "self-determined, competence-elevating experiences" and avoidance or escape. There are both seeking and escaping dimensions to choosing leisure. There is also boredom in leisure related to attitudes, values, and levels of involvement. Sustained intrinsic motivation (i.e., an awareness of the values of the experience) seems likely to lead to commitments of particular activities— to serious leisure.

The spectrum of leisure motivations and satisfactions suggests a dialectic between involvement and escape. There are both engagement and disengagement poles to this dialectic. Leisure is not just a single meaning, dimension, or kind of activity. Rather, it is complex, as experience is complex. There are choices and constraints. There are deep involvements and shallow entertainments. There are challenges of skill and easy escapes. There is no one kind of leisure, in either form or meaning.

Figure 7.1 Continuums, Not Dichotomies

Involvement:	Intense..	Escape/Entertainment
Frequency:	Regular..	Occasional

Leisure that is both intense and regular is most likely to be serious leisure. Activity that is both occasional and escape would often be dabbling. However, ordinary activity, such as watching television, can be both regular and escape/entertainment, while episodic sport engagement for many adults is intense and occasional.

Serious Leisure

There have been a variety of approaches to serious leisure. One focuses on the sequence of skills acquired over a career with an activity. This is called *specialization*. Another focuses on the individuals who make such commitments because they find the activity so satisfying. They are called *amateurs*. Other approaches refer to "high-investment" activity. The underlying theme, however, is the same. There is a commitment to developing skill and experience in an activity that becomes central to the participant.

Specialization

The specialization metaphor began with a study of fishing. Bryan (1979) observed a progression of styles of fishing among those who do stream fishing with dry fly lures. His own fishing experience paralleled that of others in moving from simply casting lures to catch the most fish to the more refined fly-casting method of catching fish to concentrating on the skill of casting and selecting the best backcountry sites and then releasing the fish. The experience changed from one of using instruments to extract a limit of fish to a refinement of skill largely for its own sake. In the process, the methods and environment came to be the center of the experience in which the challenge was enhanced and the results de-emphasized.

The same process has been observed in other activities. Rock-climbers at higher levels of skill forego many of the technologies of climbing to master the rock face without pitons and ropes. Musicians may choose to play on difficult ancient instruments to maximize authenticity as they specialize in particular past eras of music. Birdwatchers try to identify a few rare species rather than maximize sheer numbers. Painters select challenging materials and media. Magicians avoid the packaged tricks to develop their own dexterity and skill. Hunters select environments and equipment that call more on their own skills. Specialization stresses personal skill, not outcomes. The specialist becomes more selective of equipment and environments, and more concerned with developing a personal style than running up a score.

The common dimension is the development of skill over time. The specialist seeks a challenge appropriate to the developed skill and an environment that offers that level of difficulty. The experience becomes one of immersion in the play rather than of display.

Amateurs

Robert Stebbins (1979) employs the term *amateurs* for those who make an avocation central to their lives. Amateurs, as the term implies, are those who love a particular activity. Stebbins began with his own commitment to string music and expanded his study to a wide range of activities—baseball, magic, archeology, theater, and others. In fact, the schema can apply to almost any skill-based activity. Characteristics of the amateur include:

- A long-term commitment to developing appropriate skills.
- A high standard of performance, essentially the same as that of professionals.
- Developing the skill for the experience rather than to make a living.
- Having a "career" of participation.
- Constructing a set of values, resource expenditures, and schedules around the activity.
- Employing symbols of the commitment in social environments.
- Becoming involved in communities engaged in the same activity.
- Identifying the self with the activity, sometimes even more than with occupation.
- Always accepting the challenge of increasing one's skill level.

Stebbins argues that such serious leisure is in part the result of work limitations. Many people have a series of jobs rather than a progressive career. Many jobs are quite limited in the skills required and the challenge of personal development. As a consequence, amateurs may turn to a leisure commitment for challenge, personal development, identity, and community. They may become cellists who work in a bank, or baseball players who work in construction.

Such leisure can also be called "high-investment" activity. The amateur has a long-term view of engagement. She or he receives instruction, invests in equipment, practices the required skills, and associates with those who share the activity at that level. At extremes there are those who seriously impoverish other aspects of their material lives to invest in the activity. Many who raise and show horses are quite literally "horse poor." Some give up higher-paying jobs to live near the ski slopes or scuba-diving reefs. Such commitments are serious indeed.

There is often a kind of progression in the commitment process. At some time, often when young, the individual finds the activity deeply satisfying. There is feedback indicating some talent for the required skills. Other activities become peripheral to this central commitment. Over time the commitment becomes greater. Almost all one's friends share the same activity. Skill levels become critical. Even vehicles and clothing are selected to support and symbolize that central engagement. Over time the individual comes to define the self in terms of the activity. It becomes central to who one is.

All this is contrasted with those who take up an activity when it is convenient and drop it when it is inconvenient or something else comes along. Most of those who do any activity are dabblers, always inconsistent in their participation. They are the 80% who do an activity only occasionally. Amateurs are the 20% who consistently develop their skills.

Social Worlds

It has been suggested that we live for the most part in "small worlds." We recognize we are citizens of a city, a state, a nation, and even of the world. But day-to-day our lives find their meaning in much smaller contexts of friends, families, work groups, neighborhoods, and leisure groups. This is especially true if we believe that those larger worlds are outside our influence—that what we do and think makes no difference. Even institutions, such as hospitals and medical service organizations, schools and universities, and local government agencies, directly touch our lives and seem to have their own impersonal rules and procedures. In the era of downsizing and cost-efficiency, employers tend to treat even long-time workers as just cost of production factors. It may be primarily in our leisure and our homes that we have a sense of significance and belonging.

An analysis of the game of contract bridge focused on the social world created around the activity (Scott, 1991). There seem to be two kinds of bridge players: the "social" and the "serious." Social players play the game occasionally with friends, are casual about their skills, and tend to make the social setting more important than the game. Serious players play regularly, continually read and practice to upgrade their skills, join organizations that sponsor tournaments, and schedule their social lives around bridge events. Their friends tend to be bridge players and their time investments bridge-related. They are, in this sense, "bridge players" who live in the small world of bridge. They are quite conscious about their levels of skill and the contests that measure that skill.

The same small worlds develop around any similar activity. It may be showing dressage horses, singing in amateur musical productions, joining the senior tennis circuit, involvement in a great books group, or dedication to a religious organization. In time, an individual may be unable to imagine life apart from the activity and its small world. The involvement, then, combines those two critical elements of significant leisure: skill investment and community. The meanings are both personal and social.

Challenge

As with all leisure, the experience itself is central to the meaning of participation. One of the questions concerning serious leisure is "Why?" Why engage in that level of investment, commitment, effort, and cost? What is there about serious leisure that commands such devotion?

There are the social aspects. The activity provides a social context for interaction and relationships. There is the involvement itself. Over time we become invested in the activity just because we have acquired equipment, skill, and associations—but there is something more.

Mihaly Csikszentmihalyi (1990) calls that something more *flow*. His first analysis was that flow is the skill response to a stimulus of challenge. When the skill is greater than the challenge, then one's condition is boredom. When the challenge is greater than the skill, the result is anxiety. When the two meet in a range that produces effective action, then the actor experiences flow. Flow is a total focus on the activity in which time and the external world seem to disappear. There is total concentration on the exercise of the skill in the face of the challenge.

Csikszentmihalyi first located this experience in both work and leisure situations in which the individual responded to a clear challenge. The condition was one in which there was a minimum of uncertainty about the goals and the context. It might be a sports event in which the rules and aims are known and accepted and the focus is on playing the game. It might be a surgeon in the operating room, a mathematician solving a problem, or a writer before a word processor. Flow was found in the focus of the actor, the consistency of the context, and the clarity of the challenge. In later work, he expanded the concept to include any skill-based response to a challenge.

While flow has been found more in work situations than in leisure, there is an obvious connection with serious leisure. Why can such leisure become so important to amateurs? The experience itself has to be central. In times when we match our developed skills with clear challenges, we are most likely to have that deeply involving experience. It is the experience that draws us back to the activity and to a career of involvement.

Again, in a time when many kinds of work are becoming routine, serious leisure may offer an alternative possibility of the deep meaning of flow. As the computer and other technologies reduce the skills required for many jobs, serious leisure may offer the opportunity to develop skills in a disciplined way and exercise them against challenge. In a mass society, such experience may become the basis of a demonstrated identity of being a competent person.

It seems evident that for younger people who have not yet entered the world of full-time work, various games, contests, and activities may be the primary context of testing and exhibiting ability. Now research also indicates this is the case for older adults. Roger Mannell (1993) reported studies in which a regular engagement in high-investment activity best distinguishes older adults with high levels of satisfaction. Those who report regular experiences of flow have the highest levels of positive emotional states. Even in retirement years, the experience of responding to challenge with competence and ability is important to life. Then, such experience is most likely to be found in serious leisure, whether in a skill-based activity or in some kind of community or personal service. At the center of life satisfaction is the experience of meeting challenge with ability. Just being entertained is not enough.

Escape and Entertainment

Of course, serious leisure is not what most people do most of the time. Studies of time use show clearly that absorbing the entertainment of television is far ahead of everything else done outside work in our waking hours (Robinson & Godbey, 1997). On average, Americans watch about 15 hours of television a week. That is more than convenience—it is also a choice.

The growing industries of leisure are primarily designed to provide entertainment. There are businesses based on acquiring and exercising skills. The big investments, however, go to the mass media, popular culture, and megadestinations such as Las Vegas and the worlds of Disney. Probably the fastest-growing leisure industry is gambling as casinos spring up in all sorts of unlikely places where they are legal. Investment drives business. Supply creates demand. In the leisure field, investment is directed toward creating markets for goods and services that are cost-intensive and repeated. The renewable resource is entertainment that comes with a new fee for every experience. The profit in equipment that lasts ten years is low. The profit is high for big-ticket toys and experiences that require a daily or even hourly fee. The exception is entertainment that is paid for by advertising and that is based on the entire consumption demand of an economy. There will always be a renewed supply of entertainment. There will be more variety and perhaps even higher quality, but there will be more and more.

New technologies seem to offer the possibility of challenge and involvement rather than passive entertainment. Computer games and the World Wide Web offer involvement and variety for those who invest in the equipment and gain the skills. Game players, however, remain a minority. The World Wide Web becomes more a medium for selling and consuming with its interactive possibilities relegated to a minority of users. The vast communicative potential of the technology threatens to be taken over by selling and exploring new ways of consuming.

Even children's toys most often offer entertainment rather than challenge. There are toys designed to stimulate creativity and abilities to make something new. Most models, however, are precut and by the numbers. Battery-powered toys, many based on movies or cartoons, provide the action while the child watches and then becomes bored. The excitement is in what the toy does, not what the child does. More and more entertainment is available on cable and satellite television, DVD/videos, and computer disks. The challenge of mental learning and physical dexterity is overwhelmed by all the entertainment that is so easy, so available, and so stimulating.

Of course, there will continue to be serious leisure for those who seek it out, pay the price of dedication, and mine its deeper satisfactions. There will be all sorts of developmental games and toys for children of all ages. Such play will, however, be one choice in an overwhelming offering of goods and services for which the cost is money rather than personal investment. Serious leisure will still be a personal choice based on a history of challenging activity and an investment in skill.

Psychologist Douglas Kleiber suggested another possibility in studies summarized in a text on the psychology of leisure (Mannell & Kleiber, 1997). It may be that leisure alternates between engagement and disengagement. This rhythm or dialectic is related to the demands of other roles, the time of day and day of the week, energy levels, and perhaps even seasons. Some persons seek more challenge and engagement; others more relaxation and disengagement. The aim is to find a balance that is appropriate to the person and to current life conditions.

Debate: Leisure is primarily escape.

YES

- Entertainment and escape are what people do. Television not only occupies far and away the most discretionary time but also it creates a dependency on such easy entertainment. It is just too easy to be entertained and so hard to meet the demands of high-investment activity.

- Even excitement can be obtained without any real challenge. Movies and television become more and more stimulating with their required car chases, violence, and sex. Gambling, especially in machine form, yields suspense without effort. Skill is just too demanding.

- The entertainment industry will provide whatever people are willing to pay for. Especially entertainment that is cost-intensive and that has to be paid for at the time of each experience will command corporate investment. Then the media will use its persuasive power to sell such offerings. It is no wonder that single corporations own television networks, movie producers and distributors, gambling mecca hotels and casinos, and tourist resorts. It's all one industry that the investment firms call "leisure."

- After all, we do need relaxation. Just living in urban areas is stressful. Economic insecurity is stressful. Family life is demanding. We need to be able to separate from all these roles and relax. That is the primary function of leisure.

- High-intensity activity is and will remain the exception. Just look at the participation figures. One might even argue that serious leisure is elitist, requiring skills related to higher education or a high cost. Mass entertainment is there for the masses (i.e., most people).

- Entertainment is what people want. It is excitement with low demand. As such it fits the lifestyles of most people who just want to be happy, not deliberately seek out pressure and demand.

NO

- The leisure most important to people, that they least want to give up, is usually serious or social. It involves those people important to us in contexts that require communication and interaction, or it involves activity in which we have developed interest, skills, and relationships over a period of time. Once we have experienced such activity, entertainment is not enough.

- Unrelieved entertainment is boring. It is no wonder that movies, television, and even professional sport become more violent and sexy. There is a limit, however, to the stimulation that can be provided to passive viewers. Just filling time is not enough to look forward to. Entertainment is fine in its place, but we also need the challenge of learning, testing, and exercising abilities.

- Nor is work enough. Increasingly jobs are routine and workers are replaceable. There isn't much challenge to an automated position that can be learned in a few hours or days. For all those whose work is no longer a skill-based craft, there is the alternative of repeated entertainment or investment in some more stimulating and challenging activity.

- Such activity has an infinite number of forms. It may be a common activity, such as rebuilding old cars or gardening, as well as more elite activities. It may be line dancing as well as ballet. There is serious leisure available for everyone.

- It is human to learn and grow. We are not satisfied to stay the same, never to develop into fuller and more competent human beings. Look at children. They become most excited when they are really learning, not just watching. That drive toward development may be repressed and stifled, but it is still there throughout life.

- Often it is in leisure contexts that we inaugurate, develop, and express the relationships important to us. We are social beings. The drive toward efficiency in most workplaces allows for little social interaction. Rather it is in the leisure contexts of doing something together that we are most likely to express our social selves.

- The entertainment industry is seductive. New technologies make it more so. Yet, there is also a resistance to even the most exciting technologies. There is a desire to get away from all the screens and stages to do something that is real. We need real people, real action of body and mind, and real meaning to what we do. The virtual is just not quite enough.

- What is most deeply satisfying? What have been the best times of your life? Is it what you have done, usually with other people, or what others have done to or for you? There is a rhythm of life and leisure. We do desire and need separation and even escape part of the time, but we also need engagement with meaning and challenge, involvement with real people, and the excitement of real play. No entertainment, however high-tech and elaborate, can fulfill the human need to act, develop, and even create.

Discussion Questions

1. What kinds of activity are "serious" and yet most satisfying? Why?

2. Give examples of "amateurs" who really love their special activity. Are they exceptional?

3. How are specialists and amateurs reliable markets for leisure goods and services?

4. Have you experienced "flow?" If so, give examples. What are the conditions for flow?

5. What gets children really excited, especially in repeated events?

6. Is escape always negative and challenge positive? Are there examples of worthwhile escape and damaging challenge?

7. Do we spend the most time being entertained because it is easy or because it is what we really want?

Resources

Bryan, H. (1979). *Conflict in the great outdoors: Toward understanding and managing diverse sportsmen preferences*. University, AL: University of Alabama Press.

Crandall, R. (1980). Motivations for leisure. *Journal of Leisure Research, 12,* 45–54.

Csikszentmihalyi, M. (1990). *Flow: The psychology of optimal experience*. New York, NY: Harper and Row.

Ehrenreich, B. (1990). *The worst years of our lives: Irreverent notes from a decade of greed* ("The cult of busyness"). New York, NY: Pantheon Books.

Goffman, E. (1967). *Interaction ritual: Essays in face-to-face behavior.* Garden City, NY: Anchor Books.

Havighurst, R. (1957). The leisure activities of the middle-aged. *American Journal of Sociology, 63,* 162–182.

Huizinga, J. (1950). *Homo ludens: A study of the play-element in culture*. Boston, MA: Beacon Press.

Iso-Ahola, S. (1980). Toward a dialectical social psychology of leisure and recreation. In S. Iso-Ahola (Ed.), *Social psychological perspectives on leisure and recreation* (pp. 19–37). Springfield, IL: Charles C. Thomas.

Iso-Ahola, S. (1989). Motivation for leisure. In E. Jackson and T. Burton (Eds.), *Understanding leisure and recreation: Mapping the past, charting the future* (pp. 247–279). State College, PA: Venture Publishing, Inc.

Kelly, J.R. (1978). Leisure styles and choices in three environments. *Pacific Sociological Review, 21,* 187–207.

Kelly, J.R. (1983). *Leisure identities and interactions.* London, UK: Allen and Unwin.

Mannell, R. (1989) Leisure satisfaction. In E. Jackson and T. Burton (Eds.), *Understanding leisure and recreation: Mapping the past, charting the future* (pp. 281–301). State College, PA: Venture Publishing, Inc.

Mannell, R. (1993). High-investment activity and life satisfaction among older adults: Committed, serious leisure, and flow activities. In J. Kelly (Ed.), *Activity and aging: Staying involved in later life* (pp. 125–146). Thousand Oaks, CA: Sage Publications.

Mannell, R.C. and Kleiber, D.A. (1997). *A social psychology of leisure.* State College, PA: Venture Publishing, Inc.

Neulinger, J. (1974). *The psychology of leisure: Research approaches to the study of leisure.* Springfield, IL: Charles C. Thomas.

Robinson, J. and Godbey, G. (1997). *Time for life: The surprising ways Americans use their time.* University Park, PA: The Pennsylvania University Press.

Scott, D. (1991). A narrative analysis of a declining social world: The case of contract bridge. *Play and Culture, 4,* 11–23.

Stebbins, R. (1979). *Amateurs: On the margin between work and leisure.* Thousand Oaks, CA: Sage Publications.

Stebbins, R. (1992). *Amateurs, professionals, and serious leisure.* Montreal, PQ: McGill-Queen's University Press.

Chapter 8
Society and Leisure

The approach to leisure in the previous chapter is individual. It focuses on the experience of the individual person. This focus is partly psychological—a state of consciousness and accompanying emotions. It is partly physical—the reality of the body in motion or at rest. It is existential—a process of becoming for the individual who is always developing through decision and action. There is a necessary attention given to the multidimensional experience of the individual actor.

But there is a second approach as well. It focuses on the social nature of leisure. Individuals are, after all, profoundly social. We do not become human in isolation. We learn to become who we are. Even our attempts to understand our experience are in the form of a language that we have learned in a particular society. We are social—even in our leisure.

Leisure Is Learned Behavior

Of course, there are instincts for play. Animals, such as puppies and lion cubs, play with each other. They engage in make-believe combat in a combination of instinct and learned behavior. For the infant, the first game seems to be peek-a-boo, a social game of recognition of seeing and being seen by another person. In a way, all play seems to be some version of self-and-other interaction. As such we learn to recognize the symbolic actions of others, interpret them, and respond appropriately.

There is very little of anything that we do that does not involve some elements of learning. Before we are a year old we learn to recognize that certain sounds and gestures have meaning. Soon we begin to employ those verbal symbols—words—to communicate our feelings and thoughts. We refer to objects that are present and then those that are absent. We begin to have some sense of the self with a word and a given name. In fact, we have no memory of a time when we did not use the learned language to make sense of our selves and the world around us. We are biological beings, animals with behaviors that spring from our biology. Research indicates that a portion of our personalities has a genetic base, although we cannot really separate the inherited from the environmental—nature from nurture. We are also, however, the animal that thinks, that is always learning.

Leisure, then, is part of that process that we call *socialization*—interactively learning to be who we are in a world with all sorts of structures and expectations. Through leisure, we may begin over half of our adult activities in childhood. More than half of all activities are begun with our families and immediate communities. That is, however, only the simplest level of learning leisure. Our interests, skills, attitudes, values, and styles of interaction are also learned in a lifelong process. However, much of this learning is not conscious or intentional. As individuals we do not exist separately from society nor society from us. We are part and parcel of society and thus both produce and reproduce, construct and reconstruct our leisure.

What do we find of interest or pleasurable and why? Are we playful or serious? Do we seek demanding physical activity or are we more oriented toward the mind? Do we read and listen to music? Do we want a lot of social interaction? What are our styles of leisure? There are so many factors in our histories that there is no way of sorting them all out. What is clear, however, is that we have become who we are as social beings. We have learned to be ourselves—and are still learning.

Leisure Is Contextual

Some leisure is solitary. We may want to get away from pressures, routines, and demands. However, even solitary leisure is consciously drawing away from something; that is, from the ongoing flow of life. Imaginative leisure, daydreaming, is usually about involvement with other people. Leisure is not a separate realm of life; it is contextual.

To begin with, a high proportion of leisure involves those with whom we are in primary relationships. They include friends, family, children, lovers, neighbors, and other intimates. Other than watching television, more free time is spent in social interaction than any other kind of leisure. Vacation trips tend to be with others with whom we have close relationships. We eat out, go to parties, entertain, and take walks with others. We even engage in sports and go to concerts and movies with friends and family. In fact, the primary meaning of many leisure activities is in the expressions of the relationships rather than the form of the activity. Further, such associations may dictate the meaning of the activity. Playing ball with a child is likely to be more nurture than a competitive event.

There is withdrawal in leisure. It may be the inner renewal of meditation or contemplation. There may be an encounter with a book in hours of reading. We may want to be alone on a walk or even watching television. A high proportion of leisure, however, is interactive. We are with others in an interactive process that may be communicative, physical, emotional, or some combination. In one set of community studies, affection and intimacy were rated by adults as their most important kind of nonwork activity. Even when we are alone, we are dealing with media of the culture and the things produced by the economy.

Leisure is contextual and situated in the complex, multidimensional system we call society. It is in places to which we have access according to social arrangements. It is in time frames set by economic and political institutions. It is either within legal prescriptions or deliberately violates them so the illegality becomes part of the meaning. It takes into account all the social expectations that go far beyond the law in shaping behavior.

Pierre Bourdieu (1984) developed the concept of *habitus* to refer to all the systems of language, thought, behavior, style, and value we learn through our lifelong socialization. These become so thoroughly a part of our lives that we take them for granted. They are mental and behavioral schemes by which we make our way through the social world. They express not only our culture in general but also the particular class, gender, and ethnicity that are the context of our ordinary lives. They are the habitual ways of behaving and interpreting the world of our families and communities. Leisure is fully embedded in such habits and in learning that is so deep as to be unnoticed and unquestioned.

Leisure Is Cultural

As already suggested, we use the socially learned means of communication and interpretation—a specific language—to think about meaning. Any language has its particular forms, syntax as well as vocabularies, that give form to the ways we think and communicate. We recognize that words often do not express just how we feel. Any language is limited as well as expressive—but that is only the beginning.

All our thought forms are part of the particular culture and subculture in which we live and learn. For example, in Western culture we tend to understand social situations in competitive terms. Even learning becomes a competition for attention, status, and, of course, grades. We often forget that in Eastern cultures learning is understood as more of a group process. Learning is *with* rather than against others. In fact, Western culture seems preoccupied with the individual rather than the group—with the self rather than society. As a consequence, we interpret events in a competitive mode and measure them by how well we have done in comparison with others. Even in team sports we keep individual statistics and see the game in terms of an individualistic star system. The culture obviously has a considerable impact on leisure—on how we play games as well as what we play. The old joke that the local symphony played Beethoven and Beethoven lost may be more than a joke.

Of course, the forms of leisure are also products of the culture. The group games of one culture may be very warlike and those of another more cooperative. Games are gendered, reflecting sex roles of aggression for one gender and nurture and sharing for the other. The expectations for behavior at a party are learned and tend to be gender and age-specific. The ways we do everything are learned in a culture that specifies what is acceptable and rewarded according to social identification. We learn how to behave in different situations and become quite skilled at meeting those prescriptions. Even events without predetermined outcomes, such as parties, become arenas of skilled social negotiation as we present our individual selves on a stage where there is general scripted action and interaction.

Bourdieu proposed we do not come into situated interaction with exactly equal resources. Rather, social class is distinguished by "cultural capital" that reflects the conditions of our histories. There are social distinctions based on our command of skills related to the culture of arts, sports, science, politics, and all other realms of acquired knowledge. In our leisure, we differentiate and identify ourselves by our use of such capital so that we will be accepted in social groups distinguished by their cultures. For example, command of the culture of stock car racing or professional wrestling may serve well at the Daytona track or local bar but fail completely at Pinehurst Country Club or a United Nations cocktail party.

All life is, in this sense, ethnic. That is, it is composed of specific taste cultures allowed and learned in the subsystems of an overall society. Again, what we do and how we do it are shaped by our opportunities and particular history of learning. Style distinguishes status. Listening to music as a general activity tells us little about the listener. However, when we know what music is preferred, where, and with whom it is heard, then we can infer a good deal about the listener—age, social class, and ethnic background. Leisure is not some transcendent state of being; it is thoroughly embedded in particular cultures and subcultures.

Leisure Is Based in Economic Roles

Leisure is not determined by economic roles. Knowing an occupation does not predict leisure engagement with any reliability. Nevertheless, who we are in the economy is significant for leisure.

To begin with, in a society in which most leisure resources are distributed through the market, income is important to what we can and cannot do. The wealthy can travel further, join clubs that offer privacy and access, visit resorts in which the comfort and service levels are extraordinarily high, and pay others to take care of the little details of life, such as children. Those with higher levels of income are more likely to be constrained by shortages of time rather than cost. The masses have access to a multitude of priced resources that meet the limitations of their incomes. The poor are generally ruled out of all but low-cost or free opportunities.

Income, however, is only the beginning of the power of economic roles. There is time. Some have considerable control over their work schedules. Even though they may work long hours, they can control the pace and spacing of those hours. Others, however, work on a rigid schedule determined by the structures of the factory or office. Now there are the service-sector employees whose weekly schedules are cut up by timetables based on seven-day-a-week and 24-hour operations. The assumption of regularity and control applies to fewer and fewer in the paid work force. Time for leisure may be out of sync with most opportunities and programs as well as other household members.

Most American households include a "second shift" of home and family responsibilities outside the paid employment schedule. Since most childcare and home provisions remain the assignment of women, they tend to be most burdened by the second shift at home. Economic institutions are just beginning to adjust work conditions and schedules to support valued female employees or men who want to take a full share of household work.

Economic roles also are a factor in access to resources. Some employers provide a range of recreation opportunities to employees who are especially valued. Perhaps more important, such workers are most likely to be able to arrange their schedules to take mini-vacations or partial days for leisure. High-level managerial and technical workers receive club memberships and subsidized trips as part of their income packages, while replaceable workers are told when to take vacations at the employer's convenience.

There are also the associations and expectations that accompany economic roles. All kinds of community organizations recruit and reject members based on their economic status. In some cases, those in particular professions and businesses are expected to belong to certain organizations and even to play the right sports and attend the appropriate concerts and social events. Economic position may yield immediate access to some kinds of leisure venues while others would be considered socially unacceptable. Many drinking establishments, for example, are clearly differentiated in terms of their appropriate clienteles. Few truck drivers would go to "The Office" after work and fewer lawyers enter "Joe's Bar" or the "Silver Bullet Exotic Lounge." The symbol system of the leisure culture tends to be quite effective.

Economic roles are related to cultural capital and social expectations. They also are structural as they shape timetables, control over time and space, access to resources, and cultures of association.

Leisure Has Roles

Leisure itself has roles. It is self-evident that games have rules and structures. The position roles in team sports determine where one is positioned and what functions the player tries to fulfill in the overall scheme of the game. Catchers and centerfielders do quite different things in softball as do safeties and flankers in football, and so on. Leisure events have structures. Even at a cocktail party there are roles of host, special guest, helper, and stranger that determine how one will act and interact. We present ourselves in quite different ways from one role to another.

Such structured role expectations and even requirements are part of any social setting, including leisure. Further, they symbolize certain things about us. We tell others a lot about whom we are by how we act. Who we are, not just in general but in that specific setting, makes a difference in whether we are central or peripheral to a group, how we enter and withdraw from a conversation, and even where and how we sit or stand.

Such roles are always gendered as will be further detailed in Chapter 13. There is our general gender identity as male or female that has considerable influence on how we walk, talk, dress, and symbolize who we are in countless ways—many of which have been so thoroughly learned as to be habitus. We may also present ourselves in ways that symbolize our specific identities in relation to our gender identifications. We may choose to exhibit varying levels of aggressiveness, compliance, humor, or knowledge. Our sexual orientations may become part of our presentation in ways that are clear or ambiguous. Some leisure has definite rules of inclusion or exclusion based on gender. Certainly the gendered roles of performers at a university football or male basketball game are specific and unambiguous. Often we make the mistake of assuming males are more competent than females in some kinds of activity—especially those requiring physical strength, endurance, or aggressiveness.

Leisure roles may also be specified by age. Some kinds of leisure are not considered appropriate for older adults, teens, or children. Some events are open only to those of certain ages. Often we assume ability is determined by age. We assume the young and the old are less competent. There are roles assigned by age in a society in which we have both entry and exit—formally or informally—as indexed by age.

Leisure is as structured and institutionalized as any other aspect of social life. In fact, the role expectations in some leisure settings may be more subtle and complex than in hierarchical institutions with clear ranks and insignia. In leisure, we may have to find out who others are, how they fit into the relevant social scheme, and what are appropriate ways of dealing with them. Dress and demeanor may give clues, but in leisure settings status may not always be clear. The negotiation of the self in leisure events may be quite a complex process. The costs of error, however, begin with embarrassment and range through humiliation to exclusion. Again, the exhibition of various kinds of cultural capital may become much of the meaning of leisure events.

Leisure Is Institutional

Many of the tastes, interests, and skills of leisure are based in educational histories. Leisure styles come out of the entire set of institutional connections for any individual—school, religion, work, family, and community.

Perhaps the most clear institutional relationship is with education. There is a demonstrated connection between a person's range of interests and amount and quality of education. The school has as a central purpose the development of cultural interests and skills. Further, the school organizes a range of sports and recreational activities available to students at low or no cost. The longer one stays in school and the better the quality of the school, the more opportunities to gain interests and develop skills are afforded. This is most evident in the high percentage of people with at least some college education that do and appreciate the arts. School is a place to acquire cultural capital. Just as important is the fund of cultural knowledge that comes with higher education and allows the individual to interact comfortably in higher levels of the stratified social system.

Religion is also important. Some churches teach that many ordinary leisure activities are unacceptable for their followers. Many also provide a set of alternative social and leisure opportunities that substitute for market provisions considered dangerous to the faithful. Such religious organizations attempt to provide a total social context for their members. Other "mainline" churches are more accommodating with the mainstream culture. Their adherents are more likely to participate in a wider range of general leisure activities and to be comfortable with the culture. In some cases, religion combines with ethnicity to reinforce separation from the general culture and to offer special celebrations with long cultural histories.

As will be examined in Chapter 12, leisure is also closely related to government. The state provides some kinds of resources, regulates others, and prohibits some kinds of activity. In licensing and taxation policies, the state may support some kinds of leisure investments and raise the cost of others. In general, the tacit political policy in the United States and other capitalist countries is to assign to the market sector all leisure provisions not otherwise assumed for reasons of equity, efficiency, and environmental management.

Of course there are leisure institutions as well. Some are governmental such as land management, community programs, and financial support of certain approved kinds of activity. Some are religious such as congregational community or "family" centers, summer camps, conference centers, and programs in the arts. Some are private associations such as YMCAs and YWCAs, Jack and Jill, Boys and Girls Clubs, Jewish Community Centers (JCCs), sports and arts organizations, and community clubs. Many are from the market sector such as bowling alleys, fitness and sports centers, the tourism business network, and all the other market provisions. Leisure is thoroughly a part of the institutional system of a society. Its organizations have the same structures and dynamics as other organizations. It is subject to the laws of the state and of the marketplace. There is often conflict among such institutions for control of resources and access to their clienteles. The social system does not always work smoothly, especially for those at the margins of the society.

Leisure Is Contested

The history of leisure, as outlined in earlier chapters, often involved conflict. Religious minorities attempted to enforce their moral codes on majorities. Racial and ethnic minorities have been labeled, restricted, and cut off from resources. Times and spaces have been protected from "unacceptable" leisure. There have always been eruptions—public or in secret—of activities considered immoral or dangerous by those with political and cultural power.

Michel Foucault (2001) has analyzed the pervasiveness of power in society. Power is central to the dynamics of the economy, institutions, and the culture. The individual both acquiesces and resists power in a continual process. There is submission and conflict. For the most part, the demands of the culture dominate. In leisure, however, there are time and places in which resistance is central to the meaning of activity.

Some leisure activity is illegal. Some kinds of gambling are prohibited and yet are readily available to those who know the system. Use of illegal drugs is widespread among the affluent as well as the poor. There is a long history of so-called "blood sports" in which animals fight, often to the death, in hideaways where followers bet on the outcomes. There are speed contests with cars and motorcycles that break the law. Unlicensed backroom businesses have long provided places for drinking and gambling. Age regulations for drinking are routinely broken. The sex industry flourishes despite laws against most forms. In fact, there is a stratification in the business from high-priced call girls for visiting businessmen to the sex traffic of the streets.

In some leisure there is conflict over control. In the early days of baseball there was a struggle between players and owners for control of the professional game. The owners won and set the pattern for all professional sports that has been interrupted only occasionally by players' strikes. In the motion picture industry there was conflict between theater owners and film producers that was settled for a time when the major studios took control of major theater chains. Skateboarders "do battle" with business owners and police as they seek new challenges outside of skateboard parks. Teens and youth conflict with shopping mall proprietors who want to ensure that the mall does not become a teen hangout, yet welcome seniors who hang out at the mall to walk and socialize. On a local level, there are struggles between various interests over financial resources.

Perhaps the most contested terrain has been just that—conflicts over the control of land. In urban parks, various groups may use threats and force to control space and exclude designated others. Parks may become gang terrain. In any community, public outdoor space is allocated by scheduling and designed for one set of users in ways that exclude others. Federal lands are quite contested: mountainsides are leased by ski operators with trees slashed or preserved for their environmental values. Fragile deserts may become cut up by off-road vehicle users who believe they have a right to use public land for their recreation. Rivers may become polluted by recreation users camping alongside or running powerboats. Waterfront land is especially contested when private owners fence off access to nonowners, including locals who have used the beach for generations. Space on beaches may become the object of age and subcultural warfare with musical tastes as a central issue. Development of desirable land for any purpose almost inevitably creates conflict with former and current users.

There are other contested nonphysical terrains as well. Males have traditionally excluded females from some drinking and card-playing places. They have denied women access to some golf courses except at designated off-hours. They have harassed females who dared to enter such places such as bars and pubs, gyms and playing fields. Further, males have often dictated the terms on which females might enter some venues. They are accepted only when they are willing to take subservient roles or act as ornaments to male leisure.

All Western societies have long histories of racial discrimination. Cities in the United States have closed public swimming pools rather than have them integrated. For decades after the Civil War, Jim Crow laws and customs severely limited the leisure opportunities of African Americans. All over the country, it is only in the last few decades that African Americans were not relegated to the balcony in movie theaters and excluded from most hotels and motels. In Great Plains towns, Native Americans have been systematically excluded from many kinds of public and private places. It took the conflict of the Civil Rights movement to change such legal and social exclusions. Racial discrimination has not disappeared, but takes less visible and more profound forms. Laws may exist to ensure equality of opportunity, but not feeling welcome still constrains and shapes participation. Further, racial exclusion is cumulative when denial at one point in life prevents anyone from gaining the skills and attitudes necessary for later participation (Gramann & Allison, 1999).

The poor, of course, are excluded from leisure resources in so many ways. As will be discussed in Chapter 23, the market system excludes according to discretionary income and access to credit. The poor, however, are made to feel unwelcome in all sorts of subtle ways when they venture onto the terrain of the established classes. The condition of homelessness excludes one from even signing up for programs if they do not have an established addresses, proper identification, and acceptable attire.

Foucault's (2001) argument is that power is at work everywhere—in every setting and every history. As a consequence, attempts to exercise power by securing control over a place, an event, or a situation may be met with resistance or even outright conflict. Leisure is not excluded from such conflict, but reflects the divisions and power differences found in any society.

Leisure Is Capitalist

Chapter 11 on the economics of leisure introduces the ways in which a capitalist system shapes and biases the leisure of such a society. The most obvious way, of course, is reliance on the market for most leisure resources and provisions. Chapter 23 outlines how the market sector offers an incredible variety of leisure resources. Especially in urban areas, a spectrum of entertainment, recreation opportunities, and places for leisure gatherings respond to all kinds of market segments.

These resources and opportunities mean society is heavily dependent on such business provisions. There are all the in-home electronics that command so much time and attention. There are all the sites where people gather to eat and drink. There are the entertainment locales for movies, plays, concerts, circuses, and other entertainment. There are the professional sports contests for spectator viewing and television programming. There are all the businesses that sell and lease big toys such as boats and little toys such as racquets and balls—and there is the massive industry of tourism.

Businesses are operated to obtain a return on investment. To obtain capital, a business has to present a plan that promises a return commensurate with the risk. Of course, many fail. The strategy of capitalist business, however, is to secure a viable market that will yield a substantial return in excess of ordinary interest.

This means more leisure resources are oriented toward investment. The business may advertise and offer an experience. Even in Las Vegas the shows—volcanoes, sea battles, circuses, roller coasters—are there to attract visitors to the central experience of gambling and its estimated $7 billion yearly income. The investment is clearly oriented toward bringing money to the machines and tables. Of course, there is no recreational experience as effective as gambling at extracting money from the players. The principle is no less operative for the most natural experience-based business, however. Guiding canoeists into the wilderness of pristine lakes and streams is also designed to yield a regular profit in a short season of operation.

Even the forms of such recreation and entertainment are designed to maximize profit. Restaurants may make most of their profit on alcoholic beverages sold at a 300% markup. Resorts make money on equipment rentals, the bar by the pool, and arranging excursions as well as room rentals. They also rent space to shops at high rates to attract those who travel to shop. In North American football, the rules and styles of play have been altered over the years to make the spectacle more exciting. For television, sports uniforms are designed to be strikingly colorful on the small screen. In all sports, stars are promoted over team play to attract crowds willing to pay high ticket prices.

The nature of leisure is transformed by its capitalist base. First, the market sector provides most opportunities. Second, those provisions are designed to maximize profit. The experience is commodified as something that can be promoted and sold. It becomes standardized, routinized, and repetitive for cost-efficiency. It is a product to be sold. As a consequence, the active engagement of the participant is channeled into routines that are easier to manage. Further, they tend to be commodity intensive. The experience of skiing is surrounded by boutiques, dress codes, equipment upgrades, fancy lounges, and new technologies, such as heli-skiing, that come at a high price. All these become part of the package that comes at excluding prices. The emotional rush of a controlled run down a quiet mountainside is submerged under the complex arrangements designed to attract a paying crowd. Leisure becomes a commodity to be marketed in a capitalist economic system.

Leisure Is Social

Leisure is social since it reflects the social system and culture in which it exists. It is not a separate realm of the mind and spirit. It is not a state of consciousness that requires only having the right thoughts or attitudes.

In a competitive culture, leisure participation is designed to pit participants against each other with the aim of determining a "winner." In segregated societies, leisure is divided by race, ethnicity, and social class. In gendered societies, there are clear differences in what is open, safe, and rewarded for females and males. In capitalist economies, the aim of many leisure provisions is to produce a profit so that investment is biased. All the substance of cultures and subcultures, the socialization of combined institutions, and the pervasive role expectations that shape practices are part of leisure. Access is opened and closed by social status as well as by price. Styles of leisure practice are learned and often enforced in particular settings. Leisure is, then, thoroughly social.

Further, leisure has a place in the overall system and culture. It is related to the full set of social institutions—the economy, school, religion, family, and government. No leisure transcends its context. Even the philosophical majesty of classic Greek leisure was based on a social and economic system of slavery and gender oppression. Leisure, then, is part of the institutional system. It may be given high value or be of only secondary value in relation to work or family. It may change and even become a factor in changing cultural values. Yet, to understand leisure, it is necessary to understand the multidimensional social system in which it takes time and place.

Leisure Is Practice

Leisure is primarily a matter of practice, of what people do in the ordinary and extraordinary times of their lives. As such it is embedded in the social system and the learned culture in which we all live. Its meanings as well as its behaviors express—and sometimes challenge and transform—the values, cultural orientations, and organization of the social system. Leisure, then, cannot be clearly isolated from its social context.

There may be no one "best" way to approach leisure. It is experience, institutionalized behaviors, cultural values and orientations, social roles, economic commodities offered through the market, government provisions and restrictions, breaking outside the law and custom as well as conformity, emotion and imagination and embodied activity, and all kinds of styles and meanings for doing almost anything. Leisure may also be that "other side" of human activity—whatever we do, think, and feel for its own sake, and for the experience. There may be a dimension of play more basic to human life than any of its forms and manifestations.

Debate: Leisure is primarily social.

YES

- The entire chapter is an argument for the proposition that leisure is social. All aspects of life are social. All behavior and its interpretations are learned in a particular culture and practiced in a complex social, economic, and cultural system. The chapter specifies different aspects of this embedded nature of leisure.

- Leisure is not separated from life, but takes place in the midst of life. Even so-called "getaways" are institutionalized and marketed. Leisure is related to everything we do and are.

- Every experience is contextual. Even daydreaming is made up of the elements of our social lives. We have learned to be who we are and what we would like to become.

- Leisure reflects the culture in which we live, its basic values and orientations as well as its forms and practices. There is nothing transcendent or universal—even our ideas of life and leisure are in and of a particular culture.

- Leisure has changed as the society has changed. Chapters 3 through 5 suggested ways in which leisure has changed in various historical contexts.

- Leisure is deeply related to our primary relationships, our families and communities of consistent caring and sharing. It may be difficult to separate responsibilities from play in such relationships. There are family roles and expectations. However, the connection of play and the building and expression of relationships has its own special meaning.

NO

- Leisure is a fundamentally personal experience. The fact that it takes forms and even meanings reflecting the culture does not alter its essence. Experience is individual—not social. We employ social symbols to carry out and interpret our actions, but the experience is ours.

- Leisure is choice. We may choose out of many possibilities presented in the social context, but we do choose based on the anticipated meanings. We may be influenced by the culture, but our lives are not fully determined. We are still existential beings who choose and become who we are in our choices and actions. Each of us is unique—not a mass-produced social product.

- Leisure is clearly separated from productive activity. It is "expressive culture" that focuses on its internal and personal meaning. If we have to do it, it isn't leisure. We may choose to engage in the mass leisure culture, or we may not. We can always resist the powers and persuasions around us. Even the television has a remote with off and mute buttons.

- Leisure is existential. It is one area of life in which we have some opportunity to orient our action toward our selves and what we want to become. Much of life is routinized. In leisure we may break the routines to try out new possibilities for our lives. Sometimes leisure may even be novel, exploratory, and creative.

- Some leisure is disengagement. Some is separation from our ordinary roles and responsibilities—even escape from the society.

- Leisure is not a set of forms or activities. It is a state of consciousness that may occur almost any time or anywhere. Some commodified and marketed experiences may not be leisure at all. They are just one more form of purchase. The experience of freedom and involvement that is real leisure, however, is more than an economic or social product. That special experience is individual—not social. Its meaning is personal.

Discussion Questions

1. Where do we most often learn the interests that guide our leisure?

2. How much of our leisure involves the other people with whom we are closest?

3. How does leisure provide the symbols of subcultural identification? for youth? for adults?

4. What "cultural capital" do you possess? Do you pursue any leisure to gain such status-identifying knowledge and practice?

5. To what extent is the leisure of particular kinds of workers distinctive?

6. Are there any kinds of leisure without role expectations and requirements?

7. How does education influence cultural differences in leisure?

8. How can leisure be used to resist social expectations and even oppression?

9. What kinds of leisure are not a product of capitalism? Are you sure?

10. Is there any human activity that is not social and a product of a system and culture?

References and Resources

Adorno, T.W. (1991). *The culture industry: Selected essays on mass culture*. London, UK: Routledge.

Beaudrillard, J. (1993). *Symbolic exchange and death*. Thousand Oaks, CA: Sage.

Bourdieu, P. (1984). *Distinction: A social critique of the judgement of taste*. London, UK: Routledge and Kegan Paul.

Foucault, M. (1981). *The history of sexuality*. Harmondsworth, UK: Penguin.

Foucault, M. (2001). Discipline and punishment. In K. Schaff (Ed.), *Philosophy and problems of work: A reader* (pp. 43–58). Lanham, MD: Rowman & Littlefield.

Gramann, J.H. and Allison, M. (1999). Ethnicity, race and leisure. In E.L. Jackson and T.L. Burton (Eds.), *Leisure studies: Prospects for the 21st century* (pp. 283–297). State College, PA: Venture Publishing, Inc.

Kelly, J.R. (1983). *Leisure identities and interactions*. London, UK: Allen and Unwin.

Kelly, J.R. (1987). *Freedom to be: A new sociology of leisure*. New York, NY: MacMillan.

Kelly, J.R. and Godbey, G. (1992). *The sociology of leisure*. State College: PA: Venture Publishing, Inc.

Rojek, C. (1995). *Decentring leisure: Rethinking leisure theory*. Thousand Oaks, CA: Sage Publications.

Williams, R. (1981). *Culture*. Glasgow, Scotland: Fontana.

Chapter 9

Leisure and the Life Course: Children and Youth

Play and recreation are central to childhood and youth. The centrality of play and recreation is not only evidenced in the amount of time and money children and youth (and their parents!) devote to these activities but also in the extent to which play and recreation are seen as potential contexts for the growth and development expected during these years. It is precisely because play and recreation have been found to be contexts for learning and development that how much "free time" children and youth have and what they pursue as play and recreation during that time are issues of growing concern.

Notions of Childhood and Youth

It is only recently in the history of North America that a distinction was made between the years known as childhood and the years we now call adolescence or youth. Adolescence is not an inevitable and universal biological and psychological stage of life; rather it is a relatively recent social construction. There are cultures where the physical maturation (or puberty) we in North America associate with the onset of adolescence, instead begins adulthood and involvement in the sexual behavior, reproduction, and work of adult life. Historians note a number of factors that worked together to construct or shape current notions of life stages in North America, including the following:

- the Industrial Revolution which changed the nature of work and slowly increased the need for an educated or trained workforce;

- child labor laws restricting children's access to paid work to protect the jobs of adults or for the sake of children's physical and moral welfare;

- a growing middle class who saw the education of sons (and only sons) as necessary for the maintenance of their new wealth; and

- increasing life expectancy due to improvements in sanitation, hygiene, and medical knowledge which allowed the years of dependence to be extended.

Historical and crosscultural records suggest while children in all times and all cultures find moments of play in their lives, the cultural age norms as recently as 100 years ago were quite different from those of today. While there is certainly great variability in individuals' experiences of childhood and youth, as well as play and recreation, because of social class, race, ethnicity, and gender (as discussed later in this chapter and in Chapters 8, 13, and 15), social expectations (or age norms) up until the 20th century did not center play and recreation in children's lives. This is not to say all children and youth today have the same expectations or opportunities for play and recreation. Rather, dominant North American cultural notions of childhood and adolescence during the second half of the 20th century have portrayed these years as years of relative freedom—carefree and playful. The inconsistency between ideal norms and reality and the fact that age norms are constantly shifting (e.g., think of recent conflict-filled portrayals of childhood and youth in movies and on television compared with earlier pictures of secluded and protected life) have led to growing concerns about the free time of children and youth, the experiences they are exposed to, and what they pursue as play and recreation. This is intensified because research has shown play and recreation of children and youth, at least potentially, are contexts for growth and development as well as social and cultural resistance.

Childhood and Play

Psychologists often study children's play to understand the processes and content of children's cognitive, social and moral growth and development. Sociologists study the play of children to gain insights into the process of socialization and the role of play in preparing children for social expectations and adult roles. Children's play also provides insights into culture, age norms, and cultural variations for anthropologists. On the one hand, play is seen as a realm of life that lacks serious consequences, allows choice and spontaneity, and fosters creativity; on the other, it is also the "serious business" and "work" of childhood.

For example, Erik Erikson (1950), a pioneer developmental psychologist, identified three levels or stages of play in childhood: the autocosmic, microcosmic, and macrocosmic. In the self-world of autocosmic play, peek-a-boo and waving hands and feet enable the infant to begin to form a sense of a distinct self and assist in gaining a sense of trust and security in the persistence or continuity of self and others.

Children move into microcosmic (i.e., small world) play as they develop basic motor skills that allow more coordinated movement as well as increased control of bodily functions. Play with stuffed animals, dolls, and other toys during this stage provides a surrogate for human companionship, according to Erikson, and serves as a means of role rehearsal.

As children's social worlds expand and motor skills increase, they move into macrocosmic, or large world, play. Such socially interactive play often requires reciprocity and verbal communication. This type of play typically coincides with the psychosocial crisis of industry versus inferiority. This crisis revolves around gaining a sense of competence through mastery of the tool world (e.g., pencils and crayons, scissors, a computer) as opposed to feeling a sense of inadequacy and incompetence with budding interests, skills, and abilities. The experiences the child has in play may enhance or undermine her or his realization of a sense of industry.

Play is also a context within which children learn the rules and roles of their culture. Such roles are different for girls and boys—they are gendered. Through play children learn what the dominant culture sees as the appropriate behaviors, attitudes, and roles for one's biological sex. Such expectations may be limiting for fullest development for both girls and boys. For example, boys are allowed or even encouraged to be more physically boisterous and aggressive in their play than girls. Physical playfulness, however, has been found to distinguish creativity among girls but not boys (Barnett & Kleiber, 1982). Further, self-confidence and autonomy have been found to be positively related to girls' involvement in sport and physical activity, but the same relationships do not exist for boys (Kleiber & Kane, 1984). In other words, it appears when children are able to step outside of the prescribed limiting rules and roles, there are developmental benefits. Conversely, when children conform to social expectations (in this case, that physically aggressive play is masculine and thus appropriate for boys), the developmental benefits of play are more limited than with those given greater latitude.

This suggests is play is not only a life space and experience where children learn culture but also a context where culture is reconstructed or changed. Play may be constraining, but it is also resistant and transforming. Hence, free and spontaneous play may be especially important for the development of children. Not only may girls have some freedom to step outside of social norms and play with greater physicality and even competitiveness but also all children may overturn and even mock traditional rules and roles (Finnan, 1982). They learn to negotiate rules and structures, deal with conflict, and reconstruct the world of play. The degree to which children find such freedom in play, as well as how and to what extent they are constrained, involves the interaction of a variety of factors including race, gender, ethnicity, and social class.

Over the last decade there has been growing concern about the constraints and freedom children find in play. While there is no way to halt the changing reconstructions of notions of childhood, it may be useful to critically reflect on a few questions:

- What is a good childhood (i.e., What do you believe childhood should be)?

- How is play important to childhood?

- Is play disappearing? If so, what can public recreation and parks programs do to provide opportunities for play rather than just organized recreation?

- To what extent should adults direct play? Do adults usually enforce traditional rules and roles?

Across the centuries various philosophers and social commentators have written about the meaning of childhood and significance of children's play to children, the human race, and culture. David Elkind, in his book *The Hurried Child* (1988), drew attention to changes occurring in society and their impact on children's lives, and their play in particular. The premise is that social changes, such as industrialization, urbanization, stress on social status and economic competitiveness have affected not only the time that children have available for play but also the quality of their play experiences—and hence, the quality of their growth and development.

Debate: Children's play is disappearing.

YES

- It is not only adults' lives being affected by the pressure and the "cult of busyness." Children's lives, too, are increasingly determined by schedules and the clock. Parents' status is indicated not only by their own social calendars but also those of their children. There are parent-and-tot swimming classes, play groups, and story hour; after-school activities such as dance classes, tae kwon do, computer classes, gymnastics, music lessons; Little League, soccer, and private sport skill lessons. These activities are filling the days of some children in place of carefree hours of backyard kickball, jump rope, climbing trees, building forts, playing house, building model airplanes, doing crafts, roaming the neighborhood, and just lolling around day-dreaming. Organized sports, under the pressures of zealous parents, may come to dominate the lives of selected children. Again, Elkind analyzes the social context of current childhood pressures. Much of the pressure comes from parents who want their children to excel—just playing is not enough.

• There is also the other side of the coin. Many children seem to be less physically active due to all the easy entertainment available. Several national studies have documented decreasing levels of physical fitness among primary school-age children. This is attributable, in part, to the increasing sedentariness of children's lives. Rather than mentally, socially, and physically active play, many hours are filled with television and video and computer games. Play has given way to being entertained.

• Physical play is important because it not only enhances physical fitness and the development of motor skills but also relates to psychological factors such as self-esteem, creativity, and intellectual, social, and moral development. Erikson, for example, argued if children are not able to develop a sense of playfulness in their lives, they will suffer as adults because duty and compulsion, not curiosity and pleasure, will rule their behavior.

• For some children outdoor play may be dangerous. Some neighborhoods, especially those under siege from structural poverty, fear of violence and safety issues, constrain children's freedom to be outside, to explore, and to visit one another. In too many homes of all social classes, violence within the home in the form of physical, sexual, and emotional abuse is an everyday reality. Psychologically, playfulness may require a minimum level of basic trust. When a child feels threatened by his or her social and physical environment, it is difficult to experience the carefreeness and spontaneity of play. Similarly, the increase in the number of children living in poverty also means that an increasing number of children are not having their other basic needs (e.g., food, shelter, health) met. Nutrition, safety, and other basic needs have to be met in order for children to play.

• Children's play time and the quality of their play is also affected by the increasing number of single-parent and dual-earner families. Work conditions have disrupted family routines including recreational time together. Layoffs, downsizing, and the loss of unionized jobs with regular hours and benefits have pushed an increasing proportion of the work force into multiple low-paying service-sector jobs with few or no benefits and irregular schedules. Such parents can spend less time with their children. Their children (both preschool and school age) spend more time in structured settings or at home alone in front of the television or computer.

- Increasingly, children are entertained with television. The major toy in children's lives today is watched, not played with. Action and interaction are reduced. Even toys become marketed figures from the cartoon shows rather than ones that enhance social interaction and physical play.

- Play is the essence of childhood. When it disappears, so does childhood. Childhood is a crucial stage of life, and play is a necessary part of it. It is necessary not only because it helps prepare the individual for adulthood or a productive future but also because childhood play defines and sustains human(e)-ness. The play of childhood sets a framework for life and creates and maintains human culture.

NO

- The concerns of those who lament the loss of play have to be put in historical context and evaluated critically. Play remains important to children's lives and development, but takes different forms in different times. Further, things were not always so wonderful in the past.

- Children's lives may be perceived as too serious and devoid of play today relative to some romanticized point in the past, but just what era in history is chosen for comparison? In the old agricultural period, children were expected to work hard, and both school and play were given little priority. Of course, for Oliver Twist and other poor boys there was the workhouse. In this country's history of slavery, children of African slaves were expected to work in the yards, fields, and homes of their White "owners." In the Industrial Revolution of the 1800s, children worked in fields, mines, factories and mills—and often died young. Release from the factory and the opening of schools and playgrounds took decades of reform movements. The notion of an idyllic childhood is based on nostalgia for a very brief time in our history, such as a decade or so after World War II—and even then, only for some.

- Further, the illustrations mainly refer only to relatively privileged children. Looking across history suggests play was not central to the lives of working-class and poor children. Certainly, some of the leaders of the early playground and recreation movements in North America were concerned about the opportunities that poor children had for play, but these movements also reflected concerns about assimilation and maintaining social order in cities flooded by new immigrants. The notion there was once some *better time* for children's play seems a questionable and somewhat elitist notion.

- The images we have of children and their lives are strongly shaped by the media. The media sell the products of their advertisers which concentrate on children playing or being entertained with their toys. The images are not necessarily representative of the reality of children's lives, but are designed to sell their consumer goods. They do not depict the ordinary daily lives of children and youth. Adult concerns may also be raised by media images of dangerous and delinquent teens that represent only a small proportion of teenage behavior. Media advertising and news are not constructed to present an accurate portrayal.

- Recent research suggests the problem is not that children don't have the time for play. Instead, it is what children pursue or experience during their free time that has changed. Yet, with all kinds of new toys in a changing culture, we cannot expect play to remain static. The play of children is reflective of the culture. Its forms vary in response to societal demands and expectations. This is not bad. Rather, it assists in preparing children for a future that is inevitably different for each generation.

- Research suggests structured or rule-governed play may also contribute to children's development in different, but just as important, ways as free and spontaneous play. For example, in structured or organized play children learn—as well as challenge—the beliefs and values of a culture. They learn skills, both behavioral and attitudinal, that will allow them to become productive members of society and also to change notions of productivity. Most of adult life in work and community is in organized social contexts.

- Children resist adult domination of their lives and play anyway. Children will play, whether adults like it or not.

Youth, Recreation, and Leisure

Like childhood, adolescence or youth is shaped by gender, race, ethnicity, and social class. With physical maturation and the development of an active sexuality, sexual orientation also plays a central role in the individual's experience of adolescent development and recreation. Therefore, in discussing the characteristics of adolescence, it is important to keep in mind that there may be discrepancies between general theories and the experiences of any one individual.

A number of changes and characteristics define the onset of youth in contemporary North America. Development of a personal identity is typically seen as the central focus of the adolescent years. Erikson (1950) described the process of identity formation as involving both individuation (i.e., a sense of self separate from others) and identification (i.e., alignment with future roles and possibilities). All adolescence is not the same. Individuation, or gaining an autonomous or independent sense of self, has been found to be more descriptive of boys' identity formation than of girls'. Because of cultural definitions of gender (i.e., what it means to be feminine and masculine), many girls experience identity through attachment or connection with others more than separation. Further, due to racism, racial minority youth must develop both a positive racial identity and a positive personal identity (Gilligan, Lyons & Hanmer, 1990).

For most adolescents, recreational activities and leisure experiences are central to identity development. The social interaction of leisure is where sexual identity is explored and defined. How recreation and leisure support adolescents' development of a personal identity varies by activity type. For example, some of the recreation activities of youth have been found to be *transitional leisure* activities (e.g., sport, hobbies) because they help youth learn to find enjoyment or pleasure in challenge, effort and concentration, and hence prepare youth for adult life. Recreational activities often assist adolescents in discovering or developing interests and talents that lead to adult vocations. In contrast, *relaxing* leisure (e.g., watching television, other entertainment), while enjoyable and restorative, has little developmental import. The time devoted to such leisure is of growing concern today, as research suggests ultimately such experiences lead to a sense of boredom and emptiness (Csikszentmihalyi & Larson, 1984).

However, it is not only the form or type of leisure that shapes its developmental potential. Teens' leisure is not just neutral or positive. Exclusion and constraint also characterize many recreational experiences. For example, the extent to which youth are excluded or face bigotry in meaningful recreational and leisure experiences because of their sexual orientation, gender, social class, race, or ethnicity challenges the identity development that can take place. There is rejection based on appearance, wearing the right clothes, and possessing various symbols of social status. Further, much recreation has "losers" who are excluded because of perceived skill level or performance capabilities. Hence, it is important to keep in mind that while play, recreation and leisure potentially contribute in positive ways to development and growth, they do not necessarily do so. In fact, teen life presents many obstacles, frustrations, dilemmas, and conflicts.

Identity Development

Identity development comes to the fore during youth because of three related changes the individual is experiencing: physical, cognitive, and social. As noted previously, adolescence is marked by the physical change of sexual maturation. The development of secondary sex characteristics is a very overt indication that we are no longer who we used to be. As our bodies change we begin to think of ourselves as no longer children. For boys who mature early, there are often rewards because with physical maturation comes the ability to excel in sports. The role of athlete is highly valued for boys in North America and is a major source of status among peers.

Early maturity in girls, on the other hand, is often not viewed positively by adults for a number of reasons. First, there is the perception that with sexual maturation comes the possibility of sexual activity and pregnancy. Further, our sexual double standard (see Chapter 14) denies girls the option of being sexually active without loss of "reputation" while sexual experience may be a source of status for males. Second, early maturity in girls is viewed with concern as it is likely to "cause problems" (i.e., sexual arousal) for boys and men. Third, some maintain that in patriarchal societies, adolescent females are rewarded for physical immaturity because they then can be considered and treated as girls—and not young women.

Recreation and leisure, as is all of social life, is gendered. Cultural definitions and norms of gender and sexuality have ramifications for girls' and boys' recreation and leisure experiences. For example, research shows girls' involvement in physical activity and sport declines with sexual maturation, especially where physical contact is involved. This is not surprising given that our culture defines masculinity as having the prerogative to use the body to physically overpower or coerce others and that masculinity and femininity are conceived as dualistic or opposites. Research also indicates as female involvement in so-called masculine activities has increased, male involvement in those activities has decreased. That is, expansion in the types of physical recreation and sport in which girls participate (despite continued negative sanctions by those supporting traditional gender roles) is accompanied by a decrease in the range of physical recreation and sport in which boys participate. Physical maturity and its consequences are defined by gender.

Cognitive changes are also seen as important to identity development in adolescence. According to Piaget (1954), youth move from concrete to formal operations; that is, from absolutist, dualistic, right/wrong thinking to the ability to reason abstractly and understand *gray* or relative reasoning. Further, there may be a shift from egocentric (or self-centered, self-focused) thinking to the ability to take the perspective of others. This shift may lead to interest in more complex games and interactions requiring greater reciprocity and reasoning. In addition, the ability to take the perspective of others often results in increased self-consciousness as we become aware that others can think the same things about us as we do about them.

Learning Social Identities

As the adolescent's body and reasoning ability change, the expectations others have of the teen also change. As teens look older and can reason in more "adult" ways, others in their social network—parents, teachers, siblings, grandparents—expect different and often conflicting behaviors from them. This, too, serves to accentuate the problems of identity. As teens look older, reason differently, and face new expectations for grown-up behavior, they think about who it is they really are and what they want to become. Hence, talking with friends experiencing the same changes and emotions becomes extremely important to most adolescents. Research has found that on average, the amount of time adolescents spend with their parents decreases by half between ages 10 and 15 years, though this varies by ethnicity, social class, and gender. Studies also indicate that hanging out and/or talking with friends is teens' favorite pasttime.

Sexuality and sexual identity, fitting in and being accepted by peers and feeling part of some group, whether a school club, gang, religious organization, or team, are central during adolescence. Recreation and leisure interests, spaces, and experiences are often the venues through which such needs are realized, whether it be school band or drama club, the temple youth group, a community sports league, gathering at a parking lot for skateboarding or town square for inline skating, or just hanging out with friends at the mall or in one's room. Schools divide along many lines, so the distinction between cliques and gangs may be one of class-biased definition. This is a time in life when who you are with is at least as important as what you are doing.

Seeking social identity may also have negative elements. Identification with a group may lead to membership in gangs that promote drug use, criminal acts, and sexual violence. Symbols of inclusion involve music such as gangsta rap and underground clubs with raves and "ecstasy parties." The desire to be accepted is one factor in teen sexual behavior and pregnancy. Even in middle-class schools, leisure is a context of exclusionary behaviors that in some cases have led to hazing, alienation, and even suicide and counterviolence (Gaines, 1991). Participation in interscholastic sport may be seen as constructive or positive leisure and yet in addition to teaching teamwork and discipline, male team sports in particular appear to reproduce homophobia, sexism, and exclusion of anyone who is "different"—being a teen is not all "fun and games."

While physically and mentally mature, in North America teens are still considered to be unprepared for all of the freedoms and responsibilities of adulthood. However, this varies by social class. Working-class youth are likely to move into adult roles (e.g., worker, spouse, parent) earlier than middle-class youth (Rubin, 1976). Some see the extended childhood or period of partial and unresolved independence among middle-class teens as a source of adolescent delinquency and rebellion. Urie Bronfenbrenner (1979), a developmental psychologist, argues for the need to create opportunities for teens to be meaningfully engaged in the everyday life of communities and society with caring adults who act as mentors and role models, rather than ghettoized in a teen culture. Indeed, research indicates teens would like to have more interaction with caring adults and would like more opportunities for engagement in meaningful activity.

School and Development

Much research also shows the one place where youth spend a significant portion of their day—school—is not likely to be experienced as very meaningful by many youth. Rather a significant proportion of youth report school is boring. This raises a number of questions:

- Can recreation and leisure after school hours make up a for meaningless and even damaging school experience? How?

- Are there ways to make schools more enjoyable? Is there even a connection between learning and enjoyment?

- Should school and learning be more fun, or is the institution really preparation for the grind of adult life as it really is?

- Should schools be redesigned (in process and structure) so that going to school is more enjoyable?

Today there are many critics of public schools. Many people criticize public schools for a variety of problems including students' misbehavior and lack of discipline, the failure to learn at world-class standards, and irresponsible spending of school funds. Behind many of the different criticisms is the common perception that schools are not teaching youth (or youth are not learning) the basic skills they need to become productive citizens and responsible adults.

The diverse solutions offered by these critics include increased discipline, school uniforms, returning to a back-to-basics approach, student-centered classrooms, increased school funding, specialized schools, experiential learning, smaller classrooms, an expanded program of extracurricular activities, increased parental involvement, multicultural education, and charter schools. However, there do not seem to be any certain solutions.

Developmental psychologists Csikszentmihalyi and Larson (1984) have argued one issue underlying the problems seen in schools (and work) today—deviance, high rates of absenteeism and dropping out, poor performance—is lack of intrinsic motivation. Based on the work of White (1950), they contend that a need for competence and mastery is a basic human need. If there are not socially acceptable ways for individuals to satisfy this need, behavior defined as deviant may be pursued. Individuals gain a sense of competence when their skills are challenged but not overwhelmed by situational demands. This state of optimal arousal called *flow* (see Chapter 7) becomes self-motivating. When in flow, there is a merging of action and awareness, altered time consciousness, a sense of control, and feelings of enjoyment or pleasure. Hence, the more flow (and enjoyment) that youth experience in school-based learning, the more meaningful they will find school and the more motivated they will be to learn.

The growth of computer games, based on weapons-aiming technologies, raises another issue of teen leisure. Those dedicated to such games report high levels of involvement, even "flow." Evidence also suggests such dedication can result in social isolation. Further, the violence endemic in many games, including physical assault on females, at the very least does not teach the kinds of values society claims to foster and value. Even "flow" can become exciting in less-than-developmental ways.

In contrast to this social psychological explanation of the failure to learn and consequent rebellious behavior, others argue the problems schools face are shaped by relations of power within society that are reproduced in schools. Specifically, youth who feel alienated and excluded from society and its opportunities for any reason are likely to also feel that way in schools. Schools reproduce the social relations (and inequalities) of the larger society. Hence, "getting into trouble" is one way marginalized youth express their resistance to and rebel against what they perceive as their exclusion. Leo MacLeod (1995), whose research focused on urban lower-class males' experiences of schooling, found schools reproduce class, gender, and race inequalities. The low-income males he studied constructed spaces where they could create their own action and express identities consistent with their backgrounds. They perceived schools as middle class in orientation and felt teachers were trying to change them into something they were not and did not want to be. From this perspective, it may be that youth gain a sense of control (and enjoyment) when they are free to create their own action consistent with their cultural values and beliefs, even if that action is seen as disruptive and deviant by others (Corrigan, 1979).

These are just two explanations for the many problems of schools today. Of course, there are also those who would argue schooling is not about enjoyment or fun. Rather, schooling is about acquiring the knowledge, skills, attitudes, and behaviors necessary to become a productive worker and citizen. This means learning the expectations and rules of organizations focused on productivity—not enjoyment or satisfaction.

Debate: School reforms

Should schools be changed to make them more enjoyable for youth? How do we learn best? Are there insights from play and recreation that might assist educators in trying to deal with these problems? It is possible intrinsic motivation may be as central to the classroom as to the playground. Just how would you change schools—including higher education? Who would likely support these reforms, who would not, and why? Develop a debate for and against such school reforms.

Discussion Questions

1. Is play the child's work or is it really fun?

2. What kinds of play are most important for development? Why?

3. How were children treated as small adults in the 18th and 19th centuries?

4. Do computer games promote skill development, or retreat and alienation?

5. How is childhood changing?

6. Are there any kinds of societies in which play is not gendered?

7. How is leisure central to the crucial developmental task of adolescents—to explore, to practice, and to solidify sexual identity?

8. Should school teach discipline or creativity first? Why?

9. Is sport really important to development? If so, why do most teens quit doing it?

10. Do sexual practices limit the opportunities of females more than males? Is this a serious problem? Why or why not?

11. Is gang involvement a developmental stage that most teens outgrow? How is it different from team cohesion or other group formation?

12. What do we mean when we talk about "at-risk" youth? Is every teen "at risk"?

References and Resources

Barnett, L. and Kleiber, D.A. (1982). Concomitants of playfulness in early childhood: Cognitive abilities and gender. *The Journal of Genetic Psychology, 141,* 115–127.

Bronfenbrenner, U. (1979). *The ecology of human development: Experiments by nature and design.* Boston, MA: Harvard University Press.

Carnegie Council on Adolescent Development. (1992). *A matter of time: Risk and opportunity in the nonschool hours.* New York, NY: Carnegie Corporation.

Cook, D. (2001). Exchange value as pedagogy in children's leisure: Moral panics in children's culture at century's end. *Leisure Sciences, 23*(2), 81–99.

Coontz, S. (1992). *The way we never were: American families and the nostalgia trap.* New York, NY: Basic Books.

Corrigan, P. (1979). *Schooling the Smash Street kids.* London, UK: MacMillan.

Csikszentmihalyi, M. and Larson, R. (1984). *Being adolescent: Conflict and growth in the teenage years.* New York, NY: Basic Books, Inc.

Elkind, D. (1988). *The hurried child.* Reading, MA: Addison Wesley.

Erikson, E. (1950). *Childhood and society.* New York, NY: Norton.

Finnan, C.R. (1982). The ethnography of children's spontaneous play. In G. Spindler (Ed.), *Doing the ethnography of schooling* (pp. 356–381). New York, NY: Holt, Rinehart, and Winston.

Fromberg, D.P. and Bergen, D. (Eds.). (1998). *Play from birth to twelve: Contexts, perspectives and meanings.* New York, NY: Van Nostrand Reinhold.

Gaines, D. (1991). *Teenage wasteland: Suburbia's dead end kids.* New York, NY: Pantheon Books.

Gilligan, C., Lyons, N.P., and Hanmer, T.J. (Eds.). (1990). *Making connections.* Cambridge, MA: Harvard University Press.

Henderson, K.A, Bialeschki, M.D., Shaw, S.M. and Freysinger, V.J. (1996). *Both gains and gaps: Feminist perspectives on women's leisure.* State College, PA: Venture Publishing, Inc.

Kleiber, D. (1999). *Leisure experience and human development: A dialectical interpretation.* New York, NY: Basic Books.

Kleiber, D.A. and Kane, M.J. (1984). Sex differences in the use of leisure as adaptive potentiation. *Loisir et Societe/Society and Leisure, 7,* 165–173.

MacLeod, J. (1995). *Ain't no makin' it: Aspirations and attainment in a low-income neighborhood.* Boulder, CO: Westview Press.

Messner, M. (1994). When bodies are weapons. In M. Messner and D. Sabo (Eds.), *Sex, violence, and power in sports: Rethinking masculinities* (pp. 89–98). Freedom, CA: Crossing Press.

Metheny, E. (1973). Symbolic forms of movement: The feminine image in sports. In M. Hart (Ed.), *Sport in the sociocultural process.* Dubuque, IA: William C. Brown.

Miedzien, M. (1991). *Boys will be boys: Breaking the link between masculinity and violence.* New York, NY: Doubleday.

Outley, C.W. and Floyd, M.F. (2002). The home they live in: Inner city children's views on the influence of parenting strategies on their leisure behavior. *Leisure Sciences, 24*(2), 161–180.

Piaget, J. (1954). *The construction of reality in the child.* New York, NY: Basic Books.

Pieper, J. (1952). *Leisure: The basis for culture.* New York, NY: Random House.

Rubin, L. (1976). *Worlds of pain.* New York, NY: Basic Books.

Shaw, S.M., Kleiber, D.A. and Caldwell, L.L. (1995). Leisure and adolescent development: An examination of the relationship between leisure and identity for male and female adolescents. *Journal of Leisure Research, 27,* 245–263.

Weiss, M.R. and Bredemeier, B.J. (1990). Moral development in sport. In K.B. Randolf and J.O. Holloszy (Eds.), *Exercise and sport sciences review* (pp. 331–378). Baltimore, MD: Williams and Wilkins.

White, R. (1950). Motivation reconsidered: The concept of competence. *Psychological Review, 66,* 297–303.

Chapter 10

Leisure and the Life Course:
Adulthood and Aging

Contrary to many popular images of adulthood, life—and leisure—do not end with youth. The lives of young and middle-age adults are not totally filled with concerns about work, mortgages, and parenting. Nor are the lives of retired older adults totally defined by leisure. Rather, adult life is not so different from that of childhood and youth, in that adults are continuing to adapt and grow as they experience changing psychosocial issues, social role demands, socio-cultural contexts, and physical, mental, and emotional capacities. Certainly adults face these changes with the expectation that they will be able to meet them with more independent thought and action than do children and youth. Still, just as in the first two decades of life, some individuals are better able to meet or adapt to the changes age brings than are others. Further, constructing a meaningful sense of self and an interesting or stimulating existence are important regardless of age.

In this chapter, the meaning of age is briefly discussed, followed by a description of the general characteristics and developmental changes of young, middle, and later adulthood. How and why experiences of adulthood are shaped by gender, race, ethnicity, and social class are briefly considered in this description. Further, critical issues about the meanings of leisure are presented.

The Meaning of Age

Typically if you were to ask, "What does age mean?" or "Why do we care what age people are?" most would respond age is important because it is an indi-cation of an individual's physical, mental, emotional, and social maturation or development. That is, we think because a person has lived a certain number of years then she or he should have certain capacities to move, think and reason, feel, and interact with others. However, while those abilities are influenced by age-related internal or biologically based processes of growth, they are also shaped by experiences, demands, and opportunities provided by the environment.

Further, age is not only an indication of maturation, historical experiences, abilities, and social expectations. Age is also used to assign rights and privileges (e.g., the right to vote, drive a car, drink, choose not to attend school, collect retirement benefits). In addition, chronological age indicates year of birth and hence, the historical era in which one has lived and the societal changes and historical events one has experienced. For example, older generations have lived through at least three quite different wars and were raised during the Great Depression. This notion of birth cohort is extremely important when seeking to understand leisure behavior. For example, research has shown that current generations of older adults, and especially older women, have significantly lower levels of physical activity and sport participation than younger generations which yields higher rates of biological decline. Older adults (especially older women) did not have the opportunities for physical skill development and sport that younger generations have had (and continue to have)—and previous participation is the strongest predictor of current participation in physical activity and sport. In the United States, the passage of Title IX in particular has now produced a period of almost three decades in which opportunities for girls and boys in the classrooms and on the playing fields have moved toward equality in schools that receive federal funding. While there are still significant differences in females' and males' physical and outdoor activity and sport involvement, since the passage of Title IX in 1972 the number of girls participating in sport has increased at a faster rate than it has for boys. Clearly the time in which we are born shapes how we develop and what we pursue as leisure.

The discussion thus far suggests two things. First, age cannot be examined in isolation from social and cultural change. Second, understanding why age is important to leisure practices is complex. Let's briefly examine each of these issues.

Age Cannot Be Considered in Isolation

Gender, social class, race, ethnicity, sexual orientation, and other factors are all related to age norms and access to resources. This is because gender, social class, race, ethnicity, sexual orientation, as well as age, are constructs of personal identity that have cultural meanings and shape social relations or the distribution of power and privilege—including access to leisure opportunities. For example, because an individual is a given chronological age, we expect that individual to have certain abilities and formulate our expectations for participation in recreation accordingly. For a ten-year-old, we might expect that individual to have the physical capacity to run, jump, and skip and hence, be interested and able to participate in hop-scotch and double-dutch. However, would we expect such interest if the child in question were a ten-year-old boy? As is discussed further in Chapters 13 and 15, interaction of the multiple aspects of identity have to be considered when seeking to understand leisure practices. The society is divided or stratified by age as well as race and economic level.

The Relation of Age and Leisure Is Complex

Age cannot be understood in isolation from other aspects of identity and social status because age has multiple meanings. Understanding the interactive and multiple meanings of age helps us to recognize all of the different factors and forces at work behind recreation and leisure motivations, interests, constraints, preferences, attitudes, and participation (or lack of it). Further, chronological age is not a good index of abilities. Everyone age 20 is not swift and strong, nor is everyone age 65 slow and feeble.

Adulthood: Characteristics and Developmental Changes

The questions—What does age mean? What does it matter? Why is it important to life experiences?—become particularly relevant when trying to describe young and middle adulthood. The physical maturation of childhood and youth and the visible physical changes associated with old age are obvious. In contrast, not much seems to happen during early and middle adulthood. Even the social roles and responsibilities that are often seen as distinguishing young adults from youth and midlife from youth and later life show increasing flexibility. For example, the student role is no longer confined to childhood and youth, first marriage and birth of first child are increasingly common in middle adulthood, and grandparenting does not only occur after age 65. Such changes may lead one to believe that age norms are not as important as they once were. However, research has shown that despite increasing exceptions to age-graded roles, the vast majority continue to acquire, occupy, and leave social roles in a remarkably age-ordered way (Settersten & Hagestad, 1996). Hence, the notion of sequential periods of life remains useful.

Young Adulthood

Young adulthood is often referred to as the *early establishment period* of life. Chronologically, it is generally defined as comprising the years of 20/25 to

40/45, a time when most begin roles of employment, intimate partner, and parent. Research suggests working-class individuals enter young adulthood (and later adult periods) earlier than do middle-class individuals by leaving school sooner. Those who are economically disadvantaged are most likely to follow high school with jobs and families (Rubin, 1976).

Young adults are establishing themselves in three areas: vocations or work, intimate relationships or family, and social identities. The research of Daniel Levinson (1978) revealed that as youth move into young adulthood they begin developing a dream. This dream has to do with vocational goals and career aspirations as well as overall quality of life. The dream may be to become a master carpenter like one's parent, a millionaire stockbroker by the age of 40, or be in an administrative position within the first ten years with a company. By the mid-30s, young adults often report reaching a plateau and going through a period of realignment as they become more realistic about limited opportunities, what it will take to realize their dreams, and their interests and abilities. At this point some may decide to return to school to change occupations or to specialize in a particular area at work. For some women the 30s may be a time of *dis-ease*. Those who have not worked outside the home but made the bearing and raising of children and caring for family and home their sole occupation (now a minority) may feel a sense of urgency and the need to establish themselves outside of the family and domestic sphere before "it's too late." For women who put work first since completing high school, college, or graduate school, the 30s may also be a time of dis-ease if the woman wants to bear children and she begins to feel the pressure of the ticking biological clock.

The second area in which young adults are establishing themselves is in intimate relationships. According to Erik Erikson (1950), intimacy versus isolation is the psychosocial crisis or ego issue of young adulthood. For Erikson, intimacy is the ability to share oneself, both emotionally and sexually, and sustain a committed relationship with another person without fear of losing self or without becoming enmeshed with the other. Isolation is experienced as a deep or abiding inhibition or dread about getting emotionally and sexually close to another. Intimacy is not something we are automatically capable of establishing. Rather, dating and serious relationships provide practice in intimacy, and through such relationships we learn how to share ourselves without losing ourselves.

The research of Carol Gilligan and her colleagues (1982) indicates that because of dominant cultural notions of gender, many women and men enter young adulthood from different developmental histories. Women are more likely to enter young adulthood from a sense of self as relational and dependent while men are more likely to come into young adulthood from a perspective of autonomy and independence. Hence, for young women and men interested in heterosexual relationships, there may be tensions or disagreements around just what constitutes an intimate or committed relationship.

Individuals in early adulthood are also seeking to establish social identities. They are looking for a sense of competence, and social recognition for this competence, in fulfilling the social roles that are expected of them. Being competent as a worker, as a friend or lover, and as a community member are all ways that individuals establish or realize social identities in early adulthood. Competence is closely related to the establishment period focus on productivity in work, family, and community.

Middle Adulthood

Midlife, the years between 40 and 45 and retirement, are commonly seen as comprising middle adulthood. However, according to Neugarten and Datan (1981), middle adulthood is delineated from other age periods not so much by chronological age as by the positions occupied within the different contexts of life—the body, the work career, and the family. Midlife is expected to be a period of productivity and ability. It is also a time when certain social and economic rewards are expected.

A number of interrelated physical changes serve to indicate to individuals their entry into midlife, although there is considerable variability in experiencing and coping with such changes. For example, a gradual decrease in physical strength, flexibility, and endurance, often coupled with an increase in body fat, is common. However, the extent of such physical changes depends on the health behaviors (e.g., diet, amount of physical activity or exercise) of the individual. Acuity of the senses may also begin to decline. Hormone levels change, too, with a reduction in the production of testosterone in males and estrogen in females leading to menopause. Midlife women also report an increased awareness of changes in physical appearance while men in midlife report changes in health and sexual performance as markers of middle age. Given our cultural notions of femininity and masculinity (See Chapter 13), this is not surprising. For women who are married or in relationships with men, the *body monitoring* of their partners becomes more important than the body monitoring of themselves. On the other hand, the shorter life expectancy of males and the increased likelihood of ill health or death due to heart disease and some types of cancer among men in their 40s and 50s may produce a new sense of mortality and life's limits.

Psychologically, individuals report a number of changes during midlife. For example, sometime in midlife, adults tend to switch from thinking of their lives in terms of time-since-birth to time-left-to-live. This is partly due to the personalization of death during these years as ill health and/or death of peers and/or parents become a reality. *Generativity vs. stagnation* is the ego issue of midlife according to Erikson (1950). With generativity there is a renewed productivity and sense of responsibility for succeeding generations and the creation of social heirs. The issue of *agency* (i.e., an independent sense of self) may be as important for women as generativity, particularly for those primarily involved in nurturing future generations through parenting and other caregiving. Midlife is also a time of evaluation and revision. The question of meaning and satisfaction in work, partnerships/marriage, and community comes to the fore. The realization that many goals may not be accomplished and that time is running out leads to what has been labeled the *midlife crisis* for some, but not all, in their 40s and early 50s. For most, however, there is some reevaluation of life and possibilities for the future.

While adults in midlife may want to *feel* young again, most have no wish to *be* young again. This may be because midlife is also experienced by many to be the *prime of life*. According to Neugarten and Datan (1981), midlife can be a "period of maximum capacity and ability to handle a highly complex environment and highly differentiated self" although this perception varies by social class. Those experiencing success in achieving goals with the privilege of influencing self and others likely see themselves as a part of the *command generation*. However, those denied access (because of level of education, ethnicity, race, or gender) to the *culture of power* tend to see midlife as no different from earlier or later stages of life. Further, women and men often report dissimilar experiences. For some women in midlife there is a sense of increased freedom and possibilities, especially if childrearing or other caregiving responsibilities begin to disappear. Some men, on the other hand, may report a sense of increased job pressures or boredom. Trying to get that final promotion or significant pay raise can cause significant stress. Or because there is no hope of further advancement and work presents few challenges, boredom with and emotional disengagement from work may occur. These gendered experiences have been found to lead men to become more affiliative and women more agentic or independent in orientation in late midlife. That is, men often turn more to family and personal relationships for meaning and identity while women may seek to increase their sense of an autonomous, self-determining self.

Of course, the extent to which individuals in midlife experience these changes depends on the contexts of their lives. For example, an increasing number of midlife adults are caring for aging parents and/or parenting their grandchildren. Such responsibilities in midlife have led to the concept of midlifers as the *sandwich generation*—those with obligations to both younger and older generations. Changing family structures due to the increased incidence of divorce, never marrying, single-parenting, and *blended* families means the tasks of middle-age are changing.

The unpredictability of life and realization that one cannot control everything is believed to be a source of an increasing externality in midlife (Kleiber, 1985). While an internal sense of fate control may serve individuals well during the adolescent and young adult years when a competitive achievement motivation assists one in becoming independent and established, it may not be adaptive in mid- and later life when adapting to rather than seeking to conquer the worlds outside the self. Overall, then, midlife is a period of significant change—an age when life's demands call for changes of the self in both identities and orientations.

Later Life and Aging

As the fastest growing segment of the U.S. population, later adulthood is commonly associated with the years 65 and older based on the mistaken notion that most (male) workers retired at that age. Due to increases in life expectancy and more common retirement several years prior to age 65, later life is now often divided into two subgroups: the *active old* and the *frail elderly*. The active or *young old* are seen as competent, relatively independent, and as major markets for travel and other leisure. The frail or *old old* are marked by a loss of independence and of physical and/or mental capacities. Nevertheless, 95% of those over the age of 65 are living in communities and outside institutions of special care.

Because of advances in public and environmental health knowledge, on average both women and men are living longer with more years of functionally healthy life. That is, the onset of functional impairment or debilitating health conditions has shifted upward toward the eighth and even ninth decades of life. In fact, those 85 and older are proportionally the fastest-growing population segment. This is quite a contrast with the late 1800s when average life expectancy was about 47 years; today, it is 78 years. Hence, the meaning and experience of old age has been radically altered in a very short time.

Old age puts many demands on the individual. A number of major social role changes typically occur during these years: retirement from paid employment, grandparenthood, caregiving for frail parents, and widowhood. Some also face relocating and making a new home because of reduced income, changes in health and functional ability, establishing new relationships, and finding fulfilling leisure interests. According to Erikson's psychosocial theory of development, in later life one is challenged to accept life for all that it has and has not been, to gain a sense of wholeness or completeness (i.e., *integrity*) while acknowledging the inevitability of death while still seeking to create a meaningful present and future.

Three factors are powerful in shaping individuals' experiences of old age and leisure: income, health, and social expectations. For individuals who were employed outside the home, income is the strongest predictor of successful adjustment to retirement from paid employment. In terms of income, older persons are no more likely to be poor than any other age category. Those forced to live on incomes below the poverty level are distinguished by gender and race strongly in later life because of the lifelong experiences of disadvantage and exclusion. In general, older men are less likely to be poverty-stricken than older women, but older European Americans of either sex are less likely to be living in poverty than older Hispanic, African, and Native American women and men. Another significant proportion of the older adult population are near poor and many live on fixed incomes that make their financial well-being unpredictable. At the other extreme, the segment of the population with the greatest wealth is also over age 65. Inequality in wealth increases with age.

Health also is central to adaptation to and satisfaction with life in old age. Like income, health constructs opportunities to be involved in day-to-day life. Research suggests people do not perceive themselves or others as old until they have manifest health problems. Further, changes in health put many older adults in unfamiliar roles and social contexts (e.g., roles of dependency, roles in medical/clinical settings). Declining health may challenge presumptions about the future, and alter experiences of time. Older adults report that *time weighs heavy on their hands* and passes slowly when interactions and activities are limited by losses in functional health. In addition, thoughts often shift from the present and future to a time past *when things were better*. Orientation to the past rather than the present and future is also associated with mental illness (Eisenhandler, 1989). Hence, aging requires that men and women face and respond to changes in health in an adaptive way.

Personal health is the result of the interaction of multiple factors and forces. For example, heredity and biology predispose some to disease or illness, such as diabetes, glaucoma, high blood pressure, heart attacks, and some types of cancer. Lifestyle also is a significant factor in health. Whether and how much we choose to smoke, drink, eat fatty foods, cycle without a helmet, drive without a seatbelt, or exercise or engage in other physical activity regularly all have potential health consequences. However, lifestyle and health are shaped not only by individual choices but also by social contexts and opportunities. For example, the poor are more likely to live in a neighborhood with greater environmental hazards such as air and water pollution. They are also less likely to have access to regular healthcare and opportunities for exercise and physical activity. Employment is more likely to be sporadic and low wage. Hence, less money is available for costly fresh fruits and vegetables and other nutritious foods. It takes a tremendous amount of resourcefulness and energy to establish and maintain a healthy lifestyle when poor in environments of danger and damage.

In addition, social and economic programs and policies, such as Social Security, Medicare and Medicaid, and wage and tax laws, all contribute to constructing the reality of individual lives in old age. While some are advantaged by these programs, others are disadvantaged. For example, at the end of the 20th century females' life expectancy is greater than that of males and the life expectancy of European Americans is greater than that of African Americans. Yet, economic and social programs and policies are not designed for these differences. Medicare does not fully address the chronic health conditions more likely to be experienced by older women (Rodeheaver, 1987). African Americans are disadvantaged by Social Security and other age-based retirement programs because African Americans are less likely to live to age 65 (or 67) when benefits without penalties are available (Gibson, 1994). Of course, sexism and racism do not only shape the lives of the old, but the socially constructed dependency of old age also intensifies the consequences of societal discrimination.

In addition to income and health, and sexism and racism, social expectations and cultural beliefs about and images of old age are also important to constructing life in old age. Because of its economic system, the United States is a society that values independence and economic productivity—and individuals who display these attributes. As with women who work in the home and in childrearing, the economic contributions of older adults who are not in paid employment are often forgotten or ignored. Such contributions include volunteering in community service agencies, schools, religious institutions, and arts organizations; parenting or raising of grandchildren; providing housing and support for single parent or divorced adult children; and owning homes and paying property taxes. However, the body is a form of *physical capital* and as long as the form, activities, and performance of old bodies are not valued by society, their productivity and contributions are unlikely to be recognized (Shilling, 1993).

Images of old age in the media (e.g., movies, television programs, advertisements) present a mixed picture of what it means to be old. Old people are portrayed as being gray, stoop-shouldered and wrinkled; dependent and helpless; sexless or sexually silly; forgetful and confused; cantankerous and stubborn; physically frail; wise and knowing; out of step with the times; family-oriented or lonely and abandoned. These images shape not only how old folks see themselves and their abilities, but also how they are perceived by others. For example, despite some changes in the portrayal of older adults, few images of older adults as physically active and athletically skilled exist in the print media, even in publications that are oriented to an older adult market. Further, the lack of such images both constrains older adults' interest in participating such activities and constructs the opportunities that are and are not provided.

On the other hand, many older adults resist such images and construct lives full of activity and competence. There is considerable evidence that most older persons do not think of themselves primarily in terms of age, but as much the same persons they have been most of their lives (Kaufman, 1986). They seek contexts to demonstrate competence and worth as they did at age 25 or 45.

Images of old age and beliefs about the process of aging in later life are important in that they *frame* the problems we see and the action we believe should be taken. For example, if we believe old age brings inevitable decline and the process of decline is due to internal biological processes, then we may also believe disengagement of the individual from society and society from the individual is not only natural but also healthy. That is, we are unlikely to believe exercise programs, travel opportunities, demanding volunteer roles, continuing education, and opportunities for athletic, artistic, and intellectual performance are worthwhile. On the other hand, if we believe that while the process of aging in later life is influenced by internal biological factors and activity can alter biology, then we will likely think that interventions make a difference. The question then becomes both practical and ethical: Should opportunities and interventions be implemented because they lower costs of care for those who become prematurely frail and enhance the quality of life of older adults and those who might have to care for them? Further, what kinds of opportunities and supports are really responsive to the needs and desires of most older adults?

There is also the issue of equity. Are there particular social responsibilities toward older persons who have been denied and disinherited through their earlier lives and reach later life deprived of common resources? For example, are we willing to support costly revisions to ensure Medicare benefits are available to all who need them? Many problems of aging begin much earlier, in inadequate schools and discriminatory work opportunities and rewards. Will we support equitable public schools funding and enforcement of equal opportunity in the work force for women, racial minorities, and recent immigrants? Do older adults deserve equal provisions of leisure resources as do children? How can self-reliance best be enhanced? Do people become less important because they are old?

Leisure in Adult Life

Of course, most of this book is about adult leisure. However, the perspectives of developmental changes and contexts that typify young, middle, and later adulthood provide critical approaches to the meanings of leisure through the life course. Adult life shapes leisure motivations, constraints, and participation, and recreation and leisure also shape adult life. For example, recreation and leisure are contexts within which friendships are established and nurtured. Leisure with friends and family is highly valued across all ages.

The life course has powerful impacts on leisure. For example, research has shown the birth of a first child has a dramatic effect on the time, energy, and money that individuals have for leisure. This effect is gendered. Despite some change, the impact of children on mothers' lives and leisure is greater than on fathers' lives. Among heterosexual couples, despite ideologies of sharing, mothers contribute much more to the domestic and leisure aspects of parenting and fathers more to the financial aspect of parenting, even when the mother is also working full-time outside the home (Horna, 1989). This has tremendous implications for both parenting and leisure. For example, while fathers' satisfaction with being a parent is enhanced by playing with children, mothers' satisfaction is unaffected by such interactions (Freysinger, 1994). Fathers are also more likely to perceive their time with children as leisure than mothers. This is because fathers have more choice in being with children than mothers due to gendered parenting roles. The politics of gender become quite apparent in this situation, especially when contrasted with same-sex couples' experiences of parenting and leisure. For example, research on lesbian couples suggests greater flexibility and equity in fulfilling the parental role and domestic tasks and responsibilities (Bialeschki & Pearce, 1997).

Work, both inside and outside the home, paid and unpaid, also constructs adults' leisure lives. Research has not demonstrated any direct relationship between paid work and types of leisure. Rather, work is one element in the overall life conditions that provides contexts and resources for leisure. Lillian Rubin (1976) studied the work and family lives of working-class young and middle-age adults and found leisure was both escape from and compensation for meaningless and damaging employment. Regardless of social class, the time and energy required by and the resources gained from work certainly shape the time, energy, and resources adults have for recreation and leisure.

Leisure is related to both affiliative or relational and agentic interests in adult years. Leisure may be a source of marital/couple satisfaction or dissatisfaction, cohesion, or instability. Parents report shared leisure is a means of enhancing the positive development of children. Older adults find leisure central to the development and maintenance of relationships.

However, leisure not only is a space where the relational self is realized but it also may provide young, middle-age, and older adults with a sense of agency or self-determination. Specifically, leisure can be a context for self-expression, learning and development, challenge and accomplishment, and recognition and credibility. The expression of competence and ability are significant to a positive sense of selfhood at any age.

Leisure also provides an opportunity to disengage from everyday demands and concerns and reengage in experience that is more personally meaningful. Psychologically, there tends to be a shift in middle adulthood that continues on into later years from an external to a more internal orientation (or sense of motivation and meaning). Individuals in these stages of life tend to want to look more inward, rather than outward, in constructing a meaningful life. Perhaps this is because of the shifting time perspective and generative concerns of middle adulthood and the exclusion of older adults productive roles as well as their preoccupation with integrity. At least potentially, leisure provides an opportunity to step back, open up, and reengage—a context within which to escape, experience change, or step off the *fast track* and shift perspective (Kleiber, 1985).

Of course, the extent to which leisure holds any of these meanings for adults varies by their understanding of leisure and self as well as by what society allows or makes possible for them. The life conditions of adults vary widely in leisure resources, opportunities, and constraints. Some adults place a high value on leisure and construct life patterns that make a major and consistent place for leisure. Others fit leisure into their primary relationship and economic roles. Through the adult life course, there seem to be rhythms of leisure that rise and fall as other elements of life become central and recede. New relationships, parenting, caregiving, retirement, widowhood, health traumas, and other conditions have their impacts on what is possible and what is desired. The athlete becomes a parental youth sports coach and in time possibly a seniors participant or avid fan. The pianist turns from performance to nurturing the abilities of a child then back to skill development. For most of the life course, however, leisure is part of the balance that adults seek in productive, relational, and expressive activity.

Debate: Older adults should have special programs provided for them.

This debate returns to an issue introduced earlier: What is the significance of age and how should it be regarded? It asks you to think about whether there is justification for the age-based provision of recreation and leisure programs and services. Given the magnitude of the expected increase in the proportion of the North American population who is 65 and older early in the 21st century (i.e., 20–25% of the population), this issue is one that will confront every community.

YES

- The physical capacities and needs of older adults are different. Vision, hearing, and sense of taste, touch, and smell are less acute. Strength, endurance, and flexibility are decreased. Balance and coordination are more uncertain. Reaction time is slower. Many older adults are dealing with chronic health conditions, such as arthritis, high blood pressure, osteoporosis, diabetes, and glaucoma. These changes in physical capacities and functioning require adaptation in activities so old folks are not only able to participate but also so they feel comfortable and competent and, hence, enjoy participating.

- The success of programs such as Elderhostel, Senior Olympics, and other age-graded programs is evidence of the validity of special provisions for older adults.

- Psychologically, older adults have different abilities and needs from younger folks. Learning something new may take longer. Short-term memory may not be as accurate. There may be less of a drive toward competition. As noted by Erikson (1950), integrity and interiority, or self-reflection, may turn interests away from social status and constant comparison. Further, older adults are likely to know themselves better and to understand their strengths and weaknesses. They may not be interested in trying lots of new activities, not because they cannot learn new things, but because they have spent 65 or more years learning what it is they are good at and interested in. While adolescents and young adults are out to prove and to establish themselves and are subject to external motivations, older adults are more intrinsically motivated.

- Socially, older adults are experiencing role loss and changes. If identity was found in paid employment or childrearing, those roles are reduced or ended. There may be time for reinvolvement in activities relinquished under pressure, or continued or increased involvement in familiar activities.

- The social environments of age-designated leisure may be especially attractive. Age peers are sources of social support both because they have lived through similar historical circumstances and they share current changes.

- Because of restrictions put on income-earning in later life or because of lifelong experiences of disadvantaged work, special programs are needed because many older adults cannot afford to purchase recreational and leisure services and programs privately.

• Recreational and leisure settings are contexts for social comparison. Compared to younger people, older people may feel less competent or skilled. Or, they may feel that younger people really don't want them around. Further, some older people, especially older women, have no interest in being involved in activities with children in which they are often put in caregiving roles. They have been there and done that.

• Older adults deserve special programs because of contributions they have made to society across their lives. They have not only borne and reared the younger generations, their energy, ideas, sacrifices, and efforts have built and supported society.

• If special programs are not provided for older adults, then they will be forgotten. The provisions for special programs and services included in the Older Americans Act when it was first passed in the early 1960s were included because the needs and interests of the growing older adult population were being ignored. While most old folks can *look out for themselves* and have the resources to do so, a significant number do not have the economic resources, health, knowledge, or social skills to provide adequate life contexts for themselves. Some are, indeed, frail.

NO

• The low number of older adults who currently participate in special programs such as those provided at Senior Centers (i.e., 10–20%) suggests that the vast majority of them have little interest in age-segregated public programs. Providing such programs serves a very limited number of older adults. It would be a better use of resources to give adequate support to necessary programs for *all* those in real need rather than persist in provisions for those who don't want them.

• Labeling special separate programs for older adults only serves to reinforce negative stereotypes of old age as problematic, deficient, and different. The empowerment of older folks is undermined. Inclusion and integration would break such negative stereotypes as abilities are demonstrated and recognized. Why should anyone have to accept a negative designation to enter a leisure program?

- Research indicates older individuals' sense of themselves is largely ageless. Older people do not define themselves primarily by age. They do not enter some different realm of selfhood at 65 or any other age. They recognize change, but in a continuity of selfhood. This *ageless self* resists labels such as *golden age* and even *senior* programs. Even more, age-segregated and age-specific programming is usually rejected by the *active old* as for the *really old*.

- The organization with the highest proportion of older members is the church/synagogue/mosque. For the most part religious organizations are not age-segregated (although some mistakenly think they should be).

- There are many benefits to be gained from intergenerational interaction. Older adults have the wisdom and experience of their years. They have much to offer younger individuals and society in general. Recreation and leisure providers should encourage integrated programming. Positive marketing symbols and work-hour scheduling can make programs attractive to older adults without ageist labels and restrictions.

- Provision of public programs and services should be based on need, not age. While about 25% of the older adult population is poor or near-poor, 75% are not. Most older adults can pay their way in leisure as well as other spheres of life.

- Age may be a poor index of ability. There are also younger folks who have vision, sensory, or ambulatory limitations; have restrictive or debilitating health conditions; and live on restricted incomes. All age groups are tremendously heterogeneous. To provide programs and services based on age ignores this reality. Activities and programs should be organized by schedule and ability—not age.

- The money is just not available. If the demographic age-distribution changes that are occurring continue, most communities will not be able to provide special programs and services for older adults. The shrinking proportion of tax-paying youth, young adults, and midlifers cannot support such an increase. Further, arguments can be made for spending our limited resources elsewhere—that is, on segments of the population who will most benefit from such expenditures (e.g., on the young who need a healthy start so that they can become productive members of society). Resources should be focused on the truly needy.

• Programs should support resourcefulness, not dependence. They should provide opportunities for challenge and competence, not reinforce inability. Oftentimes, age segregated programs reinforce stereotypes of need, dependence, and inability.

Discussion Questions

1. How do war and Great Depression experiences change attitudes and values toward work and leisure?

2. Is age valued or disvalued in American society? How? How might recreation and leisure contribute to the valuing of old age?

3. How is the society stratified by age? What kinds of resources and opportunities are opened and closed by chronological age?

4. Why is it especially difficult to be old and poor?

5. Is a midlife crisis common? Give examples. How might leisure help individuals to cope with the changes of midlife?

6. Is retirement more a crisis or opportunity? How does retirement differ for men and women? How and why does leisure change in retirement?

7. How does the 50% likelihood of divorce affect adult life for women? for men? What are some likely effects of divorce on recreation and leisure participation?

8. What are the implications for providers of leisure and recreation programs and services of the fact that most married women will be widowed if they are not divorced?

9. Which life transitions are most important to leisure? How?

10. What is the best time of life? Why?

References and Resources

Achenbaum, A. (1978). *Old age in the new land: The American experience since 1790.* New York, NY: Johns Hopkins University Press.

Bialeschki, M.D. and Pearce, K. (1997). "I don't want a lifestyle, I want a life:" The effect of role negotiations on the leisure of lesbian mothers. *Journal of Leisure Research, 29,* 113–131.

Eisenhandler. S.A. (1989). More than counting years: Social aspects of time and the identity of elders. In L.E. Thomas (Ed.), *Research on adulthood and aging: The human science approach* (pp. 163–181). Albany, NY: SUNY Press.

Erikson, E. (1950). *Childhood and society.* New York, NY: Norton.

Freysinger, V.J. (1994). Leisure with children and parental satisfaction: Further evidence of a sex difference in the experience of adult roles and leisure. *Journal of Leisure Research, 26,* 212–226.

Freysinger, V.J. (1995). The dialectics of leisure and development for women and men in midlife: An interpretive study. *Journal of Leisure Research, 27,* 61–84.

Gibson, R. (1994). Reconceptualizing retirement for Black Americans. In E.P. Stoller and R.C. Gibson (Eds.), *Worlds of difference: Inequality in the aging experience* (pp. 120–127). Thousand Oaks, CA: Pine Forge Press.

Gilligan, C. (1982). *In a different voice: Psychological theory and women's development.* Cambridge, MA: Harvard University Press.

Horna, J. (1989). The leisure component of the parental role. *Journal of Leisure Research, 21,* 228–241.

Kaufman, S. (1986). *The ageless self: Sources of meaning in late life.* Madison, WI: The University of Wisconsin Press.

Kelly, J.R. (Ed.). (1993). *Activity and aging.* Thousand Oaks, CA: Sage.

Kleiber, D. (1985). Motivational reorientation in adulthood and the resource of leisure. In D. Kleiber and M. Maehr (Eds.), *Advances in motivation and achievement: Motivation and adulthood* (pp. 217–250). Greenwich, CT: JAI Press.

Levinson, D. (1978). *The seasons of a man's life.* New York, NY: Alfred A. Knopf.

Neugarten, B. and Datan, N. (1981). The subjective experience of middle age. In L. Steinberg (Ed.), *The life cycle: Readings in human development* (pp. 273–283). New York, NY: Columbia University Press.

Rodeheaver, D. (1987). When old age became a social problem women were left behind. *The Gerontologist, 27,* 741–746.

Rubin, L. (1976). *Worlds of pain: Life in the working-class family.* New York, NY: Basic Books.

Settersten, R.A. and Hagestad, G.O. (1996). What's the latest? Cultural deadlines for family transition. *The Gerontologist, 36,* 178–188.

Sheehy, G. (1976). *Passages: Predictable crises of adult life.* New York, NY: Dutton.

Shilling, C. (1993). *The body and social theory.* Newbury Park, CA: Sage.

Steinberg, L. (Ed.). (1981). *The life cycle: Readings in human development.* New York, NY: Columbia University Press.

Stoller, E.P. and Gibson, R.C. (1994). In E.P. Stoller and R.C. Gibson (Eds.), *Worlds of difference: Inequality in the aging experience* (pp. 120–127). Thousand Oaks, CA: Pine Forge Press.

Chapter 11
The Economics of Leisure

Everything has economic dimensions. Leisure is no exception. Resources for leisure are distributed through the economic system. Leisure goods and services are a segment of the economy. Less evident, however, is that the kind of economic system is a major factor in the kinds of leisure that are possible, permitted, and promoted. Further, economic systems change over time. The current system is quite different from previous periods and is still changing.

The New Economy

The American economy today is significantly different from that of 200 years ago, 150 years ago, or even 50 years ago. Those changes have made our lives quite different from those of our forebearers.

The Industrial Revolution

America once had primarily an agricultural economy. Cities were few and small centers of culture and finance—mostly seaports connecting the new land to the Old World. Until the Civil War, this was a largely rural society composed of small towns distributed within a day's buggy ride of most farms. Open land drew many farmers westward. Opportunity meant new land. By the mid-19th century industries were developing, but still were usually suppliers of the rural areas and their transportation needs.

The Civil War was one mobilizing force in the drive toward industrialization. Chapter 4 gave more details of this industrialization and urbanization. Here we will only suggest this economic sea change had powerful implications for leisure. The city became the site of situated leisure provisions: amusement parks, professional sports, and halls for entertainment. The factory schedule became the source of timetables for living with a clear demarcation between work and nonwork time. Most workers received wages that became the means of market participation including leisure consumption. In industry there was a drive for productivity that shaped working hours and conditions and, surprisingly, leisure. Many efforts were made by manufacturers and other employers to control leisure—to make it preparation for work rather than escape and dissipation. Further, the worker was to become a rational consumer and, in Henry Ford's Detroit even the possible owner of the Model T car with all its leisure potential. This "Fordism" united work, wages, productivity, and conformity with family and leisure-driven consumption. In this industrial age, work time and leisure time were clearly separated and both important.

During the period between 1850 and 1950, except for wartime, the average workweek was consistently reduced: from 70 hours in 1850 to 65 in 1870, 62 in 1890, 55 in 1910, and 45 in 1930. This was a 35% reduction in 80 years. Factors included labor organization and resistance marked by thousands of strikes as well as a recognition by mill and mine owners that shorter hours were more productive. Further reduction of five hours every two decades would have yielded workweeks of 40 hours by 1950, 35 by 1970, and less than 30 by 2000. A continuation of a proportional trend would have brought us to 42 hours by 1950, 40 by 1970, and 37 by 2000.

What has occurred is a double change in the trend. The proportional reduction began to level off after 1960 at about 40 hours a week or a little less. Industry resisted further reduction on the grounds that the investment in a worker's skills made it inefficient to further reduce productive time. The second change, to be outlined in the next section, was the creation of the postindustrial economy. Industrialization in the 19th and early 20th centuries produced the city, wage labor, the separation of home and work, replacement of the agricultural social timetable with industrial time, and the designation of leisure as a separate domain of life outside work time. It was a radically different world from the former agricultural society.

The New Economy

There has been, however, another major economic shift. It goes by a number of labels. The most common is *postindustrial*. There is, of course, still productive industry just as there was, and is, still an agricultural segment of the economy. The simplest sign of change was that since the 1980s, most jobs have been in services rather than productive industry. In fact, all employment growth since about 1970 has been in the service sector—retailing, human services, health, support services, travel, hospitality, and recreation. This shift has had important implications for investment, employment, education, and even for leisure.

Contextual Factors

The major contextual change has been that every domestic economy is now thoroughly part of the world economy. National borders mean less and less as protections give way to a regular flow of products, capital, management, and even labor. Some of the results are:

- Production is movable. Production follows standards of cost and efficiency. Parts for a car are made in many countries, often on contract, and assembled near final markets or transportation hubs. Factories are closed and moved to low-wage locations. There is even a cycle in which formerly low-wage zones, as on the Pacific Rim, move production to the "new" areas. Selling on world markets, price and quality competition cannot be restricted to a country or region. Labor has become a variable and movable cost of production.

- Distribution is also worldwide. Clothing in the local discount store may be from anywhere. American footballs and baseballs are made in China. American movies and videos are displayed in every world city. There are no impermeable economic walls. In the new information age, there are few secrets about products or price.

- Finance is also international. Banking and stock markets operate by satellite over all of the world. Almost all major corporations are international conglomerates with international ownership, marketing strategies, and management. Investment capital moves across former borders without cost or attention. One implication, of course, is that there is little loyalty or rootedness in any particular locale or "home."

- In such far-flung operations, the only goal for management is return on investment to the dispersed and anonymous corporate owners. This raises the pressures to produce regular profits, increase productivity, lower the costs of production, and integrate goals, strategies, and control. The emerging instrument of management and control is *information* with countless technologies of transmission. Some even argue control of information is the center of corporate power.

- Finally, although there are some enclaves of resistance by managed economies and dictatorships, this world economy is fundamentally capitalist despite different forms and levels of state involvement in national economies. It takes investment capital, from some source, to participate in the process. Capital is rewarded first and labor is an instrument of production. Capital is the source of power, not production or distribution. This has led to a continued centralization of economic power through the capital-rich corporations. What used to be designated as "developed" and "developing" economies are now often referred to as "central" and "peripheral." The measure is not geography, but instead, the control of capital.

Work Today

In this economic context, the structures and contexts of work have changed significantly:

• Most employment is now in the service sector rather than production. Job growth has been in food service, retail sales, healthcare, residential support, recreation, and hospitality. Further, considerable labor-intensive production moves to low-wage areas. This has caused a decrease in opportunities in factories, in unionized jobs, and in long-term work careers in production. At the same time, there has been an increase in entry-level service jobs with accompanying high turnover.

• Women have entered the work force through many doors. In the United States, a sign of the change came when a majority of women with preschool and school-age children were in the paid work force. Many jobs are in services such as retailing and healthcare. Others are in electronics manufacturing where women are alleged to be better than men at fine-motor-control production. This gender shift of the work force is worldwide. With few exceptions, female-dominated occupations have lower wage rates.

• Services tend to have different schedules from the factory. Many are in operation seven days a week and 24 hours a day. Work schedules in the service sector tend to be irregular and spread throughout the day and night. In this pattern, more jobs are part time—less than 30 hours per week and without security or health and retirement benefits. At a discount retailer, up to 80% of the sales and stock personnel may be part-time and without benefits. This has led to long and irregular hours and households with all adults employed in multiple jobs.

• The average workweek appears to have leveled off for those employed "full-time." The statistic, however, may obscure more than it reveals (Schor, 1992). What is more significant is the variation around the average. As suggested, some with more than one part-time job may exceed the 40 hours a week. Others in high-pressure professions and positions also commonly may work 50- and 60-hour weeks. Those whose functions are considered most productive and most important to profitability are often under extreme pressure to work long and hard. They are the managers, developers of new technologies and products, and frequently those in sales. For such workers, the new economy has not brought more leisure, but greater time scarcity. As was introduced earlier, imagine the mother of preschool children working in one of those high-pressure long-hour positions. That is what we call the "time crunch."

- The so-called "work career" seems to have become more rare. As factories close, corporations downsize, and small businesses fail at a 50% plus rate, a stable work trajectory from entry to management seems less and less common. The work "career" would seem to be more a zigzag than a rising curve. The vanishing career seems to be based on the factor of "replacability." Those who are costly to replace and whose functions are central to profitability are rewarded both with income and security. Those whose skills and experience are easy to replace are paid less and let go more readily. This means that *current* skills and career-long learning are required to have even a good chance at moving through a stairstep sequence of positions. Note also the profitability factor. In the services, it may be more difficult to demonstrate costly-to-replace skills in settings where job-specific training is continual and brief.

- In this work context, one issue is whether work is now more central to life or instrumental. In noncareer service-sector positions and even more in part-time employment, does the job become primarily a means to an income that supports the elements of life that are really important? What happens to company loyalty and identification (i.e., "I am a Boeing worker") when layoffs come with every market downturn or move to lower costs? Is employment primarily a matter of income with no long-term identification with either the corporation or the type of job (i.e., "I am a machinist"). When the issue of the "work ethic" is raised, the employment context cannot be left out of the discussion. What is the meaning of work in the postindustrial economy?

- The income distribution patterns are also changing. According to the Congressional Budget Office, from 1971 to 1994 the top 1% of incomes went up 72% adjusted for inflation (Galbraith, 2000). The top 20% increased 25%, the middle 20% showed no change, and the bottom 20% decreased 16% in real income. This trend has continued into the 21st century. Those crucial to productivity and profitability, usually due to special skills or experience, are gaining more income and wealth while those in the middle have stagnant incomes and those at the bottom are falling further behind. In a market economy, such disparity further divides the society on economic lines.

Leisure Today

Leisure is more than the other side of work. Nevertheless, the two are related. Changes in work conditions have implications for leisure. One, explored in Chapters 5 and 6, focuses on the nature of leisure activity, meanings, and consumption. Here we will introduce impacts of economic change on leisure as a sector of the economy.

- Leisure is now a recognized segment of the economy. Estimates of its size vary, but $300 billion a year is not an exaggeration. Estimates are that 97% of the direct spending on recreation is in the market sector. Financial houses have leisure industry departments. Further, leisure is considered to be a growth sector. For decades, about 6–6.5% of household income was directly spent on recreation. That figure is now up to between 7–8%. But indirect expenditures for transportation, clothing, recreation space in the home, eating out, and travel with a leisure component are even more—especially for households with higher incomes. The added economic impact of tourism will be examined in Chapter 22 and popular culture in Chapter 16.

- Leisure has its basic product components. There are golf clubs, beachwear, snowmobiles, skis, and other equipment. There are pleasure boats, outboard motors, fishing gear, and surfboards. There are also the places for use, instruction programs, and activity-based group travel. As outlined in Chapter 23, that is big business. Probably as important, however, is all the auxiliary business that service recreation-centered events. Just driving down the road on the way to a recreation destination gives a sample of the businesses dependent on the beach and seashore, the forest or mountain park, the sports arena, or some other leisure venue. Leisure is an economic octopus with its tentacles in real estate, travel, transportation, food, clothing, communications, and a hundred other types of business. Leisure as consumption may be most evident in the entertainment and tourism industries, but a drive through the shopping mall reveals much more. How much of the floor space of the local Wal-mart or Target is devoted to leisure-related items? How many of the services in the yellow pages are based on some kind of leisure activity? There are toys for all ages and diverse leisure styles.

- A large proportion of leisure service businesses are quite local in scale. They are retail outlets or tied to a local resource. There are also, however, the major international corporations, especially in tourism. Some are activity-specific and based on a single locale. Others are worldwide in their markets and diverse in their product lines.

- How does leisure fit into the economic spectrum? It is, by definition, not necessary. It is not food and shelter. One proposal is leisure is the new incentive for work. As suggested earlier, work careers may not be all that satisfying. In most developed economies, food, housing, transportation, and other "necessities" are assured for most of the population. Has leisure become the added incentive to work regularly and productively? Is leisure more the special goal—the "something more" that is never satisfied? Economic theory posits the "insatiable consumer" who always wants more. To what extent has leisure become that area of life in which the consumer will always work for something new, more stylish, or at least different?

Leisure Markets

In a market economy, there are always business interests seeking to bring together some goods or services with consumers. There is always investment capital whose managers are seeking profit-making enterprises. Nevertheless, most businesses fail. Small businesses fail at a high rate, about half in less than two years. The central concept is *marketing*—arranging an economic meeting between the buyer and seller. In some ways, leisure-based marketing is like that of other goods and services. In some ways, it is different (Kelly, 1985). For example, by definition leisure spending is not necessary. There are always alternatives, including not making the purchase at all. Further, leisure consumption is based on some nonwork activity. The kind of activity, its forms and meanings, determines the nature of the markets. Some special approaches to leisure-based marketing are a little different from selling cars, refrigerators, business suits, and garden tools. As with clothing, leisure goods are signs of style and status.

Market Segmentation

Marketing always identifies particular markets—those most likely to purchase the particular items offered. Any marketing gives attention to available income and ability to pay. In leisure marketing, however, some of the other market identification factors have particular meaning:

1. **Access to resources:** The special places of leisure—such as ski slopes, country clubs, fitness centers, lakes, courts, playing fields—are generally closed in some ways. The limitations may be cost, membership, distance, or climate, but access is always a limiting factor.

2. **Age:** Many leisure activities are segregated by age. Sports, especially, are almost all age-graded in competitive programs. Being in a school is required for entrance into many activities for children and youth. Other activities are just not as appealing to most older persons. There are age regulations for admission to many places of entertainment. In other cases, such as rock concerts or game arcades, almost all the clientele is in a certain age group.

3. **Education and leisure style:** Education remains one of the best indices of the range of leisure interests for most people.

4. **Gender:** Despite opening many kinds of activity to females, gender remains a differentiating factor for many activities.

5. **Culture and ethnicity:** Language and cultural history divide populations in leisure as well as in other aspects of life. Some activities are especially ethnic.

Insofar as leisure styles are a part of overall lifestyles (see Chapter 6), then everything that affects patterns of leisure is potentially useful for market segmentation. Leisure, for the most part, fits into overall lifestyles. The more marketers know of the elements of those styles, the more precise they can be in identifying markets.

Activity Investment

Leisure markets are different from others in that they depend on voluntary participation in activity. No one has to play golf, fly to Colorado to ski, invest in an expensive home entertainment center, or eat out. There are always alternative activities and often alternative resources. Unlike the markets for refrigerators and transportation, one can just not do it at all. Therefore, the activity must be attractive enough to win in competition with other possibilities including just staying home in front of the television. There may be all kinds of social pressures, status factors, and role-related expectations involved in leisure, but there is also generally some choice involved. This puts a premium on the quality of the experience that is anticipated and remembered. As a result, there are some special characteristics of leisure markets. (See Chapter 23 for further analysis.)

Frequency of participation varies widely in leisure. Many of those who play tennis or golf, swim or picnic, and go to movies or concerts do so only once or twice a year. Others engage in their central activities with great regularity. They make many kinds of investments in the activity, including time spent gaining skills, equipment cost, joining associations, reading specialized periodicals, and gaining access to resources. About 20–25% of those who do any leisure activity do so more than occasionally (Kelly, 1987). For most activities, a minority of participants are regular. Others start activities but drop out. They do not invest themselves significantly in gaining skills or in other requirements that make participation satisfying. The major markets in leisure are those invested in the activity.

Market Cycles

Every area of marketing has its fads — new items that appear — are promoted and often given notice in the media, and then fade into obscurity. Other products fit into established markets and maintain a viable level of demand. Occasionally something new, the video game for example, creates a new market. Fads reach a peak quickly and as quickly decline. New products, such as fiberglass skis, enhance the market for a sport. All markets eventually reach a peak, level out, and may even decline. There are *NO* exceptions. The cycle may be brief or take years, but it is there. Racquetball, for example, has declined to a level far lower than predicted by its promoters. Most racquetball clubs have now diversified into "fitness centers." The issue in investing is to identify the current stage in the cycle and invest (or sell out) in a timely fashion. The trick is to distinguish fads from those activities or technologies that correspond to established life patterns. Further, in leisure markets, a viable business can be based on an activity that regularly attracts less than 1% of the adult population.

How the Market Works

Classical economics holds that "demand creates supply." When we need more cars, the market will produce more cars, eventually at a price that yields an adequate but not excessive profit. In current markets, especially those based on technological development and investment, that is not enough. Economic growth requires new goods and services and growing markets. To minimize loss, the equation is reversed. Supply creates demand (Galbraith, 1967). This seems to be especially true in leisure markets. There was no demand for snowmobiles, Jet Skis, DVDs, or many other new products until demand was created by demonstration and advertising. The product, with its activity and resource base, created its demand. This is always the case for new goods and services. Even products that improve performance or satisfaction in an established activity—graphite racquets or golf shafts—have to be promoted, often with star endorsements and demonstrations. After all, no one *needs* a Jet Ski or windsurfer. The market is a creation of the product and the activity. Through advertising, products are visualized as essential to status, images, and lifestyles.

Note that marketing is always directed toward those who can pay—preferably at a level that will yield a significant profit. Marketing innovation is not aimed at the poor, or even the middle mass. It is directed toward those whose demand may be most profitable. That is the nature of a market economy. As a consequence, a disproportionate market effort is directed toward the affluent. Destination resorts are designed for the upscale markets—those willing and able to pay the highest prices. As a result, those upscale markets tend to be saturated, leading to bankruptcies. The bias of investment capital is always toward anticipated profit. It is more profitable to create a market among the affluent than to compete in a crowded market for those on a strict budget.

Further, the most attractive markets are those that need replenishing. Producing a good, competitively priced item that will last for a decade limits the market. It is better to enter markets that require new purchases with regularity. That is the meaning of *style*. As goods go out of style, they must be replaced even though they may be functional and serviceable. In the leisure industry, there is the continual effort to market new styles of almost everything to create demand—and style may have nothing to do with functional quality.

The bias in investment in market economies is evident. There is no market sector investment in such resources as walking trails that produce little in the way of new markets (although there are now specialized "walking" shoes). There is tremendous investment in gambling boats and casinos with their ever-renewing market. There is investment in cost-intensive items and in their "improvement" to renew markets. The aim is always the same: to create or improve a cost-intensive market. That means the activities promoted will be those based on a technology or access to a resource that can be controlled. It will develop a Disney World or a Six Flags Amusement Park—not a hiking path or forest. It will prefer affluent adults over poor children, and cost over personal development. The market works; the question is "for whom and for what?"

Debate: The market allocates (leisure) resources best.

The assumption of classical economics is always that the market system is the best way to link the producer and the consumer. The alternative is some sort of command economy in which some agency of the state employs rational or even ethical principles to allocate resources to production and to distribute goods and services. On a community level, both the public and market sectors are leisure resource providers. On the national level, both sectors manage valuable land and water opportunities. Who does it best?

YES

- The market is most responsive to the wants of the consumer. The consumer enters the market able to make an immediate decision as to purchase. Further, the consumer is able to make decisions as to priorities. Market decisions by individuals and households are made with a recognition of scarcities—in the case of leisure scarcities of both time and money. The bureaucracy, on the other hand, is far removed from the consumer. Bureaucracy is a cumbersome machine at best. Market decisions by the persons who will use the product require no complex process, no special expertise, and no expensive bureaucracy.

- The "sovereign consumer" is the right locus of decision. No one should decide for others whether they should prefer hiking boots or concert tickets. In some areas, medical care for example, there may be the need for expert opinions. In leisure there is none. Only the individual consumer is able to assess the probable value of the experience and the resources that maximize that experience. We know our own leisure wants and needs better than anyone else. There is no need for experts. Further, the market enables us to maximize our freedom. Any bureaucracy, however benevolent in intent, tends toward control, often control for its own sake. Experts (i.e., "professionals") make a career of asserting they know better than ordinary people. If there is any area of life in which we ought to be able to make our own decisions, it is leisure.

- The market is immediate and flexible. Bureaucracies are slow. They lag behind what is current. If we want to try something new, even a fad, the controlling agency will resist. The market, always alert to new demand, will respond most quickly. In fact, the market system is always in the process of developing new goods and services that may create demand. The profit motive is a great stimulus for flexibility and innovation.

- The market is relatively free from political trading. Of course, there are regulations for some kinds of activity. For the most part, however, the market works through the exchange of goods and the portable media of money and credit. Whenever there is some political agency of control, it will be operated for the political (and often economic) gain of those involved. For example, the recreation systems of large cities are used to buy votes at least as much as they are to respond to evident need. In socialist systems, leisure resources have been used to reward the bureaucrats. Combining political and economic power can be inequitable and even dangerous. Control systems distort the market with an overlay of privileges that are both inefficient and unjust.

- Even public recreation is moving more to a fee-for-service basis of allocation. Tax revenues are limited and competitive. Using a quasi-market system, public agencies are able to pay for services and respond to what their constituents clearly want because they are willing to pay for it. There are no fully accurate methods of indirectly measuring the preferences and values of large populations. The market provides the most direct measure.

- Market rewards increase productivity. Rather than decide for workers what they want in recreation, employers would do better to raise wages and let the worker decide. When income is tied to productivity, the incentive to produce is clear and unambiguous. Corporate recreation programs, on the other hand, admit all workers by category and have no clear connection with productivity.

- Market economists usually argue that the market is not inequitable. Rather, there may be (and are) inequities in the distribution of income. The proper response to inequity is not to decide for workers what services they should be given free or at a subsidized rate. It is to address the distribution of income directly and through taxes so that all may be free to act as sovereign consumers. The poor should have higher incomes—not services determined in a government agency.

- The market is the basis of society. Society exists through the exchange of goods and services. The system through which this is done is the market system, the division of labor, and money as a medium of exchange. Anything that distorts this exchange subverts the entire system. When such distortions are made in a bureaucracy far removed from the actual lives of citizens, then it is largely by accident when there is an accurate response to wants and desires. The market may at times get out of balance and overproduce or misdistribute, but in time it adjusts to reality. In the meantime, there is generally enough flexibility for consumers to adjust their lives to what is available.

NO

- The market seeks a return on investment, not the development of human life. Leisure is more than consumption. It has a developmental or existential component fundamental to human life. The market responds to price, not need. Resources are allocated according to potential profit, not the potential to support and enhance life. The toy or faddish gewgaw that offers a high profit margin may have little to do with the dimensions of human action, significant bonding with others, and personal development. There is little profit in open space or forest paths, but the potential for life may be immeasurable.

- The market creates an imbalance in investment. On a different level, the market is not used to allocate resources to education because children produce little direct profit. Rather, we believe that it is good for the society that all children be educated, not just those whose families can pay high fees. The market just doesn't allocate well for all elements of the common good. The same is true for leisure. Do we want only the children of the wealthy to learn to sing, dance, and play sports? Do we want only the suburbs to have open space? Do we want only a few to see the Grand Canyon with price being the sole decision factor? If it were up to the market, we would have more of Las Vegas and less of Yellowstone, as gambling produces a higher profit than camping. Try to imagine just what our communities and country would be like if we were to evaluate every resource decision solely by demonstrated ability to produce a high-income return.

- The market emphasizes commodity-intensive activity. The market will promote Jet Skis and powerboats—not swimming. The market will stress expensive electronics—not playing the guitar. The market will sell uniforms and equipment—not space for children to organize their own games. Further, the "best" equipment will go out of style or wear out quickly. The more expensive and temporary the equipment, the better. Yet, walking is one of the few activities increasing in participation. There is no known correlation between the cost of equipment and satisfaction—short- or long-term.

- Further, the market will respond to high-end consumers first. Those who have the money to pay high prices for equipment, locales, access, clothing, and other leisure items will receive disproportionate attention in a market economy. The big money is in residential resorts, not campgrounds near public beaches. That is why the multimillion-dollar resorts proliferate. Opportunities for the wealthy are overbuilt while they are crowded for the middle mass. In time, the market will expand to lower-end consumers, but priority always goes to those able to pay the most and yield the highest return on investment.

- The market is short-term. Corporations seek profits this quarter and this year—not a decade down the line. As a consequence, resources tend to be overused and even badly degraded in order to maximize current use and income. When a resource is to be preserved for generations to come, such as national parks, the market does not tend to manage it well. Further, market allocation will often use land and other resources intensively rather than sustainably. Planning and management for the long term is imperfect at best, but seldom done well by those with corporate investors given first priority. Planning is long term when done well; the market takes the short view. It is by definition immediate.

- The market is inequitable. Few would defend a system of income reward in which stock sales produce higher incomes than teaching or dealing 21, or more than caring for the old and infirm. Then, a market system of distribution is totally dependent on available income. Those with chronic health expenses have little for leisure, even though care-givers may most need a break. The market makes no allowances for anything, especially not for need. In the United States, with its enormous differences in income, the gap between the wealthy and the poor is widening, and 20% of households are poor. To distribute all of any good entirely by market price is inevitably inequitable. Until the income distribution is changed, the market at least has to be augmented with tax-subsidized goods and services.

This argument is fundamental to more than leisure. It may be the most important ongoing debate of the 21st century. Is ours a market society, a welfare society, or some combination of the two? There will be different approaches to the debate in Chapters 12 and 21.

Discussion Questions

1. Did the Industrial Revolution create modern leisure? How?

2. What are the implications of postindustrial changes for leisure?

3. Realistically, what are the conditions of most jobs today? Give examples.

4. Is there any real security in this kind of economy?

5. What does being in a world economy mean to a part-time wage worker?

6. Give examples of recent leisure fads, and sustained markets. How do they differ?

7. How has public recreation become commercialized?

8. What is the best way to offer leisure opportunity to the poor?

9. How is resource conservation an issue for recreation?

10. What does the leisure market fail to provide?

References and Resources

Driver, B.L., Brown, P., and Peterson, G. (Eds.). (1991). *Benefits of leisure*. State College, PA: Venture Publishing, Inc.

Galbraith, J. (1958). *The affluent society*. Boston, MA: Houghton Mifflin.

Galbraith, J. (1967). *The new industrial state*. Boston, MA: Houghton Mifflin.

Galbraith, J. (2000). *Created unequal: The crisis in American pay*. Chicago, IL: University of Chicago Press.

Hunnicutt, B. (1988). *Work without end: Abandoning shorter hours for the right to work*. Philadelphia, PA: Temple University Press.

Kelly, J. (1987). *Recreation trends toward the year 2000*. Champaign, IL: Sagamore.

Kelly, J.R. (1985). *Recreation business*. New York, NY: John Wiley.

Kotlowitz, A. (1990). *There are no children here: The story of two boys growing up in the other America*. New York, NY: Anchor Books.

Pine, B.J. and Gilmore, J. (1999). *The experience economy: Work is theatre & every business a stage*. Boston, MA: Harvard Business School Press.

Rojek, C. (1985). *Capitalism and leisure theory*. London: Tavistock.

Schor, J. (1992). *The overworked American: The unexpected decline of leisure*. New York, NY: Basic Books.

Schor, J. (1999). *The overspent American: Why we want what we don't need.* New York, NY: HarperCollins.

Thurow, L. (1980). *The zero-sum society: Distribution and the possibilities of economic change.* New York, NY: Basic Books.

Wilson, J. (1988). *Politics and leisure.* Boston, MA: Unwin Hyman.

Wilson, W. (1987). *The truly disadvantaged: The inner city, the underclass, and public policy.* Chicago, IL University of Chicago Press.

Chapter 12
Politics and Policy

What does government have to do with leisure? Isn't leisure a personal matter—a matter of choice, personal preference, and taste? We may remember totalitarian states have used organized recreation and sport for their political purposes. There have been youth organizations designed to teach the ideologies of "National Socialism" in Hitler's Germany and of the communist revolution in the Soviet Union. There have been state-supported sports programs, especially for the Olympics, to demonstrate the glory and power of particular governments. There have also been leisure privileges granted to those with political power or influence, but that has been characteristic of dictatorships and centralized power. In a democracy with a market economy, what does politics have to do with leisure?

How Is Leisure Political?

One answer is that everything is political. That is true in the sense that decisions made in the political process, whatever it may be, are ultimately about the use, distribution, and control of resources. For example, the funding of a highway system supports travel by private car. Congressional legislation on timber sales from national forests effects recreation resources by building access roads, destroying forests, and polluting rivers and steams. Community planning reserves fields for playgrounds or opens them for commercial development. All such decisions are made through political systems in conditions requiring the negotiation of conflicting interests. There are a number of ways in which leisure is clearly political.

1. Space is usually scarce and, therefore, subject to political decision. Access to public space—in both natural and built environments—is decided by government. Are national monuments and parks free

and open to all, or restricted to those who pay user fees? Is the public golf course reserved for adults—or even male adults—before 3:00 p.m. on Saturdays and Sundays? Is the school gym open for pickup basketball in the evening? Does the community have laws that require setting aside a percentage of land being developed for housing for parks or recreational use? Who decides on scheduling recreation facilities? Do children have priority over adults, fee-payers over those in open programs, organized activity over self-organized play? Are snowmobiles and trail bikes permitted on fragile dunes and deserts? These and a thousand other issues are adjudicated in some political process in which some have more leverage than others.

2. How are hunting and fishing permits allocated? What hours must bars open and close? What kind of "entertainment" is permitted in particular zones of a city? There are all kinds of regulations governing leisure. Both public and private facilities have hours, maximum user limits, fire and safety rules, and other regulations. Use of some chemical substances is prohibited. Alcohol cannot be consumed in some places or during particular time periods. We tend to think of "blue laws" regulating behavior as largely in the past, but there are still many regulations—Some are even former religious prohibitions. Others are based on safety or interference with other activities. Even private property is restricted from actions that pollute the environment or disrupt the lives of neighbors. None of these regulations, however common or long-standing, is exempt from political action.

3. Taxation is, of course, political. Through taxation the government supports some activity and restricts other. There are luxury taxes on yachts, excise taxes on alcohol, sales taxes on tobacco, bed taxes on hotels and motels, taxes on rental cars to capture the tourist dollar, fuel taxes on travel, and property taxes on vacation real estate. Conversely, the second-home industry is supported by allowing federal income tax deductions on Aspen condo and Northwoods cabin interest payments. Boats and airplanes as well as gourmet meals can be written off as business expenses under certain conditions. Taxation is a major way through which the leisure of some is subsidized and that of others rendered more expensive. It may be no accident the support tends to favor those with the greatest political influence.

4. There is also all the infrastructure that makes various kinds of leisure possible. There are roads for car travel, sewers and utilities for vacation developments, airports and airways for distance travel, safety

protection, and all the tax-supported facilities and services that make living away from home possible. Where are highways located? Which area gets sewers first and at what cost? Which beaches have public access, parking, and maintenance? Which forests are given fire suppression and which are allowed to burn? Again, these are political decisions.

5. The United States is one of the few countries that provides little direct government support for elite international sports teams and athletes. There are, however, generous tax benefits for corporate sponsors. In most countries there is some direct support of national teams, training programs, and travel. The purpose, of course, is political: to make citizens feel good about their government.

6. The mass media are also a political area of allocation and dispute. Television and radio frequencies are allocated—free or through auction—to particular corporations. They then control this resource with all its potential for profit and persuasion. The decision as to allocation through price or some criteria of public welfare is political. Restrictions on content are decided in the Congress. Whether or not to support and control public media in television, radio, and print is a political decision that varies from one nation to another. The constitutional right to free speech and access to the media is tempered by concerns about damaging or dangerous material and messages. When does regulation become censorship? Can the market provide adequate control? Now there is the Internet and concern about sexually explicit material available to the young, and bomb construction details offered to potential terrorists.

Leisure is political. There is implicit and explicit policy underlying the laws, regulations, and provisions of every level of government. The task is to analyze how political processes produce policy and open and close many doors to leisure.

What Is Politics?

The previous outline suggests many of the dimensions of politics in relation to leisure. In the beginning, the political is based on a struggle over space. When the commons of old England was enclosed for the commercial use of particular individuals, then the struggle was under way. Where was it permissible to walk, hunt and fish, graze animals, and plant a garden? No longer was there common land open to all. The state protected the right to private property, even that which had previously been held in common for the entire community.

Now the control of space remains central to the relation of the polity to leisure. On the immediate level, there are conflicts over the use of public space, such as gyms and parks, by different user groups. Some parks have even become the "turf" of gangs or are under the "protection" of particular drug dealers. Other parks are built due to the political influence of real estate and developer interests who are investing in housing in new areas. In some cases, there may be conflict between those who would preserve land for open space or agriculture against development interests with public park and recreation departments offering a compromise between common ground and private use. Many kinds of activity—from walking to sports—require dedicated and often designed space. Space is opportunity. Without space there is no freedom to choose. The control of space, however, is political. Even the act of making land available for market-sector use rather than holding it in public domain is a political act.

Any struggle over scarce resources is political. For example, is a national park managed to maximize visitor use with a minimum of damage to the environment, or is it managed primarily to preserve a unique environment by allowing limited recreational visitation? The priorities are decided in political arenas, sometimes by legislation and sometimes by struggles within management agencies. A U.S. Forest Service chief ranger may have the final decision between opening an area to mining and grazing or closing it to protect wild animal habitats. In such a case, the organized efforts of those with opposing agendas and aims may be brought to bear with as much political weight as possible. The classic conflict is over the highly protective designation of land as wilderness versus multiuse management that permits roads, mines, grazing, logging, second homes, and resort development.

A decision may be termed political whenever one group attempts to gain or maintain power over another. The conflict may be local, such as allocation of a budget among activities, neighborhoods, or facility use. It may be legislative in a city council, state legislature, or Congress. It may involve those who manage a park or forest, those who select personnel, or those who lobby for particular programs or provisions. All the special interest groups are not business-based. There are also those who lobby for Little League, Special Olympics, age-group swimming, and summer theater. Resources are almost always scarce. Budget allocations go one direction rather than another; the use of space for one activity limits or eliminates others, for example permitting Jet Skis on a lake may damage fishing habitats.

One persistent issue is benefits that go differentially to one population segment or another. Such decisions may favor one racial or ethnic group to the exclusion of another. In a capitalist economy, it is common to turn to private enterprise to provide some kinds of opportunities or even to manage public resources. That almost inevitably produces a bias toward those who can pay most readily, and those who can yield a profit for the enterprise. When resources have been acquired or developed with tax money involved, then any uneven or biased distribution of access and opportunity may be questioned. The boundaries between public and private may become fuzzy and inconsistent.

Leisure also becomes political whenever control of behavior is involved. Such control may be in providing resources for "patriotic" events such as commemorative parades and festivals, such as Fourth of July fireworks. Such events not only reinforce the political establishment but also provide opportunities for campaigning by those who hold public office. The inclusion and exclusion of symbols and even participants from parades and other events is a political decision. As already outlined, licensing for various entertainment enterprises may involve political influence. It also controls behaviors by limiting locations, hours of operation, and even the personnel allowed to run the business. Further, police not only "serve and protect" but also regulate behavior by custom as well as by law. Which street behaviors are permitted, and by whom, and which ones prohibited may be a matter of police discretion as well as law. The history of leisure is full of examples of groups with political power enforcing their own values on others, often on majorities. The Victorian era was notorious for its blue laws that attempted to regulate not only public behaviors but also those in the "castle" of one's own home. The informal drinking practices of the shebeen where drinks were sold in homes were soon subjected to police raids unless "arrangements" were made. During the Prohibition period, illegal drinking was common in speakeasies that paid their "tax" to the authorities, but resulted in arrests for those who violated the local political codes. Even now, many states have laws regulating the kinds of sexual practices that are permitted in private residences. Such laws are now being challenged by judicial rulings. Some chemical substances and plants are permitted in some states but not in others. Gambling is regulated everywhere, but the conditions of licensing vary widely. The violence of football, ice hockey, and boxing may take place in tax-supported stadiums in states where the violence of blood sports is prohibited. The control of leisure behaviors, on all levels, is a varied political scheme with differential power and influence channeled through all kinds of governmental bodies.

Persistent Issues

A number of issues appear in various situations and conditions in relation to leisure. Three of the most significant are the relationship of the political and the economic, public investment, and direct control of leisure.

Is the Political Determined by the Economic?

The old cliché is the so-called "golden rule"—He who has the gold rules. That is clearly too simple. There are many political coalitions of the relatively poor and disinherited—some even resulting in revolution. In developed Western economies, however, the process may be more subtle than a simple granting of power to the wealthy. Certainly local government boards and committees tend to be filled with those from the more affluent sections of the community. Almost all community studies have demonstrated major economic interests are disproportionately represented in local and state government. It requires special and deliberate organization around recognized issues for those who are marginal economically to gain even temporary political influence. Further, the funding of political campaigns in this media age means those controlling financial resources can at least buy access to those in office and sometimes even determine political outcomes.

The underlying system, however, is less visible than simply purchasing votes or influence. There is a tacit ideology in most nations that government has as a primary mission—the support of the economy. Foreign policy is at least partly dictated by securing and protecting trade advantages. The power of the government is employed to protect the international system that makes possible the operation of global corporations. A high value is placed on productivity, whatever the location of the workers. Unemployment is accepted if its "acceptable rate" is considered best for the investment return of the global corporation. And the government assists in the development of markets anywhere in the world. Consumption is necessary for corporate production of goods and services to be profitable. The ideology is not really that of government absence from an unrestricted "free market." Rather, the government intervenes in all sorts of ways—taxation, regulation, financial control in banking and currency—intended to maintain the economic system designed for corporate success as measured by investment return. One important clue to interpreting government action or inaction is always to analyze how it supports some economic interest.

Limits on Public Investment

The Federal Office of Management and Budget estimated in 1993 the government spent 0.17 of 1% of its total budget on recreation. If households allocate about 8% of their expenditures to leisure, then there is a major discrepancy. Most spending, then, is in the market sector. The market sector is the major investor in leisure provisions. Investment in provisions for leisure is over 90% in the market sector. It is assumed the market sector will be the major provider of opportunities. Public investment is limited to those resources that cannot be provided by the market sector due to factors of long-term conservation, efficiency, or the lack of profitable markets. Public community softball fields are the most efficient use of scarce space and national parks the best way to conserve unique environments.

The underlying ethic seems to favor the individual over the collective. That is, anything that can be done by the individual should not be undertaken by the state. Leisure would seem to be paramount among those aspects of life that are individual rather than collective. Leisure is not considered necessary and, therefore, can be largely left to the choice and initiative of individuals. It is a matter of personal rather than common welfare. The exceptions are considered exactly that—exceptions to the rule of individual responsibility.

This means the preponderance of leisure opportunities will be those that attract investment capital. As analyzed in Chapter 11, that will be skewed toward provisions that yield a profit. There will be limits placed on public-sector investment—billions for gambling, and a few thousands for hiking trails. Further, any enterprises that can be "privatized," assigned to the market economy, will be removed from the public domain. Public agencies will be responsible only for those projects assumed to be both important and unlikely to yield a profit. An important result of this policy is funding for public recreation will be severely limited. Only in communities with relatively high incomes will there be an abundance of programs and resources. In the meanwhile, national parks, forests, beaches, and historical monuments fall further and further behind in simple maintenance and are starved for development. Again, such allocation decisions are political. The political policies, however, are based on ideologies of market primacy and productivity.

Is Control of Leisure Largely Past History?

There are tales of Puritan repression in the colonial era. There are more recent stories of the blue laws regulating behavior, especially on Sundays, in the so-called "Bible belt" and conservative small towns. There remain residues of old laws still on the books, but seldom, if ever, enforced. They are only reminders that some organized population segments, usually minorities, will attempt to impose their moral codes on others.

Is such social control of leisure still an issue? Is political power still used to limit the choices and tastes of others? The issue may be stated as follows: a basic "right to leisure" versus enforcement of the "right kind of leisure."

Do people have a right to make their own choices as long as they do not endanger others or do irreparable environmental damage? Most would agree some regulation is necessary. We do not want off-road motorcycles tearing up fragile dunes. We do not want drunken carousing on the beach next to our family picnic. We do not want drag races down our city streets at any hour. These and other leisure behaviors do too much harm to the lives and leisure of others. But how do we feel about having where and when we can drink alcoholic beverages controlled? What is our attitude toward censoring television programs and Web sites that display sexual practices we find repugnant and unfit for the young? Should gambling be restricted because 10–20% of those who gamble develop a compulsive gambling habit? Is direct violence acceptable in boxing or other violent sports, but not on the streets or in the park? Is there a fundamental right to religious freedom that permits others to engage in sexual practices (e.g., polygamy by some Mormons) or use of controlled substances (e.g., peyote by some Native American nations) in ways that violate common norms and standards? Is there, as some court decisions seem to hold, a common set of moral standards by which a community may limit the freedom of some members? The truth is a web of law and customs do control leisure. There is also resistance to such control through secrecy, privacy, and outright challenge. Can leisure be limited when it is deemed a threat to the "common order," but be largely unrestricted when its practices are private?

Debate: Government should regulate destructive leisure behavior.

YES

- Some leisure is a threat to society and must be limited. Public demonstrations of sexuality that threaten family values and community standards of decency have to be controlled. Games and language that denigrate racial groups, ethnic minorities, or other members of the community cannot be tolerated in the name of freedom.

- Some behaviors are dangerous. The injuries they are likely to cause impose long-term costs on the community that have to be borne by those careful enough to avoid the activity. Some are even dangerous to others, such a powerboating or using Jet Skis near swimming beaches. Some reasonable regulation is simply a matter of public health and safety.

- Any society has to be based on some common moral order. Activity that threatens that order by promoting subversive values and practices have to be restricted. For example, hate groups indoctrinate the young under the guise of "survivalist" forest recreation. There is the exploitation of children in sexual practices and media. Any society has to have some limits.

- Some activity pollutes water sources or otherwise damages environments. While some localized environmental change is necessary for recreation development, resource destruction has to be regulated.

- Sometimes the behaviors of a few degrade the experience of many. Doesn't there have to be some limit on noise production in campgrounds or motorized vehicle speeds on trails also used for hiking? Such rules are not really government control, but reflect a consensus of a majority of users. Rules are necessary, however, to prevent an inconsiderate minority from stealing from the leisure of the majority.

- Some activities and environments are dangerous to children who are not prepared to exercise mature judgment as to danger. Age restrictions or requirements of adult supervision are fundamental to children's use of beaches, rivers, or mountainsides.

- Some traditional activities, known as blood sports, are cruel to the animals involved. The pleasure of a few with power over the animals cannot justify baiting animals to tear each other apart.

- Recreation should be just that, re-creating. It is to be a benefit to individuals and the society. Destructive activity cannot be permitted in the name of freedom. The social order takes priority over the immediate gratification of those who desire only the pleasure of the moment.

NO

- Leisure is the realm of the individual. Personal freedom should be maximized rather than curtailed. What seems dangerous to some may be the adventure and challenge of others. Who is to decide what is dangerous and what is legitimate risk?

- When the government exercises control, the interests of powerful minorities usually prevail over those of the majority. The political realm is too subject to influence by organized groups who want to inflict their tastes and preferences on the entire society. In leisure, of all aspects of life, personal autonomy ought to prevail over social control whenever possible. The premise of state regulation for the "benefit" of its citizens is always dangerous.

- Diversity ought to be the hallmark of leisure. Further, tastes and interests vary widely. Leisure is the realm in which the right to be different and individual should be protected first and any necessary regulation be a matter of utter necessity. State control can lead to uniformity.

- The government has interests of its own. There is a drive to control and maintain authority and power. Some in government even have economic stakes in leisure. It is quite clear from the experience in socialist states that bureaucracies tend to perpetuate themselves at the expense of citizens. Bureaucracies are just not very responsive to what people want in their everyday lives.

- Cultures change. Regulations tend to remain in place long after their purposes have lapsed. For example, secularized societies are now open to behaviors condemned by previous religious cultures. The best way to avoid the problem of cultural lag is to minimize regulation to begin with—whatever can be left to individual choice ought to be.

- After all, who is to decide for others what is beneficial and what might be damaging? There is always a tendency to try to impose our values—and even tastes—on others. One way to prevent this is to keep the government out of private life, especially leisure based on personal experience.

Does the United States Have a Leisure Policy?

Unlike many other countries, the United States has no ministry responsible for "Youth, Sport, and Leisure" or "Leisure, Culture, and the Arts." There is no one place to look for documents that enunciate a national leisure policy. In fact, recreation provisions are divided among a number of departments and agencies with responsibility for land management or health.

There may be no explicit leisure policy, but it is possible to extrapolate the possibility of an implicit policy. That policy would be that leisure is primarily a concern of the individual. Further, whenever possible, the market sector will be relied on to provide leisure resources and opportunities. The underlying ideology is one of individualism. Leisure is a matter of individual gratification. Therefore, the individual is to choose the activities, investments, styles, and equipment that are appealing. There is no public standard to meet. There may be expectations related to social status or ethnic identity, but even those can be rejected. The basis and aim of leisure is personal, not social. Therefore, the individual is a leisure consumer, making choices based on personal taste.

As a consumer, the individual makes choices from what is provided in the market. Whatever will provide the most gratification for the price is acceptable. Resources will be provided by the market whenever there is demand at a price that yields a profit. The leisure actor is, from this perspective, the "sovereign consumer." From the supply side, then, the bias is toward consumption of goods and services. The bias is toward the commodified market rather than toward the experience, as analyzed in Chapters 5 and 23.

The public sector, then, provides only what cannot be offered by the market sector. Even though over 90% of leisure spending is in the market sector, the public sector does provide certain kinds of opportunities:

- Some environments are unique, fragile, and in high demand. The major national parks, some wildlife habitats, and waterways have to be managed for long-range preservation as well as current use. As with the Grand Canyon, too many overflights in low-level paths, too many rafting trips with their impacts on the scarce landing and camping sites, and too many cars on the rims are more than the ecology can handle without severe damage.

- Some resources are more efficiently provided by the public sector. In a condition of urban space scarcity, the maximum use and access to softball fields, golf courses, swimming pools, and other space can be made available to more users at lower cost through public management. It makes no sense for a family or club to own a forest so they can camp once a summer.

- Some segments of the population cannot gain access to significant recreation opportunities unless the public sector subsidizes their participation. As long as 20% or more of the population is in poverty, there will be millions of households, and especially their children, who require tax-supported programs. This principle of equity historically was the beginning of the public recreation movement in urban America.

Such public provisions, however, still fall within the ideology of the primacy of the market. Public programs have to be justified as exceptions. As indicated above, resource preservation, efficiency, or equity are used as arguments for public recreation. Further, the benefits of public programs are justified by their contributions to economic productivity, health, and community values

(Driver, Brown & Peterson, 1991). They are claimed to be something more than activities for their own sake. Rather, they increase productivity by relieving stress that promotes emotional health or are exercise that promotes physical health. In other cases, they distract those, such as "at-risk youth," who might otherwise be a danger to the community.

In such a mode, efficiency is likely to be given greater weight than equity. Recreation for the poor is justified by the potential damage that might otherwise be caused to the larger community. The argument is that it is cheaper to build gymnasiums than prisons. At the other end of the cost spectrum, it is more efficient to allot scarce harbor space to rationally assigned boat slips and moorings through the public sector than have wealthy individuals or private clubs claim all the available space. On the other hand, when the market can be claimed to allocate according to the choices of consumers and investors, the market sector tends to be given priority.

Debate: Leisure is a public responsibility.

YES

- Many crucial resources are both scarce—even unique—and fragile. Their preservation is important to the quality of life for future as well as present generations. They must be managed with more than current profits as the primary consideration.

- Those without the financial resources to participate in market-provided leisure should not be cut off from important opportunities. This is especially true for children and youth. Sports, the arts, forests, beaches, and so forth should not be out of reach for 20–30% of the children of any community. Social equity requires public provisions for those who are marginal economically.

- The market allocates by price. There should be some allocation of resources by need. Children, the disabled and those requiring special access, and others who may be excluded by price have recreational needs that can be filled only through public programs.

- Leisure is part of the balance of life. There is a public responsibility to provide at least a measure of that balance for all citizens.

- Public resources can be managed to maximize use and access. The market is not always as economically efficient as public planning that can make the optimal use of scarce space—indoors and outdoors.

- As analyzed in Chapters 5 and 23, the market is biased toward provisions and investments for goods and services that yield a profit rather than a developmental experience.

- Public recreation can yield a sense of community and commonality. Festivals, summer sports, and parks offer times and places where people of a community gather with a sense of solidarity—of cohesion rather than division.

NO

- Leisure is an individual matter. Public programs attempt to enlist as many as possible in the same prescribed activities.

- For the most part, the market is the most direct and efficient distributor of resources. In the market, no bureaucratic planner decides for the individual or community what is best. If you don't want it, you don't buy it.

- Bureaucracies are unresponsive and lag behind current interests. They tend to become entrenched in their ideas and programs rather than change. The bureaucratic ethos is to be careful, avoid mistakes, and take no risks—but without risk, there is no change.

- Government bodies cannot be trusted to be apolitical. Leisure provisions will be used for political ends. For example, city parks and other recreation opportunities will often be directed toward districts where some incumbent politician is threatened and needs support. What appears to be rational planning is actually part of a partisan political process.

- Those with power, usually economic, will manipulate public providers for their own ends. For example, parks will be located to benefit developers rather than based on a careful analysis of neighborhood use and need. Corporate interests will direct which mountainsides are bulldozed for ski runs and which corporations get the leases. There is often little correlation between population needs and equitable allocation on the one hand and political decisions on the other.

- Leisure tends to be defined as a reward for productivity or even political cooperation rather than as a human right.

Discussion Questions

1. How is leisure space contested in your community?

2. What is the basis for the allocation of recreation resources in your community?

3. Are there still areas of control over leisure by government? How are they justified?

4. What is the basis for political power in the United States? It is really "one person, one vote" or combinations of powerful interests?

5. What are the limits on public investment in leisure resources?

6. What kinds of public provisions are most important in your community? in the nation?

7. Should public recreation be limited to those opportunities the market cannot provide?

Resources

Clarke, J. and Critcher, C. (1985). *The devil makes work: Leisure in capitalist Britain.* Urbana, IL: University of Illinois Press.

Cross, G. (1991). *The social history of leisure since 1600.* State College, PA: Venture Publishing, Inc.

Driver, B.L., Brown, P., and Peterson, G. (Eds.). (1991). *Benefits of leisure.* State College, PA: Venture Publishing, Inc.

Hargreaves, J. (1986). *Sport, power, and culture: A social and historical analysis of popular sport in Britain.* New York, NY: St. Martin's Press.

Hunnicutt, B. (1988). *Work without end: Abandoning shorter hours for the right to work.* Philadelphia, PA: Temple University Press.

Rojek, C. (1985). *Capitalism and leisure theory.* New York, NY: Tavistock.

Wilson, J. (1988). *Politics and leisure.* Boston, MA: Unwin Hyman.

Chapter 13
Gender:
Girls and Boys, Women and Men

In our culture, gender is a central aspect of individual identity. It is also central to the structure and process of society and culture. This chapter explores how and why gender shapes leisure and recreation as well as how and why leisure and recreation may perpetuate or transform beliefs about gender. What is the meaning of gender in relation to notions of sex and sexuality? Why is gender such a powerful force in our lives? How do we explain sex differences? How does gender affect leisure? This chapter concludes with a discussion of whether this difference necessarily means inequality, and a related debate on leisure in patriarchal cultures.

The Meaning of Gender

Gender, sex, and sexuality are distinct but related concepts central to our identities and, hence, our leisure. To understand the meaning of gender, it is useful to first define sex and sexuality. The term *sex* refers to an individual's biological make-up. Specifically, females and males are distinguished by their chromosomes, hormones, and anatomy. *Sexuality*, on the other hand, is an expression of our selfhood and how we perceive ourselves in relationship to others. We are sexual beings, and how we relate to others sexually is a central aspect of our selfhood (see Chapter 14). Sexuality has both biological and social meanings. *Gender* is the set of social expectations attached to biological sex. That is, certain behaviors, physical appearance, social roles, attitudes, expressions of sexuality, and abilities are expected from individuals based on their biological sex. Prescriptions of femininity and masculinity describe what a culture expects from and allows an individual to do based on the perceptions of biological sex.

Some think of gender, sex, and sexuality in essentialist and categorical ways. That is, we believe that gender, sex, and sexuality emanate from a mutually exclusive and dualistic biological basis. An individual is either male or female, heterosexual or homosexual, masculine or feminine. Further, these categories are typically believed to exist as opposites; that is, if masculinity includes being physically aggressive then femininity means being physically passive.

However, while such understandings of sex, sexuality, and gender may seem simple and straight-forward, more recent thinking about these aspects of identity suggests they are quite complex. This is because sex, sexuality, and gender are relational, dynamic, and political. What it means to be female and male, feminine and masculine, heterosexual and homosexual are given meaning in relationship to each other. Further, the meaning of these dimensions of individual identity are constantly changing because they are socially constructed and historically embedded. For example, while today in the United States pink is associated with femininity and blue with masculinity, until the 19th century just the opposite was true.

In addition, while our culture is prone to view gender, sex, and sexuality as "either-or," in reality there is considerable variation among and within individuals in their experiences and expressions of gender, as well as sex and sexuality. For example, heterosexual and homosexual are no longer the only categories or sexual orientation; categories of bisexual and transsexual have been constructed as well. In terms of expressions of gender, *metrosexual* is now a category of masculinity—a heterosexual male who is interested in what are commonly seen as more "feminine" pursuits such as massages, manicures, and fashion. Gender is an ongoing process produced, negotiated, reproduced, and transformed in people's actions across time or history. The concept of "sex role" is sometimes used interchangeably with gender. However, this concept is more limited because gender also is about relationships of power. Gender is not a static role that is given, enacted and neutral, but instead a dynamic construction that produces and politicizes difference.

The Focus on Sex Differences

Much leisure research now focuses on and reports sex differences. Recreation agencies commonly differentiate their programs and services based on sex. While an emphasis on sex differences may highlight social inequalities and different life experiences and allow them to be addressed, such an emphasis also may also serve to reify and perpetuate those differences. The differences come to be seen as natural and inevitable. What is most important in thinking and talking about sex differences is to reflect on why they exist and why there is so much resistance to changing beliefs about them.

Over the years various explanations for sex differences have been put forward. For example, some argue the differences we see between females and males generally—and in recreational interests, behaviors, and experiences specifically—are primarily due to biology. Particularly, anatomical and hormonal differences are believed to underlie differences in individuals' physical, psychological, and emotional functioning. On the one hand, the average higher production of testosterone in males is seen as the source of male competitiveness and aggressiveness. On the other, the higher production of estrogen in females, as well as the fact that only females bear children, is credited for female nurturance. Similarly, the average larger frame of males and the average greater ratio of body fat to muscle in females is used to explain average strength differences in females and males and lower female participation in various forms of physical activity and sport. Such explanations ignore at least two things.

First, while on average females' frames are smaller and their physical strength is less than males today, some females have larger frames and have greater physical strength than some males. Further, as females continue to have opportunities and encouragement to engage in physical activity and sport, the gender gap in physical strength and performance is narrowing with greater gains being made by females. It may be that male physical potential has reached its peak (without the use of performance enhancing drugs) and the upper limits of female physical potential will not be known until females' opportunities to develop such potential are equal to that of males. Hence, beliefs about the biological basis of physical performance differences in males and females are changing. By most measures, there is greater difference within genders than between their means. This notion of "overlapping lines" demonstrates how many focus on between-sex averages rather than the greater variation in size, strength, and speed within either sex.

Secondly, difference does not mean lack of interest or ability. The range of body sizes and strength among males does not mean that smaller or less strong males cannot participate in physical activity and sport. Rather, skills are developed and team sports positions assigned that take advantage of physical attributes.

Nancy Chodorow (1978) provides another explanation for current psychological sex differences. Building on Freudian theory, she asserts that in the first two years of life children begin to develop a sense of their biological sex and the behaviors expected of them. Since mothers have been (and continue to be) the primary caretakers of young children, for boys to develop an *appropriate* sex role identity they need to separate, detach, or become independent from the mother. Such independence is reinforced across childhood and adolescence in a variety of ways. For example, boys are allowed more freedom of movement in their play than girls. Boys who cling too much to their mothers are labeled "momma's boys"—a pejorative term. Therefore, central to boys' sense of self is autonomy and independence.

On the other hand, girls need to stay attached or connected to their mothers to develop an appropriate sex role identity. Such relationality is reinforced by the social environment that encourages girls to think of themselves in relation to others. One example of how girls learn nurturance is that when they are punished for misbehavior, adults are more likely to stress the impact girls' misbehavior has on others rather than breaking rules. Central to girls' sense of self, then, is affiliation and relationality. Chodorow's theory suggests that if the caretaking of children was more equally shared between mothers and fathers or if fathers were the primary caretakers, the development of gender in girls and boys might well differ.

Chodorow's theory also incorporates another explanation for sex differences—socialization. Sex differences and gender are taught, practiced, and learned. We learn gender expectations through the behaviors of females and males and the images of masculinity and femininity presented in books, television, music, families, schools, synagogues, churches, and mosques. We are constantly surrounded by models of, and messages about, what we *should* be like if we are biologically female or male. To deviate from these norms has consequences that can range from teasing to rejection and even serious or life-threatening actions such as sexual assault and gay bashing.

Others contend sex differences are about power and privilege. When differences advantage and disadvantage individuals based on an unequal valuing of those differences, then sex differences and gender are about power. In studying the play of children, Janet Lever (1976) concluded boys are advantaged by their play in ways girls are not. In the play toward which boys are directed, boys learn skills, such as working with large groups, teamwork, negotiating conflict, and competition, that prepares them for economic (i.e., work) roles as adults. The play in which girls are encouraged to engage, on the other hand, is more likely to occur in small groups or dyads and teaches them cooperation and nurturance—skills important for domestic roles, but not for valued and rewarded as economic roles.

Eleanor Metheny (1973) also studied the play of children and youth, particularly their participation in physical activity and sport. She noted Western cultures' constructions of masculinity and femininity have defined gender dualistically (or as opposites) and have assigned to masculinity the prerogative or right to use the body to physically overpower, coerce, or dominate others. Hence, males have the right to engage in activities that require such behavior (e.g., sport, war), while females do not. In fact, female involvement in such activities challenges and threatens constructions of gender and male privilege. It is for this reason, as well as the extent to which involvement in such activity provides access to scarce valuables (i.e., money, prestige, power or influence), that the inclusion of females in masculine activities such as sport or the military is so fiercely contested.

Beliefs about sex differences have such a long history that many have come to see them as natural and universal. However, one does not have to look back far to see how dynamic are images of what it means to be biologically female and male. For example, during the Victorian Era, females were seen as physically, mentally, and emotionally frail and fragile. Physicians advocated girls and women should not engage in anything physically strenuous, mentally challenging, or emotionally demanding as it would damage their reproductive systems and undermine their true purpose in life—motherhood. Such attitudes prevailed among the middle and upper class in particular, who saw working class and poor individuals as more primitive and less developed than themselves. Hence, strenuous labor was acceptable for lower-class women. Being nonsexual and a virgin was also valued for middle- and upper-class males as it was believed that "reckless spending of their seed would lead to the production of runts, feebles, and females" (Ehrenreich & English, 1973). Norms of masculinity and femininity change across time and are strongly shaped by social class, though such beliefs permeate and affect the lives of females and males of all classes and races (Ehrenreich & English, 1973; Henderson, Bialeschki, Shaw & Freysinger, 1996).

Today increasing numbers of females are involved and very successful in physically, mentally, and emotionally demanding activities. In fact, girls' and women's involvement in sport and physical activity is one factor in changing stereotypes of gender, and what it means to be female and male. Also, increasing involvement of some males in nurturant and caregiving activities has provoked many to rethink beliefs about presumed biological differences between the sexes. However, significant inequities based on biological sex still exist in the distribution of opportunities and resources.

Gender, Recreation, and Leisure

Gender is important because it frames our lives—how we define ourselves, others' perceptions and expectations of us, our resources and opportunities, and the distribution of power. In talking about gender we acknowledge the social, cultural, and historical basis of definitions of biological sex. Leisure and recreation are both affected by and affect gender. They reproduce or perpetuate dominant notions of gender in some ways, and challenge, resist, and transform in others.

Considerable research has focused on the gendered experiences of play and recreation in childhood and youth. This research suggests while historical changes have occurred in the play and recreation of girls and boys, there is much continuity as well. For example, just as in the past, males today are more likely to engage in sport and physical activity in childhood and to continue with such participation throughout adolescence and adulthood. Males are more likely to participate in video and computer games. Boys' play and recreation also are likely to involve large groups, have changing leadership, and take place outside or away from the home.

The play and recreation of females, on the other hand, is more likely to be physically passive, involve sport and physical activity where body contact is not required, emphasize physical appearance (what has been called the *glamour-consumer role*), and to take place within or around the home (Henderson, Bialeschki, Shaw & Freysinger, 1996). Marketers continue to advertise different toys for girls and boys, and adults continue to provide girls and boys with different opportunities for play and recreation. Despite the passage of Title IX in the United States in 1972 that requires educational institutions receiving public funds to provide equitable opportunities for females and males, schools continue to struggle with actually meeting this mandate. There seems to be much resistance to sharing the scarce valuables that sport provides (e.g., status, prestige, money). Further, female accomplishments in sport also threaten traditional notions of masculinity and femininity.

Relative to the not-so-distant past, however, expanded opportunities and a greater diversity of role models are now available. While the female high school ice hockey or football player or male synchronized swimmer or cheerleader still garner media attention, such "crossovers" in sex-role performance more often pass without comment. In physical activity and sport, both gains and gaps seem most apparent. In women's professional basketball, select images of the women involved that reproduce stereotypical notions of femininity (e.g., physically attractive, heterosexual, nurturant, motherhood) are promoted for the media. One professional basketball league, the American Basketball League (ABL), and the women's professional soccer league, the Women's United Soccer Association (WUSA), have folded due to a failure to grow as anticipated. Similarly, men today are more likely to say that males should be involved equally in childcare and domestic tasks. Research, however, shows that regardless of their employment status, women continue to be more likely to actually carry responsibility for most of those tasks. In fact, increases in the time males give to household tasks seem to have leveled off.

Such "facts" are important to understanding leisure and recreation participation in adulthood. Studies of adults over the past 20 years have indicated that meanings of leisure vary little by sex. In North America both females and males associate leisure with a perception of choice, lack of obligation or necessity, or relative freedom. However, the "containers" of leisure—that is, forms of activity and the social, temporal, and physical contexts where leisure is experienced—differ by gender. For example, males and females are likely to engage in different physical activities and sports (e.g., females in aerobics and males in weightlifting). In addition, males are still more engaged in physical activity and sport.

Further, women and men often experience the same activities differently. For example, playing with children is more likely to be experienced as *pure leisure* by fathers and *semi-leisure*—a mixture of choice and role obligation—by mothers. This is common even though (or perhaps because!) mothers spend more time with their children in play, regardless of their own employment status or the ages of the children. The consequences of such play also differ for fathers and mothers. One study found the parental satisfaction of fathers was enhanced by play with children while it had no effect on mothers' parental satisfaction (Freysinger, 1989). At the same time, other forms of activity, such as socializing with family and friends, are as likely to be important or highly valued leisure for men as they are for women.

Research has also indicated women are more likely than men to experience leisure when outside the home and not only with children present. For men, home is more often a site of leisure than for women because it is more a place of relative freedom and choice for men. Constructions of gender still tend to place primary responsibility for domestic and childcare tasks on females. Home, then, is a site of more responsibility rather than freedom for many women. Some women may even see staying late at work or working overtime as a more attractive option than going or spending time at home (Hochschild, 1989).

Another container of leisure is time. Here again gender is an important factor. However, a variety of other factors, such as age, social class, race/ethnicity, and employment status, mediate the impact of gender on time for leisure. For example, in general men have the most free time and employed, married women with dependent children the least. However, this varies by social class as affluent women are able to pay others to take care of some childcare and domestic work. Conversely, women and men with lower incomes and less secure jobs may well work two or more jobs, leaving them little free time. Similarly, age shapes leisure since widowed, retired women do not face the *second shift* of the employed working-class single mother with dependent children. In other words, while gender is a powerful force in our lives and leisure, its impact varies as discussed in Chapters 9, 10, and 15.

Does Difference Necessarily Mean Inequality and Oppression?

Three primary perspectives about gender differences have been identified. Some scholars contend few differences between males and females are not socially learned. They advocate changing the structure of society (e.g., in terms of the distribution of resources and opportunities) and seek to reduce the focus on sex differences. Others believe important sex differences exist and the sources of these differences are both biological and sociocultural, such differences will always be with us, and equal opportunity within this social system is most important. Still others accept a biological basis for sex differences and gender, believe that differences are natural and even "God-given," and hence do not acknowledge that gender inequities or sexism exists. They tend to see reformers as the problem.

From the first two perspectives, there is no difference that makes a difference. That is, whatever difference might exist between females and males, and for whatever reasons, it is culture that puts meaning on and attaches value to those differences. For example, the second perspective would say that while females learn to be cooperative and males to be competitive, the problem is not with the learning of this difference but with a society that values competition more than cooperation and that doesn't provide equal rewards. In other words, difference doesn't have to mean inequality and oppression.

However, according to the first perspective the problem is with the social system. Difference is used to justify the stratified distribution of power. It inevitably leads to inequality and oppression because differences define access to resources. Power in North America is dependent on having resources such as material wealth, knowledge and education, and/or fame and prestige. Such resources yield power to determine one's own life and the lives of others. The distribution of power is distinguished by gender, sex, and sexual orientation as well as by economic position. This issue of whether difference necessarily means inequality and oppression is central to the following debate.

Debate: Women are leisure for men and make men's leisure possible.

As suggested earlier, females and males differ in their access to and experience of leisure. Some argue that because of both formal laws and policies as well as changing attitudes, the United States is no longer a sexist society. Others contend sexism permeates everyday lives and social relations because this continues to be a patriarchal society structured to privilege males and disadvantages females. Social relations throughout the society are gendered in inequitable ways. From this perspective, leisure is seen as a realm of life where sexism may be reproduced or perpetuated through relations overtly and implicitly unequal in self-determination.

YES

- Women are the "social organizers" of their family's, including (for those who are married) their husband's, leisure. Women do most of the work in preparing for holidays, vacations, family gatherings, and other social leisure (Bella, 1992).

- Mothers, regardless of their own employment status and age of their children, spend more time with their children and more time in play with their children than do fathers. This potentially provides fathers with more time without childcare responsibilities or more free time. Fathers are also more likely than mothers to pursue their leisure without their children.

- Women work a "second shift," making possible men's leisure by having primary responsibility for the emotional and physical care of children and the physical day-to-day care of the home. It is still women who usually cook the meals, wash the clothes, clean the house, see that homework is done, transport children to activities and doctors' appointments, and have responsibility for the routines of household maintenance. This reduces their free time and increases men's. Some research even indicates that most husbands add to household burden more than relieve it (Baber & Allen, 1992).

- To the extent that pornography depicting females and prostitution with females is pursued as recreational or leisure experiences by men, women provide men with leisure. Further, the penalties for women providing such services are greater than those for men who are consumers of such services (MacKinnon, 1995; Malamuth & Donnerstein, 1984).

- Women and girls are spectators, dancers, ornaments, and cheerleaders at male sporting events. They provide men and boys with recognition, support, and an audience for their displays of physical skill. Their costumes signify that they are sexualized adjuncts to the real event.

- Women serve as escorts (both paid and unpaid) and provide men with enjoyment through their presentation of self (e.g., physical appearance or dress, manner or behavior). They are ornaments to men's presentation of status and power. Why else is appearance so important to the selection of female companions for high-status males? This glamour-consumer role may be perceived as enjoyable but is also work for females. In fact, constructing and maintaining the "ideal" body may actually be hazardous to health (Bordo, 1995).

NO

- While it may be true that most married women with children are primarily responsible for childcare and homemaking, this is not true of all women. There are slowly increasing numbers of families in which men more equally share homemaking and childcare tasks. Also, many women are not married, do not have children, and/or are not involved with men. Their lives and leisure are more independent. Conversely, many men do not have partners to provide such services for them. Both women and men may choose not to be part of an unequal caregiving relationship.

- While in some families women may have primary responsibility for homemaking and childcare, it is inaccurate to say men don't contribute to those families. Men are more likely to be involved in economic roles in families that also support leisure for all family members.

- Some women with traditional role orientations prefer to be the primary caregiving parent and homemaker. They may even discourage spouses from taking such responsibilities. They do not see making leisure available to men as problematic.

- Increased opportunities for independent leisure are available to women, especially for those who have the economic means to purchase childcare and domestic services. All kinds of services are available in the market economy. Now that most adult women are in the paid work force, more are able to use part of their incomes to relieve household burden and purchase their own leisure.

- The market is responding to this change with more leisure opportunities oriented toward women, including women-only clubs, sports, and travel packages. Independent women are a growing leisure market.

- Revised body images of girls and women as strong, adventurous, and active have emerged. Television commercials, popular music, and magazine copy and advertisements increasingly portray women pursuing their own interests and having the right to do so. Women are portrayed as having their own lives rather than just as companions to men.

- It is unfair to say this is all one-way. Men also make possible women's leisure by supporting them financially, escorting them to leisure and recreation events, providing protection in some threatening environments, and paying for recreational and leisure events. Most couples negotiate their leisure choices.

- Leisure can be a realm in which females resist male domination and take independent actions. Greater economic independence can lead to greater self-determination in all of life. This is especially the case in a society in which purchasing power is equated with choice. The new images of women's leisure are more and more supportive of opportunities that express the freedom and empowerment of women. The culture is at least more ambivalent about gender relations despite many sites of continued sexism.

Discussion Questions

1. How is sexuality shaped by gender roles?

2. Give examples of how children learn sex roles.

3. Does gender have to mean power and privilege? Are there situations that are gendered but equal?

4. How can the greater involvement of fathers in parenting change the gender socialization of boys? of girls?

5. Are there significant changes in childhood with girls more involved in larger-group play and competition? Should sports be sex-segregated for young children?

6. Are there any social situations that are not gendered? in which there is no determinative awareness of gender identities? Give examples.

7. How do the high divorce rate and the greater number of single adults affect gender roles? shared custody after divorce? adult leisure?

8. Do most young women prefer to be ornaments rather than agents? What is your evidence? What are the implications for leisure?

9. How does leisure provide possibilities for women to resist secondary gender roles?

10. Is exercise more for appearance or health? Are there gender differences?

References and Resources

Aitchison, C.C. (2003). *Gender and leisure: Social and cultural perspectives.* New York, NY: Routledge.

Baber, K.M. and Allen, K. (1992). *Women and families: Feminist reconstructions.* New York, NY: Guilford Press.

Bella, L. (1992). *The Christmas imperative.* Halifax, NS: Fernwood Publishing.

Blair, S.L. and Lichter, D.T. (1991). Measuring the division of household labor: Gender segregation of housework among American couples. *Journal of Family Issues, 12,* 91–113.

Bloch, P.H. (1993). Involvement with adornments as leisure behavior: An exploratory study. *Journal of Leisure Research, 25,* 245–262.

Bonen, A. and Shaw, S.M. (1995). Recreational exercise participation and aerobic fitness in men and women: An analysis of data from a national survey. *Journal of Sports Medicine, 13,* 297–303.

Bordo, S. (1995). Reading the slender body. In N. Tuana and R. Tong (Eds.), *Feminism and philosophy: Essential readings in theory, reinterpretations, and application* (pp. 467–489). Boulder, CO: Westview Press.

Chodorow, N. (1978). *The reproduction of mothering: Psychoanalysis and the sociology of gender.* Berkeley, CA: University of California Press.

Ehrenreich, B. and D. English. (1973). *Complaints and disorders: The sexual politics of sickness.* New York, NY: The Feminist Press.

Frederick, J.C. and Shaw, S.M. (1995). Body image as a leisure constraint: Examining the experience of aerobic exercise classes for young women. *Leisure Sciences, 17,* 57–73.

Freysinger, V.J. (1989). Leisure with children and parental satisfaction: Further evidence of a sex difference in the experience of adult roles and leisure. *Journal of Leisure Research, 26,* 212–226.

Green, E., Hebron, S. and Woodward, D. (1990). *Women's leisure, what leisure?* London, UK: Macmillan Education Ltd.

Henderson, K.A. (1994). Broadening an understanding of women, gender, and leisure. *Journal of Leisure Research, 26,* 1–7.

Henderson, K.A., Bialeschki, M.D., Shaw, S.M., and Freysinger, V.J. (1996). *Both gains and gaps: Feminist perspectives on women's leisure.* State College, PA: Venture Publishing, Inc.

Herridge, K.L., Shaw, S.M., and Mannell, R.C. (2003). An exploration of women's leisure within heterosexual romantic relationships. *Journal of Leisure Research, 35*(3), 274-291.

Hochschild, A. (1989). *The second shift: Working parents and the revolution at home.* New York, NY: Viking.

James, K. (2000). "You can feel them looking at you." — The experiences of adolescent girls at swimming pools. *Journal of Leisure Research, 32*(2), 262–280.

Larson, R.W., Gillman, S.A., and Richards, M.H. (1997). Divergent experiences of family leisure: Fathers, mothers, and young adolescents. *Journal of Leisure Research, 29*, 78–97.

Lever, J. (1976). Sex differences in the games children play. *Social Problems, 23*, 478–487.

MacKinnon, K. (1995). Sexuality, pornography, and method: Pleasure under patriarchy. In N. Tuana and R. Tong (Eds.), *Feminism and philosophy: Essential readings in theory, reinterpretations, and application* (pp. 134–161). Boulder, CO: Westview Press.

Malamuth, N.M. and Donnerstein, E. (1984). *Pornography and sexual aggression.* Orlando, FL: Academic Press.

McRobbie, A. (1991). *Feminism and youth culture: From 'Jackie' to 'just seventeen.'* London, UK: Macmillan Education Ltd.

Metheny, E. (1973). Symbolic forms of movement: The feminine image in sport. In M. Hart (Ed.), *Sport in the sociocultural process* (pp. 227–290). Dubuque, IA: William C. Brown.

Shaw, S.M. (1999). Gender and leisure. In E.L. Jackson and T.L. Burton (Eds.), *Leisure studies: Prospects for the 21st century* (pp. 271–282). State College, PA: Venture Publishing, Inc.

Wearing, B. (1998). *Leisure and feminist theory.* Thousand Oaks, CA: Sage.

Chapter 14
Sexuality

Chapter 13 introduced definitions of sex, gender, and sexuality. *Sex* is the biological identification as male or female. *Gender* is the socially constructed set of expectations, roles, and symbols attached to biological sex. It is specific to a society and, therefore, is varied and changing. *Sexuality* is the expression of biological sex in gendered modes of behavior and communication. This chapter focuses on those expressions, especially as they are socially located in leisure. The central theme is variety—in forms, contexts, uses, values, and meanings.

Sexuality and Identity

Sexual identification is fundamental to everything we do. We are unlikely to remember a time when we did not know ourselves to be gendered—little girls or boys—even though the meanings might be strange, mysterious, and even arbitrary. From early childhood learning to be male or female makes a difference. Many of the old prescriptions have changed. For the most part, it is now okay, even rewarded, when girls develop and demonstrate physical competence. Conversely, aesthetic aptitudes may be encouraged in boys. We hear less about "tomboys" and "sissies." Nevertheless, we also know there are differences that go everywhere and affect everything.

More than gender, we also know we are sexual beings. Especially as we enter adolescent and adult years, sexuality becomes a dimension of almost everything. We have sexual dreams and daydreams, hopes and fantasies, apprehensions and fears, images and uncertainties. As teens we are powerfully sexual and deeply insecure as to just what it means. We look around and see conflicting images. We look ahead and see little we can count on. We look at ourselves and see multiple meanings of being sexual. All this has become more complex in a time when greater diversity in sexual expression has come to be recognized.

It is difficult enough to understand and adapt to normative sex roles—the sets of social expectations that go with gender. Sexuality is something more: It is a biology of identification and sexual relatedness. It is learned behavior that is taught in ways filled with ambiguity and ambivalence. It is fascinating and fearful, fundamental and surrounded with taboos. It has meanings that are biological and social in ways no one seems fully able to disentangle.

It is no wonder many people retreat to a kind of "essentialism" in which biological identification is said to explain everything. The argument is females and males are biologically different and, as a consequence, different in every other significant way. As presented in Chapter 13, this argument does not hold up in a world in which nothing is *that* clearly divided. Rather, we have come to learn who we are as gendered beings. Further, we are continually learning to explore and express our sexuality.

For example, sexual orientation is not just a matter of either/or. Most males and females are lifelong heterosexuals, some lifelong homosexuals, some bisexual, and some experience shifting orientations through the life course. There are stories of gradual discovery and of sudden revelations. There are lone and lonely pilgrimages and the influence of significant other persons. Further, in different historical epochs in European-American as well as other cultures, sexual orientation and expression have been fostered, required, prohibited, flaunted, repressed, hidden, and honored in different ways. Sexual orientation is complex, not simple.

Learning Sexuality

The basic premise is that we learn sexuality. Children are taught that certain sexual actions are taboo. As a result, things sexual become hidden and communication is repressed. In many cultures, males are given tacit consent to be aggressive and even predatory toward females, and females are warned over and over that they must defend themselves, and their family's "honor," against such activity. This creates an overarching set of gendered orientations that intensifies curiosity and secrecy, stifles exploration, and inhibits communication. Such a system may have had a biological basis prior to contraceptive technology, but now is learned from a powerful cultural system. There are always changes in sexual cultures, partly propelled by violations of the codes. There are also deep contradictions between the messages of moral culture or prohibition and a media culture of exploitation. The messages of home, church, television advertising, and MTV may be profoundly conflicting.

This is no casual or peripheral concern. Everything is sexual. How we dress, walk, talk, work, play, and everything else have gender identification, and consequently, some degree of sexuality. One of the great changes in Western societies is women and men may be together almost any time and anywhere. We work together, study together, and play together without former rules of separation or family protection. Sexual identities are one theme of all sorts of conversations, exchanges, gestures, and symbols at work and play. Flirtation not only takes place at the cocktail party but also in the mailroom and around the watercooler. Sexuality is more than intercourse. It is a dimension of all kinds of human relatedness, in its suppression as well as expression. It is, after all, inextricably who we are.

Social Change

The context of sexuality changed radically in the last 100 years. The 1890s is often identified as the beginning of the "sexual revolution" in North American culture. Increases in divorce rates, women's self-determination, public discourse about sex, medical attention to the sexuality of both men and women, and other changes became more explicit. In the 1920s, women's sexuality was symbolized by more revealing attire and acceptance in leisure sites such as bars and night clubs. Then, the technologies of contraception began to disconnect sexual intercourse from reproduction. Sexual activity was more accepted for its own sake—even for pleasure—which also disconnected it from marriage and the family. Sexuality has become more open, accepted, public, and diverse. Some try to reinstitute the "old ways," but are fighting a rearguard action against a changed culture.

The profound changes are seen in increased divorce rates close to 50%, more singleness in adult years, open diversity in sexual orientations and styles, twice as many adolescents active sexually as in 1950, greater use of explicit sexuality in media, and most women now out of the home and in the paid work force while few men are in the home as primary caretakers. Whether or not this adds up to a "sexual revolution" or major evolutionary change is less important than the very different culture in which young males and females now learn to be sexual.

Sexuality and Play

As analyzed in Chapter 13 and summarized here, our sexuality is central to who we are no matter where we are. We take, or play, many different roles through the life course. In all, we have sexual identities. In most, we have sexual purposes, even though they may be primarily symbolic display. We do very little in social settings in which we are unaware of how other persons read the symbolic codes of our actions and presentations. For most, we are always aware of the presence or absence of sexually identified others (Goffman, 1959). We "notice" others and respond to whether and how they notice us.

Children's Play

Ways in which children's play is gendered have been presented in Chapters 9 and 13. Even in a time in which new opportunities in sports and other recreation have been opened to females, these differences remain. A dramatic increase in sports participation by girls is far more than a temporary response to legal mandate. It involves different images of females and female bodies as strong and competent.

Sexuality in play, however, is something more. There is play with and curiosity about one's own body. There is precocious sexual play in which children experiment with what they fancy to be adult behaviors. There is direct fondling, kissing, and physical exploration. Just how first-graders become aware of and intrigued by kissing, hugging, and grabbing may be difficult to analyze. Sexuality is, after all, all around them, and they learn early on that they are significantly gendered. It is clear, in any event, that explicitly sexual behavior does not wait for puberty. Further, some young children are coerced into sexual behavior by those physically or socially more powerful. Sexuality may turn from being playful to victimization—even in the family.

Most important, however, is the fact that at every age we are aware of gender images and identifications and something of what they mean for how we should behave. This is demonstrated by the observation that most play becomes different if both sexes are involved. Even when play roles are not differentiated by sex, and they often are at very early ages, interaction with those who are seen as "different" affects the modes of play. In play, children are continually learning and reinforcing early versions of what it means to be female and male.

Teens

Some cultures do not identify a long "waiting period" of adolescence in which those who are sexually able are still defined as in a period of preparation. In North American culture, the teen years are a time in which there is acute self-consciousness about appearance. This is manifested in all the symbolic hats, shirts, jackets, shoes, and other apparel that signify membership in particular cliques, gangs, or cultures. It is also evident in concern about the body. Females especially are expected to be conscious of the body images the media exhibits as appropriately feminine and even sexy. The inability of most teens to meet such rigid standards leads to feelings of inadequacy and eating disorders among females and "macho" behaviors among males in vain attempts to meet the presumed standard. All of this for both males and females is in the felt "gaze" of the "other;" the leisure of adolescent females in particular may be strongly shaped by the "gaze" or surveillance of males (Frederick & Shaw, 1995; James, 2000). To demonstrate sexual acceptability is a central aim of social behavior, self-presentation, and concern with appearance.

Play, then, is often display. Looking right may be as important as skill. Play takes place in the sexually charged, if often ambiguous, atmosphere of school and leisure. Add to this the insecurity of those who are uncertain or different in the nature and orientation of their sexuality, and adolescence becomes a period of both sexual preoccupation and anxiety. One fundamental developmental task, however, is to learn what it means to become a man or women with those of the same and other genders. As with many other aspects of development, there are losers as well as winners in this complex game.

The central social environment of this process is leisure. It is out of the classroom and away from the family that much sexual exploration and expression occurs. It may be at a party, shopping mall, concert, sporting event, or just "hanging out" or driving around. Music, clothing, car decor, and language are all symbols of the self-presentation that attempts to identify the self as an acceptable, correct, and even sexual being. This is not peripheral. It is central to self-development, and to becoming a full person in a society still ambivalent—if not confused—about sexuality.

Human development has its central dilemmas. The persistent dilemma is said to be between challenge and security (Gordon, Gaitz & Scott, 1976). This dilemma is expressed most acutely in the sexual dimensions of teen life in drives toward both acceptance and independence. The peer group has standards of sexual expression and even performance. The family generally has more protective and conservative standards. As a result, this central preoccupation becomes more and more separated from the family and immersed in the peer culture. That culture, filled with sexual symbolism, is inconsistent as to how sexual identity should be exhibited and expressed by females and males in a variety of settings. Further, there is the mixing of social norms, body prescriptions, and personal self-definitions in this complex process of becoming. In almost every social setting, there is a continual testing of who one is and is becoming. For the most part, the social contexts are both gendered and sexual. It is far more than coping with changing bodies and hormones. It is how one walks, talks, dresses, dances, drives, parks, and explores various sorts of touching. It is public and private, aggressive and protective, bold and fearful. Whatever else, it is leisure in its most intense and significant mode.

Adults

As already indicated, adult sexuality exists in a social milieu of profound change. The "women's movement" is based on comprehensive change as most adult women have entered the paid work force. This gives them greater mobility, wider social environments with those of the same and other sex, and fuller resources for action. Families in developed economies have fewer children on average and in more compact periods. Sexuality has become more open for both sexes. Sexual orientations and expressions are more diverse and accessible. The media are saturated with sexually based images. Sexual interaction is no longer restricted to monogamous marriage. In addition, there is acute conflict among those who would regain old standards, those who embrace new freedom and opportunity, and those seeking to create new ways of channeling sexuality.

Expectations for relationships seem to be rising in the midst of such change. In marriage and other committed relationships, partners are expected to be lovers, leisure companions, and supporters of personal development, all while meeting the traditional economic and household role expectations. It no wonder up to half of marriages end in divorce, and many others become "arrangements" without significant intimacy and sharing. It is possible relationships fail more because of higher expectations than indifference. In any case, many social settings, especially for leisure, are still based on the premise that people come in couples. Recreational travel arrangements are priced for "double occupancy." Dinner parties are seated for even numbers. And for the most part, people are expected to leave with those with whom they came.

Despite all the pair-based social arrangements, more adults are now single. They may be single, by choice or circumstances, for a lifetime. They may be looking. They may be in a time of transition between relationships. They may have ended a relationship or been left by a partner. They may be divorced or widowed. There are singles throughout the life course—and the society is still learning to cope with their status, social needs, and sexuality. Both public and market providers are responding to this population segment. They are not only viable markets but they also may be more leisure-oriented than those with multiple household roles. Further, there are singles who are living alone, singles with resident children, singles in group housing, and singles who are mobile and transient. They are not all young. Many are poor. Some are lonely as well as alone; some are quite integrated socially. They are all persons with their diverse social needs and values. One important aspect of their condition is singles' sexuality is defined somewhat differently from those presumed to be half of a couple in a committed relationship. Yet, as for all adults, there are sexual dimensions to just about every relationship. As introduced in the chapter on the development of consumerism, leisure environments and consumption have become the preferred context of romantic relationships and events (Illouz, 1997).

One set of problems emerges when that sexual dimension is used to exercise power and control. Since sexuality is a social construction as well as a biological element of life, it can be defined in a particular situation to the advantage of those with the power to define. This is evident in college and professional athletic events in which females are given roles of objectified figures in brief and tight costumes to enhance the entertainment for the male gaze. The male power to define gender in sports/entertainment events rewards females only when they accept particular sexualized roles. In more informal settings, the male patrons at a bar may greet and interact with a small group of women as though their arrival was a sexual gesture. Their intent to discuss some work issues away from the office environment would be disrupted and even thwarted by the looks and remarks of men who impose sexuality on the situation. In competition swimming, for example, the attire required to lessen water drag may be defined sexually by males in ways that distract female athletes from their sport performance. In general, in our culture it is possible for males to sexualize a social situation. The party, bar or club, or even sports event is defined as an opportunity for demonstrating and gratifying male sexual pleasure regardless of the wishes or purposes of females. As simple an act as "dressing up" is defined by men as being done for their visual sexual pleasure and even as an invitation to further interaction. Any social situation can be defined by those with the greatest social power. In gendered events, males usually have that power unless subverted by female resistance (Wearing, 1996). It is no wonder that women may prefer to avoid such environments when they do not have equal social power to define symbolic meanings or physical power to determine physical outcomes. Legal definitions of sexual harassment may be partly developed for the workplace, but tend to be much more fluid and potentially degrading or even dangerous in the leisure setting. Even in relatively neutral settings, many males tend to take for granted this power to define interaction sexually. The extreme of this use of power is in the "date rape" that may involve physical force as well as alcohol and drugs. Of course these "typical" power relations may well be altered in leisure contexts where heterosexuality is not the norm.

Issues associated with sexual orientation are embedded in misunderstanding, prejudice, discrimination, and even violence. Despite increased recognition of gay, lesbian, bisexual, and other orientations, there remain legal and cultural definitions and biases that impact the lives and especially the sexuality of nonheterosexuals in every aspect of life. Homophobia takes forms, both overt and covert, that make life for nonheterosexuals a constant practice of protection. Leisure is one realm of life in which communities of acceptance and exchange can be developed. Conflict over sexual norms, however, continue to make fuller understanding and inclusion difficult. At the very least, the assumptions of heterosexuality as normative are challenged by a diversity of sexual orientations. In addition, sexuality under conditions of conflict becomes even more problematic and central to development and expression.

Styles of Sexuality

Sexuality takes many different forms in contemporary society. Again, these meanings are socially constructed, generally by those who benefit from the definition. Such constructions are based a long history of heterosexual relationships still undergoing change.

Sex as a Contest

Studies of courtship in the 1950s were full of references to the "double standard." This concept presupposed that gender roles had shaped the sexual expectations and norms of females and males quite differently. Males were expected to be aggressors who would gain as much compliance as possible from females. In the language of sport, males were said to "score" if they were successful in having intercourse with females while avoiding any commitment that might be enforced in court. Females, on the other hand, were expected to be passive and even strategic defenders. They were responsible for protecting themselves from male aggression while still engaging in appropriate social interaction.

In this uneven contest, the responsibility for the level of sexual interaction rested on the female. However, young women who permitted intercourse were labeled "easy" or worse and often named as trophies in male social contexts. As a result, males were likely to engage in intercourse with females they did not intend to marry. Conversely, females were most likely to have intercourse with males they did intend to marry. With the added potential cost of pregnancy, the contest was a much more serious game for females than males. Further, the power to gain one's ends, physical or social, was not equal.

Even the term "courting" now seems outmoded. Both the expectations and contexts of sexual expression outside of marriage have changed. Sexual activity begins earlier for a large percentage of teens. In some subcultures the question has become "Why not?" rather than "Why?" Couples live together, sometimes for convenience more than as a trial relationship. Just as important, women students have become more decisive about their own lives and less willing to allow men to define every situation in terms of their constructed privilege and power. As women increasingly have lives with goals other than marriage and motherhood, they enter the contest with greater equality in resources.

Nevertheless, there are indications the game is not over. Despite ideologies of equality and self-determination, sexual intercourse is still defined by some as a conquest. It is something less than a fully shared relationship when there remain aims of winning, scoring, and social prestige accompanying "success." A high-prestige date may be a "trophy" for either young men or women. When that prestige, based on social position or physical attributes, is used to obtain sexual compliance, then sexual activity becomes a kind of "commodity" even when the exchange is not in money. Sexuality may be in display as well as action, in public gestures of compliance rather than actual intercourse. The basic meaning of such sexuality may be in the contest rather than the developing relationship.

Some sexual interaction may be clearly defined as nonserious. In the process of exploring relationships for their own sake rather than with power agendas, there may be such playful activity as "flirting." The little drama of "What if?" may be played out—sometimes in moments—with both persons knowing they do not mean it. There are times and places when sexuality may be a dimension of interaction in a playful game with no winners or losers. At these moments, sexuality is truly leisure—not a contest.

Sex as a Commodity

Some say that sex work is the "oldest profession." More likely the priesthood is older. Forms of prostitution make sexual activity a commodity for sale as an economic transaction. With illegality raising the price, men, women, and children sell their sexual participation quite directly on the streets of cities and through brokers who also manage the services of more expensive companions and escorts. In some cities in Europe and Asia and near Las Vegas, the sex industry is licensed, regulated, and advertised. It may be seen as a kind of leisure service for the purchaser. Studies indicate some purchasers prefer to buy the activity rather than negotiate with commitments of time or emotional involvement. Others prefer activities outside the range accepted by most voluntary partners.

Traditional prostitution is only a small part of the sex industry, however. There are clubs with explicitly sexual entertainment in styles that attract particular clienteles. They may be strip clubs with female performers, shows oriented to homosexual patrons, and clubs where the public activity is a prelude to other backstage action. The alternative newspaper in a midwest city may have a half page of classified ads offering a variety of sexual occasions for a price. Twice the space may be devoted to similar ads for escort and companion services. Some European college towns are known for their student sex trades that attract visiting participants. In the United States, the industry employs students, typically female, working to pay the bills. At airports all over the world, free visitor guides have advertising for "escorts," "massage parlors," and special clubs. "Sex tourism" in some form is found almost anywhere as persons seek sexual experience in the relative anonymity of a distant city or resort. The infamous sex tourism in Bangkok, based on leaves from the nearby Vietnam War, expanded into a variety of forms, including the virtual slavery of young girls sold from their rural villages. All this and more is the direct part of the sex industry frequently linked with leisure businesses in urban entertainment, gambling meccas, and tourist destinations. Engagement in the industry is frequently not voluntary—especially for the young or poor.

More inclusively, the sex industry uses many other ways to sell sex on the market. There are "R" and "X" movies and videos. Some video shops specialize in pornography, while others have an age-restricted annex. Magazines are edited for a variety of sexual styles, preferences, and orientations. In tourism there is everything from the explicit package through the singles-oriented Club Med to the cruise ship for older singles with mild hints of shipboard romance despite the usual 10:1 sex ratio.

Sexuality is at least one, if not the central, dimension of most entertainment. As suggested earlier, even sports contests are augmented with females in sexualized attire and dance routines. The fantasy lives of soap opera figures move from one sexual relationship to another. Magazines on supermarket stands try to attract buyers with hinted revelations about the sexual activities of celebrities. Even the most conventional tourist packages frequently picture the old "sun, sand, and sex" appeals. Television advertising employs all kinds of sexual images and symbols to sell everything from cars to toothpaste. Music now uses videos with often extremely sexual images and actions, often only vaguely related to the music. Parents and grandparents complain about the sexually saturated atmosphere in which their teens and preteens live. They may ignore the reality that their own media environment is also filled with sex designed to market something—directly or indirectly. Even business deals and political pacts may be sealed and celebrated with the expense-account sexual encounter.

The sex industry is not biased as to orientation. It responds to demand from any viable market and creates demand with all sorts of new opportunities. It is important, however, to recognize the largest segment of the industry involves females trading some kind of sexual compliance for money. In most industry contexts, males with dominant economic and political power exercise that power over women. An extreme is found when fathers in extreme poverty sell daughters into sexual subjugation for the survival of the rest of the family. Even highly paid performers still meet the tastes and demands of males who desire the power they can purchase. As in sexual contests, males and females seldom come with equal resources and power. With few exceptions, the sex industry exhibits a profound gender-based exploitation that permeates the entire enterprise.

Sex as Leisure

If sex as work implies it is marketed for a price and used for commercial ends, then sex as leisure suggests it primarily for its own sake, for the experience. Of course, real life is seldom that clearcut. Commonly sexual activity is one part of a more comprehensive and complex relationship. There may be multiple meanings in sexual interaction related to the nature of the relationship, social status, and other external outcomes. Nonetheless, analyzing sexual activity as recreational or relational does focus a basic issue.

Recreational Sex

One traditional theme of sexual ethics in Western culture insists sexual activity be serious—for greater ends such as reproduction or bonding in marriage. There is, however, another approach to sexual expression that defines it primarily as a pleasure medium. Sexual activity, with its intense and varied potential for physical pleasure, is defined as recreation—a self-contained kind of activity. The satisfaction from a sexual encounter, as in any other recreational game, comes from the immediate experience. It may, like a sport, combine elements of skill mastery, physical expression, diversion from role requirements, and communication with another person. The satisfaction is both intrinsic and social, but the experience itself is foremost.

Sexual activity may be recreation in the sense that it allows the participant to emerge more fit for other activities and responsibilities. As in an athletic event, there may be moments of "flow" in which the self is merged into the experience and awareness of time disappears. From this perspective, sexual activity is worth doing for its own sake without reference to its place in building relationships, creating the family, or cementing committed relationships. Especially since the introduction of contraceptives has largely disconnected heterosexual intercourse from reproduction, sexual activity has become less "serious" in its meanings and consequences. The possibility of sex for its own sake is a reality. Further, the play element of sex leads to display in which sexual relationships become symbolic of social status and even adult independence.

Some analysts argue a "new hedonism" has become the reigning sexual ethic. Sexual expression is seen as play—self-contained in its meaning and a particularly intense form of social leisure. The primary meaning of the act is in the experience rather than in external goals or consequences. It may be a game with implicit rules and outcomes confined to the single event. Even the spread of HIV/AIDS and its loss of immunological defenses have brought about practices of caution rather than abstinence. Multipartner recreational sex is not as risk-free as formerly assumed and requires even more careful protection. The potentially fatal results of casual encounters, however, have not ended recreational sexual activity.

Relational Sex

Ample evidence suggests sex has become a preoccupation in American culture, even a commodity to be sold and to stimulate buying. Some see this
development as a retreat into self-centered indulgence, while others applaud
a greater emphasis on freedom and self-expression. The two opposing camps
can be identified as those who espouse sex for its own sake versus those who
believe sex is one dimension of fuller relationships. Some stress pleasure, and
others personal and social responsibility.

Defining sexuality as something more than physical pleasure does not
imply a negative attitude toward sexuality. Sexual activity can be and frequently is deeply enjoyable and intensely satisfying. Further, sexuality is a
profound part of human selfhood that needs to be accepted, understood, and
developed along with other elements. We are sexual beings as well as social,
cultural, decisive, embodied, thinking, self-conscious, and responsible beings.
If life is good, then our sexuality is good.

Nevertheless, sexual expression seems to be different from tennis in more
than the amount of space required. Sexual relations involve two persons—
not just two bodies. Various forms of sexual interaction are demonstrations
of affection and intimacy—not just bodily exercises. Intimacy such as sexual
intercourse is enjoyable. It is also important for the development and maintenance of significant relationships. It takes place in the context of such relationships and is an expression of the quality of the relationship. It is a sharing of
bodies and emotions—not just a using of the other.

As one dimension of a stable or growing relationship, sexual expression
may be termed *relational.* It is more than an obligation. It is chosen as an
expression of a multifaceted relationship of sharing and communicating. It has
meaning intrinsic to the experience, but is also embedded in the ongoing
relationship. Intimacy is more than physical; it is a full sharing of oneself with
another. It is trust, communication, companionship, interdependence, commitment, and physical expression. It is part of a full relationship. It is more than
doing something together; it is a demonstration of relatedness, and a medium
of communication as well as pleasure. In addition, it may change, reflecting the
career of the relationship as well as the trajectory of personal development
of each partner.

Debate: Sex can be recreation.

YES

- Sex is a physical and emotional interaction with its meaning in the moment. It is immediate and self-authenticating. It is experience diminished by outside dimensions and distractions.

- Sexual activity is enhanced by the attraction of novelty. It becomes dull when routinized and repetitious. Sexual activity is heightened by a variety of partners, settings, and symbolic contexts. It is an exploration, not just more of the same.

- Sex is an event with preparation, culmination, and recollection. It is like a game in containing its own meaning.

- Like other recreation, sex has performance elements. One may become more skillful and demonstrate that skill through a sequence of encounters, settings, and relationships.

- Contraception has largely compartmentalized sexual activity for heterosexuals. There are still consequences and even dangers, but that is true for many kinds of activity. In sex as in rock-climbing, there are devices and techniques for minimizing the dangers.

- It is silly to try to make something that special out of sexuality in a culture saturated with it. Sexual activity may have been something special and almost sacred once, but no longer. Sexual symbols are continual in all the media. It is impossible to put the magic genie back in the bottle.

- Sex industries are now too powerful and pervasive to suppress. They may be regulated, but will continue to offer a spectrum of opportunities in every culture and a variety of markets.

- Sexuality is part of our species nature—not simply an instrument of social institutions such as the family. It has a life of its own.

NO

- Sexuality is not separate from the whole person. It is integrated into our selfhood. We are social beings. Our sexuality is one dimension of that nature of communicative and sharing relationships.

- Sex separated from fuller relationships becomes exploitative—the using of one person by another. As such, it expresses inequalities of social power, most often the use of females by males.

- Exploitative sex frequently involves coercion—emotional or physical. A definition of sexuality concentrated on the self with others to be used for pleasure opens the door to the exercise of social, economic, or physical power over the relatively weak. It violates any ethic of the worth of every human being and of fundamental self-determination.

- Sex is most pleasurable when in the context of fuller relationships. It is the deep expression of intimacy, not just coordinated physical action. It is most fulfilling with dimensions of trust and a history of relating.

- No technology can totally separate sexual activity from conception or sexually transmitted diseases. It is still best to know one's sexual partners well.

- Sex is not a contest; it is intimate sharing. The experience is one of a union of body and emotions in a demonstrated relationship. It is not winning a contest and displaying the trophy.

- Sexual expression develops and changes with a developing relationship. It parallels changes in a relationship through the life course. It may enrich and consolidate a relationship, yet has the potential of novelty and renewal. It is a dimension of the wholeness of life. It is who we are, not just something we do.

Discussion Questions

1. Is there any part of life in which gender and sexuality are totally irrelevant? What and how?

2. What are the most important contexts in which we learn who we are as gendered beings?

3. Is sexual orientation genetically determined, inborn, socially learned, or a complex process? What is your evidence?

4. How is leisure central to the social development of teens?

5. Is there still a double standard? Do sexual norms and practices change as cultures change?

6. Is this now a sex-saturated society? If so, what are the implications?

7. Is the sex industry growing? Where and how?

8. What is different for adult singles socially and sexually? in leisure orientations?

9. How has entertainment become sexualized? for whom? Give examples.

10. Do the rules of sexual expression change with marriage? How and why?

11. What forms and expressions of sexuality are rewarded or penalized? Why and for whom?

12. Is sexuality still the least understood and most emotionally charged aspect of life? If so, why?

References and Resources

Blackshaw, T. (2003). *Leisure life: Myth, masculinity, and modernity.* London: Routledge.

Chapkis, W. (1997). *Live sex acts: Women performing erotic labor.* New York, NY: Routledge.

Frederick, J.C. and Shaw, S.M. (1995). Body image as a leisure constraint: Examining the experience of aerobic exercise classes for young women. *Leisure Sciences, 17,* 57–73.

Goffman, E. (1959). *The presentation of self in everyday life.* Garden City, NY: Doubleday.

Gordon, C., Gaitz, C., and Scott, J. (1976). Leisure and lives: Personal expressivity across the life span. In R. Binstock and E. Shanas (Eds.), *Handbook of aging and the social sciences.* New York, NY: Van Nostrand Reinhold.

Henderson, K.A., Bialeschki, M.D., Shaw, S.M., and Freysinger, V.J. (1996). *Both gains and gaps: Feminist perspectives on women's leisure.* State College, PA: Venture Publishing, Inc.

Illouz, E. (1997). *Consuming the romantic utopia: Love and the cultural contradictions of capitalism.* Berkeley, CA: University of California Press.

James, K. (2000). "You can feel them looking at you." The experiences of adolescent girls at swimming pools. *Journal of Leisure Research, 32*(2), 262–280.

Messner, M. (1992). *Power at play: Sports and the problem of masculinity*. Boston, MA: Beacon Press.

Money, J. and Tucker, P. (1975). *Sexual signatures: On being a man or a woman*. Boston, MA: Little, Brown.

Stockard, J. and Johnson, M. (1980). *Sex roles: Sex inequality and sex role development*. Englewood Cliffs, NJ: Prentice Hall.

Walby, S. (1990). *Theorizing patriarchy*. Oxford, UK: Blackwell.

Wearing, B. (1996). *Gender: The pleasure and pain of difference*. Melbourne, Australia: Longman.

Chapter 15

Ethnicity, Race, Social Class, and Leisure

Our lives and leisure are strongly shaped not only by age and gender but also by ethnicity, race, and social class. They frame leisure interests, activity participation, resources, and opportunities. Ethnicity, race, and social class are dimensions of personal identity that are socially constructed; that is, society gives meaning and value to customs and practices, skin color and other physical features, and levels of education and types of occupations. Hence, like gender and age, these dimensions of personal and social identity are political issues in that they stratify power (i.e., influence over self and others) and privilege (i.e., advantages). In this society, these factors make a significant difference.

Further, those who due to their gender, age, ethnicity/race, and social class are part of the dominant culture and therefore most advantaged in terms of access to resources and opportunities are often unaware of their privileged status and advantage. They are likely to take their position for granted and ascribe their success largely to their own and their family's hard work, effort, abilities, or talents. While individuals may not feel they have more power and privilege because of race, ethnicity, or social class, they still have the advantage of having the "right" identification in a social system that structurally distributes access to resources and power according to factors other than personal merit. For example, current tax laws advantage those with higher incomes when tax breaks are given to those who can afford to buy a home and even a second home. Further, college students from low-income households are less likely to be helped by scholarships and other forms of financial aid than those with higher-income backgrounds. Investigations also show race is a factor in lending decisions of banks, so Latino-Americans, for example, have a more difficult time obtaining a mortgage or business loan than European-Americans even when relevant qualifications are identical. In the realm of leisure, some country clubs, fraternal groups, and business associations continue to exclude on the basis of race and ethnicity (Chideya, 1995).

There are still many examples of racism within intercollegiate and professional sport in positional segregation and assumptions about the "natural ability" and particular characteristics of African-Americans. Some argue, "Things aren't so bad" because they are "much better than they used to be." It is true, for example, that participation in many (but not all) competitive sports has been opened to athletes of all racial identification (Collins, 2003). Improvement, however, does not make any racism acceptable. In a country where equality of opportunity is proclaimed as a founding principle, any discrimination is a violation of core values. Further, equality of opportunity requires more than noble words.

Power, privilege, and resources vary across time and situation in ways that combine social position factors. Social position factors are additive and cumulative. Children from African-American families with college educations and stable incomes have far more opportunity than those from poverty-stricken families. Yet, race and gender still make a difference in the corporate world in which jobs are tracked by race and "glass ceilings" or when limits to advancement in employment exist for women. Ethnicity, race, and social class intersect each other, and need to be considered along with gender, age, and sexual orientation when explaining the distribution of power, privilege, resources and opportunities—even in the realm of leisure.

What Are Ethnicity and Race?

The whole conception of ethnic groups is so complex and vague that it might be good to abandon it altogether.
—Max Weber

Ethnicity is typically defined by some combination of country of origin, physical traits, language, religion, food, holidays, and other customs. An ethnic group is a group of people who share these qualities. Race has been defined by physical characteristics or traits passed on from generation to generation. There are many contradictions in such definitions however. For example, everyone has some characteristics of ethnicity or historic family culture, but only a minority of those are socially defined as being part of identifiable *ethnic groups*. In the case of race, there are no clearly defining genetic markers in the sense that they are found in only one labeled *racial group*. Ethnicity and race are socially defined in ways that change over time. Further, it is a social construction as to whether those identifications make a difference. Identification leads to discrimination only in selected cases. The

Irish, for example, are no longer defined as inferior and are now allowed in the best restaurants in Boston.

In other words, there are several complications and even contradictions. First, defining ethnicity and race is not simple or straightforward. Because of the inclusion of physical characteristics, concepts and beliefs about race are assumed to have a biological—and thus inevitable or natural—basis. Yet, even without generations of reproductive mixing, there are no genetic characteristics exclusive to any designated "race." What is selected as distinctive in physical traits is very much a social construction. Why are hair texture, skin color, or facial features seen as sufficient to distinguish race? Just how much whiteness, brownness, or blackness separates racial identities? Yet there has been a revival of so-called "scientific" genetics, even in universities. The traditional Southern "one-drop rule" is rendered absurd by a long history of mixed parentage and movement across color lines. The reality of race is in how people are identified and treated by those with dominant social power. What appears to have a biological basis is actually given significance or meaning by changing cultural standards.

For example, a tall, well-proportioned male walks down an urban street at night. A European-American female walking her dog nervously crosses to the other side of the street because in the shadows the male seems to have dark skin. She defines this high-school math teacher by what she perceives as a racially defining characteristic—that is, because of the perception that he is a man of color, he is dangerous or a threat.

Or, the National Basketball Association's player personnel is about 90% African-American. Some see this fact as a triumph for a long-disinherited group, and others see it as a marketing problem. Some ascribe the disproportionate distribution to biology, presuming a greater incidence of so-called "fast-twitch" muscles in athletes of different races. Others point to the social condition in which young African-Americans see basketball as one of the few avenues of opportunity open to them and focus their efforts on that sport. The biological explanation ignores the fact that no group has a monopoly on any kind of muscles or nerves. The social explanation is reinforced by the fact that the media promote limited role-models of success via a medium available in almost every home—the television. Is African-American success in basketball explained by biology? If so, then why not tennis or other sports with much the same motor requirements? Are there more basketball hoops than tennis courts and golf courses in economically disadvantaged neighborhoods? Is the racial designation of some football positions a matter of biology or of discriminatory judgments?

In a social system that discriminates, it may seem difficult to separate perceived physical and mental attributes from culture and opportunity. This is as true for ethnicity and leisure as it is for race and sport or gender and math test scores. This has led some, for example, to measure the extent to which ethnicity—or a shared culture, not to mention arbitrary census categories— distinguishes leisure preferences and choices. This research suggests choices based on an ethnic history or culture will be influenced by the extent to which individuals identify with ethnic groups (Gramann & Allison, 1999). Yet most often in these studies, ethnicity and race are measured by some vague and arbitrary census categories rather than by self-identification of social situation. The current controversy over racial and ethnic categories and the addition of one responsive to social change such as "mixed" or "multi" suggests the problem. The presumed neatness of racial and ethnic identity breaks down under examination.

Despite Weber's observation, understanding ethnicity and race as social constructions and not biological or natural categories does not mean that ethnicity and race do not matter and are not important—in fact, just the opposite. While race is not a clear genetic category, it is significant on at least two levels—self-perception and others' perceptions, and self-defined identity and socially defined identity. First, race or ethnicity is a valued source of identity and community. Life is given meaning through the cultural practices that are part of our ethnicity and race. Race and ethnicity are sources of strength, and leisure practices are often contexts of racial and ethnic affirmation and celebration. Secondly, resources and opportunities for leisure, education, work, community life, friendships, and family depend on social identifications. Even self-concepts and self-esteem are constructed in a categorizing and discriminating social context. That is, the attributions others make about us because of ethnicity and race shape life chances generally and access to education, occupations, and income specifically. In the research on recreation and leisure, much attention has been put on the latter—that is, the importance of race and ethnicity in distinguishing opportunity—and very little on the former. In so doing we have "problematized" racial difference (i.e., being a racial or ethnic minority) rather than "whiteness" and racism itself (Fine, Weis, Powell & Wong, 1997).

What Is Social Class?

Social class is also a challenging concept to define as the cues or indicators of social class are both overt and subtle, and often inconsistent. Typically some combination of income, occupational status and level of education are used to determine social class. The higher one's income, occupational status and level of education, the higher one's social class. Occupational status is indexed by income, required education, responsibility and autonomy, power exercised, gender composition, physicality, and dirtiness of the occupation. The more females in an occupation and the more physical and/or dirty the occupation, the lower is its status. Weber summarized all this as *life chances*.

While income, education, and occupation level are the more overt or obvious indicators of social class, they are not always simple and clear. For example, whether income is "new money" or "old money" and is gained legitimately or illegally is important. Further, the type of institution of higher education one attended—Ivy League, community college, or public university—also is a factor.

Class designations are also complex and changing. A traditional set of categories was that of upper, middle, and lower classes. In the era of high industrial employment, there was general agreement that a *working class* could be identified by *blue-collar* employment. Now the growth of service employment and the reduction of factory jobs makes the white/blue collar distinction outmoded. Many service jobs are lower income and less secure than industrial employment. Further, there seems to be a *new class* of technicians, research and development personnel, financial managers, and others with skills or experience that raises them above any middle-class or middle-mass category. They are highly rewarded, but seldom have family or inherited wealth. They are not in the class of the "elite wealthy," but they have considerable discretionary income, especially when households combine two rewarding positions. It is clear the old middle class is dividing among the "new class," the service sector, and the shrinking old industrial working class. The lower or poverty class, however, remains at 15–20% of households.

Social class also plays a part in determining social status, what Weber called *lifestyle*. Status includes more subtle cues having to do with cultural knowledge and practice, material possessions, and prestige. Symbols include type of cars, neighborhoods, shopping and eating venues, destinations for holidays or vacations, and beverages such as beer or a wine. These and many other lifestyle factors enter the calculation (see Chapter 6 on leisure styles).

Then there is power in the community—influence over self and others through serving on the school board or the town council, being an officer in church or synagogue, or being in limited membership community organizations such as Rotary, exclusive clubs, or status groups such as the Symphony Guild. Of course, there is a difference between prestige and real power. In most communities, major decisions are made by a closed set of persons with economic and political power. Social status can be seen as a cultural continuum or as real social divisions. Some status is available to anyone who can afford the material symbols. However, there are even more subtle cues—vocabulary, grammar, accent, attitudes, dress, and physical appearance.

Whether or not we like to admit it and are aware of it, we all use such signs to both display our status and assess others.

In the United States, many are particularly averse to admitting social class is important. Perhaps this is because we like to think everyone has the opportunity to achieve in terms of education, occupation, income, and material goods. There is also widespread support for the concept of *meritocracy* in the United States—the belief that the hard work and efforts of individuals are rewarded and thus are the root of success. Yet, many see meritocracy as more myth than reality. Many work very hard with minimal financial or prestige rewards. Working hard certainly does not guarantee success. About 50% of small businesses started by ambitious and industrious entrepreneurs fail. There are many hard-working people who are not and never will be economically successful or even secure. Hence, an uncritical belief in meritocracy often leads to a blindness to unequal opportunities and to "blaming the victim"— the belief that people are poor because they must be lazy or of weak moral character since hard work and effort are rewarded.

Just as with ethnicity and race, social class may be difficult to define or measure but is very important to individual lives. It not only influences resources (e.g., time, money, skills, health) for education, work, and leisure, it also shapes expectations and perceptions—those we have of ourselves and that others have of us. *Life chances* vary from the moment we are born until the day we die.

The Relationship of Class to Race and Ethnicity

Despite laws intended to eliminate discrimination, material resources and everyday opportunities continue to be stratified on the basis of race and class. If "whiteness" and "middle class" are assumed as the standard, the *less-white* or *more lower-class* one is and appears to be to others, the more constraints are faced in gaining access to resources of all kinds. Again, the fact that ethnicity, race and social class are complex and problematic constructs does not mean that they are not powerful forces. Further, the fact that some individuals from ethnic and racial minority groups are wealthy and that some whites are living in poverty, that some have beaten the odds, overcome the constraints and *made it*, does not mean that race and class discrimination no longer exist in the United States. Rather, such discrimination may take different forms and operate with greater degrees of subtlety at higher levels of work, community, and leisure (Philipp, 1999; Stodolska & Yi, 2003).

While laws have begun to redress some of the more overt elements of unequal opportunity in the United States, life conditions remain unequal.

For example, for two individuals to have an equal chance at a job, they must come to that job from equitable conditions—in this case, educational backgrounds, previous employment experiences, and other human capital. *And* they must be evaluated without regard to social identification, by race, gender, or background. In another example, for two individuals to have equal opportunity to buy a new home, they must have not only the same material qualifications but also the same opportunity to take out a mortgage and be seen by seller and realtor to have the same right to live in a particular neighborhood. But communities and neighborhoods that are homogeneous racially and by social class remain the norm.

Which is more invidious in American society—racial or class division? Some argue law and custom have now reduced racial discrimination to the point that poverty is the real issue. Others see changes as more partial and limited. Racial and ethic discrimination may have gone underground or become more indirect and subtle, but they remain quite operative in a divided society. Still, there is evidence of change. Marriage across religious, ethnic, and racial lines is increasing to the point that hundreds of thousands now identify themselves as "mixed" or "hyphenated." Even the corporate boardroom is admitting more Latino-Americans, African-Americans, and second-generation ethnics still seen as minority. The changes are slow, but seem to be going in one direction—toward a diverse society with elements of integration.

On the other hand, ample evidence suggests race and ethnicity continue to matter (West, 1994). Every index of public health, quality of education, employment, and housing indicates that social position factors are additive and cumulate. Problem conditions are worse for those who are poor and first-generation, African-American and living in an urban ghetto or rural poverty, Latino-American and old, and other combinations rather than any single problematic identity, location, or condition. Further, more than one generation in negative conditions makes the problems cumulative. Several generations of moving from chattel slavery to Mississippi delta sharecropping to a Detroit ghetto without viable work opportunities is far more difficult to overcome than single-generation marginality due to a parental health condition. Conditions are cumulative and interactive—not simple and linear. It is no wonder it takes more than a few antidiscrimination laws to bring about inclusive and fundamental change.

Those who believe in the meritocratic system typically support the notion of equality of opportunity. However, what the meritocratic ideal ignores is that the "playing field" is not level to begin with. A principle of sport is that the game begins with the score even—Life is seldom like that.

Leisure: Impacts of Ethnicity, Race, and Social Class

Because of the complexity of ethnicity/race and social class, there is little agreement as to how these social factors relate to recreation and leisure. The tendency has been to focus on a single aspect of the complex relationship.

Race and Ethnicity

One attempt at explanation of ethnic and racial differences in preferences and choices is "ethnicity theory." According to this "theory," ethnicity and race are important to leisure because they shape values, norms, customs, and attitudes. That is, the leisure of various ethnic and racial groups differs because of cultural differences. This explanation assumes there is a culture common to all members of an ethnic or racial group and ignores the diversity of values, attitudes, and norms that exists within any group. It also assumes leisure is essentially a matter of personal choice with only marginal limiting factors.

Another explanation of ethnic/racial difference in leisure is "economic marginality." Many differences are based on cost. The poor seldom ski, travel to Europe, or join fitness clubs. Different economic resources seem to differentiate leisure participation among various ethnic and racial groups. Again, what is ignored is that not all members of an ethnic or racial group are of the same social class or have the same economic resources. "New class" minorities travel, ski, and go to the theater, especially when they have higher levels of education.

Neither single-focus explanation has been found to be very useful in understanding the impact of ethnicity and race on leisure. Rather, research suggests that the history and experience of discrimination and inequality in opportunity or access to leisure is at least as important to choices and interests as culture and economic resources. Multiple factors are cumulative and interactive. Further, measures of racial and ethnic variations have been inconsistent and weak. Within recreation and leisure studies, the relatively little research tends to be limited and simplistic. More useful insights come from research in disciplines such as sociology, communications, cultural studies, and education its growing composite fields of feminist/gender, ethnic, and racial studies.

Historically there have been some racial differences in leisure preferences and patterns. Differences related to economic resources, such as high-cost sports of skiing and golf or travel, largely disappear for the rising Black middle class. Some differences are cumulative results of long patterns of discrimination such as segregated swimming pools and a lack of opportunities in the rural South, urban ghettoes, and the border towns of the southwestern United States. While improvements in access to resources are changing those differences, leisure continues to reproduce racism at the same time it is a means of *selective acculturation*. Leisure is even a context for *ethnic boundary maintenance* where differences in leisure practices are based on important and valued cultural histories of music, food, religion, and family composition that people seek to maintain (Gramann & Allison, 1999). In this complex relationship three generalities seem accurate:

1. Racial differences are rapidly changing as the culture, resources, and opportunities change.

2. No simple explanation can account for all the factors developed over time in a discriminatory society.

3. Race still matters.

Social Class

Social class interacts with leisure in a number of ways. The most obvious is that level of education, income, and occupation all shape skills, money, health/energy, and time for recreation and leisure. Early efforts to discover whether the relationship between type of occupation (e.g., blue collar or white collar) and leisure interests or styles yielded no consistent or powerful relationships. The availability of credit, the disappearance of many high-income manufacturing jobs, and the variety of white-collar service occupations make it difficult to find a predictable connection between occupation (as a measure of social class) and leisure. Further, class distinctions in *tastes* or lifestyle are often subtle and difficult to discern in survey-type research (see Chapter 6). For example, upper middle-class and working-class individuals may both indicate in a survey that their recreation includes boating or fishing. But the style of boating or fishing—on a yacht, cabin cruiser, or rowboat or from the banks of the local lake, on a deep sea fishing expedition, or fly-fishing in Wyoming—often highlights the distinction that social class makes in leisure and is unmeasured in national surveys. As the market sector is more and more the primary provider of leisure opportunities (see Chapter 23), social class and economic resources may come to have greater impacts on leisure in the 21st century.

Social class is related to leisure in more indirect ways as well. For example, a major concern for many in the United States is the increasing gap between the "haves" and "have-nots." The second half of the 20th century saw the rich getting richer, the poor getting poorer, and the middle class both shrinking and working harder to hold onto their way of life. This has several implications for leisure. As the middle class shrinks, the tax base for and the composition of those using public services changes. A declining middle class reduces both tax revenues and user support for public services. Further, if urban public recreation becomes increasingly associated with poverty, participation of the middle class may be reduced as they avoid unwanted associations. Those who have the income to purchase things like education and recreation privately may become increasingly segregated from the poor of all racial and ethnic backgrounds. Those not using public programs may then be less willing to support new or increased taxes for public education, recreation, parks, and other human services. Further, as contact across classes decreases, the affluent will lose touch with the reality of everyday life for the majority of Americans. This is a problem since the more affluent are in positions of authority or power and make decisions regarding what is needed for the public welfare (Ehrenreich, 1989).

The leisure of the wealthy is almost entirely in the private sector. They travel more and further. They gain privacy by belonging to private exclusive clubs and owning land, second homes, and even lakes and beaches. They can afford all sorts of "pricey" venues and activities, such as Broadway theater, condos at Aspen, London apartments, and private boats, airplanes, and sports lessons for their children. The rich *are* different. They play largely separated from both the middle mass and the poor—especially now that the private or corporate jet is the new symbol of real wealth.

In addition, some suggest that just as the leisure of the elite in ancient Greece was supported by slaves, women, and the poor (see Chapter 3), the leisure of the middle and upper classes today is supported by the work of the lower class or minimum-wage worker. That is, in the labor-intensive service industries, such as retailing, entertainment, or domestic work, the line worker is often paid low or even minimum wage. Leisure industries including tourism depend heavily on such low-wage service workers. Further, those workers are unable to afford most market-sector leisure opportunities. At the same time, at ski and beach resorts, affluent clientele drive up the prices of housing, food, entertainment, and transportation, leaving low-wage service workers unable to afford housing, food, and recreation in their own communities.

One function of the middle class in a capitalist society is to act as a "buffer" between the rich and the poor. When there is a large middle class, the poor are more likely to believe that they have a chance to work their way up. Further, the argument goes, a large middle class ensures a larger tax base for public services such as education, and in the long term, more opportunity for all. Lower- and middle-income households usually pay a higher proportion of their incomes in sales and income taxes. Conversely, the wealthy are able to *shelter* more income from taxes.

In summary, ethnicity, race, and social class are factors important to understanding recreation and leisure participation, contexts, styles, and resources. They shape life chances and a lifetime of access to resources for leisure, such as money, time, health, knowledge, and skills. Opportunities for recreation and leisure continue to be distributed or denied to individuals based on their ethnicity, race, and social class. Given the potentially positive relationship between recreation and leisure and personal and societal health and well-being, this becomes an issue for the entire society.

Debate: Recreation and leisure construct and reproduce stereotypes and inequalities of ethnicity, race, and social class.

Some scholars argue recreation and leisure are sources of negative stereotypes of ethnic and racial minorities and the lower social classes. Rather than building community, recreation and leisure only highlight difference and reinforce fears and prejudices. Others, however, maintain that recreation and leisure are sites where negative images and stereotypes are most likely to be challenged and changed. For example, it is in music, sports, and other forms of entertainment that ethnic, racial, and class boundaries are most likely to be broken down and a common humanity and sense of community experienced—or is it?

YES

- As forms of leisure—television, games, books, theater, movies, toys, magazines, newspapers, and music—may construct and reproduce negative and divisive images or stereotypes of different ethnic and racial groups and social classes. Television sitcoms attempt to produce humor through stereotyped racial and ethnic identification. Even classics of theater such as Shakespeare's *Othello* and Bernstein's *West Side Story* have negative images. Stereotypes have been presented in *All in the Family, Roseanne, Married With Children, The Simpsons*, and *South Park* and in the portrayal of criminals and cops (the "good guys" and the "bad guys") in shows such as *N.Y.P.D. Blue* and *Law and Order*. Perhaps Little Black Sambo is gone, but there are style dolls and games with negative slants. The images and messages presented to us in these forms of leisure construct and reinforce beliefs about various groups of people, who is "good" and "bad," who is attractive and who is not, who is intelligent and who is emotional, who is lazy and who is hard-working. Rarely do they challenge the dominant culture's biases and prejudices or highlight the commonalties we all share as members of the human race and the richness and strength gained from diversity and difference. Given that these cultural products (and television in particular) are in most homes for hours each day, they cannot help but have profound impacts (see Chapter 16).

- Most leisure remains segregated by race and class. Interethnic or interracial contact within leisure settings is relatively rare, and when it does occur, it may be defined as a "problem" rather than an enrich-ment. Most leisure is pursued in ethnically and racially homoge-neous settings. The rich and poor are clearly separated. Voluntary inclusion is most often within small circles. Sunday morning ser-vices are still segregated by race and ethnicity. Costs and class reinforce the divisions. Residential segregation prevents children and youth from playing together. Suburbs especially are segre-gated by race and class. Even small towns still have an "other side of the tracks." It takes legally enforced desegregation to integrate and even then, schools are divided socially. Leisure is separated by cost except for television (see Chapters 11 and 23). Further, the con-text in which ethnic and racial minorities and working-class whites are allowed into many market-sector leisure settings is as service workers which only serves to reinforce beliefs about differences between ethnic, racial, and social class groups.

- Sport may seem to be an exception. It is leisure for participants and spectators. It may be a means of social mobility for racial minority and lower class youth. However, the percentage of high-school athletes who continue athletic careers in college and the percentage of collegiate athletes able to move into the professional ranks are very small—about like being struck by lightning. Pro-moting sport as a way out of poverty is to give unrealistic expecta-tions. It can be a cruel deception that diverts efforts from more realistic avenues of advancement. Emphasis instead should be placed on improving the quality of education available, ending racism and opening up opportunities in all occupational realms (and not just that of entertainer or athlete). Even on the stage and court, minorities are still performers for the entertainment of those with real power. Who, after all, is in the sky boxes and owners' offices?

NO

- One of the benefits of leisure is that it can be inclusive and build community. All television, movies, and theater do not portray negative images and stereotypes of ethnic and racial minorities and lower social classes. They may portray real people coping with real problems. Even toys and games may be inclusive and diverse. These forms of leisure may also present ethnic and racial minorities and the working class and poor in a more positive light and in nontraditional roles, such as judges and opera singers. Further, they present individuals regardless of ethnicity, race or social class with common, as well as unique, life experiences. The images and messages presented on television can become a source of critical reflection and discussion. The issue is not television or movies or music itself but how the individual *consumes* or interprets and processes the images and messages. There are serious efforts being made in the media to portray diversity in a positive light.

- Despite limitations, participation in sport is a means of social mobility for some working-class and racial minority males in the United States. Athletes are more likely to attend college than their peers and even to achieve higher occupational status (Vogler & Schwartz, 1993). Title IX opened such opportunities to females of all races and classes. For example, while in 1979 (the year that Title IX legislation was interpreted to include sport) only about 20% of high-school-age girls were involved in sport, in 1998 over 60% of high-school-age girls played sports. Even a few thousand persons with opportunities are worthwhile.

- Sports teams present an image of persons of different identifications working and playing together, trusting each other, and even caring for each other.

- Recent research also suggests sport and other extracurricular activities are a way to keep *at-risk youth* in school, off the streets, and out of trouble. Youth who are poor are more likely to live in settings that place them at risk, where crime rates are high, violence common, and good jobs rare. Sports and the arts are gateways to education, economic opportunities, and positive self-images. Helping youth who are surrounded by various addictive behaviors, teenage pregnancy, and school dropouts avoid these behaviors is a way to increase their life chances and opportunities for social mobility.

• Many community recreation programs are integrated. If a child is to play baseball, softball, soccer, and other sports, it will be in an integrated setting. Organized recreation, especially public programs, break down the neighborhood barriers and bring children and youth together in an experience of common action where only skill really counts. Public-sector summer camps and arts programs are usually integrated. The crucial factor is children are doing something together that unites rather than divides them. It may not transform the society, but it is a start. The problem is not leisure and recreation. It is a society increasingly divided by income and persistent racism. Every experience across barriers in children's and youths' activities, every positive image, is a contribution to breaking down the stereotypes of segregation.

Discussion Questions

1. How often does your family share a meal with someone of a different racial, ethnic, or social class identity?

2. Is your school more integrated or divided? How and why? What forms of school recreation are most segregated by race and social class? Why?

3. Give examples of positive and negative images in current television and movies.

4. Will dating and marriage across lines eventually make race and ethnicity irrelevant? When and why or why not?

5. Are your school sports teams a force for integration or segregation?

6. What are the issues concerning Native American sports symbols and mascots? Are the "tomahawk chop" or "dancing Indian" mascots really harmless? Why or why not?

7. Do White kids really want to "be like Mike?" What does this mean?

8. Why are ethnic and racial symbols appropriated by majority youth in music, clothing, and language? Does this mean that racism no longer exists?

9. Is there hope for a diverse society that does not discriminate? for integration without losing valued identities?

10. What, if anything, can recreation and leisure service providers do to promote such a society?

References and Resources

Bloom, J. and Willard, M. (Eds.). (2002). *Sports matters: Race, recreation, and culture.* New York, NY: University Press.

Chideya, F. (1995). Don't believe the hype: Fighting cultural misinformation about African Americans. New York, NY: Plume.

Collins, M. with Kay, T. (2003). *Sport and social exclusion.* New York, NY: Routledge.

Dunier, M. (1992). *Slim's table: Race, respectability, and masculinity.* Chicago, IL: University of Chicago Press.

Ehrenreich, B. (1989). *Fear of falling: The inner life of the middle class.* New York, NY: Pantheon Books.

Fine, M., Weis, L., Powell, L.C., and Wong, L.M. (1997). *Off White: Reading on race, power, and society.* New York, NY: Routledge.

Gramann, J.H. and M.T. Allison. Ethnicity, race, and leisure. In E.L. Jackson and T.L. Burton (Eds.), *Leisure studies: Prospects for the 21st century* (pp. 283–298). State College, PA: Venture Publishing, Inc.

Henderson, K.A. and Ainsworth, B. (2001). Researching leisure and physical activity with women of color: issues and emerging questions. *Leisure Sciences, 23*(1), 21–35.

Holland, J.W. (2002). *Black recreation: A historical perspective.* Chicago, IL: Burnham.

hooks, b. (1994). *Outlaw culture: Resisting representations.* New York, NY: Routledge.

Kincheloe, J.L., Steinberg, S.R., Rodriguez, N.M., and Chennault, R.E. (Eds.). (1998). *White reign: Deploying whiteness in America.* New York, NY: St. Martin's Griffin.

Levine, L.W. (1988). *Highbrow, lowbrow: The emergence of cultural hierarchy in America.* Cambridge, MA: Harvard University Press.

MacLeod, J. (1987). *Ain't no makin' it: Aspirations and attainment in a low-income neighborhood.* Boulder, CO: Westview Press.

Marable, M. (1996). *Speaking truth to power: Essays on race, resistance, and radicalism.* Boulder, CO: Westview Press.

McPherson, T. (2003). *Reconstructing Dixie: Race, gender, and nostalgia in the imagined South.* Durham, NC: Duke University Press.

Naylor, L. (1998). *American culture: Myth and reality of a cultural of diversity.* Westport, CT: Bergin and Garvey.

Philipp, S. (1999). "Are we welcome?" African American racial acceptance in leisure and the importance placed on children's leisure. *Journal of Leisure Research, 31*(4), 385–404.

Schorr, L.B. with Schorr, D. (1988). *Within our reach: Breaking the cycle of disadvantage*. New York, NY: Anchor Books.

Shinew, K., Floyd, M., and Parry, D. (2004). Understanding the relationship between race and leisure activities and constraints: Exploring an alternative framework. *Leisure Sciences, 26*(2), 181–200.

Stodolska, M. and Yi, J. (2003). Impact of immigration on ethnic identity and leisure behavior of adolescent immigrants from Korea, Mexico, and Poland. *Journal of Leisure Research, 35*(1), 49–80.

Stoller, E.P. and Gibson, R. (Eds.). (1994). *Worlds of difference: Inequality in the aging experience*. Thousand Oaks, CA: Pine Forge Press.

Vaz, K.M. (Ed.). (1995). *Black women in America*. Thousand Oaks, CA: Sage.

Verney, K. (2003). *African American and U.S. popular culture*. New York, NY: Routledge.

Vogler, C.C. and Schwartz, S.E. (1993). *The sociology of sport: An introduction*. Englewood Cliffs, NJ: Prentice Hall.

Weber, M. (1968). *The economy and society: An outline of interpretive sociology* (G. Roth and C. Wittich, Trans.). New York, NY: Bedminster. (Original work published in 1922)

West, C. (1994). *Race matters*. New York, NY: Vintage Books.

Part IV

Forms of Leisure

Chapter 16
Popular Culture and Mass Media

Popular suggests lots of people like it. In food it is McDonald's rather than French cuisine. In music it is "easy listening" or MTV rather than the Chicago Symphony. In drama it is the sitcom or made-for-TV movie rather than off-Broadway theater. A more careful analysis, however, discloses that popular culture is divided among a multitude of taste cultures, many of which are quite specific to a segment of the population designated by age, region, or ethnicity. *Mass* denotes use by most of the population as distinct from special minorities. Yet, even the most popular television programs attract no more than 20% of viewers, relatively few people go to spectator sports, and almost no one reads the entire newspaper. Further, popular culture and mass media may be just the place to look for expressions of contemporary culture. Popular culture may be of high quality and mass media reflect the deepest issues of life. Even the most absurd of television talk shows may touch some dimensions of life's struggles. Nevertheless, the terms do suggest what most people do as distinct from elite or specialized activities.

What Is Popular Culture?

Popular culture may not last through the centuries, but it is what most people are doing now. Printed media, visual media, music, and other forms of entertainment are common leisure fare for many and big business for the economy. In terms of time use, television is in a class by itself. Yet with cable, video, and various pay formats, television is characterized as much by its variety as its mass quality. Popular culture is in the marketplace and supplied by those who attempt both to respond to and to shape consumer choices. In radio it is characterized by *narrowcasting* that specifies listener markets by age, ethnicity, and taste with no attempt to reach the "masses." It is culture that is sold, yet may also symbolize exactly where a person or group is in the social spectrum. It symbolizes specific group identity, often in conflict with the majority. As such, the music of a teen group has to be different—not just like that of everyone else.

There is a familiar dialectic here. On the one hand, popular culture is marketed, promoted, and sold in the crassest ways to create demand. Further, from a marketing perspective, the ideal is for a product to be in high demand one month and then replaced by something else the next. On the other hand, even that transitory piece of music or drama may touch on something deep and real to create that demand. What is popular both creates and responds to what is contemporary in the lives of some target market. This is just as true of reruns of *The Lawrence Welk Show* for oldsters as it is of rap for teens.

Popular culture is everywhere. It is there whenever one turns on the television or the radio, sees the movie multiplex signs, or reads the entertainment section of the Sunday paper. It is so thoroughly woven into the culture, including mass sports, that it is the most common topic of conversation at lunchtime or at the workplace. It is a different form of Bourdieu's (1996) "cultural capital" by signifying general social acceptance rather than social class differentiation. It is safe and inclusive conversation. It signifies inclusion in the immediate group rather than difference.

Historically, popular culture is the romantic ballad of the time, the singer everyone knows, and the movie star whose picture needs no caption. It is light comedy in theater, the circus coming to town, and the rise of professional sports. It was Babe Ruth and then Hank Aaron, Joe Louis and then Muhammad Ali. It was Bing Crosby followed by Frank Sinatra, John Wayne and Tom Cruise, Mary Pickford and Ingrid Bergman, Billie Holliday and Aretha Franklin, Alfred Hitchcock and Steven Spielberg, Harry Belafonte and Spike Lee, the Beach Boys and the Beatles. There were the ballads and traveling shows of the 18th century. The emergence of *mass culture,* however, probably came with the rise of the city and industrialization. Only the city could produce the crowds to create major entertainment events. Only technology could produce the new heroes such as Thomas Alva Edison and Charles Lindbergh. Then the World Wars pulled masses out of their regionalism and parochialism into a national culture. Now the electronic media have created an emerging global mass culture that transcends former barriers of distance, religion, culture, and language.

Another perspective is that of the life course. Popular culture is not just for teens. It is there throughout life. For example

Children have television and their toys modeled on television shows. They have labeled clothing and shoes, comic books and cartoon shows, and prescribed "heroes" from media and sport.

Youth have rock and rap, dancing and MTV, mass concerts, "Walkman" radios and CD players, surround sound and boom. Teens are the largest movie market and a television target audience. Symbolic identification calls for the right brand of clothing in the current style. Every item of culture has social meaning.

Adult singles are not all flying to Cancun and driving BMWs, but they are a new market. Media, cars, travel, clothes, and culture identify the young adult with purchasing power, a desire to "connect," and an image to project.

Parents have a more home-centered culture for family and entertainment. "Pop" culture becomes more conventional with more long-term investments in equipment, family travel, and home-based media.

Older adults are still markets for entertainment. The culture, however, is more one tied to the past and tastes retained from former times. They also join in consumption of popular entertainment, such as hit movies and television shows, televised sports, and even romance paperback books.

What Do People Do?

There are a number of ways of measuring how people spend their time. One requires recollection and estimates. Another involves keeping diaries with entries of place and activity at specified intervals. There is a relatively high degree of consistency for major categories of activity, such as sleep, employment, travel to and from work, and watching television. More informal activity or doing several things at once are most difficult to report and measure. Further, reporting average times spent in categories of activity may reveal little about just how the day is constructed and negotiated. The variations may be more important than the averages. Nonetheless, some of the structure of the day can be seen in such general reports.

What Do People Do Everyday?

An older study of time-use asked what people did every day (*Where does the time go?* 1983). The most common free-time activities in order were: watching television, reading the newspaper, listening to recorded music, talking on the phone, exercise, and talking with friends. Less common were reading books and magazines, hobbies, and gardening. Teens watched more television, talked more on the phone, and exercised more. Those ages 65 and over also were more likely to watch television every day; read newspapers, books, and magazines; and have hobbies. The same study focused on television; its results appear in Table 16.1.

Table 16.1   Hours Watching Television and Hours Available for Leisure

	Average Hours per Day Watching Television	Average Hours per Day Available for Leisure
Teens	3.97	5.85
Ages 65+	3.50	6.18
Singles	2.89	5.45
Parents, children grown	2.78	4.44
Single parents	2.68	3.64
One-income parents	2.52	3.41
Married, no children	2.42	5.22
Duel-income parents	2.24	3.25

Source: *Where does the time go?* 1983

Watching television seems to involve two main factors: the availability of companions for other activity and the amount of time available. This suggests that at least some television use is residual—done when nothing better is available rather than a choice of high priority. Nevertheless, it remains the greatest consumer of leisure time for all ages. Other studies also report teens watch the most television and those in early adulthood the least. Television viewing decreases with education level and income. For males, Sunday is the big television day with almost double the weekday time. In all categories, women watch less than men by a margin of about 25–30%.

Recent time-diary studies in the United States by Robinson and Godbey (1999) reinforce the centrality of television as well as that of informal social interaction. Further, comparison with similar studies from the 1970s and 1980s indicates that television viewing is increasing to an average of 18 hours a week in 1995. Television captured 18 hours a week as a primary activity and five more as secondary. This compares with a weekly average of seven hours given to outdoor recreation, sports, crafts, hobbies, the arts, and other recreation. Social activities such as going to events, restaurants, parties, and informal socializing accounted for an average of 7.3 hours. Television, then, accounts for about 40% of all free time. This figure does raise a question about all the people who claim they experience severe time pressure.

A current study of trends in leisure activities finds only two major activities other than gambling that are clearly and consistently growing in participation (Kelly & Warnick, 1999). They are walking and golf—both of which reflect the aging of the population. The other major trend is that of greater participation in sports by younger women reflecting greater opportunity and social approval.

Leisure patterns include special events that punctuate and highlight the routine of life. They may be important in ways that far exceed the amount of time given them. This may be true of the vacation trip, the dinner out, a sports contest, or even an hour of quiet reading. In the hour-by-hour routines of life, however, popular culture and mass media take a central place. Along with television, people read a little, mostly newspapers and magazines, listen to music, and talk about the common culture. Along with the weather and other people, the ordinary topics of conversation are entertainment figures and events, sports, and media gossip. Informal interaction and conversation (e.g., "hanging out" for teens) is a major use of time. Even then, however, popular culture mediated through television is a central topic of discourse. Popular culture is not only what people do; it is what they talk about.

Debate: Most people just watch television most of the time.

YES

- Just look at the statistics on time use. Like it or not, nothing rivals television in time use.

- Television is residual. When we have nothing planned or organized, we watch the tube. It is no wonder that the time adds up.

- Television is easy. It is available all the time. There are almost no constraints or costs. It is always there.

- Most studies find that people like television. There are a variety of modes of entertainment. Networks do their market research so they can respond to what people want. Through the entire life span, television is available and attractive.

- There is a diversity of offerings for a variety of tastes, especially when we include free TV, cable, the satellite dish, videos, and pay-per-view.

- Urban life is stressful. It takes time and effort to go anywhere in the city. Other activities tend to be costly. Therefore, the convenience and low cost of television is magnified.

- Watching television requires no skill or effort (except for programming the VCR).

- Costs for television sets have declined to a level almost anyone can afford.

- Almost everyone under age 55 has been raised with television. They are part of a television culture in which television is like air.

NO

- Time diaries are misleading. Often the television is on when people are actually doing something else. People talk, read, doze, iron, and vacuum before the television. It is often background rather than the primary focus. The intensity of watching television varies. All that time doesn't count dozing, daydreaming, talking on the phone, or other distractions. Often people tune in and then tune out.

- Remote controls permit zapping and surfing. As a result, reports of television viewing are highly inaccurate since they assume that people watch one program for its duration without interruption. Many of those hours the television is just on, but barely watched.

- Social interaction is primary and more important. Most television viewing can be and is interrupted for conversation, children's questions, or even the phone.

- People enjoy television, but when asked which activities they would "least like to give up," television usually comes in behind activities to which there is a high commitment and social interaction with those most important to us.

- The events that punctuate the daily round are more important than their frequency indicates. They are most memorable and significant when we can't remember the plot of last night's sitcom.

- Television is too easy. The low levels of effort and challenge mean that it has a low impact.

- When there is a time crunch, television is often the first activity reduced. See the figures for working mothers and other parents.

- Many popular programs are fads that rise and fall in viewership by the year or even the month. There is little continuity.

• Slowly increasing household budgets for leisure suggest people are seeking alternatives to television for time that is increasingly valued.

The Mass Media

There are three main kinds of media: print, visual, and auditory. How common are each in contemporary culture? How do they differ in overall lifestyles?

Print Media

Publishing is a major industry and consumes over 10 million tons of paper for newspapers alone. People still read for pleasure as well as for information. The variety of interests is suggested by the shelves of the large new bookstores, magazine racks, and newspaper stands. Reading, however, is not a growing industry. The bookstore chains are driving independent stores out of business and engage in cutthroat competition with each other. Many general-interest magazines have failed. The growth market seems to be specialized publications based on interest in particular leisure activities, such as collecting or World War II history. Many cities now have only a single major newspaper, and polls show television is the major source of news for most people.

Many books are not for leisure purposes. They are textbooks, standardized tests, reference works, and technical manuals. In the year 2000, almost $34 billion was spent on all books with $12 billion of the total for paperbacks (U.S. Census Bureau, 2002). About one-third was spent on trade (i.e., pleasure reading) books and 10% for children and juveniles. The good news is only 12% were college textbooks and 35% were general trade books. The trade books include not only fiction but also biography, history, the arts, sports, travel, and all sorts of how-to books. Popular paperbacks are sold not only in bookstores but also in supermarkets, airports, drug stores, and discount stores. They are published for mass markets, follow sales trends, and returned to the publisher if not sold in a matter of weeks. Reading as leisure, then, is a varied enterprise marketed for many tastes, interests, and intellectual levels. Some reading is primarily escape and relaxation; some is more demanding and read for learning and personal growth. In addition, more than any other leisure activity, reading is done alone. The major exception is books read to children.

Books, however, are only one kind of reading material. In 1995 there were over 12,000 newspapers in the United States, but only 1,700 daily. The growth has been entirely in weekly papers with the number of dailies remaining constant since 1980. Those published only on Sunday had a total circulation of 61 million and dailies 58 million. Sunday circulation increased about 7 million since 1980 and dailies shrunk 4 million. Many papers are read by more than one person, therefore some newspaper reading seems to be a daily occurrence for a majority of Americans. Much such reading, however, is limited to selected sections of the paper. Some is for business purposes, and some primarily for pleasure. Some takes place in offices or while commuting to work and some at home. Some people read only the sports or financial reports; others at least turn through the entire paper.

The production of periodicals is more complex. There are technical, farm, professional, and hobby magazines. There are also magazines for hunters, homemakers, professional women, travelers, gun collectors, boat owners, skiers, and a thousand other leisure specialists. There are periodicals that are solid text, some that are all pictures, and a majority with both. There are comics and art journals. In fact, magazines, like radio, are characterized by their relatively narrow target markets. They are on almost every conceivable topic, and sometimes limited to members of a particular society. Most important, many are financed almost entirely by their advertising with subscriptions barely paying the mailing costs. Like television, they are marketing tools as well as entertainment.

Visual Media

Television is, of course, the major consumer of time outside of work and sleep for American adults. As already suggested in the debate, some of the figures may be misleading. The fact that a television set is turned on does not mean that the entire household is watching or even that anyone is actually sitting in front of the set giving it primary attention. Nevertheless, in general, time diaries indicate most Americans watch television at least two hours a day—a substantial time allocation.

Statistics on television are almost like quantifying breathing or daydreaming. The medium is there all the time, always available and frequently on in the background of another engagement. It may be on during meals, when going to bed, or when cleaning house or getting ready for work or school. It is company for those who are alone, a distraction for those trying to have a discussion, and a babysitter for tired or occupied parents. It is the primary contact with spectator sports, the theater, and the news. With cable or satellite there are programs available 24 hours a day. Video/DVDs add specific movie programs that are self-scheduled. Some viewing is focused and of relatively high intensity, and some is diffuse and low intensity (Kubey & Csikszentmihalyi, 1990) Some is social and some alone. Some becomes a topic of conversation and some is immediately forgotten. The main fact, however, is that it is always there. Televisions are in over 98% of homes. The average number of sets per home was 2.4 in 2000. Over 85% of homes had VCR or DVD players and over 68% of television-owning households subscribed to cable or satellite (U.S.

Census Bureau, 2002) Television sets are now found in almost any room of the house. As a comparison, in 1996, 91% of Americans ages 18 and above watched television, 75% in prime time, but then only 9% had Internet access with the latter figure increasing about 3% each year.

Unlike magazines and radio, most television programming is *broadcasting* that seeks to attract a wide viewership. There are, however, increasing numbers of specialized channels for sports, history, and the arts. They are vastly outnumbered by those that rerun sitcoms and old movies. The exception is the number of religious channels with both local and national programming.

Television, because of its immediacy, has the power to bring together the population of a nation and even of the world around a particular event. The nation gathered before the screen at the assassination of a president, and the world stopped before the death of a princess. In 1978, the eight-day series of Alex Haley's *Roots* had 130 million viewers and was a common topic of daily conversation, even among Whites who had never given much thought to chattel slavery. In sports, the Super Bowl usually has the highest viewer total of the year; however, the baseball World Series has had a reduced number of viewers, even in prime time evenings. Television, more than any other medium, has the power to reach those of different regions, religions, ethnicity, ages, and lifestyles. Once national and now global, television produces a common culture, often experienced simultaneously in a way unimaginable two decades ago. For better or for worse, television *is* the world culture.

Now new electronic technologies offer more choice and diversity. First it was the VCR and cable. Now it is the satellite and fiber-optic cable with interactive communication. Now major markets are able to order almost any kind of programming at any time of the day or night. Such technologies will be more expensive than the current formats. Nevertheless, they may have a dramatic impact on the networks and others that depend on delivering consumers to the advertisers who sponsor the programs. As the audience becomes more fragmented, the value of the remaining mass set of viewers is reduced. Further, it is precisely the most sought-after target markets, the affluent consumers, who may be lost first.

Motion pictures are quite a different story. (How recently were pictures still silent?) The mode of presentation changed from the little storefronts of silent films to the movie palace and the multiplex. The industry now has multiple markets. Films have a primary domestic market in theaters and secondary markets in theaters all around the world. Just as important, however, are the "aftermarkets" of videos, DVDs, and television. The life of movies is now almost eternal with the "classic" videos and the television channels running ancient films over and over. The distribution of films has become complex and diffuse. All kinds and ages of movies are all over the world.

Total movie attendance in 2000 was 1,465 million, up slightly from 1990. The motion picture industry was a $50 billion enterprise in 2000 with about $7.4 billion each in theater and video revenues. Revenues have increased gradually during the 1990s. There are always productions that try for "blockbuster" status and inclusive markets. Many fail to recoup their multimillion-dollar costs, even with millions spent in promotion. Other films are targeted at more specific sets of viewers, such as teens, families with young children, art-film clients, and even ethnic groups.

The long-term picture of the industry, however, is one of decline. There was a 65% drop in movie theater attendance from 1950 to 1990, and a loss of theaters of over 25%. Drive-in theaters are almost all gone despite their "passion pit" uses by teens. The number of films produced was halved between the end of World War II and 1970 alone. The reason, of course, is television. The paradox is television depends on the motion picture industry for much of its product. The former competition has now changed with domestic made-for-TV movies released to theaters in other parts of the world. The production facilities are often used by both television and movie producers. Stars from one medium jump to the other.

Movies are a medium that draws a disproportionate amount of its clientele from one end of the age spectrum. Studies have found 70% of moviegoers are under age 30 and more than half under the age of 20. For teens, of course, the movie theater is a place to meet as well as an entertainment venue. Often the darkness and measure of privacy are as important as the film itself. The greatest growth market, however, is in the home. The most common use of the VCR/DVD is to play rental movies rather than recording from television. Again, the medium is marked by variety, in programming as well as in markets. The multiple outlets around the world have had an impact on the kinds of movies produced as well as on the distribution and sources of income.

Auditory Media: Popular Music

Again, the new element in music is that it goes everywhere. There is still the high-fidelity home electronics center with surround sound and the potential of spending thousands of dollars on the set up. Now that sound can be put into the car or pickup. Compact disks (CDs) have transformed the recorded music market at home, but also can be downloaded and played with pocket-sized devices. Sound recordings costing over $12 billion were sold in 1998. That is an increase from $7.5 billion in 1990. The biggest markets are those under age 25. Classical recordings were only 4% of the market with rock 33%, country 17.5%, pop 12%, urban contemporary 10%, rap 8%, jazz 3%, and gospel 3%. Recorded popular music is a major industry, although it is threatened by digital music downloads, drops in CD sales, and the burning of one's own CDs for personal use.

Of course, such music is heard on the audience-focused radio stations, on television, in movies, and in concerts. The industry depends heavily on promotion of the current hit singles, albums, and videos. Such promotion depends on a synergy of television, recordings, movies, and concerts. The essence of the marketing is that certain items are promoted heavily for a short period and then replaced by others. The latest recordings are to be listened to intensively for a short period. Then different products, even if by the same performers, move to the top of the sales charts. The marketing is in a "fad" mode of quick rise and equally rapid fall. The supply of hit music, however, is never-ending.

The youth market is the largest and most enthusiastic. There are other segments, however. Some are regional, some ethnic, some religious, and some oriented to a particular style of music and performance. Western music is distinct from general country styles. The pop religious music of the Bible Belt is different from soul and African-American gospel. Many buyers, on the other hand, cross ethnic boundaries in an allegiance to styles that originated in different cultures. Such segmented markets attract thousands of recording producers who hope to find the right combination of performer and music. There are still, however, more general markets that feature established musicians with a wide appeal that may endure for decades. Themes of romance predominate with themes varying from nostalgia to the outright sexual. This is an industry that has been transformed by a technology—the transistor is now imprinted silicon that has expanded and diversified an entire industry.

Popular Culture, Taste, and Social Identity

One side of the popular culture picture is the supply side. It is an enormous industry, hundreds of billions a year, depending on what is included. It is also a high-promotion industry. It is common for movies costing $10 million to produce to spend another $3 million on promotion. What is more significant is that the industry is interlocked in one great promotion enterprise. Cable television, videos, movies, concerts, radio, billboards, magazines filled with articles on celebrities, the use of stars in advertising, and other promotions make exposure to the entertainment industry almost constant. From the saturation, popular culture is a central topic of conversation. About the only way to avoid the promotional atmosphere is to go home, turn everything off, and read an old book. All this is no surprise when the corporate giants that dominate the industry are in almost all phases of entertainment. Most book publishers are owned by a larger publisher that is owned by one of the multifaceted entertainment giants that produces movies, television, music, and just about everything else.

The corporate supply side of popular culture is enormous and global. Certainly there are a thousand little recording companies trying to edge into the market. Most, if they are successful, will be bought out by a giant. Television may have a few local stations, but even they purchase old programs from the corporate distributors. Most national channels are owned by a few corporations, merging and buying each other at a rate that is too fast to follow. GE and Westinghouse compete with Disney for network control. It is no wonder such an industry is successful in commanding most of the available time of youth and adults. It is also no wonder those most susceptible to such promotion, the young and those with less education and fewer resources, become major markets.

Taste and Variety

The industry offers almost everything in entertainment. The "narrowcasting" of radio is only one example of how finely the markets are segmented. When a television program is in the early stages of development, the target audience is specified and the likely advertisers contacted. Magazines are directed to those with special involvements or who fit particular demographic profiles. Market research done every year in massive studies can identify the magazines, television programs, and leisure activities of almost every conceivable population segments indexed by region, age, education, gender, race, income, and other variables.

The purpose is to locate *taste cultures*. Taste cultures are the primary markets for particular kinds of music, television, movies, magazines, travel packages and destinations, and other popular culture. Such taste cultures are not only identified; they are also created and cultivated. The media create a synergy by attacking such market segments from all sides. The attempt is to create a lifestyle based on the consumption of a particular entertainment package from hats to shoes, and from CDs to sitcoms and MTV. The supply side is quite sophisticated in its supply of entertainment for taste cultures. The promotion of popular culture is an essential part of the industry with its own budgets amounting to hundreds of billions of dollars.

To create and supply such taste cultures, the industry specializes in variety. Some critics write about "mass" media as though everyone consumed the same amusements. They refer to the "Disneyfication" of popular culture. There is, of course, a major concentration on "middle America" and common tastes. Disney is especially adept at attracting such tastes. It is at least as accurate, however, to focus on the almost infinite variety of popular culture. The variety of musical styles, movie types, and other offerings demonstrate there are many taste cultures. Whenever they are considered to be a viable market, there will be entertainment aimed at them. Popular culture becomes the symbol system by which subcultures are identified and differentiated. Even within one high school, there are often multiple subcultures with their own identifying dress, music, and even language.

Popular Culture and Social Identity

The variety of youth cultures is the most obvious example of the symbols of social identity. Even within a single community or school, teens are divided by age, social class, race, and cultural styles. Each group has its insignia, mostly the adoption of elements of popular culture. There are dominant groups and counterculture groups. There are those that adopt the mainstream of whatever is being promoted that month and those that resist to identify themselves as outside the mainstream. Labels, colors, and styles of clothing are only the beginning of such symbolic identification.

One side of all this is supply, the constant promotion of popular culture. The other side emerges from the real-life circumstances, issues, and dilemmas of development. For example, sexuality and sexual identity are central to the lives of most teens. Sexuality is also central to all the media, especially to rock, rap, and other musical styles. The culture is responsive to what is really going on in the lives of teens in ways that evoke what is often a powerful response.

Teen cultures have their mass elements, but they are also divided and subdivided. There are those who are central to a school culture, but at least as many who are more marginal. The drive to identify with some group creates many subcultures. Some resist the institutions so strongly that their differentiation and resistance are marked by clear symbols. They listen to a different kind of music, talk differently, and form their own groups. Nevertheless, they are still consumers. They still have to appropriate something that is offered in the incredible variety of popular cultural styles and subcultures. Even unique sets of cultural symbols are constituted of marketed items. Indeed, there is mass culture offered by the mass media. However, there are also countless taste cultures that in some specific way provide an identity for those who want to be different.

Debate: "Disney" is just what most people want.

YES

- By "Disney" we mean not only the Disneyland/Disney World/Disney Productions/Touchstone/ABC/etcetera enterprise, but also all the popular culture that appeals to most of middle America. It is also specific. After all, Disney World is the world's premier tourist destination. The multifaceted giant is probably the most successful entertainment corporation in the world. Disney is the standard for the industry. In general, they go for the mass market.

- Disney means clean, neat, safe, and well-organized. It also means inoffensive, unchallenging, and fake. It means entertainment without real challenge or risk.

- For example, real cities are strenuous. Disney's fake cities around EPCOT's lagoon are neat convenient little places that manufacture a few symbols that bring the real down to size. Main Street has none of the variety or conflict of a real small town—and somehow the great world theme parks manage to appeal to almost all ages. Disney's new "wild animal" kingdom combines real creatures with animated fakes, real forest with a concocted tree that has a theater inside, and a pretend safari in a jungle created by bulldozers—all in the safety and cleanliness of the Disney style.

- Real travel is difficult. There are languages, crime, and strange cultures. The Walt Disney World maximizes ease. There are no skills required to travel Disney style.

- The wonderful world of Disney is much the way we wish the world might be. It is an escape from all the problems of real life and real people into a fantasy that somehow recreates the ordinary into the ideal. History Disney-style is a world of heroes who say only nice, safe, affirming things about the okay world.

- Disney is a simulated world, recreated into an environment that, for a price, serves our every need—except even the needs are redefined by the concoction. We don't need love; we need entertainment. We don't need to learn; we need to be reassured. This is simulated in a world that walls off reality and seems, from the inside, to be complete.

- There is no challenge in this world. When we can afford the entrance fees, we are protected from anything that might test our skills—physical, mental, or communicative. Rather, we are immersed in a consensus culture of a world that can pose no danger to us or to the world we would like to believe really exists.

- You can't argue with success, and Disney is the popular culture icon of success.

NO

- Disney is only occasional. Even devotees of Disney World tend to go there only every five years or so. The day-to-day world of social life is much more varied. In general, we seek a balance of different elements of life, not a complete diet of Disney.

- Anything as safe as Disney World would become boring after a few days. It is a neat occasional destination, not an environment for life.

- In the progression of tourism, leisure travelers often go to conventional and safe places at first and then become more exploratory. There is a desire for more challenge and variety than can be offered by one-walled simulation.

- Disneyland/Disney World markets are important, but they may be shrinking. Even television is now responding to varied interests as well as to mass markets. Tourism is characterized by its variety as well as its packages. Real society is too diverse to make Disneyland/Disney World its symbol. After all, MTV is not Disney—yet.

- After experience with the real, the fake becomes ridiculous. The more people travel, learn, and have a variety of experience, the more absurd the world of Disney will seem. The diversity of the world is more a symbol of the future; Disney is from the past. The Disney World version of history has now become embarrassing.

- EPCOT was in reality something of a failure. It so lacked attraction that the Disney Corporation had to actively advertise Disney World for the first time—and they are careful not to measure how many visitors are disappointed. The tourism world is diversifying. Television ratings suggest that the mass media networks are losing market share. Disney is an attractive symbol of homogenized culture, but it may symbolize a past that is being replaced by a culture too diverse to simplify.

Discussion Questions

1. Why is popular culture popular: because it is marketed, or because it represents realities of life?

2. Is the amount of time devoted to television a problem? for the individual? for society?

3. Are there symbols of social identity in your school? How deeply do they divide the school and the community?

4. How intense is most television viewing? Is it a focus of attention or just background? Explain.

5. Do people still read? Is reading becoming an elite activity? primarily for old folks?

6. Who goes to movies now? Is price becoming more of a constraint?

7. How many varieties of popular music are on the market today? What do they symbolize?

8. Is popular culture more a "mass" culture or a diversified set of cultures and styles?

9. Is the "Disneyfication" of American leisure a problem, or just a symbol of middle-mass taste?

References and Resources

Bellah, R., Madsen, R., Sullivan, W., Swidler, A. and Tipton, S. (1985). *Habits of the heart: Individualism and commitment in American life*. Berkeley: CA: University of California Press.

Bourdieu, P. (1996). *The rules of art: Genesis and structure of the literary field*. (S. Emanuel, Trans.). Stanford, CA: Stanford University Press.

Dulles, F.R. (1965). *A history of recreation: America learns to play* (2nd ed.). Englewood Cliffs, NJ: Prentice Hall.

Ewen, S. (1976). *Captains of consciousness: Advertising and the social roots of consumer culture*. New York, NY: McGraw Hill.

Friedman, J. (Ed.). (2002). *Reality squared: Televisual discourse on the real*. New Brunswick, NJ: Rutgers University Press.

Gans, H. (1974). *Popular culture and high culture: An analysis and evaluation of taste*. New York, NY: Basic Books.

Kelly, J.R. and Warnick, R. (1999). *Recreation trends and markets: The 21ˢᵗ century.* Champaign, IL: Sagamore.

Kubey, R. and Csikszentmihalyi, M. (1990). *Television and the quality of life: How viewing shapes everyday experience.* Hillsdale, NJ: Erlbaum.

Lewis, G. (Ed.). (1972). *Side-saddle on the golden calf: Social structure and popular culture in America.* Pacific Palisades, CA: Goodyear.

Robinson, J. and Godbey, G. (1997). *Time for life: The surprising ways Americans use their time* (Rev. ed.). University Park, PA: Penn State Press.

Rojek, C. (1996). *Decentring leisure: Rethinking leisure theory.* Thousand Oaks, CA: Sage.

U.S. Census Bureau. (2002). *Statistical abstract of the United States* (Section 1230. Arts, Entertainment and Recreation). Washington, DC: U.S. Government Printing Office.

Where does the time go? The United Media Enterprises report on leisure in America. (1983). New York, NY: Newspaper Enterprise Association.

Chapter 17
The Other Side of Leisure

Recreation is usually defined in positive terms as activity that "re-creates" persons to better assume needed roles in the society, polity, and family. Leisure is defined more inclusively. Yet, most attention is given to activity with potentially positive outcomes. Leisure is said to have benefits that range from supporting physical health through exercise, mental health through relaxation and stress reduction, personal development in challenging activity, and social cohesion in various forms of interaction. This chapter is something else—it is about the "other side" of leisure.

A variety of terms may be used to refer to leisure that has measurably negative outcomes. It may be *deviant* in violating the common norms of the society. It may be *amoral* in ignoring the moral standards of the culture. It may be the *other side* of activity that is otherwise acceptable, such as the violence of sports or the drug culture of rock music. From any perspective, there is a negative side to leisure that is quite real, common, and even involves billions of dollars in costs and investments. It is always there, even if slightly obscured behind cultural veils so we can pretend it does not exist in *our* community.

All this is not totally neglected in the rest of the book. There have been images of leisure that is primarily entertainment without challenge, skill, or developmental potential. The previous chapter introduced media versions of such easy entertainment. There are all the ways in which leisure becomes a commodity to be purchased. In chapters ahead there will be other types of leisure with at least some negative aspects. Chapter 18 discusses the violence of commercialized sport. Chapter 20 introduces recreation that is destructive of natural environments. Chapter 22 outlines costs of tourism to host cultures and economies. Chapter 23 on the market sector again raises the issue of consumption as leisure and the massive investment made in such provisions. For example, in Las Vegas an operative hotel was recently blown up to be replaced with a new $800-million edifice to house those who come for an estimated $7 billion plus of gambling per year. Chapter 14 sketched the omnipresent sex industry with its exploitation of the weak and poor, especially women and the young. In the United States alone, there are hundreds of thousands of teen and preteen prostitutes on the streets of our cities without protection from multiple hazards.

Sometimes this is referred to as *deviant leisure* (Rojek, 1999). The problem with this label is the difficulty in drawing any lines of distinction. What is the standard by which an activity is judged deviant? From what clear and accepted standard does an activity deviate? For example, gambling is a growth industry sponsored by states, cities, and even churches. There are X-rated videos readily available at almost every neighborhood video outlet. Sex tourism is advertised in the free brochures available as one gets off the plane in almost every major airport in the world. Where do we draw the line between "normal" and "deviant?" Even more, as many decry, there is plenty of sex and violence offered into the home every day and night on television, much of which is unacceptable to many of those who subscribe to the cable and satellite services. The fact is there is no clear and unambiguous set of criteria for leisure in the contemporary variety of taste cultures.

Mini-Debate: Whatever people do is OK if it is what they want.

YES

- The essence of leisure is freedom. No group has the right to impose its standards on those who differ.

- There are countless taste cultures in a modern society with conflicting interests, pleasures, and standards.

- There is no way of enforcing a single standard amid such diversity.

- Anything goes today unless it is directly destructive. That's just the way it is.

- After all, standards are relative and constantly change. Regulation always lags behind reality.

NO

- A complete lack of standards will weaken the moral order and in time destroy the society.

- People often do not think out the consequences of their actions. They have to be protected from themselves as well as from others.

- Human weakness may not only be dangerous to others but also may be self-destructive. Many people are weak and will be exploited by those with something to gain from their frailty.

- The collective wisdom of a culture is greater than the preferences of individuals.

The World of Indulgent Leisure

Many forms of leisure range from the self-indulgent to the destructive. Just think of the spectrum of possibilities available in the modern city. What is available, at least to those who can pay, when one arrives at any major airport? Is there anything not for sale somewhere—legally or illegally? In this chapter, we can only sketch some of the most common forms of the other side of leisure. Note that many of these activities are only the most evident examples. There is a downside to almost anything.

Gambling

Statistics on gambling are always questionable due to the gigantic illegal side of the industry. Estimates range up to $600 billion a year for legal and illegal gambling. In 2000, casinos, not including hotels, did an estimated $13 billion with a yearly increase of over 10%. The FBI estimates that $2.5 billion was bet illegally on the 1997 NCAA basketball tournament and $80 million legally. The numbers on illegal betting especially are subject to question since profits are laundered and hidden. Also, the extent to which the growth of various forms of legal gambling have displaced illegal betting on "numbers" and sports is not clear.

What is clear is gambling is a major growth industry. In the United States, Atlantic City was rebuilt around gambling to rescue the dying resort city. Of course, the major destination is Las Vegas. Even with all its shows, pools and golf courses, Las Vegas is still primarily developed to attract gamblers. What may be surprising is the extent to which those gambling visitors are just "ordinary people"—the banker, farmer, druggist, and little old widow from around the corner. What may be less remembered is the number of resorts developed around gambling in the past. Did you know about the special trains in the 1920s that ran from Chicago to tiny French Lick, Indiana, to take its participants to spas-turned-casinos and that these casinos may be reopened?

Gambling is not something new, distant, or esoteric. Almost every small town has had its backroom poker games sometimes with the chief of police as a regular player. Bingo has been a common fundraising and social enterprise for Roman Catholic parishes for decades. The newspaper shop has often been the neighborhood "bookie" where bets could be placed on horse races thousands of miles away. Gambling on "numbers" has been endemic in most urban neighborhoods. Business and professional men have had their regular poker nights—and prestigious country clubs have had their cards rooms and even slot machines in the era of gambling prohibitions.

Now, of course, there is legal gambling almost everywhere. States have licensed "riverboats" that hardly leave sight of the dock as full-service casinos. Native-American nations have used exemptions for tribal lands to open casino gambling—some with high profits, some marginal, and some failing usually due to location. Gambling permits are highly sought after and legislators subject to considerable pressure (and financial inducements) to permit new casinos, especially near cities. No one needs to go to Las Vegas or Atlantic City to gamble. There are a variety of forms, but the table games such as 21 (i.e., blackjack), roulette, and poker are giving way as more space is allocated to the electronic machines, especially video poker. Skill and social interaction is minimized on the casino floors. The latest form of gambling is online. With established credit it is possible to engage in a variety of wagering without leaving the home. It is unclear, however, how the gambling mafia can break the kneecaps of those who don't pay up through the Internet.

Estimates of gambling participation vary. One national study found the following:

- 14% of adults visited a casino in the last 12 months

- Less than 2% did so more than ten times

- Atlantic City was the most common venue followed by Las Vegas and Reno/Tahoe

- Over 45% had purchased lottery tickets in the past 12 months

- Over 20% had done so once a week or more with weekly drawings the most popular (*Simmons study*, 1990)

One study of gamblers in the Midwest found low-income families wagered 7% of their income on average, but those with middle and higher incomes less than 3% (Abbott & Cramer, 1993). Higher income gamblers were less likely to play bingo and more likely to visit casinos. Gender differences were slight—especially for the married who went to gambling venues together. Men, however, tended to bet higher amounts with the exception of bingo.

At this time, the growth in legal gambling is spurred by its greater availability. There is a race among government jurisdictions to open new businesses for off-track betting, riverboat and other casinos, and lotteries. The tax revenues along with incentives offered directly to government officials in various forms, including campaign contributions, are powerful factors. The fact that gambling is a very expensive method of obtaining money from citizens is usually ignored. Of course, there are also other problems. The highest proportions of income spent on gambling are by those who can least afford the loss—the poor. It is a highly regressive form of revenue production. Legal gambling is often accompanied by interests outside the community, including organized crime. Money lost in gambling is not spent in the community on other purchases—housing, cars, hardware, clothing, and even food. There are lost jobs and tax revenues as well as gains. Finally, there is the "problem gambler" with incredible stories of resources lost and lives ruined by an inability to control that drive to wager. Even if such problem gamblers account for less than 10% of the total, the costs to individuals and families of regular gamblers may be great. Most economic analyses find legalized gambling produces greater costs than benefits to local communities *unless* most of their patrons are from outside the area.

Gambling is, by its nature, exploitative. Requiring little or no skill, it attracts many who dream of the million-to-one or less likelihood of the big win that will transform life. As such, it appeals most to many who have the least chance of gaining wealth in any other way. It is, in a sense, the ultimate commodification in which everything is promised in return for the purchase. Nevertheless, it is more popular than golf (but not gardening). It is exciting without any cost except "money." It deals in something everyone knows, uses, and seems to desire—money. Its rewards are clear and quantifiable—and now it is legal and, perhaps, respectable. It is leisure on the boundaries of morality and social acceptance.

Substance Use

Substance use is another activity that has, in part, moved from illegality to legality and from the fringes of society to respectability. "Designer drugs" are the center of entertainment at exclusive parties. Crack and other cocaine- or opium/heroin-based drugs are sold on the streets in the most destitute urban ghettoes. Marijuana and the latest concocted drugs are available on street corners and in back alleys near middle schools as well as high schools. Campuses are major distribution centers, but even prisons have their systems of supply. Illegal "experience-enhancing" drugs are everywhere in every region of the world. No society is too poor and none too knowledgeable about costs and consequences. Even bankers and government bureaucrats doff their "suits" on weekends and bring current substances along with the bottle of wine to parties.

Again, the total costs in the illegal drug trade are only estimates and depend on the level of distribution at which the measurement takes place. Street values are high multiples of the costs from production to transportation to central distributors to final sales. Prices are escalated by the illegality of such substances and adds a risk factor to scarcity. At the downstream end of the system, small operators run the highest risk for the lowest profit. At the other end are international cartels whose shipments run into millions of dollars a day. In between are regional distributors, sometimes organized-crime families and sometimes interlinked street gangs. Current fashionable drugs have their faddish moments until the word is out about their destructive power, while the old standbys never seem to go away. In any case, much of the use is clearly leisure, chosen for the intrinsic experience rather than extrinsic ends.

At the end of the system are the users. They may be teens who think that drugs are "cool" and a temporary form of play. They may be the desperate and the disinherited for whom substance use is an momentary escape from prison of poverty. They may be the elite wealthy who display that they can afford to be above the law and ordinary conventions. They may be performers in the arts or sports who become part of a special drug culture. Drug-based subcultures develop around particular rock groups and jazz scenes. Users may be almost anyone who is introduced to drugs and comes to value the experience over the longer term costs—and almost all begin by believing that addiction only happens to other people who are weak and don't know when to stop.

Of course, there are more common legal drugs. It is clear now nicotine in tobacco is a drug, enhancing some kinds of experience and usually addictive. The current revelations from tobacco company records about additives in the manufacturing processes and advertising campaigns that target women, teens, and racial groups make it clear that tobacco is an addiction-based industry. The effectiveness of attacks on the industry in North America will be measured over the next decades. In the meantime, antismoking campaigns have had only limited success—especially with the new markets of women and racial groups. Even if markets are limited in North America, exports are increasing and tobacco use is on the rise in most of the world. Multimillion-dollar legal judgments and settlements seem to be only temporary blocks to an industry that refuses to go away despite overwhelming evidence of health costs and dangers. Again, considerable smoking is fostered in leisure environments—especially in peer groups of the young.

The "drug of choice" for students is alcohol. It produces an experience of emotional release that may be associated with violence and sexual exploitation. Most date rapes have alcohol as a central factor. Yet, alcohol is relatively cheap and available—even for those below legal ages of consumption. Reports on one campus bar in 1998 were that over $10,000 worth of beverages were sold on one Friday evening with up to half to those under the legal age of 21. In urban settings, campus areas, and almost every town in America, alcohol is big business. The styles of consumption may involve exclusive "call brands" of liquor, high-price aged wines with exclusive labels, and even "designer" beers. Or they may still be the traditional blue-collar Blue Ribbon or Bud after work in home or tavern. There are cheap wines on the streets and costly beers at elite parties. There is alcohol in almost every style, price, and variety. For some drinkers, the aim is to get drunk. For some addicted alcoholics, consumption is out of control and destructive of almost every other element of life—even one's most valued relationships. Most drinking, however, is for leisure purposes. It is a "social lubricant" believed to enhance the experience of social interaction, or to make the evening more pleasurable. This belief, of course, adds to the group pressure to join in.

In some cultures like that of the French and Italian, alcohol (usually wine) is a regular part of at least the evening meal. In other cultures, alcohol is associated with more segregated environments. In any case, it is a mood-altering substance, sometimes addictive, and associated with all styles of leisure. A British or Irish pub may be the social center of a neighborhood. Alcohol may be a required element of entertaining—even when alternative beverages are available for sober alcoholics. Alcohol may be the common drink in cultures where water is contaminated. What is clear is alcohol is too thoroughly a part of the social life of many cultures to banish it entirely. National "Prohibition" in the United States is usually pointed to as the prime example of the impossibility of a total ban. Almost any campus area demonstrates that even age-based regulation is seldom successful. Alcohol in some forms and consumption styles is the "drug of choice" in the leisure of most cultures throughout the world.

Violence

Violence itself may be a form of leisure—both for participants and spectators. The relationship of violence, on and off the field, to sport is outlined in Chapter 18. In the game, violence is part of many sports: the hitting in football, fights and checking in hockey, and the direct infliction of damage in boxing. This is distinct from the risk element in many sports that can result in injury or death. This is the "other side" of activity that also has many positive meanings and outcomes.

This connection of sport and violence is not incidental. Many games have been designed to be practice for warfare with skills of aggression and implements similar to weapons. Sport in many cultures explicitly teaches violence. It was the late General Douglas MacArthur who proclaimed, "On the fields of friendly strife are sewn the seeds which on other days, in other fields, will bear the fruits of victory." Now there are new games that mimic warfare, such as paintball with its weapons, "kills," and stalking of the enemy. War games, especially when organized for the young, are direct socialization into a culture that makes war a glorious game rather than a destructive horror. Of course, such games are also connected with versions of manhood and masculinity. Complex electronic games include all kinds of violence, including the rape and torture of women and the use of nuclear weapons.

There is also a long history of "blood sports." They include not only boxing and various forms of one-on-one combat but also pitting animals against each other and against humans. The Roman arena brought humans before hungry carnivorous animals. In colonial America, there was bear-baiting in which dogs were set on chained bears, dog fights with specially bred and trained dogs, and cockfighting. All these "sports" were usually to the death with the losing animals buried (if that). In parts of the United States, these contests continue as a regular part of the leisure culture. There have, of course, been many attempts to outlaw such activities as cruelty to animals. However, the culture of violence seems too deeply embedded to make such prohibitions effective. In Latin cultures, bullfighting with rings in the centers of the great cities not only involves the slow death of the bulls but also the goring and disemboweling of horses used in the spectacle. Some forms of blood sports are found in many cultures in all eras and regions of the world. Some involve risk to human participants as well as to the animals. In all, animals are sacrificed for the pleasure of humans. The connection of sport violence with demonstrations of male physicality and power will be explored further in the next chapter.

There are many other forms of leisure-related violence, including hunting and some sexual practices. One that has gained the most attention in recent years has been gang activity. There has been the direct violence of random and targeted "drive-by" shootings with the common murder of innocent children and adults who were in the "wrong" place. There are the "turf" wars over space, in the neighborhood as designated by streets or even in public parks. These are a form of war games that may have elements of negotiated rules and conventions. In some cases, even theft has been presented by the gang members as a form of game with goals, skills, and risk. There is excitement in risky behaviors even when the opponent is the law. Some descriptions of gang theft sound like a sport with members playing designated positions on the "team." When other opportunities for excitement are closed, then even breaking the law may have some of the meanings associated with leisure. They are, in a way, games of chance. The outcomes, however, may be violent, destructive of life and community, and involve the dangers of drug addiction, prison, and even death. The leading cause of death of African-American males under age 40 in some cities is violence. The other side of the picture is that the gang provides social acceptance and identity for those left out of other communities by economic, social, and racial discrimination.

Ordinary Activity

In examining the negative side of leisure, there is often a tendency to stress a sense of "otherness." Those who engage in such activity may be seen as different, exotic, or members of other cultures. Conversely, it is possible to argue there is no essential element of such behavior that is clearly foreign. Rather than "normal" and "deviant"—two distinct kinds of behavior—there is more of a spectrum of activities and styles engaged in that have leisure dimensions. A few examples follow.

Driving may often be an "other side" leisure activity. For some there seems to be a thrill in breaking the law. Others make driving a more competitive sport with aggressive behaviors of challenging speed, weaving, and take-offs from stops. Perhaps the most extreme style of such driving is "road rage" in which there are deliberate attempts to harm those who offend the player in some way. Probably more common among otherwise law-abiding citizens of all ages and genders are impromptu and organized "drag races" where the power of one's ride can be displayed.

In sexual activity, there is also a range of exploitative behaviors. In its milder forms males gain sexual compliance as a kind of contest in which the players keep score and in which the other person is just an object or trophy (see Chapter 14). Beyond this nontrivial "sport" there is a variety of ways in which sexual compliance is gained through social power, the use of alcohol or other drugs, and direct physical force. The common reports of date rape on campuses are usually leveled against male students who otherwise seem unexceptional. There is a range of forms of sexual coercion that turn something good into something else. Such behaviors are more than the exception. Rather, they seem to be based in a sexual politics that connects masculinity with physical power, especially over women (Messner, 1997).

In many cultures graffiti (i.e., illegal writing on walls or other flat surfaces) has become an important kind of political protest, often against repressive governments. Outdoor art may be encouraged to cheer up urban spaces, especially in deprived neighborhoods. It is difficult to draw a line between such decoration and political symbolism and graffiti that violates the norms and regulations of a community. In any case, outdoor art presents a range of symbols and messages—from beautiful to the obscene.

The same may the true for any art. For example, in the diversity of music labeled "rock" there are messages of grace and love contrasted with those of violence and the degradation of human beings. In contemporary arts, it becomes increasingly difficult to draw lines between the beautiful and the grotesque, the constructive and destructive.

As an example related to a particular device, there is the motorcycle gang. Roaming the roads on a sunny weekend in California, there are "cycle gangs" of families with their children, geriatric riders taking their discounts at the fast-food stops, students getting out of the classroom and on to the open road for a break, a variety of other groups, and even the "Hell's Angels" with their culture of violence. Motorcycles of different styles are used on racetracks, motocross hillsides, and in fragile desert and dune environments. Some of the behaviors are aggressive and dangerous; some are relaxed and social. There is nothing inherently good or evil about the motorcycle itself. It is a device that facilitates leisure that may be seen as free and healthy or deviant and dangerous.

As presented in Chapter 20, no kind of leisure activity is generally viewed more positively than getting into natural environments, to the peace and beauty of the forest, mountain, or water. Yet, there are also many outdoor recreation behaviors that are destructive of the very environments that attracted the visitors. There is littering, motorized vehicles that tear into fragile surfaces, horseback camping that pollutes isolated mountain lakes, aerial sightseeing that destroys the quiet of the canyon, ski slopes that are a visual blight in the summer, and boats that drop their waste and oil slicks into the harbor or lake. As indicated earlier, the forest may be used for contemplation or war games. There is nothing inevitably noble and restoring about increasingly crowded natural environments.

There is no clearcut distinction between good and bad leisure—between the positive and the negative. Some of the distinctions are a matter of taste and culture. Some form a continuation of styles and behaviors from the clearly constructive to the clearly destructive. Some standards and judgments change from one historical period to another. Almost any activity can be used for negative ends. For example, the outdoor recreation of the "Hitler Youth" and the political use of Wagner's music by the Third Reich. One person's amusement is often another's exploitation—and the power to define leisure "moralities" is political.

Criminal Leisure

Most controversial, however, is illegal activity. There have long been calls to legalize at least some substances, such as marijuana, on the grounds it is a harmless form of leisure. Harmless or not, one can go to jail for possession with intent to distribute. There are all the illegal private sexual acts of consenting adults. Many kinds of illegal behavior are accepted as legitimate leisure when they are conducted in private and do not disrupt the social order. Gambling may be the most common form of leisure that has been illegal in most forms and places at some time.

Some have argued, however, there are leisure dimensions to outright criminal activity. There is the Bonnie-and-Clyde aura placed around those who have broken the law in seemingly glamorous and riskful ways. Looking far enough into the past, Jesse James becomes a western folk hero rather than a common bank robber. The question is whether that aura of risk, danger, and even glamour can be ascribed to those who break the law now. It certainly may be within certain cultures. Those who flout the law and profit in the process may be heroes in some cultures with extremely limited economic opportunities. The outlaw may be defined as a figure of political protest— even labeled a "Robin Hood" when some of the gain is shared.

Breaking the law for personal gain is never just a sport in which the winner violates the rules. Yet, there may be elements of challenge, excitement, camaraderie, winning and losing, and symbols of success. It may be going too far to call such activity leisure when it emerges out of a context of poverty, racism, and repression. There may be some common dimensions between leisure and gang-based street violence and carrying deadly weapons. The use of the weapons, however symbolic and exciting, is something different from activity focused on the experience. Yet, when possibilities of positive leisure are closed off, who can say for sure there is nothing parallel to leisure in risky, identity-symbolizing, criminal behavior?

There may be no absolutely clear line between those who choose to drive too fast when they aren't going anywhere and those who break into a warehouse. Breaking rules as a game is not unknown in the office and factory as well as on the streets.

Nevertheless, most will assert there have to be laws, regulations, and rules to protect others from the actions of the careless as well as the criminal. Living together in a society requires compromise and consideration. The problem is some will go beyond individual expression to engage in activity that is dangerous and destructive. Leisure may imply freedom, but there have to be limits. The issue is where to draw the line.

Debate: Destructive leisure should be banned.

YES

- Violence is exploitative. It harms the poor and the weak—those without the resources to withstand greater power. The exercise of exploitative power *against* others has to be regulated.

- Opportunity creates participation. If an activity is dangerous or degrading, then allowing it as free expression will draw more into it. At least some forms of gambling, for example, exploit the poor and are most likely to foster addiction. There have to be limits.

- Some people just do not consider the consequences of their actions. That is why we place age limits on some activity. The personal and social costs of some activity may be too high for a society to allow.

- In many leisure activities, a minority lose control. They become addicted to a substance or even an activity. Such addiction destroys lives—often innocent children and families. Some addiction may be a form of mental illness. In any case, it may be better to prevent the illness by controlling access to the activity or substance rather than to have to deal with the consequences.

- In almost any activity, some will go beyond any reason. That is why there have to be regulations on the use of natural resources, including banning some destructive activities. We cannot rely on everyone to exercise good judgment.

- There is also a waste of limited resources. The market may operate when it comes to expanding Las Vegas or tourism, despite how much some may want the investment directed elsewhere. When the resources are limited, fragile, or unique, however, then protection may require banning some kinds of activity or access.

- Any society needs some forms of control. People cannot do whatever they please whenever and wherever they please without invading the rights of others. Even leisure may be so invasive or destructive that it has to banned for the common good.

NO

- Where do we draw the line? There is no way of writing a law or regulation that does not invade individual liberty. There are too many examples of trying to enforce the tastes or preferences of the majority, or often a vocal minority, on others. Those with political and economic power will often use the law to enforce their tastes on others.

- Regulations become censorship. How much of MTV would pass the censors? It wasn't that long ago that married couples were placed in twin beds by the Motion Picture Production Code. No lawmaking group can be trusted with the power to enforce its own standards on a society. The ineffectual attempts to regulate television programming illustrate the problem.

- In a diverse society, there has to be room for many tastes and cultures—even when there is conflict. The standards of a group with political power cannot be levied on everyone.

- Prohibition doesn't work. People will do what they really want to do, even if there are elements of violence, exploitation, or the possibility of addiction. All banning does is drive such activity underground where it cannot be regulated and becomes more dangerous.

- Social pressure is the most effective social control. People are more likely to violate the law than the norms of their peer group. That makes education more effective than law for discretionary activities such as leisure.

- We learn best by experience. There has to be some opportunity to try things that seem attractive to learn that the costs far outweigh the benefits. Nothing can teach the dangers of gambling any quicker than for a teenager to lose his or her limited savings.

- There does have to be some structure within specific contexts. There are legitimate issues of safety on a ski run or at a beach. Arbitrary or excessive regulation, however, simply prompts some to take up the game of testing the limits. Clearly sensible regulation is one thing; attempts to control styles of leisure are another. It is one thing to regulate hunting to preserve the resource; it is another to ban it because some people find it offensive.

- Freedom is fundamental, to life as well as to leisure. It is better to err on the side of freedom and responsibility than control.

Discussion Questions

1. Is leisure always free, developmental, and positive? Why or why not?

2. Can we rely on the market to regulate leisure investments, or will some provide anything for money?

3. What is the distinction between normal and deviant leisure? Give examples.

4. Where can we draw the line between a variety of tastes in television programming and unacceptable sex and/or violence?

5. Why is gambling a growth industry? Is it likely to peak and decline like other activities?

6. Is substance use leisure? Why or why not?

7. Is violence "as American as apple pie?" Give evidence for your answer.

8. How can breaking the law be leisure? What about its costs?

9. If prohibition does not work, how can dangerous leisure be controlled?

10. Why is there so little about the other side of leisure in the mainstream leisure and recreation literature?

References and Resources

Abbott, D.A. and Cramer, S.L. (1993). Gambling attitudes and participation: A Midwestern survey. *Journal of Gambling Studies, 9,* 247–263

Gottdiener, M., Collins, C., and Dickens, D. (1999). *Las Vegas: The social production on an all-American city.* Oxford: Blackwell.

Messner, M. (1997). *Politics of masculinities: Men in movements.* Thousand Oaks, CA: Sage.

Rojek, C. (1995). *Decentring leisure: Rethinking leisure theory.* Thousand Oaks, CA: Sage.

Rojek, C. (1999). Deviant leisure. In E.L. Jackson and T.L. Burton (Eds.), *Leisure studies: Prospects for the 21st century.* State College, PA: Venture Publishing, Inc.

Simmons Market Research Bureau. (1990). *Simmons study of media and markets.* New York, NY: Author.

Chapter 18
Sport

Sport is everywhere. Children play their versions of sports wherever they can find a little space. Schools require some sport participation in classes and offer a wide spectrum of sport opportunities after class hours. Television has a constant stream of sport programming from all over the world 24 hours a day. Universities have multimillion-dollar varsity sports programs for men and women with stadiums—some of which seat over 100,000 spectators. Sports provide the basis for billions in gambling revenues. Sports events are also a daily topic of conversation wherever people gather—at work or at play.

Yet for adults, sport participation is quite limited. The only connection most American adults have with sport is through television. There is a great drop-off in playing sports when women and men leave school. The easy access to facilities and organized programs of school is left behind and sports require more self-organization and become more costly. There is a later decline in sport participation when the minority still playing become more involved in midlife roles and may lose some of the physical ability of youth. Sport may be important in the culture and as entertainment even though most adults do not play sports regularly.

In this chapter, a number of issues will be addressed: sport as entertainment, sport as activity, the nature of sport, and why people engage in sports, and sport as business. In all this analysis, there will be a fundamental theme: There is something about sport that is different from most other activities. What is it that makes sport so special for many people?

Sport: Who Is Watching?

Watching sports is a major leisure activity in contemporary culture. Further, attachment to particular teams and athletes seems to provide a kind of social identity for many children, youth, and adults. Some illustrative statistics provide a foundation for an analysis of sport as spectacle.

Table 18.1   Total Attendance at Selected Spectator Sports, 2001

Major League Baseball		73,881,000
Basketball—	NCAA men's	28,949,000
	NCAA women's	8,825,000
	Professional	21,436,000
Football—	NCAA	40,481,000
	NFL professional	20,590,000
Horse racing, all forms		37,000,000 (1999)
National Hockey League		21,957,000

Source: U.S. Census Bureau, 2003

Trends vary. Horse racing attendance is declining due to off-track betting, TVG Broadcasting and other betting opportunities, but the industry is steady and continues to show growth in its parimutuel turnover. Men's NCAA football and basketball are steady. Women's collegiate basketball is increasing. Professional hockey is increasing slightly. Except for strikes, professional football and baseball show no significant changes, but professional basketball has been increasing in attendance. Of course, all attendance figures are of total admissions with many fans attending several times. Although about $4 billion is spent on sports admissions in a year, less than 10% of the adult population attended any sport event in the past week.

While the totals are impressive, most sport viewing is on television, not in the stadium. The average professional football game draws 10% of the national viewing audience and the Super Bowl more than 40%. About 20% watch a baseball World Series game in daytime. Between 100 and 500 people will be watching a nationally televised game for every one there in person. The Simmons Market Research Bureau 1994 survey of 18,000 households found substantial proportions of the adult population watching sports on television. For example

- 6.7% watched auto racing occasionally and 2.3% frequently

- 19.6% watched professional baseball occasionally; 11.2% frequently

- 11.7% watched college basketball occasionally; 7.0% frequently

- 14.1% watched professional basketball occasionally; 8.9% frequently

- 9.2% watched golf occasionally; 4.4% frequently

- 19.6% watched professional football occasionally; 22.0% frequently

Televised sport is big business. For the 1997 Super Bowl there were 58 advertising slots. The price was $1.2 million for each 30 seconds. FOX paid the league $1.6 billion for television rights. In 1998, Disney, which owns ABC and ESPN, paid over $10 billion for its television football contracts. ESPN's deal for nonprime NFL games was almost $5 billion. Professional leagues have systems for sharing television revenues so that small-market franchises can remain competitive with the teams in New York, Chicago, and Los Angeles. Franchises are sold for hundreds of millions of dollars. They become profitable through television income as well as through the tax write-offs in which players as well as stadiums can be depreciated over their useful life. On the collegiate level, the television rights to the 1997 NCAA basketball tournament sold for $209 million, but gate receipts were only $17 million.

It is not only in university towns that sport may well be the major topic of casual conversation at work as well as in leisure venues. Small towns may identify with their school teams as they lose their retailing and service functions. Year-end tournaments bring together supporters even for schools where the stands are largely empty during the regular season. Betting pools spring up everywhere as the NCAA basketball tournament begins with its selected 64 teams. Super Bowl parties are held all over the country, often organized by nonfans who are not sure who is playing and who may not watch the game. Much of this is social rather than a devotion to the sport. (What team lost last year's Super Bowl?) Nevertheless, sport is more than a game. It is a cultural phenomenon with multiple meanings and dimensions.

Who Is Playing?

The question of who plays sports is quite another matter. Most children do, often informally as well as in organized contexts. Many youth engage in sports even though they have been excluded from school varsity participation. In high schools and colleges, there are intramural leagues and clubs as well as self-organized games. Sport participation is a significant, if minority, set of leisure activities for students. The picture for those out of school, however, is quite different. Further, most adults who play any sport do so only occasionally. As with most leisure, there are also age, gender, and social class differences (see Table 18.2, page 276).

The overall picture is one of low participation rates. Further, most adults who play a sport at all do so infrequently. Only 2.6% of adults play golf more than 40 times a year. Swimming attracts 25.5% of adults but only 5.1% swim 40 or more times a year. About 1.7% play basketball, 1.2% soccer, 2.2% softball, and 1.6% volleyball 40 or more times a year. Further, for most sports,

Table 18.2   Sports and Fitness Participation, 1994

	Total (millions)	Total percent	Percent male	Percent female	Percent times per year
Bowling	33	17.5	19.3	15.9	5.9 (20+)
Golf	21	11.1	15.1	7.5	4.7 (20+)
Tennis	12	6.3	7.2	5.5	3.1 (10+)
Racquetball	8	4.4	5.9	3.0	3.1 (5+)
Inline skating	2	1.9	2.2	1.6	
Fitness walking	48	25.6	22.1	28.9	10.0 (10+)
Jogging	17	8.8	10.2	7.5	3.5 (10+)
Basketball	9	4.8	7.5	2.6	
Football	6	3.4	5.2	1.6	
Softball/Baseball	8	7.4	9.5	5.4	
Volleyball	13	7.1	7.4	6.8	
Swimming	48	25.5	25.4	25.5	9.7 (20+)
Bicycling (outdoor)	21	11.3	12.5	10.1	5.9 (20+)
Downhill skiing	7	3.9	4.5	3.3	
Waterskiing	8	4.2	5.2	3.3	
Distance running	7	4.0	4.2	3.7	

Source: Simmons Market Research Bureau, 1994

especially team sports, males have higher rates than women. The gender difference, of course, reflects opportunities over a lifetime as well as current interest. Gender differences are, however, narrowing for most sports. In the over 25 years since the passage of Title IX, the number of high-school females participating in competitive sports has increased almost 700%.

Age is another matter. There is a consistent downward trend in sport and fitness participation related to age. A few examples from the Simmon's study (1994) will illustrate the picture:

• Swimming declines from 41% for those ages 18–24 to 31% for those 25–34, 16% for ages 55–64, and 10% for 65 and older.

• Jogging declines from 19% for ages 18–24 to 4.6% for ages 45–54.

• Tennis goes from 13% for ages 18–24 to 6% for ages 45–54 and 2% 65 and older.

• Softball declines from 15% for ages 18–24 to 11% for 25–34, 8% for 35–44, 6% for 45–54, 2.4% 55–64, and 2% 65 and older.

• Basketball drops from 13% ages 18–24 to 6% 25–34, and 1% 55–64.

There are two exceptions:

- Golf starts at 17% for those ages 18–24 and remains relatively high at 13% for those 55–64 and 65 and older.

- Fitness walking actually increases from 25% for those ages 18–24 up to 30% for 45–54, 26% for 55–64, and 25% for those 65 and older.

With the aging of the population, it is no surprise that golf and fitness walking are the two physical activities increasing in total participation.

There are other factors in sport participation. Most sports have a marked decrease related to income. That is no surprise for costly sports such as downhill skiing and golf, but is also the case for tennis, jogging, and swimming. The income factor is, however, less strong for team sports such as basketball, volleyball, and softball. Race and ethnicity, insofar as they are correlated with income and discrimination, also shape sport participation.

Sport participation statistics have a problem with seasonality. Many sports played primarily outdoors have seasons of peak participation and low seasons, especially in regions with winter climates. Such seasonal sports have participation numbers somewhat biased by seasonality. One trend in sport, however, is to offer year-round opportunities through indoor facilities and travel to warm climates. Such opportunities usually come at higher cost and are limited to higher income participants.

Sport begins with relatively high participation levels in school—at least for occasional players—and diminishes to generally low levels through the life course. As suggested before, the only exposure most adults have to sport most weeks is on television.

Special Issues of Sport

At one time, it was assumed sport was a good thing for both participants and spectators. Now critical analyses of sport are common. Sport is associated with violence, racism, and sexism.

Violence is part of some sports as they are played. Boxing is the practice of beating another person into unconsciousness. American football is a contest of violent collision as well as skill. Rugby has an even higher injury rate. The physical struggle near the basket in basketball is an essential part of the game. Some players are known for their physical play and called *enforcers*. And everyone knows about those who "went to a fight and a hockey game broke out." The accidents and intimidation are accentuated in auto racing with spectacular flaming crashes repeated over and over on television sports reports.

There is also crowd violence. International soccer/football matches have had to be canceled because of fan riots at the stadium and after the contest. Even in relatively controlled university basketball arenas, individual fans exhibit verbal and physical behaviors that are at least symbolically violent. Sport, after all, is a contest. There are sides with winners and losers brought into a concentrated time and space of opposition. It should not be surprising the confrontation may get out of control, on the playing surface and in the stands. Concern over such violence goes back to the Roman arena as well as to the blood sports of deadly combat that have emerged in almost every culture.

Violence and Gender

There is an especially sinister element to this violence that has gained attention more recently. It suggests one target of this violence is women. The place of women in sport has been secondary to the playing of the sport by men. Until recently, women were discouraged or even barred from physically demanding and highly competitive sports. Competitive sports were not considered "lady-like," and there were suggestions that such activity would be injurious to the delicate physique of women. Now with Federal Title IX standards of gender equality in educational opportunities and new images of strong and active women, such exclusion is diminishing.

Still common, especially in mass spectator sports, is the use of women to heighten the spectacle for male viewers. The Dallas Cowgirls became a national symbol of such barely clad dance lines. Institutions of higher learning select female students for body type and parade them in tight costumes during football and basketball games. Female students are even selected to help with recruiting of prize athletes in ways that may suggest they represent part of the attraction of the university. In short, women as sexual objects are part of the mass sport entertainment package picked out by television cameras in ways that have no relationship to the game.

The connection of this sexual exhibition and suggested availability with violence has gained attention as athletes, both university and professional, have been indicted for physical attacks on women. Of course, one possibility is that the "problem" is created by media attention, and such violence against women is thoroughly a part of the culture. It may have no special connection with sport. One study of campus reports, however, indicates the rate of reported attacks is as much as six times higher for athletes than the general male population. The question, then, is whether there is something about sport that provokes or even teaches such sexual violence. Do athletes expect sexual compliance and learn to meet resistance with violence? If so, then the general socialization and citizenship values of sport become subject to question.

There are also the images of masculinity and femininity. Competitive sport may symbolize what "real men" are supposed to be: aggressive, strong, and capable of violence. "Real women," on the other hand, are supposed to be passive, nurturing, compliant, and gentle. Traditional sport roles support such images. Such images have been found even in Little League contexts and banter as well as among older athletes (Fine, 1987). But traditional sport roles are changing. Now women may be admired and rewarded for strength, speed, grace, and even competitiveness. Yet, the dance lines continue and football is the essential men's sport while figure skating really belongs to the women.

Mini-Debate: Sport reinforces gender stereotypes (Messner, 1992).

YES

- The major revenue sports emphasize masculine violence. Women more often receive acclaim for sports stressing grace.

- Females are underrepresented in the controlling roles of sport— coaching, ownership, and management.

- In the past, there have been different rules for female sports, emphasizing their supposed inability to play the "real" game.

- Both professional and university sports employ "sexy" females to supplement the entertainment while the "real game" is for men only.

- Sport socialization for males stresses the masculine attributes of being tough, "playing through pain," being able to "take it and dish it out," hitting hard, and even inflicting injury. Overcoming opposition is through conflict, not reconciliation. There is a deep relationship between violence and masculinity.

- The competition ethos is one of men against men with high rewards to the winner. In the "star system," the rewards are not only financial but also social status with power over others. In former times, this ethos was claimed to produce good soldiers for warfare, now the competition is more in economic and sexual spheres.

- One outcome of sport, fellowship and friendship, can also be seen as male bonding that excludes women. The infamous locker-room talk may reinforce this distinction.

- Gender is a social construct in the sense of being taught and learned in a culture. We learn as children what is expected of us as gendered beings. Sport is one social arena in which this is taught, exemplified, and rewarded. In fact, sport is central to our images of what it means to be masculine and feminine.

- Men, retaining most power in the economic and political fields, define the world according to such gender constructs. Sport vocabulary is everywhere. The world is described in the metaphor of sport contests of men against men with women on the sidelines.

NO

- That old world is changing rapidly. Women now play the competitive sports: basketball, soccer, volleyball, and even rugby. They are admired for being fast and strong. The old images of femininity are being left behind.

- Opportunities for women in sport have also changed. Now there is a new generation of females who were encouraged to engage in strenuous sport as children. They have access to facilities and better coaching. Early starts are making all the difference. Females no longer run and throw "like girls." In track and swimming women now go faster than men's world records of a few decades ago. As increased opportunities change abilities, images change as well.

- There are no longer just "feminine" sports. Women's basketball and soccer are hard, fast, and competitive. Some males may not like it, but women are presenting new images of high competition and competence in formerly male provinces.

- As a consequence, there is a blurring of former gender stereotypes. The culture is changing. Sport demonstrates the more aggressive images of women as the home demonstrates that men can be nurturing. The problem is some men and women just haven't caught up with the change.

- There is a reconstruction of gender roles that includes the physical competence of women. One possible reason for the seeming increase in reports of sexual violence is that women are saying "no" and fighting back.

- Fundamentally, many women no longer accept the old stereotypes. This deep cultural change may provoke some gender conflict for a time, but eventually men will come to accept and even value partners who are independent and strong, in life as well as in sport.

Sport and Race

Another critique of sport has been that it has been racist. This may seem a thing of the past because so many professional African-American, Latino, and increasing numbers of Asian and immigrant European, stars in basketball, football, or baseball are rewarded with multimillion-dollar contracts. They are celebrities employed to promote products to consumers a majority of whom are European American. The old racism of sport, decades of exclusion and separation, may seem past. Sport is valued also by the previously excluded just because it provides avenues to wealth and models of success.

Yet, there remain suggestions of continued racism. Too often men and women involved in sport utter pronouncements and remarks are based on the old racial stereotypes and judgments. There are now African American and Latino coaches, officials, and managers. They are, however, in a distinct minority. In the professional leagues, owners with the real power to rule the sport are almost all European American. That may reflect the economic distribution of wealth rather than racial exclusion, but the fact remains. Media roles are opening only gradually. There is some opening of formerly "racial" playing positions to those who had been judged less capable of performance requiring certain skills. Yet, most quarterbacks are still White and most cornerbacks Black, and those of Asian descent are believed to not have the "right body type" for professional basketball despite evidence to the contrary. Is there no racist discrimination in this?

Sport has become more open to non–European-American males than business or the university. There has been great change from the old days of segregated leagues and outright exclusion. Many remember well when Jackie Robinson took incredible abuse to be the first African-American big-league ballplayer. Change has come fast. Perhaps now sport reproduces the racism still embedded in the culture rather than exemplifies outright exclusion. It is more subtle and beneath the surface.

What Is Sport?

Listing sports is easy. Of course, there may be some borderline cases. Is the nonphysical game of chess a sport? It certainly is competitive enough. Is the physical activity of jogging a sport when it is not competitive? In general, however, we know what we mean by sport. Sports are contested, have accepted rules, and usually involve physical action. Narrow definitions require traditions of structure and even special spaces. They refer to competitive, institutionalized sports. They exclude mental contests or more spontaneous "new games" that are more cooperative than competitive. More inclusive approaches just list common dimensions such as having uncertain outcomes, organization, and some kind of measured completion.

The most persistent themes of sport are physical activity and effort, a degree of regularity and form, and competitive formats and outcomes. Sport involves forms that allow for a measurement of relative skills, whether by external judging or a competitive score. There is an element of play in the outcome uncertainty and freedom of participation. One inclusive definition is "Sport is organized activity in which physical effort is related to that of others in some relative measurement of outcomes with accepted regularities and forms" (Kelly, 1996, p. 214).

A more relevant question is "What is so special about sport?" How have a number of games come to have such social and cultural significance in society after society?

Sport has long been a center of excitement and attention in Western societies. The Olympic games began in ancient Greece, at first for amateurs and eventually for sport specialists sponsored by the wealthy. The World Cup of soccer/football becomes an obsession for those nations whose teams gain the final rounds. In the United States, baseball may have been replaced as the "national pastime" by televised professional football. In Indiana, basketball is the state sport from small towns to the universities. Sport is given an incredible measure of attention for something that is by definition contained and confined to its singular time and place.

There are a number of factors. In school the prestigious sports are a major source of social status. Sport provides a direct means of self-testing with its immediate feedback and the more recent growth of statistical measures. It is integrally related to self-images, sex roles and identities, and identification in mass culture. As a consequence, sport has been both exalted and attacked by social philosophers and critics from diverse perspectives. Even athletes themselves have joined in criticizing the "overemphasis" on sport, the adulation of stars, and the exploitation of players by business interests and universities.

Christopher Lasch (1977), a historian fascinated by sport, reflected on both the contributions and corruption of sport in contemporary society. He began with the intrinsic satisfaction of sport participation. The intensity of concentration is a pure form of engagement without external consequences. The "ideal conditions" contrast with the moral confusion of most life. The game begins new and fresh in conditions of temporary equality, the action is self-contained, the form set, and the outcome uncertain. Once the game begins, external factors are irrelevant. In a routinized world, the immediate feedback of sport is clear and unmistakable in the artificial context of the game.

Lasch argues that there is nothing inherently evil about the spectator element of sport. Rather, the spectator is able to join in the drama of the contest through an identification with the players and the action. The vicarious participation yields some of the same meaning and engagement of actually playing the game. Further, being part of a collectivity of spectators yields a sense of community and solidarity often missing in a fragmented world. The spectator becomes part of the contested drama, enhancing the meaning for the players and for the society.

Problems emerge when the containment of sport is lost. The sport itself may be changed to heighten the intensity of emotion and identification in a mass setting. In vast stadiums and now on the small screen, the game may seem distant and trivial. So the rules are changed and styles of play altered to make the game more exciting, more dramatic, and even more violent. As Roman gladiatorial combats became bloodier as they were fought to the death, so modern spectator sports have been changed as well. In football, even the shape of the ball is different. Now the media-transmitted impact and appeal becomes the purpose of the game. The contest is manipulated to grip spectators who are defined as a market rather than a community. Play leads to display. Individual virtuosity replaces team coordination. Stars become more than athletes who are part of a team. Rewards vary by magnitudes of millions of dollars. The game is no longer a set-apart contest with its own intrinsic meaning. Some of this distortion comes with a preoccupation on winning rather than playing. Any contest has losers as well as winners. When the meaning of the game is focused entirely on the outcome, then the experience of play is devalued or even lost. This reaches extremes in the Olympic Games when the media define the second-best gymnast in the world as a "loser" in an event with only one winner. The nature of sport is recast when "winning is the only thing."

Some would argue using sport for other ends is nothing new. Many sports in earlier cultures were preparation for war and combat. Walter Camp proclaimed that the do-or-die spirit of football held the line in World War I. As suggested earlier, images of masculinity have been tied to the aggressive and contested nature of sport. Sport has been extolled because it promotes physical competence, health, and even moral character. Lasch argues that whatever the external aims, sport is transformed by being used for other purposes. What is lost is the focus on the experience of the measured and regulated contest *for its own sake*.

Some attempts have been made in youth sports to minimize the external meanings of sport. There are rules requiring that all team members play.

Statistical records are not kept from game to game. All-star games and playoffs are eliminated. Every effort is made to concentrate on each game as it is played. Coaches are taught to emphasize the team effort, the development of skills, and involvement in each game. The stress is on the experience—the risk, feedback, focus, and skill of playing the game. There is some hope that such programs will restore an uncorrupted kind of sport insulated from business, politics, and exploitation. The history of sport, however, suggests it will continue to reflect its cultural context. In a competitive, status-conscious, and materialistic society, sport is unlikely to be just a pure engagement in a structured contest for its own sake. There will probably continue to be a dialectic between playing the game for its own sake and the organization of sport for personal and institutional gain.

Why Play Sports?

One paradoxical matter is those who care most about sport are often the most severe critics. Those who have experienced the excitement and involvement of a game played on equal terms by well-matched opponents know sport at its best. They know the fullness of meaning of the risk, involvement, and immediacy of the game. They know the satisfaction of the disciplined gaining of skill that engages the whole self: body, mind, and emotions. They know the heightening of meaning of such engagement in a world that is often routine and unchallenging.

It is this experience that is at the center of sport. Mihaly Csikszentmihalyi (1975) identified sport as one arena in which challenge and skill may meet in a way that produces the deep experience of "flow." The agreed-on structure of sport enables players to focus on their engagement. The skills of sport are exhibited in fixed forms. The feedback is immediate and clear. The game becomes its own limited world of meaning in a meeting of challenge and skill.

Along with the experience itself, there are other meanings to sport. One is clearly the relation of physical exercise to health (Godbey, 2003). Abundant evidence suggests regular physical exertion supports health throughout the life course. Dedication to exercise, however, is difficult for many. The proportion of adults who begin programs of regular exercise and discontinue is near 80%. Exercise itself does not seem to be that attractive for many. Persistence is enhanced by feedback and sense of accomplishment. Exercise is supported by social ties with others who join in the exercise. The value of sport as a context for exercise is the experience. Sport is intrinsically satisfying, socially engaging, and offers a sense of efficacy. For many, it is the best context for regular physical exertion. There are at least two problems, however. The first is injuries that prevent participation. The second is most adults have not had lifetime experience in which sport has been satisfying.

The reward of social status is somewhat different. Several studies found sports are the most important factor in social status in secondary schools. Of course, in earlier times this meant male sports gave status to varsity athletes and association with those athletes gave status to females. It may be the system is more complex in most schools now. It seems to be the case, however, that sports still are a central basis for status among children and youth. Insofar as that is true, it raises certain problems. It directs attention to one kind of ability to the exclusion of others. Physical maturity becomes a major factor in school rewards. Attention and reward are given disproportionately for skills and accomplishments that may have little relation to adult achievement. Praise, notice, sexual attractiveness, and status accrue to the athlete rather than to the scholar, artist, or person engaged in service to others. Further, this reward system is gender-biased and skewed toward particular images of masculinity and femininity.

There are indications of change. Female athletes are beginning to receive more attention. School sports are more often played to empty bleachers as the social organization of schools fragments. The stars on televised sport may replace local heroes. Status rewards are dependent on the importance of sports in the school culture. In schools divided by race, class, and material status symbols, sport may just not be as important as previously. Sport may no longer be as central a symbol of community and cohesiveness.

Sport As Leisure and As Business

Insofar as sport participation is based on the experience, it is leisure. Sport may be a special kind of leisure—challenging, exciting, involving, strenuous, community-building, and satisfying. The previous analysis also suggests that sport is part of the social system. It may be used for political purposes—as a spectacle to distract citizens from other issues. It may be an economic enterprise with investments of hundreds of millions of dollars in stadiums, franchises, and players. It may be central to the development of children and youth by providing experience of demonstrated competence and social bonding. It may also be problematic for some since every contest has losers as well as winners. Competition may be seen as the context for the experience of sport rather than its sole meaning.

On the other hand, sport is spectacle and entertainment in the modern media culture. As such, it is big business, integrally a part of the investment and promotion systems of capitalist economies. Some argue the essence of sport has been transformed by the media and its incorporation into the economy. Players are now commodities—stars who are bought and sold and depreciated as investments. Spectators are consumers of the entertainment. Athletes are defined exclusively as those performing in the vast arenas in games that attract media coverage. Sport is not something we do; it is something we consume. And it is marvelously provided as mass entertainment for which we pay in money rather than disciplined effort. That is the leisure of sport for most adults.

Debate: Sport is now primarily business.

YES

- Sport is an integral part of the capitalist economy. Hundreds of millions of dollars are invested in franchises, stadiums, and teams. The media, leagues, cities, and owners are part of the system. The aim, as for any investment, is a profitable return. Even horses are sold into syndication as investments. The media buy the contest to resell it as advertising for other sectors of the economy. That's the way most experience sport—as entertainment business.

- Major sports events are sponsored to advertise business products, such as golf tournaments and the Nextel Cup in auto racing. Football bowls and golf tournaments are renamed for corporate sponsors. Billboards line baseball fields and figure-skating arenas. The entire event becomes a stage for advertising.

- There is also the status factor. Owners become celebrities along with their purchased players. Stadiums have prestigious sky boxes sold to businesses that write them off from their taxes as a business expense.

- Cities make their own investments in sites and stadiums, partly for prestige and partly to attract visitors who spend money. It is considered to be good for business to be a "big league" city even if tax revenues are used to finance the enterprise.

- University sports are now training leagues for professional teams. Not only football and basketball but also baseball, tennis, and track are more preprofessional than amateur in nature. Even the games are played with "pro-style" offenses to maximize future prospects for players.

- The federal taxation system underwrites sport business by allowing for depreciation of assets, including the athletes. High-paid stars become rapid tax write-offs.

- To maximize revenues, stars are promoted rather than teams. The media collaborate by focusing their commentary and cameras on those designated stars who are then resold in the advertising schemes of the business interests.

- Sport is controlled by the owners. Players may occasionally need to be reminded of this as their strikes fail to alter the power structures of the sports. Even free-agent players are free only to enter a market controlled by the owners.

- Television revenues are the major source of income. Revenues are shared by formula among owners and even universities to support the overall system. Sport and media are combined into a total business enterprise with all sorts of deals that stress the major markets and keep the overall system functioning.

- Even college sports have been sold to advertisers through sponsorship deals with labels displayed on uniforms, ads on scoreboards and officials' tables, soft drink franchises, and signs all over stadiums. Coaches have special income-producing deals with such sponsors to enhance their total financial "packages."

- The clothing and equipment of professional athletes have prominent brand labels. Scoreboards, tickets, and badges have advertising logos—even universities sell their teams for advertising revenue. Students may be priced out of supporting their own franchised school teams. How much of the promotion of adult-organized youth sports such as Little League comes from those who manufacture and sell the fancy uniforms?

- Most sports have their "second season," playoffs and tournaments that bring in increased revenue and provide major media events. Such second seasons are a major source of income for professional franchises and university programs.

- Playing styles are designed to provide the best spectacle. Defense may win games, but offense fills the seats and provides the best media show.

- Leagues, franchises, service businesses, player contracts, endorsements, advertising, scoreboards, television, newspapers, and networks form an economic system in which the game is just a commodity to be sold.

NO

- Interest in sport is based on playing. Those who become attached to professional and university teams usually played the game as children. Their interest is based on experience.

- Children and youth play sports because they want to. The problem is the system places too much emphasis on spectator events rather than participation. Given the chance, the young with greatest access to opportunities do play sports—even the gender gap is closing.

- Retail businesses are based on participation. Hundreds of thousands of businesses supply equipment, facilities, and instruction so that people of all ages can play sports.

- When sport is defined inclusively, many kinds of structured activities include physical exertion. Many are more available to adults than the traditional team sports, but contain many of the same meanings. Rates of participation in each sport may not be high, but the cumulative total of playing sports and games would be much higher.

- There is a renewed stress on doing sports. Participation in golf is increasing because it is available to older players and to women as well as to younger males. As opportunities are widened, participation is likely to grow.

- Playing sports is important to children and youth, especially in the school context, because it provides an important opportunity for growth and development. We are physical beings, and the experience of sport is more than a peripheral aspect of life.

- For adults still involved in sport, the experience continues to be important. The experience of sport that may even lead to the concentration, involvement, and excitement of "flow" may continue to be central to the overall scheme of life's meaning.

- Sport has significant social meanings. It is a central topic of conversation in all sorts of settings. It provides the basis for many friendships that transcend the sport setting. Sport is very much a part of the total culture.

- Historically all kinds of societies have had their sports. Many types of sport are found in different societies in different epochs. Sport is more than a business promotion; it is a universal element of cultures and social systems.

- The meanings of sport engagement—physical competence, challenge, and coordinated action—are central to what it means to be human. Business may distort those meanings, but cannot obliterate them.

- There are just too many manifestations of self-organized sport, of play for its own sake, to focus entirely on the industry of sport.

Discussion Questions

1. Is mass sport as a spectacle quite a different thing from actually playing the sport? How are watching a sport and playing it related?

2. Does television create interest in sports? Does it redefine sport in the process?

3. Is there something inherently violent and aggressive in sports? Is this necessarily bad?

4. How is sport still racist? sexist? elitist?

5. How do the meanings of sport change through the life course?

6. Are youth sports too organized and dominated by adults who love seeing their children decked out in uniforms and making all-star teams? Do parents spoil children's sports?

7. Are women still primarily ornaments for men in sport contexts? Will this change?

8. How has television changed sports at colleges and universities?

9. What is it about sport that draws people into participation? Are meanings age-related?

10. Has business spoiled sports in contemporary society? How?

References and Resources

Bloom, J. and Willard, M. (Eds.). (2002). *Sports matters: Race, recreation and culture*. New York, NY: New York University Press.

Brackenridge, C. (2001). *Spoilsports: Understanding and preventing sexual exploitation in sport*. New York, NY: Routledge.

Coakley, J. and Donnelly, P. (Eds.). (2003). *Inside sports*. New York, NY: Routledge.

Collins, M, with Kay, T. (2003). *Sport and social exclusion*. London, UK: Department fro Culture, Media, and Sport.

Csikszentmihalyi, M. (1975). *Beyond boredom and anxiety*. San Francisco, CA: Jossey-Bass.

Eisen, G. and Wiggins, D. (Eds.). (1994). *Ethnicity and sport in North American history and culture*. Westport, CT: Greenwood Press.

Fine, G. (1987). *With the boys: Little League baseball and preadolescent subculture*. Chicago, IL: University of Chicago Press.

Godbey, G. (2003). *Leisure in your life: An exploration* (6th ed.). State College, PA: Venture Publishing, Inc.

Hartmann-Tews, I. and Pfister, G. (Eds.). (2003). *Sport and women: Social issues in international perspective*. New York, NY: Routledge.

Hoch, P. (1972). *Rip off the big game: The exploitation of sports by the power elite*. Garden City, NY: Doubleday.

Huizinga, J. (1950). *Homo ludens: A study of the play-element in culture*. Boston, MA: Beacon Press.

Kelly, J.R. (1996). *Leisure* (3rd ed.). Boston, MA: Allyn and Bacon.

Lasch, C. (1977). The corruption of sport. *New York Review*, April 28.

Messner, M. (1992). *Power at play: Sports and the problem of masculinity*. Boston, MA: Beacon.

Messner, M. and Sabo, D. (Eds.). (1991). *Sport, men, and the gender order: Critical feminist perspectives*. Champaign, IL: Human Kinetics Press.

Miller, P. and Wiggins, D. (Eds.). (2004). *Sport and the color line: Black athletes and race relations in 20th century America*. London, UK: Routledge.

Michener, J. (1976). *Sports in America*. New York, NY: Random House.

Novak, M. (1975). *The joy of sports: End zones, bases, baskets, balls, and the consecration of the American spirit*. New York, NY: Basic Books.

Simmons Market Research Bureau. (1994). *Simmon's study of media and the markets*. New York, NY: Author.

Sudgen, J. and Tomlinson, A. (Eds.). (2003). *Power games: A critical sociology of sport*. New York, NY: Routledge.

U.S. Census Bureau. (2003). *Statistical abstract of the United States*. Washington, DC: Author.

Williams, J. (2004). *A game for rough girls? A history of women's football in Britain*. London, UK: Routledge.

Chapter 19
The Arts

In classic approaches, the arts have been most closely identified with leisure. The Greeks referred to music, writing poetry, drama, sculpture, and other arts that flourished in their culture. The humanism of the Renaissance glorified the human spirit, body, and creativity in artistic expression. Throughout the centuries, the church in the West was a center of support and inspiration for the visual arts, architecture, and music. Artistic expression in all cultures has usually been considered the primary evidence of their quality.

This is true of the so-called folk arts as well as the classic arts. Whole civilizations are categorized according to the remainders of painting, pottery, and sculpture found by archeologists in later centuries. There is now renewed interest in the songs and stories of cultures and subcultures as evidence of their self-interpretations. The arts are more than the exclusive culture of the elite. The arts are seen as central to every level of every culture. The arts are what people do to express and symbolize the meanings of their lives—They are symbolic representations of who we are.

Who Does The Arts?

There are marked differences in participation in the arts, especially when the focus is on the "fine arts." All people in modern societies do not attend symphony concerts, visit art museums, or enjoy opera in equal numbers. On the other hand, they do not equally listen to country western music, go to rock concerts, or buy tickets to Las Vegas shows. There is a division between "high culture" and "pop culture" that is recognized even when said to be just a matter of taste. This chapter focuses on the classic arts even though no assumption is made of their intrinsic superiority.

The arts are practiced in all sorts of environments. Public schools are especially active in music with their bands, choirs, and other musical groups. A high proportion of introduction to music is in school. It is also true, however, that such programs are strongest in districts with the highest per student budgets. There is also art in the home with consumption of hi-fi music and television drama, reading, and decoration. There are pianos, other musical instruments, potting wheels, drawing easels, crafts of weaving and woodworking, and even writing. The arts may begin with children drawing with crayons, sculpting with mud, dancing to music, making up stories, and singing wordless songs. At the other end of the life course, the retired may take up an art left behind through decades of work and family responsibilities. For all ages, vacations may include visits to a variety of artistic displays and performances.

In many communities, there is a variety of programs in which artistic work is produced and opportunities afforded for appreciation:

- Public recreation programs with both education and performance opportunities

- Nonprofit organizations, including orchestras, opera companies, community theaters, dance groups, and others

- Commercial enterprises, such as theaters and concert organizers

- Schools on all levels, some specializing in the arts

- Private instructional programs

- Voluntary organizations, such as camera clubs, art guilds, and theater groups

- Religious organizations with programs in music and other arts

Some programs are for children and others for adults. Some are at high levels of "amateur" performance and others for beginners. One aspect of the growth in the arts has been the acceptance as part of "the arts" of such forms as photography, modern and jazz dance, jazz and folk music, and new forms of the graphic arts. In some the skills required to produce something satisfying are not as demanding as in traditional arts. Barriers for participation may be lower and acceptance wider.

The arts, requiring skills that may be more personal and portable, are more likely than sports to continue after leaving school. The percentages, however, are not high. Further, they are strongly related to education. Percentages of those ages 18 and above who engaged in an art at least once in 2002 are:

- Drawing: 9% with 12% of those with some college education

- Creative writing: 7% with 11% of college graduates and 13% with graduate education

- Pottery: 7% with 9% of those with some college

- Playing classical music: 2% with 5% of those with graduate education

- Buying art work: 30% with 31% of college graduates and 34% with graduate education

- Attending a classical music concert: 12% with 22% of college graduates and 34% with graduate education

- Attending opera: 3% with 6% of college graduates

- Attending ballet: 4% with 7% of college graduates

- Attending a musical play: 17% with 30% of college graduates

- Attending a nonmusical play: 12% with 23% of college graduates

- Visiting an art museum: 27% with 47% of college graduates

- Photography: 12% with 17% of college graduates

Source: Statistical Abstract of the United States (2003)

Since there is a high correlation between education and income, rates of participation in the arts also increase with income level. This relationship gives an impression of the elitist nature of the arts. It should be pointed out, however, that small but significant percentages of those with less than a full high school education read, draw, write, and visit museums. Some of the differences may reflect costs and opportunities more than interests.

Television has had some of the same impact on the performing arts as on sports. Via the screen, videos, and satellites the great events of the performing arts may be viewed in the living room. The finest opera performances, Broadway plays, premier concerts, and even international events such as the Edinburgh Festival are available without cost in almost every American home. As a result, standards of quality are raised and the possibility of young artists being inspired toward excellence are worldwide. The negative side, of course, is that live performances may lose support and opportunities for young and amateur performers in the community will be diminished.

Trends in the Arts

Despite reductions in financial support from the National Endowment for the Arts, the *Statistical Abstract of the United States* of 2003 does not report dramatic changes in community arts production:

- In 2000 approximately 1,600 community orchestras had total budgets of over $1,126 million. Of these 37 are considered major orchestras. Half as many people attended their concerts as went to Major League Baseball games. Total attendance, however, now remains stable at about 31 million since 1993, but many orchestras are in severe financial difficulty.

- Trends in classical music recording sales are difficult to measure due to format shifts. In general, sales seem relatively steady over the past 30 years. Sales in instructional level musical instruments, however, are increasing.

- More than 1,200 companies produced opera in 2000. The 98 professional companies of OPERAmerica had budgets of more than $638 million. Budgets, attendance, and total performances show steady attendance at about 6.3 million.

- Dance appears to be a growing area in the performing arts despite financial troubles for many national and regional companies. Numbers of performances of resident and touring companies are increasing, supported by young people being instructed in dance performance.

- Theater exists on many levels. The number of commercial theaters on Broadway has declined, but regional, community, and school theater continue. As many as 100 million people attend the half million plays presented by amateur school and community groups.

In general, there is no sign of a boom in the arts. Financial difficulties exist for all performing arts on all levels. Even major urban performing arts centers face serious problems. Nevertheless, overall participation in the arts lags only slightly behind population growth. When all forms of the arts are included, the arts are a major cultural phenomenon.

The Arts in Society

The number of artists who have gained the high level of skill required to be professional is relatively small. The number of amateurs who devote themselves to gaining and improving their skills is infinitely higher. Yet, the concept of the "fine arts" connotes for many a kind of elitism or even snobbery. There are two basic approaches to the issue.

The first proposes it is all a matter of taste. Some prefer classical and some pop. Some value Shakespeare and Ibsen and some the weekly television sitcom. One is not inherently better than the other; they are just different.

Further, such tastes are acquired. The relationship between education and the arts is hardly surprising. In the educational process, there is not only exposure to the arts but also a consistent socialization as to the value of artistic endeavor. In school we are taught the tastes that we then assume are a sign of superior culture. The differences between fine, folk, and popular culture are in such acquired tastes, not in the nature of the art. Bach and the Beatles are just different forms of music although one is older and the other more popular.

The other approach stresses such elements of the arts as technical skill, difficulty of preparation, acceptance by "experts," and enduring over time. It is true that most pop musical groups and compositions last only months or a few years while the "classics" have lasted through the centuries. Further, most classical artists spend years, even lifetimes, gaining the technical skills for high-level performances. Yet, there is no clear line of division on either skill or longevity.

One other factor, according to some analysis, is social status. For example, the symphony guild is one of the highest status organizations in most communities. The annual guild dinner dance, usually at the country club, may be the major social event of the year. Skill or even musical discrimination have nothing to do with prominence in such an "arts" organization. Further, programs with lists of contributors, dinners before prestigious events, and receptions with visiting artists are signs of economically based social status. The arts reflect the community social hierarchy. In this way, support of the arts becomes a symbol of community position. The audience, then, becomes a social construction tied to the symbolic culture and institutional division of the social system (Zolberg, 1990). An exclusive focus on the arts and related tastes obscures how the arts become a symbol of social stratification. There is a clear social separation between the Metropolitan Opera and the Grand Old Opry.

This separation is intensified by location, pricing, and requirements of dress and decorum. While there has been some leveling of concert prices between the concert hall and the stadium, in general prices reinforce exclusion. Pop and rock concerts in outdoor arenas dwarf even the largest symphony or opera audiences. Further, the accepted rules for behavior at classical performances seldom include dancing in the aisles, swarming the stage, or informal attire. All kinds of arts are, after all, also a business. They are marketed to appropriate consumers in ways that clearly differentiate their social status and resources.

Debate: The fine arts are exclusive and elitist.

YES

- Participation in the arts, both appreciation and production, is strongly related to higher education. Insofar as higher education is correlated with family income, then arts and socioeconomic status go together. There are even some indications that the status of the university or college is a factor.

- Social status is symbolized by many signs, of which the arts are only one. Knowing about the arts, joining arts organizations, and being seen at prestigious performances are all status symbols. Having the "right" taste and knowing the proper vocabularies of arts discourse demonstrate higher social status to society's gate-keepers. Bourdieu (1984) calls this "cultural capital."

- The costs of acquiring skills in the arts make it likely performers will come from families with financial resources. Very few kids from the projects, however talented, will make it into a major orchestra. The exceptions are usually funded by well-endowed programs in major cities.

- In contrast to a pop or rock concert, the fine arts require "proper" conduct at their programs. One does not go to an art gallery opening in jeans, smoke cigars and drink beer at the ballet, or dance in the aisles at the opera, or enter the auditorium once the performance has started. One has to be taught how to behave.

- The fine arts have their own lines of inclusion and exclusion. While modern art may occasionally break those boundaries, traditions have great power to accept or reject. Further, educated "official" critics decide for others what is acceptable. These critics are usually based in the elite media or institutions.

- The canons of acceptance are not a matter of popular acceptance or the market. Rather, *New York Times* critics and Ivy League faculty are the authorities on what is good. The fine arts have their anointed gatekeepers of taste, quality, and acceptance.

- Perhaps most important, the fine arts are a kind of closed corporation in which all the symbols of social status—such as education, cultural knowledge, modes of communication, and connections—

come together so completely that anyone can tell in a moment who fits in and who does not.

NO

- All education includes the arts. Almost every public school provides introductions to the arts—both appreciation and performance. Now there are public high schools in the poorer sections of major cities that specialize in arts preparation. Universities provide scholarships and even seek out the talented from deprived backgrounds. Countless programs open the arts to people from all levels of society.

- The results of such programs are gradual, but real. Major orchestras are no longer just White and male. The world of the arts is opening up in a systematic program designed to break down the old exclusive barriers. Even national barriers are falling and artists may come from anywhere in the world.

- Public programs do more than admit a few scholarship students. Established artists are forming companies and educational programs in East Harlem and Watts. There is a strong conviction among those in the fine arts that there is ability everywhere and the arts are an enrichment for any life.

- The old distinctions are becoming blurred. Leading artists perform on television. Concerts are mixed in their offerings. The technical and artistic quality of some television drama may be quite high. There are "crossover" artists who play a variety of music and who refuse to make any clear separation between the classical and the popular. Who would exclude American jazz from the arts? Jazz developed in the midst of poverty and racial exclusion—sometimes in bordellos.

- There is also a blurring of the lines between the folk and fine arts. In music, ceramics, drama, dance, and other art forms, the formerly rigid standards of the classical are being broken down. Such change may be controversial, but one aim is to make art more accessible to more people. The appreciation of beauty, after all, should not require a graduate education or an investment portfolio.

- Now "stars" in the arts may come from anywhere, from Kansas to China. The arts, ideally, are a true meritocracy. In the end, all that really counts is that the artist be good at his or her art. There has long been a connection between social status and the arts, but that is really a violation of the nature of art in which all that matters is doing it well.

Creation and Appreciation in the Arts

The arts involve both production and consumption. The performing arts require those who attend and understand the performance. So there is skill involved in both production and appreciation. Further, while the artist may become totally absorbed in creation, in the end there is the presentation to others. Art is not an isolated act.

Arts Creation and Production

There seems to be something special about arts production. Doing and creating in the arts primarily for the experience, as leisure, is different from even the most informed appreciation. There is an investment of the self and an identification with what is created that is missing in appreciating the work of others. This difference may be illustrated in the engagement that Robert Stebbins (1979) calls being an "amateur."

Modern amateurs, according to Stebbins, are not just messing around with an art or an activity. The amateur is neither a professional gaining a major part of her income from the craft nor one who occasionally dabbles in the activity. Rather, there is a sustained commitment to acquiring a high level of skill. The standards for the amateur are the same as for the professional. The amateur does the art in a highly systematic and disciplined way. An amateur violinist practices regularly, obtains help in improving skills, and is a regular member of one or more orchestras or chamber groups. This investment of the self in the art or other activity is central to the amateur's identity. Further, the commitment usually involves being part of a community of amateurs who form a significant social group. For the true amateur, there is always the challenge of further improvement in skill. At the same time, there may be an immersion in doing the activity for its own sake, for the experience. The appreciative audience is only part of the context of creation.

Practice may be fulfilling in itself. It is more than preparation for the public performance. Nevertheless, the concert, show, or other performance is part of the whole experience—a time to put the skills to the final challenge. In performance, there is also feedback that is a test of the investment in skill. In the end, however, it may be the player's own evaluation that is most important. Of course, in any skill-based activity, those who have a high level of skill are best able to appreciate the performance of others. There is a deep connection between doing and appreciating, whether the activity is dance or basketball.

Performance and creation are not strange and alien activities. Expression is a part of human nature. Children draw, act, sing, and dance their way through the day. The problem is that somehow growing up seems to involve outgrowing such creative spontaneity. Some have even suggested such creative impulses diminish as children enter school. Some theory in the arts is based on the premise that creation is an unusual and esoteric activity. Others argue that being human involves imaginative and playful action. The issue is not why some try to create in the arts and elsewhere, but how have we stifled the playfulness we knew as children.

It is true, however, that it takes more than impulses to create. Howard Becker, a sociologist, found artists live in "small worlds" of interactions that shape and support their efforts (1982). The artist is not alone in his or her creation. In artistic subcultures, amateur and professional, there is a context for mentoring, leadership, innovation, and even eccentricity. Further, this subculture provides the standards the artist accepts as relevant. Artists form their own organizations to provide this social context of their art.

There is also the individual question. Many practice art, but few gain high levels of competence. All these people create in the sense of developing and expressing skill. Only a few, however, are creative in the sense of producing something truly new and unique. Research identified some characteristics of such persons. First, of course, they have disciplined themselves to gain unusual competence. Second, they focus on the art. Third, they seem to be willing to take risks, to go beyond what is conventional. They have the capacity to see things differently. These factors, however, do not explain why a few are especially creative. Perhaps they just combine opportunity and ability in a unique set of circumstances.

Creative artists do not seem to live in some special seclusion. Most writers are in the city, or even a suburb, not at a quiet seashore. Most composers are busy making a living. Mozart was preoccupied with economic survival. Bach had his children and weekly performances. Clara Schumann and Amy Beach managed households and entertained frequently. Charles Ives managed an insurance business. Scott Joplin emerged from extreme poverty, faced racial discrimination, and had to raise the funds to try to produce his operas. Leonard Bernstein was most productive when engaged in multiple projects, not when he retired from the New York Philharmonic. Most creative artists are like the rest of us — managing conflicting elements of complex lives.

Is there some artist in all of us? The forms of creativity may differ. One problem with a concentration on the classical arts is we may seem to limit creative activity to such rare domains. We may set particular standards for a traditional art that are exclusive and excluding. Yet, we all can play in the sense of trying actions that have no fixed outcome. We all can do almost anything a little differently from anyone else. We can all communicate, verbally or in symbolic action, in innovative ways. The arts do not distinguish a few people who are creative. Rather, they distinguish those who have taken their ability to play and create and welded them to particular skills and challenges.

Arts Appreciation and Consumption

Appreciation is also an important part of the arts as leisure. Some travelers build an entire summer around visiting European cities to see certain works of art and architecture. Attending plays at large and small theaters may be a central interest for residents of major cities. A selection of CDs and a good sound system are possible in any size community. Reading is not only available but also portable.

There is an obvious symbiosis between creation and appreciation. Artists perform for themselves and for their fellow artists, and for consumers. The experience of singing in a choir may fundamentally be that of producing the music together, but the appreciation of an audience is also part of the performance. Most potters and weavers like to sell some of their work, even if they make their living in other ways. Most painters like to exhibit and sell, even though they teach school most of the week. There is something intrinsic in the experience of arts creation, but there is also the performance *for others.*

One aspect of appreciation is the market. Paintings are purchased through dealers who determine what will be offered for sale. Music directors of all kinds of orchestras recruit "name" guest performers, advertise "pops" concerts, and sprinkle their concerts with tried-and-true favorites to attract paying audiences. Dance companies pay the year's bills with the holiday presentations of *The Nutcracker.* Enterprises that do not secure a market do not last.

And that is only the retail aspect. The arts may also be seen as an industry. There are management firms, promoters, and media consultants. There are financial entrepreneurs and investors. There is all the media promotion of the star system with a few performers receiving six-figure guarantees. The arts are big business for some and a constant financial struggle for most. The markets are the consumers—those willing to pay for the performance or the product. Also in the mix are the media performances and presentations, on both commercial and public television channels, that are one element of the entire industry promotion.

The second element is that of nonmarket support. As already suggested, countless nonprofit organizations and for-profit corporations support museums, performing groups, and teaching institutions. Many of those involved in such support are those deeply devoted to the particular art. Others may be involved at least partly because of the social status of the enterprise. Some support the arts as a civic duty or for public relations claims. For example, Texaco has sponsored the NPR broadcasts of *Live from the Met* since 1940.

In the United States, the National Endowment for the Arts has become a controversial agency of the federal government. Its budget has been reduced from about $180 million, and some would end the subsidy entirely. It supports not only national and major professional programs but also many regional and community organizations including those that bring the arts into schools and small towns. While the amount is a tiny percentage of the total expenditures on the arts, some argue the Endowment is an important symbol of the nation's commitment to the arts. Most of the budgets for the arts on any level, however, are from admission fees and local and regional supporting individuals and organizations. Fundraising is always a central element of arts institutions.

Debate: Public financial support should be given to the arts.

YES

- The arts are important to the entire culture. They are a central expression of the best of its values and work. They explore the meanings of human life in that culture as does nothing else. In the end, a culture will be judged more by its artistic creations than by anything else. A society that neglects the arts to pursue only economic gain will in the end lose its reason for being.

- Public support helps keep the arts from being elitist. When only the wealthy support the arts, then their status-related tastes will rule. The arts will be in danger of becoming more a prestigious display than a realm of riskful creation. Public support, especially when directed by the artists themselves, will open opportunities to the new, young, and innovative as well as to the established and well-promoted stars.

- Programs such as the National Endowment for the Arts support the arts in areas that are marginal economically and geographically. They bring performances to small and isolated towns. They help support teaching programs in the inner city. They support the youth orchestra, the exhibit of young artists, and the local dance company. Ideally, public support is directed toward those without access to private wealth.

- Even major urban arts centers are in financial difficulty. Smaller cities are finding it almost impossible to support significant performing groups, museums, festivals, teaching programs, and even public libraries. Without public support, there will be a major shrinkage in all aspects of the arts on all levels.

- Public programs encourage and nurture young artists who have not yet achieved a stature that permits self-support.

- The arts enrich the entire culture and should be supported by the public.

NO

- Most financial support of the arts is from private sources. Public support is minor and not worth the conflict.

- It is better to allow the market to decide what should be supported. Public agencies are not good judges of quality. Public support means decisions will be political. Even appointments to evaluating boards will be based on political rather than artistic criteria.

- Politics should be kept separate from creativity. There are too many ways in which the arts can be used for political purposes. When the establishment determines support, then there will be little opportunity for the critical and innovative. Political commissions will support what is safe and noncontroversial. There will even be allocations based on political favors rather than artistic merit.

- Public support perpetuates status snobbery. The arts should be supported by those who appreciate them, not by some politically appointed elite who have political influence or social status.

- If there is public support of the fine arts, then why not all the arts? How can public support be reserved for a few activities appreciated by a minority of the population and withheld from many other creative activities, such as folk arts, crafts, and new forms of creativity?

- In the arts, the creator or performer has to desire to excel. The struggle is part of the experience. Schools introduce the arts and teach basic skills. From this basis, it is better that developing artists demonstrate the commitment to persist and overcome obstacles. It is in this process that the committed create themselves as artists.

Freedom and Discipline in the Arts

In an influential essay, Josef Pieper (1952) argued "leisure is the basis of culture." He proposed leisure is a condition of openness and receptivity, a "mental and spiritual attitude." In this condition, it is possible to do more than reproduce previous forms and products of the culture. Rather, forms of communication may be produced that fulfill, reveal, and even extend the culture. They express some meaning, emotion, or coherence of existence. In other words, there is a profound relationship between leisure and the arts.

Satisfaction in Doing the Arts

For this part of the analysis, we define the arts inclusively as activity that creates what is new and different whatever the medium or material. It is the playful action of creating in some performance what is new, not quite like another that has gone before. It is engaging in that action for the sake of doing it regardless of the final disposition of the product. The instrument may be hands, voice, body, mind, or a computer. The material may be seen, heard, touched, or even imagined. The "fine arts" are only examples of creative activity.

There are differences among the arts. Those whose performance is part of a group such as a choir or orchestra may find more satisfaction in the shared contribution than as a solo performer. Dancers are more likely to report satisfaction in the physical coordination and grace than those who perform sitting or standing still. However, there are satisfactions found in many kinds of the arts. They are the satisfactions of creative play.

This connection is revealed in Aristotle's statement in the *Poetics, Chapter 26,* that art does more than imitate life. Art creates what "might be" or even what "ought to be." It is always playful rather than limited to accepted existence. What is necessary for such creative art is more than time. It is a total environment that enables playful activity, activity done for the experience rather than a predetermined outcome. Leisure, from this perspective, is necessary for the creation of art. Fredrich Schiller (1954) believed people are most human when they are at play—when engaging in creative activity for its own sake. Creative activity, then, is not a luxury, but central what it means to be human. The arts are more than self-expression; they have the potential to be at least a glimpse of the harmony and beauty that life might be. Creation is not for the sake of possession, not for the market or for social status. It is a shared vision of what life is and might become. It is a dialectic of being and becoming—and leisure is the possibility of such creative activity.

Arts participation tends to stress intrinsic satisfactions in the experience. As with sport, there may be a deep involvement in bringing a developed skill to the challenge of the performance. There may be what Csikszentmihalyi (1990) calls "flow." In the performing arts, there are times when nothing counts but doing it well, even rising to a new level of action. The arts combine long-term development of skill with experiences not quite like any that have gone before. There is an existential "becoming" for the creating self in the act of creation. As a consequence, artists report satisfactions of self-expression, mastery and competence, learning and growth, and emotional highs.

There are also social meanings to creative activity. Most such activity is done in company with others. The arts have, as analyzed earlier, their "social worlds" of support and criticism. They provide a sense of community with others who accept the same challenges and engage in the same efforts. There are also the satisfactions associated with the product that in some way is offered to the world. The products of art are never perfect, yet have meaning as they are experienced and accepted by others. What is most important, however, is in the experience itself, in doing what may be strenuous, demanding, often frustrating, frequently exhausting, and yet part of a process with unique meaning. There are costs and even failures, yet there is also something uniquely satisfying in that creative process.

Form and Freedom in the Arts

Central to the nature of creative activity is freedom. Though dance is limited by the capabilities of the body and the forms of music, theater by language and stage, painting by the textures and dimensions of the materials, there is also a freedom to create in the arts. Even within existing forms, the artist produces something that has not existed before, a work not quite like that of any other artist. The freedom to choose and the satisfaction of production are combined in the arts. In the performing and creative arts, old forms and materials are always being tested and even broken open by those whose imaginations cannot be fully contained in the past. Fantasy and play are integral to art. The composer, artist, and performer are always working toward the future—the "not yet" of the art and of life.

Paradoxically, the creative arts also require great discipline and mastery of skills. To sing, dance, act, draw, write, or otherwise create well requires a great deal of preparation and hard work. While there have been intriguing "primitive" artists, most imaginative products have come from those who have mastered the disciplines of their crafts in concentrated practice. As a result, not only does a high level of creation call for discipline and skill, but satisfaction seems to increase with such mastery. The greatest thrill of doing the arts comes when the challenge requires every bit of skill that has been painfully acquired. The skill called upon to mold a delicate platter of pottery, sing the running line of a Bach aria, play a complex Joplin rag, or communicate new depths of character in a Eugene O'Neill or August Wilson play may be incredibly exciting. They come in the union of freedom and discipline, the exercise of skill in creation. The meaning, then, is not only in the end product but also in the experience of creating. It is no wonder Aristotle had difficulty thinking of leisure apart from the arts and contemplation.

Discussion Questions

1. Is it more satisfying to create in the arts at relatively low levels of skill, or to appreciate the performance of those at the peaks of skill?

2. Will the fine arts ever become really popular? Why or why not?

3. Should schools and public community programs introduce and teach the arts? Why or why not?

4. Is art essentially a personal creation or a social offering? Is there art without appreciation?

5. Why are more women than men involved in the arts? Can this be changed?

6. Are the creative arts the highest form of leisure? Why or why not?

7. Are the fine arts elitist and marginal to what is important to most people?

8. Should the "fine arts" be redefined to include jazz and other non-traditional forms as the graphic arts now includes photography and filmmaking, and sculpture includes ceramics?

9. Is there likely to be an increase in amateur arts engagement as education levels rise? Or are there too many time pressures to allow for real involvement in arts skills and expression?

References and Resources

Becker, H. (1982). *Art worlds*. Berkeley, CA: University of California Press.

Bourdieu, P. (1984). *Distinction: A social critique of the judgement of taste* (Richard Nice, Trans.) Cambridge, MA: Harvard University Press.

Csikszentmihalyi, M. (1990). *Flow: The psychology of optimal experience*. New York, NY: Harper and Row.

Gans, H. (1974). *Popular culture and high culture: An analysis and evaluation of taste*. New York, NY: Basic Books.

Hans, J. (1981). *The play of the world*. Amherst, MA: University of Massachusetts Press.

Huizinga, J. (1955). *Homo ludens: A study of the play element in culture*. Boston, MA: Beacon Press.

Pieper, J. (1952). *Leisure: The basis of culture* (Alexander Dru, Trans.). New York, NY: New American Library.

Pieper, J. (1963). *Leisure: The basis of culture* (Rev. ed.; Alexander Dru, Trans.). New York, NY: New American Library.

Schiller, F. (1954). *On the aesthetic education of man: In a series of letters* (R. Snell, Trans.). New Haven, CT: Yale University Press.

Stebbins, R. (1992). *Amateurs, professionals, and serious leisure.* Montreal, PQ: McGill-Queen's University Press.

Stebbins, R. (1979). *Amateurs: On the margin between work and leisure.* Beverly Hills, CA: Sage.

Zolberg, V. (1990). *Constructing a sociology of the arts.* New York, NY: Cambridge University Press.

Chapter 20
Outdoor Recreation

People go into the forest to hike, camp, ride, and play. They especially seek to be near water, to be in it, to be on it, and to see it. They drive hundreds and even thousands of miles to see great vistas of mountains, valleys, and shorelines. However, people also go into the backcountry to cut trees, mine coal and other minerals, and run our vehicles. People celebrate that this country has over 300 million acres of land in public trust available for recreation. They are concerned that 70% of American shoreline is privately owned and largely closed to the public. They also question the ability of the government to manage such a significant resource well. As a consequence, public land, especially where demand is heavy, is conflicted territory. There are many unresolved issues concerning outdoor natural-resource–based recreation.

Outdoor Recreation Resources

More than 200 million acres of federal land are available for recreation of various kinds. States offer another 42 million acres and local government bodies about 10 million acres. There are forests, lakes, rivers, mountains, deserts, trails, prairies, battlegrounds, and other sites of historic and scenic importance. Of the 200 million total acres, about 50% is forest, 9% wilderness, 10% fish and wildlife preserves, and 6% parks. Federal land in the mountain and coastal West, not including Alaska, makes up almost 75% of the total (Cordell, 2004).

People come to these sites to hike, fish, swim, hunt, climb, sail, canoe, tube, soar, race, run, sun, ski, camp, drive motorized vehicles, and enjoy countless other activities. In some areas the managing agency offers facilities and access; in others there is no development of any kind. On or near some sites there are businesses that sell, rent, and repair all kinds of equipment as well as offer lodging, food, and other amenities. There is the quiet, and even desolation, of the wilderness and crowds at an urban reservoir. All this and more provide opportunities for many kinds of recreation.

According to federal and market national surveys, the most popular outdoor activities are walking and hiking, swimming, fishing, camping, and operating various vehicles and craft on land and water. The most common activity is sightseeing from the car. Least common is going into remote areas for specialized activities. In all cases, however, there seems to be something special about being outdoors, somewhere in or near the water, forests, mountains, or other such locales. The environment is central to the meaning of the experience.

National Resource Providers

The scope of natural resources held and managed by the federal government is unique to the developed world. What is now taken for granted is partly an accident of the vastness of land holdings in the West not suitable for farming and partly a result of far-sighted leaders who recognized that opportunities once lost would be impossible to reclaim. Further, there was the conviction that these resources belonged to the people as a public trust. One side of that trust is preservation of such resources for all future generations. The other side is that they should be used and enjoyed in ways consistent with their preservation. As a consequence, conflict between those putting conservation first and those promoting certain uses is inevitable.

The **National Park Service** (NPS) of the Department of the Interior began with the great parks of Yellowstone, Yosemite, and the Smoky Mountains and later added historic and archeological sites. The mission was to preserve such resources in ways that made them available for use and appreciation. No hunting, commercial development, or harvesting of resources was usually permitted. The preservation mission, however, was to be balanced by recreational use. Camping, lodging, educational and scientific programs, and other enabling provisions were to be developed to enhance enjoyment that did not degrade the resource. With almost 15 million overnights stays and 286 million visits to 300-plus national parks and monuments in the year 2000, conflicts between use and preservation are inevitable. Adding 56 million acres in Alaska in 1978 does nothing to alleviate crowding at the Grand Canyon or Yosemite. Now plans are being developed to manage uses in ways that conserve the resource and still maximize the experience for visitors.

The **U.S. Forest Service** of the Department of Agriculture manages more than 200 million acres of forest, grassland, mountains, desert, and water. The forests have multiple uses including recreation, timber harvest, mining, grazing, and other extractive industries. Mountainsides are leased and developed for skiing. Lakeshore sites are leased for resorts. Highways are developed for general transportation and scenic access. The Forest Service "land of many uses" is constantly being fought over by those with different interests, some appreciative and some extractive. Many recreation users want development of boat-launching ramps, ski runs and lifts, campgrounds, and trails. Others support closing areas to any new development with wilderness designation. Outside of Alaska the Forest Service manages most of the land designated as National Wilderness. The passage of the Wilderness Act in 1964 led to continual conflicts between developers and those who argue that once a forest is cut, it can never be restored. Often in the middle are recreation users who want to preserve water and environmental quality and still have access to their backcountry sites.

The **Bureau of Land Management** (BLM) has increasingly been drawn into the conflicts. Originally a kind of residual depository for land not designated for parks or forests, it is now recognized that the BLM manages over 140 million acres in the 50 states that have many values for the extraction of oil, minerals, and other valuable materials. There are also millions of acres of great beauty and environmental value. With over 70 million visits a year, the BLM has the same pressures for use and preservation as the NPS and U.S. Forest Service.

There are also other federal agencies of importance. The Department of the Interior includes the **Fish and Wildlife Service** with more than 80 million acres of land and water intended as habitats for fish, fowl, and wild animals. Also in Department of the Interior is the **Bureau of Reclamation** that manages a number of major water projects, especially in the West. The Civil Works Division of the **U.S. Army Corps of Engineers** has entered the recreation field with the construction and operation of waterways and reservoirs. Increasingly recreation uses such as boating have become major factors in Corps management and development. About 80% of Corps reservoirs are located within 50 miles of cities, creating 500 million recreation day uses annually.

There have also been a number of laws, regulations, and programs with recreation implications, including the Wild and Scenic Rivers Act of 1968, the Urban Open Space Land Program of 1961, the Land and Water Conservation Fund of 1964, the National Trails System in 1968, and the National Environmental Policy Act requiring the study of the ecosystem results of proposed government actions. It is evident, then, that recreation is only one component of the complexities and conflicts of natural resource management.

State recreation provisions are only about one-sixth of the acreage of federal holdings. Some growth in state resources has been funded by the federal Land and Water Conservation Fund, which has now been cut back. Some states have elaborate park systems with premier sites developed since the 1930s. Other states rely more on federal provisions and on municipal and county programs. Nevertheless, attendance at state parks increased over 400%

since 1950 to over 800 million visits. Now many states are promoting their recreation resources to attract out-of-state tourists.

There are local governments with considerable investment in outdoor recreation space. Most investment tends to be municipal areas for outdoor sports. There are, however, parks, forest preserves, and water resources offered by many cities and counties. Local recreation provisions tend to be quite uneven, especially when land values are highest in areas with the highest tax revenues.

The Market Complement

While most of the attention is given to public land and water resources, there is also the market side of the overall picture. In some areas, the recreation resources are primarily private. On seashores or islands that are highly developed by resorts, there may be little public access to water or the beaches. On Hilton Head Island, major resorts control almost all water access. In Hawaii on the island of Maui, the miles of beaches lined with resorts are dotted with small public-access entries. The aim of most major developers is to control as much of the prime recreation space as possible.

On the other hand, in many outdoor recreation areas the public and market sectors are complementary rather than competing. At or near public recreation areas, businesses may operate the launching and boat-storage facilities. They sell equipment and do repairs for the boats, windsailers, and other water toys. Near forests and lakes there are guide services, rental boats and fishing gear, rental rafts and canoes on the river, and flights to backcountry lakes. Businesses teach beginners how to kayak or sailboard, climb the rock faces, and swim underwater. They sell, rent, and repair all kinds of equipment. They are, in fact, a necessary complement enabling use of the public land and water. This relationship may be seen most clearly in those resorts located on or near attractive public resources. In such cases, public management that maintains access and quality for the resource is crucial to the success of the business.

One issue, however, is the use of public land for commercial enterprises. When hotels and campgrounds in national parks are operated by businesses, they pay a limited franchise fee and meet certain contractual requirements to maintain what is often a monopoly at a public site. Critics argue the fees tend to be too low for the businesses to pay their fair share of park maintenance and improvement. Also, in such a monopoly situation the quality of the provisions may suffer. Supporters respond that the government should not be operating facilities that can be provided better and more efficiently by private enterprise. Where contracts do not adequately protect the park or other resource, they can be rewritten and put up for bid when they expire.

There is the persistent question of who manages resources best. Proponents of privatization argue business responds most fully to the market—to the demand for quality related to price. Advocates of public management reply that unique and fragile resources must be managed for their long-term conservation as well as short-term profit. Some believe that the apparent conflict misses the reality of an essential complementarity in which the public and market sectors can cooperate in doing what each does best. Businesses may best provide services within a framework of government management for the long-term protection of the natural resource. Business may run the ski lifts and snack shops without turning over the entire mountain to entrepreneurs.

Debate: The National Parks should be run as a business.

YES

- Business is inherently more efficient than bureaucracy. Business is best at providing services and National Parks are now multiservice recreation destinations.

- The National Parks are destinations for vacation travel. Such trips are part of household budgets. There is no reason to subsidize the destination when the rest of the trip is made at market prices.

- Parks in some areas are in competition with market destinations. The valleys outside Yellowstone have upscale resorts, but the park is tax-supported. All tourist provisions should be on an equal basis.

- The park entry and facilities are a small part of the total trip cost. Market-level prices will seldom exclude visitors who can afford the rest of the trip.

- There can always be reduced group rates for educational and other special programs.

- For the most part, National Park visitors are upper-income households who can afford market prices.

- The parks are currently underfunded and facilities are deteriorating. Market pricing would support adequate maintenance and improvements. Businesses would bring the facilities to a level of quality consistent with the resource.

- Current government cutbacks in expenditures are endangering the quality of the environment as well as facilities. Premier destinations can produce revenues at levels that will protect the park and the quality of the visitor experience.

• One way to reduce crowding is with pricing. One factor in current crowding is that National Parks are such a bargain.

• National Parks are part of the entire network of the tourism industry. Yet, as prime destinations they are excluded from the overall pricing system and distort the allocation balance. Operating the parks as businesses would allow the market system to bring demand in line with costs. Imagine what Disney could do with Yellowstone Park. Piped-in pressure could make Old Faithful erupt every 20 minutes on schedule. A monorail would skim over the boiling pools. A rainbow bridge would improve viewing the falls. The lake would have a marina and paddle boat concession. "Mountain men" would roam the streets as guides to the restaurants. Theme hotels would include the "Elk" with its tame herd, the "Bear" with play areas for human cubs, and the "Trout" with stocked fishing ponds. Improvements to the rustic old park would bring it up to world-class tourism standards.

NO

• The national parks are so designated because they are unique resources and environments. They are not just ordinary destinations and should be managed as a public trust.

• National parks belong to all the people so access should not be determined by price. They merit tax support because they are national treasures, not local businesses.

• A number of surveys found most people want special environments preserved whether they visit them or not. Economists call a view that considers a longer term than next year's vacation *existence value.*

• Such environments should be managed for long-term preservation rather than short-term profit. Contracts limiting development can always be twisted or stretched. If the profit incentive is great enough, businesses will find ways to exploit the resource. Try meditating to the noise of backcountry heli-skiing.

• In publicly managed parks, private enterprise can still run the services under the terms of carefully drafted franchise contracts. Such contracts can be improved as they come up for renewal. Also, many services can be located outside the parks to reduce crowding in the parks.

- Limitations of use can, under public management, be based on fair methods and equal access rather than price and discretionary income.

- The primary criterion for management of national parks should be to maintain them for all generations—not exploit them for current markets.

- Such management should be based on scientific principles designed to put the resource first. Scientists are still learning what is best for different environments and should not be limited by long-term contracts.

- National park designation is a recognition of the significance of the resource—not a label to attract tourists.

- The Grand Canyon and other such parks are a world and national resource—not the basis for profit. The federal government is responsible to provide management based on such value—not on partisan budget fights in each year's congressional debate.

What People Do in the Outdoors

As already indicated, the variety of activities in natural-resource settings defies listing. The 1994-1995 National Survey on Recreation and the Environment (Cordell, 2004) found the ten most popular outdoor activities were walking for pleasure (83%), family gatherings (74%), visiting nature centers (57%), picnicking (55%), sightseeing (52%), outdoor sports events (50%), visiting historic sites (46%), view/photograph wildlife (45%), swimming in natural waters (42%) and swimming in pools (41%). In general, those activities that are increasing in participation are those engaged in by older adults, the growing segment the population.

Some go to natural environments primarily to experience them in some appreciative way. Others go primarily to engage in some activity requiring such outdoor space. Many combine the activities of such trips bundles related to the resource. For example, lakeside camping may combine the camping experience with swimming, boating, fishing, and hiking. One factor is the composition of the recreation group, especially the involvement of children. Camping not only offers access to the water and woods but also engages the family or other group in common activity.

It would be interesting to profile the "typical park visitor." Research, however, suggests considerable variety just in the single activity of camping. For example, there are:

- *Budget campers* use the campground for low-cost access to the resource.

- *Travelers* camp to save money.

- *Sports-car couples* pack tents and bags for urban stops on the same trip.

- *Student campers* include both explorers going where no one has gone before and party campers using the site for group celebration.

- *Family campers* focus on togetherness and nurturing, with older children who peel off to find same-age peers, and gender role-playing in which men do provider tasks and go fishing and women stay in camp to do the maintenance and caregiving.

- *Breakaway campers* seek separation and solitude.

- *Comfort campers* bring all the conveniences of home including power campers who are fully electrified, and V-campers with their RVs, TVs, and videos.

- *Toe-in-the-water campers* are unsure about the trip, but trying it for the sake of significant companions.

- *Extractors* use the campsite as a base to forage for fish, game, rocks, or anything else that can be legally removed.

The point is that there is no typical resource user. Some come in large groups for social interaction. Some come for solitude and separation. Some fish from boats with big motors and some hike out to meditate. The variety becomes a problem only when the activities conflict and one activity degrades the experience for the others—and each group seems to think that their activity should have priority and be protected from interference.

Among such users of outdoor environments are the "specialists" who focus on a particular activity. They may fish with flies in remote streams, climb unique rock faces, hike into the wilderness with minimal equipment, or take photographs of rare bird species. They are one kind of natural-resource devotee who tend to support ecosystem protection and limits on uses. At the other extreme are those who want development for their kind of activity, such as alpine ski resorts with multiple lifts, restaurants, shops, and lodges or condominium resorts on prime beaches. Most common are those who prefer management that provides for their activity, whatever it is, and limits all others.

What Do People Want in Outdoor Recreation?

Not all visitors come to the land and water resources for the same purposes. They seek a variety of experiences. They may want escape, to get away, but usually they get away together in groups. They want an experience based on the natural environment, but that environment may range from the primitive to the highly developed. They want a break from ordinary routines and environments, but in a setting in which they can "be themselves" with a minimum of external expectations. They come to a variety of places: lonely mountainsides and crowded beaches. Yet, in all cases there is something about the environment that makes the experience possible. Further, there has to be some "fit" between the resource and the kind of experience sought.

B.L. Driver of the U.S. Forest Service developed methods of examining the satisfactions of water- and forest-related recreation:

1. *Social*: family togetherness, being with friends, meeting new people, exercising leadership and sharing skills.

2. *Personal expression and development*: reinforcing self-image, competence testing, discovery and learning or creativity in personal reflection and physical exertion.

3. *Experimental (Intrinsic)*: stimulation, risk taking, tranquility, using equipment, nostalgia

4. *Nature appreciation*: enjoying scenery, closeness to nature, learning about nature, seeking privacy and space

5. *Change*: rest, escape from pressures and routines, avoiding crowds, getting away

Appreciation of the environment and the reduction of stress are common motivations for getting to the outdoor environment. Yet, there are also personal and social agendas people bring with them. Everything impacts the experience. Moods and conflicts may be brought into the wilderness. Other visitors may change the conditions for enjoyment. Even the wilderness has rules and regulations. In addition, the weather may spoil almost anything that is outdoors. Like everything else in life, outdoor recreation is a multifaceted experience.

What, then, is the purpose of setting aside and managing natural environments? Is the primary purpose to preserve them or to enable them to be used? Which is more important—conservation or recreation? Are they really in conflict?

Conflict: Users, Developers, and Preservers

Some would preserve natural environments for their own sake, simply because they have their own special value. Some would manage natural environments so they can be used optimally, for recreation now and in the future. Some see natural environments as one kind of places to be developed for the use of humankind. It is no wonder there is conflict.

There are three main interest groups. *Developers* would alter the land so it can be used for a profit-making enterprise. The enterprise may be a resort meant for recreation, timber harvesting, or mineral extraction. In any case, the developer will make major changes in the resource. At the other end of the spectrum are the *preservers*. Represented by such organizations as the Sierra Club, preservers take the long-term view and attempt to prevent any action that is damaging or irretrievable. They base their arguments on the uniqueness of environments and the organic nature of the ecosystem in which any intervention impacts all the rest. The third interest group is that of the *recreation users*. They tend to support both conservation of the quality of the resource and access for use. They would limit interventions in some cases and promote development in others. Backpackers, for example, would restrict the entry of motorized vehicles, but still develop trails and campsites by pristine lakes and streams. Downhill skiers support clearcutting mountainsides for ski runs and building access roads, but want the surrounding mountain vistas preserved from logging. Recreation users support development for their own activity, but may oppose other kinds of interventions.

Coalitions may form between two of the interest groups over particular projects. Snowmobilers may support building logging roads. Those who fish may support building roads and marinas. Preservationists may find common interest with nonextractive recreationists in wilderness expansion. Further, environmental law requires the social and economic interests of residents of an area be addressed. Developers tend to be well-represented in the legislative and legal forums. Preservationists have many effective organizations. Local residents and dispersed recreation interests, however, may not be organized for effective political action.

Such conflict involves goals as well as uses. What is most important—preservation of the integrity of a resource for all future generations, or management to enhance current uses? Which comes first—jobs based on extraction, or the ecosystem itself? Do some interventions improve the resource and others degrade it? If so, how can we measure future consequences? Are highways with all their related facilities a threat to the land and water or the primary way by which most people enjoy the outdoors? Is the noise of Grand Canyon overflights an intrusion on the experience with nature or the only way that many will ever see the unique scenic wonder?

The land and water are used in many ways, but we tend to focus on direct human use. People enter the forest to cut trees, mine minerals, hike, camp, hunt, fish, take pictures, ride trail or mountain bikes or horses, explore for rocks, study flora and fauna, and combine different activities. We live on the land, cultivate it, exploit it, study it, appreciate it, and manage it. Some uses are easily combined and others conflict. Some are temporary and others create lasting impacts. There are two main forms of management for natural resources. When the resource is in private ownership, laws and regulations are designed to prevent widespread and permanent destruction. Such laws are limited in both scope and effectiveness. When the resource is in public ownership, then the managing agencies have more control. Their power, however, is still limited by law and by previous uses. There are, for example, old mining claims in designated wilderness and developed in-holdings of resorts and residences in national forests. Further, development nearby may impact the resource of even the most treasured national park or monument.

Nevertheless, land and water planning is necessary for both preservation and use. The federal government uses a framework of the Resource Opportunity Spectrum to designate areas as primitive or open to limited or full development. The aim is to balance opportunities with the nature of the resources. The assumption is that there are places most suitable for major resorts and others so fragile that they can sustain only the most limited use. Of course, the conflict is most acute when attractiveness, access, and fragility are found in the same place.

Any planning begins with a thorough understanding of the ecology of the resource—of just how terrain, water and drainage, tree and plant growth, animal and bird life, soil composition, and all other elements of the natural ecosystem are interrelated and mutually supporting. Any change or intervention is calculated for its initial and cumulative effects. Then there are also impacts on the human communities dependent on the resource. Integrated and comprehensive planning is not only complex but also may involve conflicting interests and outcomes. The aim is not to control human freedom, but to maximize freedom and opportunity for the long term. The conflict arises when purposive interveners—human beings—have interests that foreclose the desired actions of others. Planning, then, becomes a political activity that recognizes scarcity, conflict, and the natural ecological balance.

Debate: Outdoor recreation is anti-environmental.

YES

- Some recreation is appreciation rather than exploitation. So much recreation, however, requires altering the environment that, on balance, recreation is destructive of natural environments. Ski runs strip mountainsides, pollute streams, and require roads, airports, and other massive development. Powerboats pollute water. Visitors litter everywhere. Even appreciation can turn a valley floor into virtual concrete.

- Developing recreation technologies destroy and pollute nature. Snowmobiles and off-road vehicles tear up the terrain and invade protected areas. Helicopters invade the formerly secluded mountaintops and backcountry terrain to bring sightseers and skiers. Commercial recreation providers constantly find new ways to invade natural areas with their technologies.

- Even public land is developed with long-term leases on prime locations: marinas, ski and fishing resorts, bike and horse rentals, and concessions at viewpoints. Business investment requires long-term commitments on the part of public managers. Development, once installed, can never be restored.

- The purpose of recreation investment is to maximize profits. That means using the resource to attract the largest sustainable number of users at the maximum market price. The natural resource, then, becomes a means to a greater end. It is not surprising that more and more recreation interests form coalitions with those who have other commercial purposes for public land and water against conservation restrictions. The value order becomes "use first and conservation second."

- Recreation is invasive, even when regulated. Even small groups in the wilderness leave their signs of invasion. Wildlife habitats are disrupted even by photographers. Fires may get out of control. Rescue operations are massive and mechanized. Recovery in some especially fragile areas is slow. Tire tracks in the desert may last a century.

- Even "Leave-No-Trace" users leave some impacts, especially when employing the latest backpacking gear and organized by commercial "experience-providing" businesses that return to the same trails and sites over and over.

- Management becomes more political than scientific. Those with the most influence, however purchased, in legislative and administrative bodies tend to get their way. Where is the old-growth forest, the unpolluted stream, or the undeveloped beach? The assumption in the United States that there is always more land is no longer tenable. Conservation requires saying "no" to some recreation.

NO

- Those who know and use natural resources for recreation are often the strongest supporters of preservation. Environmental organizations have hikers, campers, and other appreciative recreationists as a major source of membership and funding. Recreational use helps build support for conservation of wildlands.

- Recreation can be located in places where the activity is appropriate to the resource. Such location is a matter of planning and management that takes the environment into account. Unique environments can be protected. Cars can be banned from the Yosemite Valley and the Grand Canyon rim. Development can be placed at a safe distance from water. It is not recreation, but bad planning, poorly enforced, that is the problem.

- There are millions of acres of land available. There is space for a variety of recreational uses and for preservation.

- Many recreation uses are educational. For example, family camping and hiking will help children become adults who care about the natural environment and may be willing to support political action.

- Recreation provides a variety of ways to experience natural environments. There is at least some appreciation even in intensive uses such as skiing or extractive uses such as hunting and fishing.

- Land and water use can be regulated through licensing and access restrictions. It is better to regulate than to close off so many resources that many will break the law and use the resources in destructive ways. Regulated use also permits education for conservation.

- Recreation is often the best alternative to other activity such as tree cutting, mining, grazing, and other extraction. Recreation also provides an alternative economic basis for communities being turned away from extraction.

- Intelligent recreation planning will not destroy the resource that attracts business. Major investments have a time frame for recovery and profit that support unpolluted water and attractive scenery.

The Integrity of Nature

A total focus on recreation in natural settings may obscure an adequate view of nature itself. The perspective may always be on what is best for human-kind rather than for the total natural environment. Humans are, after all, a part of nature. In the long term, humans, too, may be an endangered species if there is too much lost of the natural environment.

For example, natural environments may be approached in terms of carrying capacity. *Carrying capacity*, however difficult to measure, is the ability of an ecosystem to accommodate use without being irreparably damaged or destroyed. Some sites are quite resilient. Others are vulnerable to damage by even minor human intervention. The assessment, however, is always made from the perspective of human use. How much use can the ecosystem absorb? How fragile is the resource and how much can we do to it?

An alternative perspective is that the natural resource has its own value apart from human use. Nature is not just a resource at all. Rather, nature is the total incredibly complex and interrelated system of which we are a part. Humans are not "in charge." Rather, nature is the greater whole. Further, any destruction within that system has wide and often immeasurable effects. We are never sure just what is "downstream" from our interventions and actions.

There may even be a kind of religious or spiritual quality to this perspective. It is that nature has its own integrity, its own wholeness. The natural environment is not just a lot of places to be used or not according to some hierarchy of human ends. Rather, nature is the context of all life, all species, and all forms. It is, in that sense, the wholeness of life. As such, it has a final rather than instrumental value. Humans, then, are just one kind of life, even if uniquely wonderful and dangerous. John Muir and Aldo Leopold are only two of the classic writers who have developed such an approach (Nash, 1967).

This perspective leads to a different approach to the natural environment. Of course, there are things there to be used, especially when they are abundant and renewable. Nature is violent and selective as well as beautiful and benefi-cent. There is always death and destruction as well as life and health. Nonethe-less, the fundamental human approach to nature may be appreciation, immersion, and even reverence. On a particular occasion, the natural environment may be an escape from the artificial and the stress of what has been built to be used.

There may be a re-union with life's sources and meanings. Nature is not just one more playground; it is special and profound.

This perspective raises the question of goals. In conflicts between use and preservation, is there an issue greater than that of optimal use over a long time frame? Is there an ethic of preservation and conservation for its own sake? Recognizing the symbolic meaning and the fragility as well as resilience of nature, we may accept the "existence value" of the natural environment. Perhaps we may someday find uses for natural processes and substances now unknown. Perhaps we may recognize that immersion in nature is something that is more than recreation; it is a basic human need. In any case, preservation is more than an assessment of alternative uses. It is that nature is the system of life itself with its own fundamental value. It is to be protected for its own sake as well as for ours. This understanding, then, leads to an ethic of relationships and wholeness rather than a calculation of costs and benefits.

Discussion Questions

1. Are there some natural environments that should be largely closed to human entry? If so, why and what are they?

2. Do you agree that "space is freedom?" Why or why not?

3. Does planning always lead to control and limit freedom, or may planning sometimes be necessary to preserve opportunity? Give examples either way.

4. Are humans a part of nature or the rulers of nature? What are the implications of your position?

5. What is special about natural-resource–based recreation?

6. What is the best way to prevent crowding—raising prices, rationing, use restrictions, or just letting dissatisfaction drive some people away?

7. Does government have the right to limit how people use their own land? Why or why not?

8. Is there an inevitable conflict between the profit motive and environmental preservation?

Resources

Burch, W. (1971). *Daydreams and nightmares: A sociological essay on the American environment*. New York, NY: Harper and Row.

Cordell, H.K. (2004). *Outdoor recreation for 21st century America*. State College, PA: Venture Publishing, Inc.

Ditton, R., Goodale, T., and Johnson, P. (1975). A cluster analysis of activity, frequency, and environmental variables to identify water-based recreation types. *Journal of Leisure Research, 3*, 282–295.

Kelly, J. (1980). Outdoor recreation participation: A comparative analysis. *Leisure Sciences, 3*, 129–154.

Nash, R. (1967). *Wilderness and the American mind*. New Haven, CT: Yale University Press.

President's Commission on Americans in the Outdoors. (1987). *Americans outdoors: The legacy, the challenge, with case studies: A report of the President's Commission*. Washington, DC: Island Press.

Schreyer, R. (1984). Social dimensions of carrying capacity: An overview. *Leisure Sciences, 6*, 387–394.

Chapter 21
Recreation Opportunity in the Community

Most recreation is in and around the home. Geographically leisure moves outward in concentric circles from the residence to the neighborhood, the community, and only then to greater distances. Of course, private transportation, the shopping mall, and then all the public and market destinations for recreational travel have transformed the community from a network of neighborhoods to local destinations, parking areas, and countless special trips. Yet, for most Americans, the residence, yard, streets, walks, and parks of the neighborhood remain central. Special trips—such as vacations, weekend mini-vacations, and regional destinations—are a part of the overall spectrum of leisure locations. Most walks, children's play, animal care, gardening, picnics, sports, arts, eating out, mall visiting, and social gatherings are in the community. Further, in most communities there is an expectation local government will provide a range of opportunities for recreation.

Community Recreation Provisions

In very small towns, there may be no more than a park for picnics that is maintained by a local service or "garden" club. In large cities, the park and recreation program may have a budget of $100 million a year and hundreds of programs and sites. In almost any community with a population of 20,000 or more, there is a mix of public and market provisions for recreation. These vary from a park or two, a swimming pool, and a few summer sports for the young to multiple interlaced sets of opportunities in a continually shifting balance among public, private, and market resources.

The Public Sector

As introduced in previous chapters, government provides a set of recreation opportunities based on principles of efficiency, equity, and preservation. Space

for recreation, such as parks, sports fields, gyms, swimming pools, and auditoriums, can be provided for regular users at the lowest cost by a public
agency that manages them for maximum use by diverse constituencies. This
is especially the case when space is scarce and costly, as in the city or developed suburb. In almost every community, there are those who cannot pay
market prices for recreation resources due to low incomes or the high cost
of special accommodations. As for children in the old industrial city, the
public sector is responsive to recreation needs for the marginal and disinherited. Finally, certain resources in a community—such as historic buildings, streams, riverfronts, lakefronts, and natural locales—are best preserved
by a nonprofit organization.

The assumption of public provisions, however, is by no means taken
for granted everywhere. Movements to limit local taxes have reduced public
support for many programs—even swimming pools and youth sports. As a
consequence, public recreation agencies are increasingly managing and marketing their programs on a fee-for-service and cost-recovery basis. Some programs and facilities are leased to market-sector subcontractors as managers.
For example, team and participation fees for Little League play escalated by
higher expectations for uniforms, lighted fields, and officiating have increased
rapidly in ways that may exclude some children. Developmental sports and
arts programs are expected to break even or even show a profit. The cost
crunch is a daily issue in recreation planning for most communities even where
tax revenues have not been reduced.

The Market Sector

In many communities, there has been a marked expansion of market-sector
recreation provisions. These include indoor facilities for racket sports and fitness programs, dance and arts, competitive and recreational swimming,
children's play areas, specialized sports instruction, equipment sales and rental, and other places for people to meet and play. This does not include the incidental leisure locales, such as shopping malls, theaters, and coffee shops.
More children's developmental programs in sports and the arts are offered by
for-profit enterprises. In some cases, even soccer and basketball leagues are
provided for the relatively affluent by businesses.

Some market-sector programs are in competition with public provisions.
When the public programs have high fees even without paying taxes, the
market offering may compete directly. In other cases, the business may offer
higher quality resources, less crowding, or exclusivity for a price. Ideally, the
market sector complements the public sector, but does not compete. Each
has constituencies with interests, commitments, and financial resources that
comprise a viable market for the provision.

The Private Sector

Many nonprofit organizations also provide recreation resources. There are the traditional programs of the YMCAs and YWCAs, Boys and Girls Clubs, schools and colleges, and local organizations supported partly by fees and memberships and partly by donations. Many religious organizations offer recreational programs in sports, camping, the arts, and social events. These provide an opportunity for voluntary segregation of populations segments by ethnicity, religion, income level, neighborhood, and other factors. They also may complement public programs. In some cases, private providers target particular areas, such as low-income neighborhoods or children and adults with special needs. The private sector includes a range of provisions from the exclusive and costly country club to the cost-free Boys and Girls Club in an urban ghetto.

Diversity and Planning

The more diverse the population of a community, the more likely there will be oversupplies of some resources and shortages of others. This is partly a result of the market that seeks clienteles able to support businesses. The bias is, then, toward households with higher incomes and larger markets. It is partly a result of the political base of the public sector. In any community, there are constituencies that are well-represented on government boards and others not organized to attain any effective representation at all. Of course, those with higher incomes also tend to be those most effectively represented in government. Add to this the income bias of private organizations, especially clubs with high-quality facilities, and the potential for inequality is evident.

One approach to this problem is community planning. The various segments of a population along with their locations are measured and mapped. Public provisions, then, are allocated in a comprehensive plan that seeks to serve the whole community. Further, in such planning, priorities can be selected according to some principles, such as those of efficiency, equity, and preservation.

A second approach to the allocation problem is community organization. It is common for those interested in a particular program—age-group competitive swimming or Little League baseball, for example—to organize and lobby for public support. It is less common for underserved and under-represented neighborhoods or ethnic and racial groups to organize to apply political pressure to gain adequate recreational opportunities.

A number of factors enter into community recreational planning. One is space—often costly and scarce in urban and suburban environments. A second is income distribution, usually differentiated by neighborhood and often by de-facto racial segregation. A third factor is that of groups with particular facilitating needs. Limitations may involve vision, mobility, mental functioning, or some other condition. In many communities, the proportion of those with such conditions makes it unlikely that the market sector will respond with any costly facilitation.

The ideal would be that a community would have a fully representative recreational commission or council that would employ professional assistance to produce a complete and constantly updated comprehensive plan. Such a plan would be based on a full knowledge of the community as well as complementary provisions from the public, market, and private sectors.

The reality in most communities is that a narrowly based board or committee responds to those interest groups with the most political clout and the most effective voices. The allocation of resources, then, becomes a very politicized process that often takes place in private negotiations rather than public forums. For example, the placement of parks is frequently decided in response to the powerful real estate and development interests rather than to a careful assessment of population composition and locations. Not surprisingly, the larger the city, the more complex and integrated into the political machinery is the recreation resource allocation process.

Public Recreation in the Community

Just how can recreation planning in a community be implemented? Three principles offer a framework for analysis: efficiency, equity, and planning.

Efficiency

Almost all decisions to allocate resources are made in a condition of relative scarcity. Both outdoor and indoor space are scarce and expensive in most communities. Even when open fields are set aside for future parks in early stages of development, there is the cost of foregone income for developers and tax revenues for the government. There are also costs of recreational development—from simple open space that is landscaped and tended to elaborate facilities.

The initial basis for such resource allocation is that most individuals or households make only occasional use of such space and facilities. Neighborhood multiuse parks may be the most often used by household members, especially those with younger children. Sports fields tend to have heavy use in prime times, but only by schedule for each team or group. Other facilities, such as gyms, pools, auditoriums, and meeting rooms, are busy because they draw users from an entire town. It is clearly most cost-efficient to make them a kind of "commons" in which the entire community shares costs and use.

Further, in crowded cities and growing suburbs such space can be saved only when designated *before* filled with housing or commercial development.

There is also the time dimension of efficiency. Household schedules, balancing multiple roles and responsibilities, and dispersal of engagements requires some overall scheduling. Otherwise, facilities will be overcrowded for brief periods and near-empty most of the time. Efficiency requires that use be scheduled in ways that maximize use and minimize inconvenience. It is no accident that ice time for hockey teams and pool time for swim team practices may be scheduled at 6:00 in the morning or other times that only the dedicated user will manage.

Equity

The first element of equity in recreational opportunity is that of cost and income distribution. That is why management is so much easier in suburbs that effectively eliminate the poor, or even middle-income households, with their housing costs. A more diverse community, urban or rural, is likely to have a proportion of poor as well as affluent. According to the Bureau of the Census in 2002, there has been a slight increase in the percentage of poor households in the United States since 1989. The very poor, those living at half the poverty level, have also increased. In the past 30 years, the income of the top 20% has increased almost 50% while the bottom 20% has lost in real per capita income. That top 20% receives half of all income. Enormous differences in income remain in even the world's wealthiest country.

The premise of public recreation is that a full range of opportunities is good for all regardless of gender, age, income, education, or race. It may be unrealistic to equalize opportunity, but it is possible to provide some measure for an entire community. The questions are "how?" and "how much?"

There are, after all, many constraints to leisure and recreation. Cost is only one. In fact, studies of constraints to desired recreation all find that time and schedule are the most significant. Others include lack of companions at feasible times, acquiring skills, distance, safety in urban parks and playgrounds, access to organizational contexts, and social factors of acceptance. Recent studies suggest those who engage in various kinds of recreation regularly are those who manage their lives to give such activity priority—not those who lack constraints.

Nevertheless, financial cost is a prior exclusion for many with low incomes—and cost is a factor that can be dealt with by providers. One way is to have no fees and finance the resource entirely through taxation. Another is to reduce or eliminate fees for those with low incomes. In some cases, those who might feel excluded, especially children, may be recruited and supported in participating in activities, such as sports and the arts.

There are also nonfinancial ways of exclusion. As communities become more diverse in ethnic background, the kinds of activities customary for emerging cultures may be ignored by the agencies that recognize no cultural preferences and traditions other than their own. There are many social factors in exclusion that often are compounded with cost.

A principle of equity calls for programs that maximize inclusion. It may even support unequal resources for low-income neighborhoods on the assumption that those with higher incomes are able to utilize private and market provisions. A combination of equity with integration may call for strategies of inclusion that bring together participants from the entire community.

No agency policy can equalize participation. It can, however, reduce structural limitations, such as cost, schedule, and physical access, including location. Public policy based on equity can reduce the constraints that have to be managed and negotiated by potential participants. There will still be differences in personal resourcefulness as well as in motivation. Even differences in ability can be mitigated with inclusive programs of skill acquisition.

Planning

Implementing programs based on efficiency and equity requires planning. Such planning may involve current and potential users of resources as well as the public, market, and private providers. It involves a recognition that there are many groups with legitimate interests. Some are organized and represented in the political process. Others, the parents of young children for example, are not organized and remain a diffuse population who vote but seldom organize or lobby.

Numerous factors may be included in community recreation planning. Almost any valid information about both people and resources can be useful. However, in this computer age, there may also be an overload of information that impedes action. The following outline of planning elements, then, is only a beginning.

- **Geography:** Most communities are neither planned nor uniform. Rather, there are different population segments in areas that have developed, changed, and deteriorated incrementally and in waves. Open space, if any, tends to be unevenly distributed. Careful analysis is required to identify household composition by area and neighborhood along with barriers to movement. Some recreation resources need to be near residences and some convenient to transportation. The geography of a community is the beginning of planning.

- **The Life Course:** While age may not be a good index of ability or interest, there are significant changes in recreation patterns related to the life course. Households with young children, for example, have both distance constraints and particular recreation patterns. Both entire communities and neighborhoods change in household composition in ways significant for recreation resource allocation and placement.

- **Access:** Railways, highways, and other barriers cut off entire neighborhoods from resources. Stairways and interior design impede access to many with mobility limitations, but physical access is only the beginning. Scheduling closes off access to many programs for those with irregular, unpredictable, or demanding work or caregiving timetables. Of course, financial cost also blocks access to many who cannot afford fees, equipment, or transportation. Lowering access barriers is one dimension of planning. It requires knowing who is in the community and where they are located.

- **Ability:** Ranges of ability exist for any activity. Many potential participants need opportunities to acquire and increase skills for satisfying engagement. Some have more acute limitations that call for adaptation of facilities, the organization of the activity, or access to the venue. When possible, the emphasis should be on enhancing ability to permit participation and on inclusion rather than segregation. For example, the wide range of abilities of older persons for almost anything suggests that age segregation is seldom useful. On the other hand, there are combinations of restricted abilities and the structure of an activity that require adaptation, and even some definitions of standards, for participation.

- **Inclusion:** Planning should be for the entire community. This means that no part of the population should be excluded, regardless of relative invisibility or lack of political clout. It also means that all resources should be part of the resource assessment, from market and private as well as public sectors. No traditions, inertia, or conflicts should be allowed to interfere with a broad and inclusive plan for any community. In such an inclusive aim, it is necessary to critically evaluate the claims of any organized interest groups as well as to identify those who are not organized or whose interests are more of need than power.

Principles and Ethics

One principle has already been offered—inclusion. As communities are changing rapidly, it is necessary to know who is there in terms of age, income, ethnicity, and other factors. Also as statistics from the last census become outdated, some new assessment may be needed especially when change is rapid.

Inclusion means more than access to the range of recreation opportunities. It also means that some adaptation may be necessary for those who do not fit the "normal" range of interests and resources. For example, more of the work force is employed weekends or evenings presenting new scheduling problems and opportunities for providers. More residents may come from other parts of the country or world with habits and traditions that do not fit the old patterns of community recreation. In many communities, the growth of youth soccer reflects such population shifts. In addition, some residents have acute limitations that prevent them from experiencing some kinds of activity unless adaptations are made.

No unnecessary barrier should close off opportunities. That is the least any public program can offer. Taking note of such barriers, especially when the numbers are small, is not a trivial or minor task for planning. Taking the next step may then require programs to increase the resourcefulness of those with limitations, whether physical, communicative, social, or financial. At the very least, there should always be the questions of "Who is left out?" and "How can exclusions be minimized?"

Underlying such planning and provisions may be a social ethic. It begins with the premise that recreation is more than a luxury; rather, it is a significant part of a full and balanced life. It is more than something to do when everything important is completed. Rather, it is important to human development, expression, and relationships. No community can provide everything for everyone. There can be, however, a social ethic that attempts to provide for the welfare of all persons in ways that are efficient, equitable, and even compassionate. Even the Preamble to the U.S. Constitution refers to the common responsibility for "life, liberty, and the pursuit of happiness." Such a concern for the public welfare excludes no one arbitrarily or by neglect. Rather, planning involves an inclusive and far-sighted view of both people and resources.

Debate: Special provisions are necessary for those otherwise excluded.

YES

- Some activity resources are simply too expensive for many who would benefit from participation. For example, equipment for some sports and arts along with specialized instruction can rule out many children and youth from even getting a start. In many communities or neighborhoods it is necessary to have some fee reduction, scholarships, or even subsidies for low-income households. That is part of what it means to be "public."

- Abilities vary widely. Youth sports need to make provision for participation by those less gifted with speed, strength, or coordination. For some, more acute disabilities require special adaptation. Just opening programs to all may not be enough. There is also a need for special opportunities and resources.

- Access always involves some restrictions, whether they are stairways, distance, costs, facilities, or the ability to read normal print. There is already too much exclusionary design and planning to tolerate any more. Some access can be revised. Some can be part of new design. In any case, access should be maximized, even if special provisions are needed.

- Competition requires that everyone have an even start. For competition to be realistic, it may be necessary to segregate and categorize by ability. We do this by age for children and older persons, but ability is really the issue. We can grade by skill level and still be socially inclusive to have real competition within ability gradations. After all, it isn't much fun to play against those either too skilled or too incompetent.

- Some recreation is therapy designed for those with special conditions in ways that are developmental as well as fun. Such therapy often requires a well-calibrated progression of challenges and ability requirements as part of the treatment program.

- Diversity means taking account of real conditions as well as of cultural preferences. Inclusion may call for special provisions rather than unconditional inclusion that actually excludes many who might benefit from the activity.

NO

- Everyone is limited by almost any measure. As there is a spectrum of abilities, there may also be a spectrum of provisions. However, any categorization of "normal" and "special" arbitrarily divides people in exclusionary and stigmatizing ways. For example, programs designated for "seniors" divide by age rather than ability and require older persons to adopt a negative definition of themselves in which old means inadequate.

- The focus should be on resourcefulness rather than *dis*ability. There are simply too many ways in which those with limitations develop their skills and adapt an activity to impose standards that rule people out of any activity.

- Any "special" programs divide the community. This is especially the case when criteria are imposed by outsiders—even professionals such as physicians or therapists. After all, one meaning of recreation is social involvement. To divide and exclude abrogates this possibility.

- "Public" means everyone. The community or other government agency uses tax revenues to include all, not to discriminate. Even different fee levels may label some participants rather than admit them on the same basis as others. There is already too much social segregation without adding to it in recreation.

- Styles of recreation do differ. People will make choices as to activities, locales, and modes of behavior. Public policy, however, should allow for such choices first rather than place people in predefined categories and groups. Inclusion means maximizing choices, not "one size fits all," and it does not mean dividing people before they choose.

- Categorization of persons always results in some stigmatization. Some are labeled inferior or at least "different." A real social ethic supports integration, not unnecessary segregation.

- Recreation is a social privilege, not a basic right. It is better to require the effort of participants rather than offer a provision that may create dependency.

Discussion Questions

1. Which sector in your community—public, market, or private—provides most of the recreation opportunities? for whom?

2. Are there "invisible" population segments in your community that tend to be underserved by recreation providers?

3. Can you identify ethnic groups that have distinctively different leisure styles?

4. Who should do recreation planning for the community?

5. What are the groups with political power in your community? How are they represented?

6. Which is the most important principle for planning recreation resources—efficiency, equity, or preservation? Why?

7. Why should recreation be provided for those who cannot afford it?

8. Give examples of necessary recreation provisions for those with acute limitations.

9. Formulate a social ethic for community recreation.

Resources

Datillo, J. (2001). *Inclusive leisure services: Responding to the rights of people with disabilities* (2nd ed.). State College, PA: Venture Publishing, Inc.

Goodale, T.L. and Witt, P. (Eds.). (1985). *Recreation and leisure: Issues in an era of change* (Rev. ed.). State College, PA: Venture Publishing, Inc.

Henderson, K.A., Bialeschki, M.D., Hemingway, J.L., Hodges, J.S., Kivel, B.D., and Sessoms, H.D. (2001). *Introduction to recreation and leisure services* (8th ed.). State College, PA: Venture Publishing, Inc.

Godbey, G. (2003). *Leisure in your life: An exploration* (6th ed.). State College, PA: Venture Publishing, Inc.

Kennedy, D.W., Austin, D., and Smith, R. (1987). *Special recreation: Opportunities for persons with disabilities*. Philadelphia, PA: Saunders.

Kelly, J.R. (Ed.). (1993). *Activity and aging: Staying involved in later life*. Thousand Oaks, CA: Sage.

Kraus, R. (1994). *Leisure in a changing America: Multicultural perspectives*. Boston, MA: Allyn and Bacon.

Chapter 22
Travel and Tourism

Worldwide, tourism may be the world's largest industry. In the United States it employs the second largest number of persons—well over five million workers. Of course, according to the travel industry, tourism includes those traveling for business as well as leisure purposes. The U.S. Travel Data Center estimates that about 23% of Americans travel overnight is for business purposes, 34% to visit family and friends, 36% for other pleasure, and 7% miscellaneous reasons. Some trips combine destinations in group travel—usually by car. Some weekend "mini-vacations" are designed to compress the travel into a limited time period. Of course, there are all kinds of day trips as well. In addition, most travel is on a budget with about 85% by car. In 1997, total global tourism expenses were estimated at $3.6 trillion with over 10% of world employment in tourism.

Why Do People Travel?

The joys of travel are not really self-evident. Traffic jams in and out of cities on weekends produce long waits in lines of carbon-monoxide emitting cars. Hours jammed into a metal tube with waits at either end make air travel somewhere between unpleasant and miserable. The common prediction in the 1960s was that the future of leisure was at home—not on the roads or in the air. Yet, all statistics on travel have demonstrated rapid increases. Why?

Some travel is just a price to pay for whatever is at the destination. The drive to the lake or seashore is not expected to be a joy. However exciting, the airport is more uncomfortable waiting than stimulation, and the thrill of air travel wears off quickly. For many trips, the purpose is the destination.

In some cases, however, "getting there is half the fun." Many driving trips are through scenic environments that are interesting and attractive. For friends and family, being together on the trip may offer a time for long-delayed communication. Just getting away from home and work routines and responsibilities may be important. Many family vacations combine one or more destinations with routes that are interesting and visits with friends and family. In most cases, the trip is more than a change. It is getting away as well as getting somewhere. The three main elements are the trip itself, the destination, and the companions. In fact some research suggests that the companions may be the most important factor in travel satisfaction.

There are many reasons for leisure travel:

• Satisfactions intrinsic to the experience—the freedom of the drive, spontaneity and a break from routines, and the different environments.

• Satisfactions in the companionship—reestablishing family coherence, uninterrupted conversations, meeting old friends and making new ones.

• Satisfactions in the destination—the wonders of water or relaxing at the sand, sun and surf, mountain vistas, and also the special destinations of the Disney World and great world cities.

• Educational satisfactions—taking children to the nation's capital or historic site, experiencing different cultures, and trips designed for learning.

• Obligations—family expectations of yearly visits, holiday gatherings, and special events.

The meanings depend on the type of trip. A driving exploration of the south of France is different from a package tour of the great European capitals. A camping trip with friends is different from a weekend in an urban hotel. Being in a different place every night or so is not the same as going to the same rental cabin in the woods every year. A cruise ship is different from rafting on a river. Leisure travel is marked, first of all, by its variety.

Styles of Travel

Travelers are different as well. In the tourism business, identifying styles of travelers is called *market segmentation*. Many studies have found that those who travel are not all alike. Not only are trips different but styles also differ as well. One study of a national sample identified six types of travelers:

• *Peace and quiet*: Middle-age people of less than average incomes who want a relaxing setting (20%)

• *Aesthetic appreciation:* Well-educated people who seek an educational experience (22%)

- *Hot winter:* Luxury and fun lovers who want to get out of the cold and onto the beach (19%)

- *Grand hotel:* Luxury vacations with service, good food, and entertainment (19%)

- *Inexpensive active:* Low-cost and active fun, meeting other younger people (9%)

- *Relatives and friends:* Family-centered vacation with shared experiences for middle-income households (12%; Burak, 1985, pp. 86–87)

The percentages may be questioned, but the styles of travel are representative. The most spectacular destinations and most-advertised tours are only one part of the entire spectrum of leisure travel. Of course, some travelers combine more than one element of style in a particular trip. In all typologies, there are common elements: (a) companions, (b) cost, and (c) lifestyle consistency. People do not become totally different when they travel. There are consistencies between what they do on vacations and the rest of their lives.

Another analytical scheme is based on such consistencies:

- *Budget travelers* (28%) are interested in travel, but always at a price. They often camp and seek educational experiences.

- *Adventurers* (24%) seek excitement and are willing to pay for it. They are younger with higher incomes. They seek challenge and like to tell of their adventures. They are the least home-oriented and traditional.

- *Homebodies* (20%) travel little and are home-centered. Older, less optimistic, and financially secure, they seldom have travel plans.

- *Vacationers* (7%) like to travel and always have plans. With lower incomes and education levels, they take conventional trips, but go a lot.

- *Moderates* (20%) like to travel, but within limits. Vacation travel is just one interest among many. Their travel is seldom related to education or sports. They are the residual category in this scheme and hard-to-define. (Perrault, Darden & Darden, 1977)

One recent change in travel patterns identified in several studies is the "mini-vacation." Rather than take only a yearly trip, more adults want multiple breaks during the year. They negotiate their schedules to have occasional long weekends in which they get away to a nearby site or fly to a special locale. Such shorter trips may comprise close to half the total leisure trips that involve some distance and being gone at least one night.

Changes in Style

Other studies suggest travelers change during a lifetime "career" of travel. Tourists may visit a new country in a group package and then return for a self-drive exploration. They may become more comfortable with making their own arrangements and going places not frequented by most tourists. Or, they may be more adventurous in their younger years and less so as they age.

The dimension of differentiation tends to be that of exploration versus security. How playful is tourism? At one extreme is the so-called "plastic bubble" in which the environment—social and physical—can be viewed from a protected position. At the other extreme is the exploration of the traveler who constantly seeks novelty and is willing to take risks. Perhaps most common is the tourist who seeks new experience, but within limits. When challenge is accompanied with too great a risk, then the desire is for a return to the security of careful arrangements.

Finally, one simple factor in tourism is so self-evident as to be often overlooked: climate. Escaping winter is central to northern Europeans fleeing to the Mediterranean coast of Spain, Canadians heading for Florida, and other sun-seeking travelers. However, there is reverse tourism as the heat or summer propels travelers north. Further, changes in the weather can drastically reduce the tourism business as when the snow fails in ski country or hurricane rains come to sunland. Climate is one major element in travel motivation.

How Is Tourism Packaged?

Tourism is business. As suggested, there is a massive and varied tourism industry. It consists of several components, all connected by computer consoles, fax transmissions, and the telephone:

- *Travel agents* handle over half of domestic air travel tickets and about 90% of international arrangements. For leisure travel, however, the travel agent is the usual supplier of information and retailer of travel packages. Vacation trips to Hawaii and the Caribbean, ski holidays in Colorado or Utah, fall foliage tours in New England, trans-Canada trains, weekend hotel packages in the cities, theater tours to New York, and hundreds of other combinations are booked in the local community through the agent. This is done on a commission basis, formerly about 5–12%. Recently airlines have changed their commission basis in ways that have squeezed the profit margins of travel agents.

- *Wholesalers* arrange the packages sold by the agents. They tend to specialize in particular destinations and regions although some offer tours and packages almost anywhere in the world. In some cases, they connect local destination businesses, such as motels and hotels, with the travel agent.

- *Tour operators* put together the combinations of travel, hotels, meals, itineraries, and all other arrangements for the packages. They buy wholesale, sell retail, and add on their management costs. They are intermediaries between the airlines, hotel chains, bus companies, and other service providers and the travel agents.

- *Hotel chains,* such as Marriott, Hilton, and Sheraton, do business in most major cities around the world. They specialize in upscale accommodations for tourists and business travelers. In recent years, they have added chains of midprice motels to reach broader markets. They have also entered the destination resort business with developments of vast complexes costing in the hundreds of millions of dollars at prime sites. Their developments usually combine beaches with golf and other sports facilities along with luxury hotels and restaurants.

- The *major airlines* also organize tour packages that begin with the travel but include all other levels of provisions. They often have hotel chain "partners" with whom they have special arrangements.

- Airlines also advertise and sell tickets on their *Web sites*. They offer discounted fares and packages in cooperation with hotel chains in an attempt to bypass the local travel agent. Even local bed-and-breakfasts advertise on Web sites so that tourists can plan their own trips on their home computers. The great change in tourism comes through the computer and fast-proliferating Web sites that offer all services—tours, tickets, accommodations, entertainment, car rentals—at prices claimed to be lower than the standard offerings of local or chain travel agents. The proportion of travel booked online has increased every year. Offerings include last-minute deals, linked discounts, customer evaluations, and Web sites of individual owners (e.g., Vacation Rentals By Owner [VRBO]). In contrast, travel agents advertise personal service, convenience, and knowledge.

- Another level of provision is in the *public sector*. Most countries and even regional destinations have their travel and tourism agencies that provide information directly to the consumer via Web sites and toll-free phone services as well as coordinate licensing, permits, land-use negotiations, and real estate deals for those who promise to bring large numbers of tourists to their regions.

Levels of Provisions

All leisure travel, of course, is not packaged. There are travelers who make their own arrangements, travel by car or train from one place to another, take their chances on finding hotels, eat at the local restaurants, find the local attractions in guidebooks, and generally mix more into the host culture. In other countries they negotiate the language, enjoy neighborhood eating places away from the tourist centers, and explore places off the beaten tourist track. In general, however, most tourism is packaged.

The different levels of provisions are found in most tourist destinations. On the Hawaiian island of Maui, there are many local hotels, motels, small businesses, eating places, and services available to those who seek them out. Most have been in place for decades and represent the older set of accommodations. Many advertise their accommodations through the wholesalers, Web sites, and tour operators as well as respond to drive-up and walk-in trade. The newest developments, however, are on a large scale. They are financed by global investment capital, designed in the head offices, and managed by specialists sent in from the international conglomerate. They tend to be on the edges of the older tourist areas so that they can control and utilize large tracts of land. Many include condominium units as well as hotel rooms. Their operations are labor-intensive with multiple services always on call. They are the growth element of the tourism developmental cycle that begins simply and expands outward to the global chains and upward in price. In 2000, simple rooms in the most luxurious Maui resort hotel were about $400 a night and deluxe suites close to $2,000 or more a night.

Again, tourism is big business. It is a large and growing industry. There remain many kinds of relatively small and local business that provide for tourists, but the trend seems to be toward consolidation. Eight-deck cruise ships, megaresorts, upscale hotels, and condominium developments command a disproportionate level of investment. The danger is saturation of mass and upscale markets leading to failures and bankruptcies. The impacts of September 11th demonstrated the fragility of tourism markets.

Electronics, however, have had an impact on tourism. On the one hand, instant communications, especially through the airline computer systems, have made reservations, ticketing, and information incredibly quick and comprehensive. Linking all levels of tourist provisions and organization has transformed the industry. On the other hand, through the Web and other media, small and local businesses are able to advertise their offerings. Travelers who want to customize their trips, stay at local "bed and breakfasts," and have the flexibility of being "unpackaged" can now make their own arrangements and construct their own itineraries.

Who Are the Tourists?

The first factor in market segmentation is, of course, income. There are, however, some interesting shifts in market segmentation—the effort to identify those most likely to travel in specified styles.

1. **Income:** The generalization is the leisure of the wealthy is distinguished by distance; they go further to engage in their leisure. For example, those with incomes in excess of $50,000 are three times as likely to travel internationally as those with incomes around $20,000. Even domestic travel is income-related, although styles of travel vary more than travel itself. Most Americans take a vacation trip most years. The differences are in cost level—from the luxury hotels and resorts to the car trip with budget motels and visits to friends and relatives. Motel chains are clearly identified as to price level with recent growth concentrated in the midprice levels. Any scheme of identifying tourist markets begins with discretionary income. Income may be seen as a resource for travel, but does not itself define interests and conditions for tourism.

2. **Age:** The demonstrated rule for travel marketing was always that the young traveled more. Most advertising was directed toward those in their 20s and 30s with the common "sun, sand, and sex" attractions. Now the tourist industry has recognized the older markets. Those whose children are out of school and who are at the peak of their incomes are a major market segment. Early retirees (i.e., the "young old") are more likely than previously to combine incomes adequate for travel with available time. They are especially sought after in the off-peak seasons when children are in school. Many destinations and tours are extending their seasons in spring and fall by courting retirees. The entry of the Baby-Boom generation into midlife and eventually retirement will focus more industry attention on this age cohort.

3. **Family life cycle:** Related to age, the family status of potential tourists is significant. Young single adults, marrying later, are a prime market segment. Young parents are more likely to stay near home and require different arrangements. Older adults free from parenting responsibilities reemerge into the travel markets, but are still constrained by

the schedule limitations of work. They do, however, often have trips in mind that they have postponed. For the industry, it may be important to reach this market before they have caregiving responsibilities for older frail parents. Current divorce rates of about 50% suggest more adults are in some period of family change and transition. Travel packages may take into account single parents traveling with children, unattached adults of any age, and those seeking to develop relationships through travel. The cruise ship business has, of course, already recognized the widow market.

4. **Education:** Education indexes both interests and styles of travel. Those with higher levels of education are more likely to travel, to seek learning experiences with new environments and cultures, and to explore. Since education is correlated with income, however, they may also be markets for higher cost tours that promise a quality experience.

5. **Time:** The "time crunch" period of the life course, when beginning work careers and families coincide, is limited for travel. The carefully arranged mini-vacation of the long weekend, usually without the children, is one possibility. Longer vacations, when they can be arranged, tend to be with children. In duel-job households, the articulation of schedules to permit a joint trip may be quite difficult. For those in the upper-income levels, time may be a more scarce resource than money. Vacations may be relatively short and scheduled full of attractions and experiences on the one hand, or escape and relaxation get-aways on the other.

Specialized Types of Travel

There is the mass market for tourism. They are the tours that go to the prime destinations and areas, include the main attractions, and are priced at competitive levels. Infrastructure of transportation, communications, accommodations, and services is highly developed. There are routines of activity with entertainment, cultural exhibitions, guided trips to special attractions, and all "the things to do." Most tourism is some variation of mass tourism with distances, privacy, luxury, and services varying by price.

There are also alternative styles of tourism including ecotourism, cultural tourism, educational tourism, and adventure tourism.

- *Ecotourism* or *green tourism* is designed to expose the traveler to the natural environments in ways that sustain those environments. It minimizes the impacts on the site and on its natural attractions. Ecotourism is a response to the mass tourism that degrades or even destroys natural environments with overcrowding. The intent is to preserve the attraction by limiting the number of visitors and their mode of entering the environment. Ecotourism is both conservation and appreciation.

- *Cultural tourism* is similar in its concern for the preservation of the environment, in this case the social rather than physical environment. It is recognized that mass tourism destroys exactly what the cultural tourist seeks—an experience with a different culture that has retained its integrity. The issue is the extent to which a culture can remain "authentic" when impacted by tourists of any style.

- *Educational tourism* is designed for learning. The resources of the site are used to provide a learning experience, sometimes with formal classes and often in some interpreted contact with the site. National parks and monuments have interpretation centers and programs. The famous Elderhostel Worldwide program combines formal and informal modes of week-long learning open only to those ages 55 and above. Other education programs are organized on-site and become part of a more traditional tourist program. Educational tourism may also be focused on children or families traveling together.

- *Adventure tourism* is exploratory. Tours are designed to go to relatively remote areas and include experiences such as whitewater rafting or mountain climbing, and exposure to more strenuous conditions. Some adventure tours are quite expensive. Other adventure travel may be self-organized and include the risk of not having everything scheduled in advance.

Mass tourism is, of course, what most travelers do most of the time. They go to the major destinations where the problems are crowding rather than primitive conditions. Mass tourism is the ships that go from one seaport to another for shopping and promote gambling and entertainment in between. It is the flight and hotel package to Las Vegas. It is the week in the mid-priced resort with golf included. It is also driving to the theme park, eating at McDonald's, and sleeping at the Day's Inn. It is important, however, to recognize that there are other styles of tourism with a variety of risk, spontaneity, and exploration.

Dean MacCannell (1976) argued tourism is a search for the authentic. The tourist really wants contact with what is real in other cultures and environments. Tourism has become a means by which modern persons attempt to understand what the world is and how it came to be. While mass tourism offers artificial attractions that draw most tourists to their entertainment, there is a deeper level to tourism. For those who move beyond the superficial, there are attempts to get into the "back regions" of life. Such tourists seek the authentic rather than the show. One issue, however, is the extent to which tourism inevitably degrades and even destroys the authentic with its "gaze." According to critics, tourism is an invasion that takes over the host culture and transforms it into a spectacle. The infusion of outside capital inevitably takes away local autonomy and places economic power in the hands of the developers and investors—the invaders.

Debate: Tourism is a fraud.

YES

- The tourist sees only the superficial—what is arranged for display. The back regions of real life are protected against intrusion. No culture can survive when the tourism invasion is total.

- The major destinations are simulations. Disney World is only the prototype of the tourism destination in which everything is fabricated for the visitor. There is nothing real there—not even in the backstage. There are only performers on the stage of the tourist site.

- Even the cultural shows are concoctions designed to emphasize those elements that appeal to the tourist and draw crowds. Since most are in competition for visitors, they stress the show and minimize the authentic. Hawaiian luaus import flashy dances from Samoa and, at least to some extent, present the Hollywood version of Hawaiian culture. Maori centers in New Zealand offer much the same show as the tourist hotels. It's all just a show with a few authentic elements submerged under the glitz.

- Tourist attractions have to be packaged. They are repetitive so they can appeal to the mass tourists over and over, every day and every season. They are standardized so they can be promoted and sold.

- Tourism offers a variety of styles of entertainment at a variety of prices. If the tourist wants to avoid what everyone will see, there is another package that offers the more exotic at a higher price. Some would argue that ecotourism or adventure tourism is just another upscale package at a higher price. The market will provide for any style for which there is an adequate paying clientele.

- Tourism requires a salable commodity. There is no profit in aimless wandering, and not much in self-organized exploration. There has to be enough standardization so that the product can be advertised and sold to an identified target market. The very nature of tourism as an industry destroys the authentic and manufactures the fraudulent.

- After all, most people travel in order to shop. The entire enterprise is a purchasing experience. The aim is to return with symbolic possessions that signify the experience. Travel packages are shopped for like cars and clothes. The outcome is not to experience the novel, but to bring back symbols that one has been to recognized destinations. There are even indigenous industries fabricating "authentic" artifacts for tourists.

- MacCannell may have described a few travelers searching for authenticity. There are some who leave their itineraries open, visit old factories and mines, and stay with real hosts. The industry, however, while accommodating such exceptions, generally makes up a product to sell—a simulated experience that has only the most tenuous connection with real life.

NO

- There are different styles of tourism. The idea of market segmentation is that everyone doesn't seek the same experience. MacCannell argued there are cycles for tourists who may come to see past the fake and strive to experience the authentic. They may not be the majority, but they demonstrate that all tourism is not fraudulent.

- There are many attempts at authenticity. Of course, past cultures and architectures may require some reconstruction. However, Colonial Williamsburg and the outdoor folk museum in Oslo represent hundreds of attempts to provide something more than a show. In addition, they attract their share of visitors who are not satisfied with what is purely sham. Disney is only one style of tourist destination, not the entire spectrum.

- Many travelers return to areas they have first visited on packaged tours to do more exploration on their own schedules and itineraries. Even the major-package tour providers offer self-drive and on-your-own tours for such repeat visitors. The package tour may be a survey that leads to the unpackaged trip.

- One of the growth areas in tourism is exploration tours that take people to the less-visited and impacted destinations. Many experienced travelers are simply not satisfied with the ordinary treks from one crowded site to another. In fact, some upscale tourists have demonstrated a willingness to pay premium prices to get away from the typical tour.

- Tourism is what the tourist makes it. If tourists want a "plastic bubble" and routinized packages, they are surely available. However, if they want the novel, exploration, the authentic, and even risk, that can be found, too. It may take a lot more effort to get to and into sites that are not drowned by mass tourists, but it is a big world. There are tourists who seek the authentic.

The Costs of Tourism

Throughout the world, nations are seeking to increase tourism. They fund agencies to develop tourism by exploiting their natural and cultural resources as attractions. They court multinational corporations and offer incentives for them to locate their resorts and hotels in their cities and countrysides. Their presumption is that tourism is one way of improving their economies and especially of gaining "hard" or convertible currencies. In the global economy, some national economies are considered "developed" or central. They have the power to control markets and provide investment capital. With higher incomes, they are the major consumer markets. There are also national economies rapidly improving their positions. These middle economies have some manufacturing and capital. They are gaining economic power by working in conjunction with the central powers. Finally, on the economic fringes are the developing economies with low incomes, little capital, and manufacturing limited to contract work at very low wages under the control of global corporations from the central economies.

Tourism development is everywhere—in New York and London as well as in the most remote African plain. It is especially desired, however, in fringe, developing areas that have so few ways of gaining income in dollars, yen, or euros. Tourism is presumed to provide income, jobs, and an undergirding of social and economic development. Further, third-world tourism is based on resources the country already has. Here are some examples:

- In Kenya there are treks to backcountry villages to see the ancient cultures as well as the wildlife.

- In Botswana there are luxury safaris to see wildlife in their natural habitats.

- In Central America the forests and rivers are sites for ecotourism that promises to make little impact on the environment in contrast with large coastal seashore resorts.

- In all sorts of remote areas, tour operators offer walk-in low-impact hikes to natural attractions and even in-home stays in unspoiled villages.

These are in contrast with the usual tourism developments that change every aspect of the host culture and environment. The examples of high-impact tourist development seem endless:

- In the Algarve coast of Portugal the hotel and condominium developments have taken over the seashore blocking off access to local residents. All the problems of crowding—such as traffic, waste disposal, crime, air and water pollution—now exist in this once lovely coastal area with small villages.

- The Algarve is only one example of what has occurred almost everywhere mass tourism has come to attractive areas. The impacts of crowding are accentuated along the prime attraction of water where every development is on or near the shore. Sun and sand produce high-rise hotels and condos, streets lined with shops and services, traffic jams, and the sanitary pollution of the very resources that have drawn the development.

- As a consequence, local residents are pushed out of their traditional locations by real estate costs, taxes, and their own low wages. Some may secure tourism-related jobs, but those jobs tend to be at low wages. The common pattern is for maintenance workers in tourist areas to be bussed in and out so they will do their jobs but not be in the way. As a consequence, they lose access to the environments that made the areas high in quality of life even when low in incomes.

What about the economic benefits? Some local businesses develop to serve tourists and provide quite adequate incomes for local entrepreneurs. There are also jobs for many local people, even though they tend to be quite menial, low wage, and insecure. Overall, areas with subsistence economies are brought into the global economy through tourism.

The benefits to the national economy are both substantial and limited. They are substantial insofar as construction provides jobs (at least until the area is filled) and that hard currency is spent locally. The economic benefit is limited, however, because the investment capital usually comes from outside. The businesses are managed by outsiders with the prime goal of any capitalist enterprise—to provide a return on the investment. The profits, therefore, tend to leave the host economy. Wages are kept low to maximize profits.

Tourism developers point to other benefits of their work. Airports, roads, sewage plants, health services, and other "improvements" come with development. Of course, they tend to benefit the tourist first and may be too expensive for local use. In the meantime, the culture is all but destroyed by the influx of tourists and their money. The beaches, forests, and other natural areas become packed with visitors and are often legally closed to locals. As on the barrier islands of South Carolina and Georgia, local residents may be actually pushed off the islands that have been their homes for generations. Now they just come in buses to clean up after the tourists.

Many host areas, especially those with democratic governments, are reacting to such impacts and losses. As in Hawaii, there are many efforts to limit development and require plans that minimize environmental losses. Crowds of tourists, however, have their inevitable impacts. While corporations that are more far-sighted now plan for the preservation of those elements of the environment that draw tourists—natural or cultural—they still have as their aim to build, fill the rooms, and sell the packages at ever-increasing prices. High-rise hotels, however landscaped and placed, bring crowds of people with all their impacts on the environment and culture. Impacts seem inevitable. How can tourists, even in small groups that do not stay overnight, not effect the lives of those in a remote Kenyan village preserved for the "cultural tourists" who want to see "authentic" life?

There is also the "other side" of tourism. In Bangkok, Thailand, there is the notorious sex tourism industry in which young girls are purchased from rural villages to meet the sexual appetites of visitors from "developed" countries. At most major airports in all countries, brochures advertise "escort services" and other types of sex tourism. A greater variety of sex-based industries are now attempting to widen the target markets. There are also the tourist meccas based on gambling rather than any natural or cultural attractions. Cruise ships offer nonstop gambling and unload thousands into ports that have become duty-free bazaars. There are all the things that many travelers do when they get away from home that they would never inflict on their own communities. When the employment opportunities provided by tourism development include prostitution, drugs, and crime, the benefits seem mixed at best. Remember the fundamental economic condition of most people in the host areas is likely to be abject poverty, especially in fringe economies. That condition is ideal for economic and social exploitation.

The question, of course, is "Who benefits?" Capitalist development puts the investors first. Next in line are often those government officials who issue permits and cooperate with the outside developers for a tidy percentage of the profit. At the end of the line are those displaced from their traditional homes and communities.

Such global tourist development has been described as a form of "colonialism." The old empires are gone, but may have been replaced by the corporations of the "first world," developed, central, or investing economies. The power to control development remains with the outsiders who provide the capital, import the designers and managers, and retain effective management control. As long as control is external, then the major benefits will be exports from the hosts to the investors.

Debate: Tourism benefits "developing countries" economically and socially.

YES

- Jobs are created in areas where unemployment tends to be high.

- With economic development come many kinds of infrastructure improvements—roads, hospitals, sanitation, and even schools.

- Locals are exposed to different lifestyles and cultures. They learn languages that enable them to function in larger settings. Their children are more likely to be educated and to be prepared for economic opportunities.

- Most investment in the central developments may be from outside, but secondary business opportunities may be more local. Tourists require many kinds of services, some of which may be supplied by local businesses. Further, tourists returning to an area may shun the mass tourism provisions and enter the local economy and culture in search of more authentic experiences.

- Third-world tourism can be planned and designed to emphasize the ecotourism, cultural tourism, and exploration that impact the environment least and tend to benefit the local economy most.

- Tourism, ideally, is based on cooperation between the developers and the local community. International corporations are becoming more aware that they must minimize some kinds of impacts or risk destroying precisely what attracts tourists in the first place.

- Tourism is a springboard for economic development. It is a beginning, not the end. It can bring in capital, technology, communications, education, and other requisites for further economic development.

- Developing economies, initially and in the "newly industrializing economies," want tourism. It is their choice based on their perception of how they want their countries to develop. They are willing to pay certain prices to move further into the global economy. Development is, after all, a process rather than a single event. Tourism is just one part of that process. The alternative is to stay in a condition of low wages and low material standards of living.

NO

- The jobs that are created are low wage and exploitative. Managers are imported from the outside and represent the interests of the investors, not the workers.

- There is a high price to pay in economic disruption. Traditional ways of making a living (e.g., fishing) are displaced by condos and marinas. Agricultural areas are used for housing, roads, and waste disposal.

- The price in social disruption may be even greater. There is no way masses of people with high incomes and touristic lifestyles will not have great impacts on traditional ways of living. There is the allure of affluence and what money can buy. Further, in areas of poverty and high unemployment, some locals will be willing to do almost anything for a price—even violate the most basic traditions of their culture.

- The sheer numbers of tourists stress the infrastructure. Water shortages are common. Beaches are polluted by various kinds of waste. Transportation and traffic jams pollute the air. There is no way that mass tourism cannot produce stress on every local system.

- This is especially the case for the physical environment. Fragile environments in such places as rivers and streams, mountain lakes, and beaches are threatened by the number of visitors. Exactly what made the area attractive in the first place may be lost.

- There are limited economic gains. They are, however, outweighed by the environmental and social costs. It is naïve to assume higher incomes are always accompanied by a higher quality of life. Further, those economic gains may accrue to a relatively few locals who gain key positions in the overall scheme of tourist development. The losses tend to be disproportionately assigned to children, the poor, and the old.

- The aim of the capitalist system is to reward investment first. The local worker will inevitably be exploited by a system in which she or he has little or no power. Labor is a cost to be kept low. The major gains leak outside the host economy to the investment sector.

- Locals lose their own leisure resources to the greater purchasing power of the visitors. Traditional play areas such as beaches may be physically fenced off to local residents.

- Overall, the costs—environmental, cultural, and social—outweigh the limited economic gains. Tourism is, after all, a world industry organized on a scale that utilizes rather than benefits the local.

Discussion Questions

1. What are the most common styles of travel? Do you travel differently than your parents or children?

2. Describe an ordinary vacation of a family with two jobs and two children.

3. Why is exploration relatively rare in leisure travel?

4. How important is climate in tourism choices?

5. Is there really a search for the authentic in travel or does Disney represent what most people want?

6. Choose a destination area and analyze how mass tourism has changed it.

7. Are alternative styles of tourism the major potential for market growth in tourism? Are many mass markets such as cruise ships saturated and about to fail? Why?

References and Resources

Burak, P. (1985). Designing products for the leisure travel market. In R.C. Mill and A. Morrison, *The tourism system: An introductory text* (pp. 86–87). Englewood Cliffs, NJ: Prentice Hall.

Cohen, E. (1988). Authenticity and commodification in tourism. *Annals of Tourism Research, 15*, 371–386.

Krippendorf, J. (1987). *The holiday makers: Understanding the impact of leisure and travel* (Vera Andrassy, Trans.). London, UK: Heinemann.

Lundberg, D. (1985). *International travel and tourism*. New York, NY: John Wiley.

MacCannell, D. (1976). *The tourist: A new theory of the leisure class*. New York, NY: Schocken Books.

McIntosh, R. and Goeldner, C. (1986). *Tourism: Principles, practices, and philosophies* (5th ed.). New York, NY: John Wiley.

Mill, R. and Morrison, A. (1985). *The tourism system: An introductory text*. Englewood Cliffs, NJ: Prentice Hall.

Pearce, P. (1982). *The social psychology of tourist behavior*. New York, NY: Pergamon Press.

Perrault, W.D., Darden, D., and Darden, W. (1977). A psychological classification of vacation lifestyles. *Journal of Leisure Research, 9*, 208–224.

Wyllie, R. (2000). *Tourism and society: A guide to problems and issues*. State College, PA: Venture Publishing, Inc.

Chapter 23
The Market Sector

When asked about our recreation, one quick response is based on a list of activities such as softball, golf, picnics, and perhaps taking walks. Such an image also turns our attention to public spaces and public provisions. The larger picture, however, requires us to refocus on market sector provisions. In fact, 97% of estimated spending on recreation in the United States is in the market sector and 3% in the public sector. When we turn to examining leisure and the market, we are dealing with most of leisure.

There are two foci in market sector leisure. The first is the everyday. The market sector provides television, popular culture, most of what we read, and most entertainment. Even sport is primarily a market phenomenon for adults who generally watch rather than play. The second focus is the special. Of course, there is the vast enterprise of tourism as outlined in the previous chapter. Vacation travel is the special punctuation of the ordinary round of life. There are also the special events of attending concerts, pop culture or high culture, movies in theaters, weekend getaways, going to the "big game," and days at the theme park or the riverboat casino. The market sector is present on every level of leisure at all ages and in all locales. Even the National Parks have franchised businesses that provide food, lodging, and trips down the river and into the backcountry. Business is everywhere.

This is no accident. As discussed in Chapter 12 on the politics of leisure, the implicit policy of many countries with capitalist economies is to assign every possible leisure provision to business. The public sector only does what business cannot do or cannot do well. As a consequence, the market sector has grown much more rapidly than the public sector in recreation.

What Is the Market Sector?

That 97% is too vast and varied to even begin to list every kind of leisure provision. However, some questions will suggest the complexity of the market sector:

- How would we travel to visit friends or some special environment without the support services for the car, eating, lodging, equipment, and onsite opportunities?

- How would public and school recreation programs continue without the equipment and supplies produced and distributed by recreation businesses?

- Where would students gather if all the commercial places offering food, drink, and entertainment were closed?

- How would we fill most evenings if all the in-home entertainment of television, music, and reading were taken from us?

- How would we plan next year's vacation or remember last year's if there were no travel brochures, guides, agents, or the marvels of modern photography and videos?

- How would we plan a special evening if all the restaurants, bars, night clubs, theaters, traveling shows, and other places of entertainment were shut down? And what if they were open but were unable to advertise through the various media?

- How do many residential developments utilize recreation facilities—exercise and meeting rooms, pools, tennis courts, and even golf courses—to attract buyers?

- What are the destination attractions with the greatest draw, both nationally and internationally? Are there not far more visitors to Disney World and Las Vegas than to the Grand Canyon or Yellowstone Park?

- Why are shopping malls developing entertainment spaces and special programs to attract potential buyers through their leisure attraction?

- How many new community facilities for sport and exercise are financed by private investment, even when they are located on public land?

- How would we get into the forest and onto the water without commercial services that in some cases have the only permits allowing for entry, fishing, or diving?

Just examine the routines and events of daily life. Our lives have some elements of recreation-related business woven through the timetables and locales of who we are and what we do. Note the proliferation of coffee shops in which people meet, drink, snack, and even read. Note the sport and leisure styling of what many people are wearing to the supermarket and the school. Note the common conversation over the hot television series the day after its showing or before the major sport event. Note all the daydreaming and planning that focus on leisure possibilities and locales. Note the tabloids and magazines in prime checkout space that feature celebrities of the entertainment and sports industries. Market-sector leisure is so much a part of our everyday life that we take it for granted.

Businesses are direct and indirect suppliers of much of our common culture. They include the manufacturers, wholesalers, and retailers of recreation equipment and apparel. They offer campsites for rent, swimming pools and sports clubs for daily fees and memberships, resorts at which to stay, contests to watch, systems for gambling, concerts to attend, and all sorts of attractions to visit. They bring the circus to town, operate the cruise ships, open the racetracks, run the bowling alleys, and plan the floor shows. They build marinas, organize tours, and offer a week at a ranch, farm, health spa, or in a jungle treetop. They guide and teach all kinds of skills to all ages. They rent the raft and provide the guide and then bus clients back to the starting point. They are all the operators of boutiques lining the streets of ski resorts selling ski togs and original art. They are the schools—onsite and in the community—where adults and children learn to dance, paint, scuba, sail, fly, and play tennis. They also offer for a price all kinds of prohibited chemical substances, sexual experiences, and ways to exploit the weak and the destitute. They are businesses, large and small, global and local, that deal directly with the customer.

Indirect suppliers are a step removed from our experience, but no less important. They advertise the products, edit trade periodicals, and provide capital for new and expanding businesses. They develop sites, such as malls, where retailers operate. They are the global conglomerates that dominate international travel and tourism—Hilton and Sheraton, United and KLM airlines. They are all the business services on the highways leading to the national park. They repair the television, string the racquets, and customize the car. They provide dirt tracks for motocross and stadiums for stock car racing. They are the mob-controlled enterprises that run illegal numbers and gambling and get the drugs imported from other continents. They are all the businesses that exist because leisure is a major part of the lives of all kinds of people.

They are the mom-and-pop grocery near the state park and the vast Disney corporation with its world network of theme parks, television networks, and studios producing the television shows and motion pictures. Over ten million jobs are provided by businesses directly in legal recreation enterprises. Conservative estimates of total recreation spending in the United States run over $500 billion a year. And that does not include the proportion of homes and cars devoted to leisure. In 1993, the Office of Management and Budget calculated that the federal government spent only 0.17 of 1% of its budget directly on recreation resources. Market-sector leisure is very big business indeed.

Why Invest in Leisure?

Why has leisure become such big business? The basic answer is simple: because investors believe the possibilities of profit are higher than for alternative investment. The conventional economic wisdom is there is no limit to the market for pleasure. A drive through any major shopping area demonstrates how many retailers are competing for the demand for appliances, clothing, cars, furniture, and office equipment. In exploring retailing opportunities, any entrepreneur seeks a "niche" market in which there is demonstrated demand and little or no competition. It is such niches that are identified as the basis for businesses offering pet supplies, art equipment, sailing gear, or bus tours arranged for retired persons (mostly widows). A leisure-based niche is based on specific demand targets, not mass markets.

Scales of Business Operations

In many cases, such markets are specific to a particular locale. The Minnesota Boundary Waters Wilderness entry points are dotted with guide and canoe supply services. Ski areas have not only major retailers but also little shops giving immediate attention to equipment repairs. Intersections of highways and rivers have boat rental businesses. At both destination areas and sending communities, businesses provide instruction in all sorts of activities. Scuba diving is taught in local pools, golf on indoor and outdoor ranges, and rock climbing on indoor artificial walls. These businesses illustrate one end of the size scale. There are hundreds of thousands of small local businesses based on participation in specific recreation activities. A viable business can be as specific as repairing Harley motorcycles or teaching and supplying hang-gliding, a sport involving far less than one-half of 1% of the adult population.

There is a trend toward consolidation, however, whenever the business is capital intensive. For example, sightseeing flights, usually in helicopters, are proliferating at tourist destination areas with scenic features that cannot be easily reached by car. The cost of purchasing or leasing a set of helicopters, maintaining them, employing pilots, financing a base for operations, licensing, insurance, and advertising can quickly exceed seven figures. To operate efficiently may require a fairly large scale of investment and management. Such a scale then involves repaying a sizable debt with interest as well as paying the operating bills. The possibility of greater profit is accompanied by greater financial risk.

The other end of the scale is illustrated by the multinational conglomerates that operate across continents and oceans. Sports equipment suppliers design for regional as well as world markets, contract their manufacturing wherever they secure the lowest prices consistent with their quality control (for example, $100 basketball shoes are being made in Pacific Rim shops paying women workers a dollar or two a day), market their products worldwide, spend millions in celebrity advertising, and attempt to dominate markets. As presented in the previous chapter, the Hiltons and Marriotts now offer a range of hotels and resorts in linked chains around the world. They even differentiate price levels by employing brand names that designate luxury provisions. Again, the attempt is to control at least a major proportion of a total global market.

There is no magic about leisure-based business investment. The same principles that apply to any business enterprise apply to leisure businesses as well. It is still necessary to have adequate capitalization, management, and identified markets. Location is crucial. Product knowledge is essential. Even with the growth of franchises that provide visibility and a management and marketing format at a price, good business skills remain basic. Loving skiing is no substitute for good accounting. Leisure businesses fail at about the same rate as other business starts, at least 50% in the first 18 months (Kelly, 1985).

Special Characteristics of Recreation Businesses

There are important ways, however, in which leisure-based businesses are different. To begin with, they are based on participation in activity that is voluntary. No one has to ski, boat, run, rent a video, or listen to string quartets. In fact, for most activities, most people do not do them and never will.

This means any recreation business is competing for the discretionary dollar. There are always alternatives. The consumer can postpone the activity, switch to something else, or just not do it at all. No one has to play golf. However much one may desire a ski trip to the Rockies, nothing basic in life is threatened by skipping the trip one winter due to conflicts or poor snow conditions. In the same way, a fiberglass boat will always last one more season, last year's warm-ups will do awhile longer, and the flying trip to Hawaii can be downgraded to a drive to Missouri. The leisure business, then, must offer intrinsically attractive goods or services that promise an experience worth the time, effort, and money. In addition, the business is always in a highly competitive climate, competing with other firms offering a similar experience *and* with those offering something else that might be more fun.

Leisure businesses have other special characteristics:

- *Many are seasonal.* They may have an income only during the beach or snow season. They may find their clients going outdoors in the summer or indoors in the winter. Even those recreation businesses that do not depend on seasonal climate have demand that varies with the school/vacation year or do most of their business in holiday seasons. This means that the income to pay the bills for 12 months may have to be gained in three or six months.

- *Many serve specialized clienteles.* As suggested earlier, they have niche markets based on commitment to quite limited participation. Overall, there are very few rock-climbers, spelunkers, hang-gliders, or even surfers. Quite profitable businesses, however, in the right place may be based on such activities.

- *Quality becomes especially critical.* When any potential consumer can just not do the activity at all or not in that time and place, then the quality of the experience becomes crucial. In a market economy, people will not consistently pay for anything that they consider to be a poor value or, in the case of recreation, not worth the time. There are always other things to do in leisure—Anyone can just stay home and turn on the television.

- Most of the market is composed of a minority of participants. In marketing there is what is called the *"80-20 rule."* This rule proposes 80% of the market for most goods and services is made up of only 20% of the relevant consumers. In recreation, this means that in any activity, only a minority do it a lot. Some analysis finds that about 20–25% of those who do any recreation activity at all do it regularly. Most tennis racquets and golf clubs are in closets most of the time. The 80-20 rule has several implications. One is most consumers tend to be knowledgeable about the activity and needed equipment. Another is that competition for that 20% of committed participants tends to be keen. They know about specialty shops, mail-order suppliers, and exchange possibilities. It also means that figures of the number of skiers, sailboaters, waterskiers, or any other recreation participants are four to five times higher than the real market size.

- One issue is related to participation trends. Too often new businesses are begun based on the identification of some participation "boom" publicized in the media. The suggestion is that the growth potential of the activity is unlimited. Again, in marketing there is another rule, that of the "product life cycle." It states that any product has a cycle of introduction, market growth, peak, decline, and plateau. Some products are fads that rise and fall quickly. Others maintain demand levels that are consistent over long periods of time. Recreation activities have a similar "activity life cycle." For example, racquetball, once heralded as the great new indoor racquet sport, peaked and receded to a modest level. All kinds of facilities based solely on the one sport went bankrupt due to the limited appeal to broad markets. No activity has unlimited growth. Some have long periods of growth and modest declines. Others come and go dramatically. One factor is the quality of the experience. Another is how well the activity fits into overall lifestyles, patterns, and investments. Planners or investors must recognize the promoters of new activities are typically wrong in their optimistic projections.

In Chapter 11, the analysis of market economies introduced the problem of investment bias. The purpose of business is to produce a return on investment capital. No matter how dedicated the business may be to clients, quality, and the community, no profit means failure. Businesses in any field have to be operated with pricing, marketing, and management that yield a return on investment commensurate with the investment risk. In leisure-based businesses, then, investment tends to flow toward provisions that promise high returns—large or affluent markets, repeat sales of the goods or services, obsolescence in style, and a relatively quick and reliable income flow. To sell a business plan to investors or lending institutions requires identification of paying markets. Market-sector leisure tends to be cost-intensive, whatever the kind of experience provided.

Commodification and Consumption

The picture of market-sector leisure certainly includes great variety in scale, activity basis, and type of experience. Some is highly participative and some largely entertainment. Some is specialized and some mass in appeal. Some consists of personal services and some mass and impersonal events. Some is constructive and even creative and some is mind-dulling entertainment or artificially stimulated states-of-consciousness.

Overall, however, the image of market leisure is cost-intensive and capital-intensive entertainment. The number one tourist destination in the world is Walt Disney World in Orlando, Florida. However successful and well-planned, it is all a simulated experience with the fake. The Magic Kingdom is based on a Main Street of retail shops surrounded by rides simulating images from Disney movies. EPCOT (the experimental prototype community of tomorrow) consists of a few American technology exhibits extolling corporate giants and cartoon representations of several international tourist destinations around a cement lagoon. The concept is one of entertainment in which the admission fees are a bare beginning of the total destination that vacuums cash or credit in its shops, restaurants, and hotels. It is a total package designed with some entertainment for everyone and the aura of quality—and yet, nothing is real or even representational. It is, indeed, its own world. It is also the ideal leisure business: capital intensive with broad markets and providing a cost-intensive and attractive experience. It is no wonder the business has been replicated in Japan and even Paris.

Perhaps the most dramatic symbol of marketed pleasure, however, is Las Vegas. Even the sight of the lighted "strip" of casino hotels as one flies or drives in is staggering. The figures are even more so. Las Vegas attracts 30 million tourists a year. New hotel complexes with their themes and image-producing fronts seem to appear yearly. In the New York–New York Hotel and Casino $400 million is invested in the complex dominated by a 529-foot replica of the Empire State Building, a 67-mile-per-hour roller coaster, and a 150-foot Statue of Liberty. In 1997 Las Vegas had 93,000 hotel rooms. In 2004, it had more than 129,000 hotel rooms with numerous new hotel, casino, and resort projects underway or projected (Las Vegas Convention and Visitor Authority, 2004). Since 1997, an upscale $1.2 billion Italian luxury hotel called Bellagio after the alpine resort town, a $500 million Paris hotel by Hilton's Bally Entertainment featuring a 50-story Eiffel Tower, and a $1.8 billion 6,000-room Venetian hotel where the Sands once stood were built (Gottdiener, Collins & Dickens, 1999).

What do people do in Las Vegas? The attempt to market it as a "family resort" did not succeed. Of course, visitors do eat, drink, go to shows, and even play golf. They go to the jai alai fronton, see Lippizaner exhibitions, go on rides, and even lounge around the pool. A relative few fly over the Grand Canyon or go to Hoover Dam. Mostly, however, they gamble. In an activity for which the skills can be acquired in an hour or less, they risk money and obtain the excitement of gambling. More floor space in the casinos is being devoted to the electronic poker slots and less to the more interactive blackjack and other tables. In Vegas, by and large, one goes to gamble alone with a machine programmed to keep a sizable percentage of its intake.

This is not to suggest that every American goes to Disney World or Las Vegas every year. Despite the growth of gambling in all sorts of unlikely places, more people still garden than gamble. Nevertheless, there is a measurable increase in such entertainment. At a time when participation in sports and the arts by adults is declining, Las Vegas is booming. Does this suggest that something is happening to American leisure?

The process is called *commodification.* The commodification of leisure is more than an increase in market-sector provisions. It is more than spending and consuming. It implies the nature of leisure experiences is more and more defined by things—buying, possessing, and displaying things from the market. There is the element of status. In a world in which most neighbors may not know how we make a living and houses and cars look pretty much alike, leisure goods offer a way of symbolizing that we have made it—as Veblen (1899/1953) analyzed, having *more* than is needed for life. There is the element of the material. Displaying things is a clear statement that requires no subtle interpretation. There is the element of identity. Toys and other symbols identify us as sailors or quarter horse breeders just as do the caps and jackets of truckers and the briefcases of lawyers. There is the element of meaning. Possessing things is available to all with discretionary income regardless of education or accomplishment.

Has leisure turned from the special experience to a commodity? Has the experience of involvement and personal investment, of social interaction and relationships at play, been replaced by owning and possessing? Has the value of the experience come to be measured by what it costs? Have we come to believe we can buy a good time or spending more will yield a better experience? Do we turn to the market more and more for our leisure?

Some have suggested the real scarcity for most people is time. Therefore, people are willing to pay more to get more of the experience in less time, often to pay others to prepare what we need. Godbey (1996) calls this phenomenon *time deepening*—a consequence of the time crunch in modern society. We trade off money for time. In opposition, others maintain most leisure spending is instrumental. We buy racquets and clubs to play the game, sound gear to listen to the music, and all-wheel-drives to get into the backcountry. A study of tournament bass fishing found that separating pride of ownership and the symbolic meanings of display from the competitive fishing experience was not easy (Yoder, 1995).

On the macro level, evidence is ambiguous. On the one hand, more money is being spent on leisure, and investments in entertainment, as in Las Vegas, are increasing. On the other hand, cost-intensive activities, such as skiing, are not increasing in participation faster than those that are relatively cost-free (Kelly, 1991). What are those two growing activities? Golf, an expensive status activity, and walking, relatively cost-free. It is likely that disentangling the material and nonmaterial, status and intrinsic meaning, or display and development, in leisure may not be possible.

Nonetheless, there clearly are symbolic display elements in leisure. Wearing the right clothing, displaying the right labels, being in style, possessing the latest implement, and so on are part of the whole experience for many. For everyone who rebels and simplifies, there are many who buy the consumption packages. Then the symbols of rebellion become a new market niche—and the market system supports this orientation. Style is an artificial way of declaring goods unacceptable. Obsolescence is a way of inducing buyers to replace things that still work. The mechanisms of the market are designed to get consumers to buy at as high a price as possible. Now the credit card makes it all so easy.

One concern is that commodification is overwhelming the "simple pleasures" of life and leisure. The glamour and glitz of consumer leisure captures our attention and resources, and turns us away from leisure that is focused on the experience—on action and interaction. Yet, having good hiking boots for getting onto the mountain trail may be purely instrumental, even when the boots are expensive. Even new golf clubs, with all their marketing hype and identification with celebrity golfers, may reduce hooks and slices and increase enjoyment. (However, don't count on it.)

Perhaps the argument turns on television. Television, that great consumer of our time, is commodity-oriented. The purpose of commercial television is to sell goods; it is a marketing tool. Programming is designed to attract selected markets. Insofar as our images come to be dominated by those of the media, then it becomes difficult not to be materialist. It is easy to become what Marcuse (1964) called "one-dimensional," focused on owning and possessing the things that give meaning to life. From an economic perspective, the growth of leisure as a segment of the economy is significant in its own right. From a cultural perspective, the development of material symbols in leisure is striking. From an individual perspective, the place of things in the meanings of our leisure is a complex issue.

Debate: We are what we buy (or she or he who lives with the most toys wins).

YES

- There is massive spending in the leisure sector of the economy, and it is growing. Including tourism, leisure is at least one of the three largest economic sectors. Further, as incomes increase, higher percentages are spent in leisure, indicating that people would like to spend even more on their pleasure. It is such leisure spending that we can display to symbolize who we are and how well we have done in this material world.

- Tourist destinations are only the most obvious type of massive leisure investment. In many communities, there are indoor sports arenas, waterslides, movie multiplexes, and other kinds of investment. Leisure has become big business on every level.

- Shopping itself is a major leisure activity. Ski resorts have more shops than ski runs. People travel the world to shop. Great new malls combine water worlds, roller coasters, and restaurants with retail stores. After all, shopping requires little skill and yields immediate feedback. It is something we can always do with multiple credit cards.

- This is a "go anywhere" culture. Much of what we do is done to see and be seen. The mall and the entertainment center relieve us from the arduous labor of skill-development and human communication. We go to be entertained.

- Television, taking up most of our unobligated time, is commodity intensive. It is a sales mechanism, in direct advertising and in its images of the "good life."

- Age and taste cultures change. Teens, for example, are socialized into a material world of fleeting symbols of belonging. It is crucial to have the latest thing, whatever it may be. Many of those things are based on leisure, not work or education. It may be hard to outgrow this learned preoccupation with the latest things.

- Competition is everywhere in the culture. One medium of competition is in symbolic display. In what we wear, show and use, we may demonstrate that we have won over the competition, whoever they may be.

- There is a mix of leisure in life. Cars are more than transportation. They are leisure displays as we crave and lease a "fun machine" that tells the world we are not ordinary. Cars are toys as well as transportation. Trips designate our social status, so we bring home items for display. The meaning is in the things we bring home.

- The nature of technology and marketing is always to produce something new. It may be better and more functional, but that is not the point. The market is there to keep consumers buying. That is its nature; and this is a market economy and a consumer culture. As with computers and home electronics, there is always something new and more powerful, whether we can use it or not.

- Things are more than things. They have meanings of taste, style, and identification. We identify who we are in the society with our things. Look at the wine industry that bases its upscale variety markets on selling to those who demonstrate their cultural superiority by learning the vocabularies of "discriminating" taste—and "taste" has little to do with the pleasure of drinking.

- Our identities are more and more leisure-based. How we present ourselves to others is signified by what we wear, where we go, what we do, and with whom we spend time. The problem is that all this is very impermanent. To keep up or improve always calls for more spending. There is always something new so there is no limit to leisure spending. There is always a bigger boat, a more stylish jacket, or a more exotic trip. She or he who can show off the most toys wins.

NO

- There may be little or no correlation between what persons spend and what they value. One study found no relationship between activities that were most valued and those that cost the most (Kelly, 1973). Rather, the activities most valued were those done with family and friends and those that required an investment in some skill.

- Ordinary leisure tends to be relatively cost-free. Walking and social interaction are not cost-intensive. Television is low cost and often low intensity. Most of the kinds of leisure emphasized in the commodification arguments are not everyday or ordinary.

- American society has an implicit policy of dependence on the market for many kinds of leisure resources. Turning to the market for equipment and services demonstrates only that the market is the supplier, not that the consumer is fixated on things.

- There is more investment capital going into leisure-based businesses because of the supply of capital. The global economy at this time needs investment opportunities and many other economic segments are saturated. The movement of investment capital tells us nothing about the motivations of consumers. Further, leisure businesses fail at least as often as others.

- One critical issue in the argument is how to classify television. It is low cost and convenient entertainment with a variety of types of programs from which to choose? Or, is television the great seller of commodities and illustrator of material lifestyles? If it is both, then is its heavy use evidence for commodification or for staying at home and not spending money? The argument against commodification tends to deemphasize the marketing nature of television and to emphasize the viewer's ability to mute the message and resist its advertising. Certainly television, in over 98% of homes, does not symbolize status since everyone has it.

- There has been some gradual increase in the proportion of the household budget devoted directly to leisure, from about 6% to close to 8% in the past 20 years. That increase, however, reflects the increase in household income more than any radical shift to leisure consumption. Leisure is still discretionary with secondary budget priority.

- Activity trends, as indicated earlier, do not indicate any great shift to cost-intensive activities. The exception may be recreational travel. In general, however, everyday leisure tends to be accessible and low cost.

- Most of the evidence for the increase in leisure consumption is at the production level. Consumption, however, is at the household and individual level. There is little evidence that household budgets have changed radically in the last decade or so.

- Much leisure spending is instrumental. Wine is still consumed because it enhances a good meal. New skis improve the experience and new boots are safer. New sailboards improve control. The purpose is the experience, not the possession. In leisure, we may show off skill more than implements. In fact, many of those engaged in environment-based activity resist style and choose to stay with old-fashioned equipment that increases the challenge. Rock-climbers, for example, may refuse to use equipment that cannot be removed from the rock face even though it makes climbing easier.

- While it seems true that taste is used to differentiate social groups, even then the consumption is instrumental. The aim is not possession, but identification. There may well be social status elements in support of the arts. Status, however, is not a thing to be possessed, but a social attribute to be displayed. For teens, the very fact that tastes change so quickly suggests their instrumental nature.

- There surely is a lot of marketing going on in relation to leisure. There is so much that often the intended targets just tune out. For much advertising, we cannot even remember the brand being promoted. The fact that advertising is so incessant and repeated is evidence it is not all that effective.

- Leisure travel is increasing. More cruise ships are on the way. Yet, tourism is occasional—not a part of the daily and weekly experience. Further, the national parks are crowded, too. Recall the "activity life cycle." Some cruise lines will oversupply and go bankrupt. Even the most intense advertising can create only so much demand. Demand is not insatiable and markets are not unlimited.

- How do we really define ourselves? Who are we? In this society of high consumption levels, who we are may still be defined more by what we do and how we relate to other people than by things. Toys are certainly there. Their existence, however, does not prove that we measure our lives by them.

Discussion Questions

1. What kinds of leisure activities are relatively costly and which are low cost? Which are most important to us?

2. How often have you turned to market-sector leisure provisions in the past week?

3. In what kind of leisure business would you invest? Why?

4. Are market providers and public-sector providers in competition for markets? Or are their offerings largely complementary? Give example of conflict and complementarity.

5. How can recreation businesses cope with the special conditions of seasonality, "80-20" participation patterns, and the activity life cycle?

6. If the market supplies most leisure resources, what does this imply for public program priorities?

7. Are most leisure purchases instrumental? Give examples.

8. Do some people define themselves by their toys? How and why?

9. Where do we get our visions of the "good life?"

10. Does spending more money produce a better experience? Why or why not?

References and Resources

Bauman. Z. (1997). *Postmodernity and its discontents*. New York, NY: New York University Press.

Butsch, R. (1990). *For fun and profit: The transformation of leisure into consumption*. Philadelphia, PA: Temple University Press.

Ellis, T. and Norton, R. (1988). *Commercial recreation*. St. Louis, MO: Times Mirror/Mosby.

Godbey, G. (1996). *Leisure in your life: An exploration* (4th ed.). State College, PA: Venture Publishing, Inc.

Gottdiener, M., Collins, C., and Dickens, D. (1999). *Las Vegas: The social production of an all-American city*. Malden, MA: Blackwell.

Las Vegas Convention and Visitors Authority. (2004). Welcome to Las Vegas. Retrieved July 7, 2004, from http://www.lvcva.com

Kelly, J.R. (1991). Commodification and consciousness: An initial study. *Leisure Studies, 10*, 7–18.

Kelly, J.R. (1985). *Recreation business*. New York, NY: MacMillan.

Kelly, J.R. (1973). Three measures of leisure activity. *Journal of Leisure Research, 5*, 56–65.

Kelly, J.R. and Godbey, G. (1993). *The sociology of leisure*. State College, PA: Venture Publishing, Inc.

Kuttner, R. (1998). *Everything for sale: The virtues and limits of markets*. New York, NY: Alfred A. Knopf.

Marcuse, H. (1964). *One-dimensional man: Studies in the ideology of advanced industrial society*. Boston, MA: Beacon Press.

Pine, B.J. and Gilmore, J. (1999). *The experience economy: Work is theatre & every business a stage*. Boston, MA: Harvard Business School Press.

Rojek, C. (1996). *Decentring leisure: Rethinking leisure theory.* Thousand Oaks, CA: Sage.

Schor, J. (1999). *The overspent American: Why we want what we don't need.* New York, NY: HarperCollins.

Veblen, T. (1953). *The theory of the leisure class.* New York, NY: MacMillan. (Original work published in 1899)

Yoder, D. (1995). *Tournament bass fishing: Commodification in a serious leisure activity.* Champaign, IL: University of Illinois. Unpublished Ph.D. thesis.

Chapter 24
The Future: Issues

How can we forecast the future? The most common method is to look at trends. This method assumes linear and evolutionary change. Of course, that doesn't always work—trends change. The product life cycle model demonstrates that markets for anything new decrease or stabilize in time. There are cycles in the economy, birth rates, and even activity participation. There are new technologies. Few are as transforming as the car or television, but many create some change even when they are incorporated into current life patterns. Most change is evolutionary rather than revolutionary, but there are exceptions. Most predictions assume revisions in a general condition of overall stability.

The world *is* changing. Sometimes the changes occurs so slowly as to be unnoticed for a time. But the world in which the current generation of 18 to 21 year olds will live will not be the same as that of their parents. Further, changes are interrelated. For example, in the world economy labor-intensive production is exported to low-wage regions creating structural unemployment. Consequent shifts to a service workforce employs more women and makes predictable careers less common. Women's employment impacts the home and childrearing as well as gender relations in the family. Time conflicts and distributions change as women become producers as well as consumers and control more economic resources. Changing gender power relations alter leisure markets and expectations and so on. All this is going on at one time, not in the linear framework of the narrative. Every real change affects everything else.

In the midst of this complex and interrelated world, what are the most significant changes? It does not require any magic to identify such changes because they are going on now. We can look into the 21st century through current social and economic change. The results of such ongoing changes are more problematic. We can, however, at least briefly raise some of the issues that will impact the future of our lives.

Issue 1: Gender and Sexuality

In these two areas, there has already been real change. The gender and sexual revolutions are not completed, but they are well in progress.

Gender

The gender revolution has a long history as women have struggled for the power to shape their own lives. Law has changed, from gaining the vote and the right to hold property to Title IX and equal access to educational and developmental resources. Economic conditions and roles have changed with most adult women, including mothers, now in the paid work force. What has not changed, of course, is that women still have primary responsibility for childrearing and often for home management as well. The amount of time given to homemaking has decreased for employed women, but there is still a time and role crunch in the years that combine parenting with employment.

There is a gradual trend for men to assume more household responsibility. This is countered, however, by the fact that almost half of marriages end in divorce with women retaining most parenting responsibilities. What is clear is many women now have greater independence and control of their lives. The problem is that social institutions are changing slowly to support these role shifts leaving many women with role overload and little increased support.

The Future: What is most likely in the 21st century? Will there be a backlash with many women resenting the scarcity of resources and increase of role requirements? Many males would join in an effort to regain their previous power and authority. Will there be a reconstitution of roles and resources that enables women to construct a balance between family and work opportunities and responsibilities? This would require developing new support systems as well as redefining gender roles. Or, will the movement toward independence and self-determination continue with women gaining equal power and resources? This would require that the present differences in income (women still have income levels less than 70% of men) and opportunity disappear.

Leisure: Some implications for leisure are clear. Women will be recognized as major markets for leisure with opportunities moving from male-dominance to near equality. This means more than opening previously male opportunities to females. It means that from childhood on there will be a transformation of leisure as females determine for themselves what leisure can mean for their lives.

Sexuality

In terms of behavior, the sexual revolution that began in the 1890s is the most comprehensive and complete of all social changes. The restrictions on sexual behavior that were enforced by law and custom a century ago are gone. Now sexuality is more often dealt with openly in all sectors of the society. We know ourselves and others to be sexual beings. Behavior has been impacted by technology with contraception severing the necessary connection between intercourse and conception. Sexual activity is no longer confined to courtship and marriage, much less to reproduction. Further, recognition of diversity in sexual orientation has further opened the society in law and custom to a variety of actions and relationships. Courts are striking down old laws that were seldom enforced. The process of dealing with sexual diversity is moving from recognition to acceptance with the eventual possibility of inclusion. While the reemergence of sexually transmitted diseases, especially HIV/AIDS, has impacted behaviors, sexual openness and activity have become firmly a part of all aspects of the society.

The Future: The dangers and costs of relatively unrestricted sexual behaviors will continue to affect modes and methods of expressing sexuality. The industries that use sexuality—especially all kinds of entertainment— will be little constrained by such dangers, however. The diversity of sexual expressions will gain increased recognition and acceptance despite resistance from conservative segments of the society. There may be, on the other hand, increased education in sexuality with debates as to the costs of the use of sex simply as recreation and diversion. It is probable that many who fully accept the sexual nature of human beings will also raise again the issue of the relationship of sexual expression to intimacy, communication, sharing, and commitment. The question is the extent to which sexual activity is disconnected from the whole person or defined as one element of being human.

Leisure: There will be a more complete recognition of the sexual nature of human interaction and, therefore, of leisure. It seems unlikely those industries that exploit sexuality for profit will reduce their products and services. The male dominance of such commodification of sex and the exploitation of the female body will, however, come under attack. Will sex be more and more a media commodity with all kinds of sex for sale, or will acceptance and education change the nature of sexual expression away from exploitation and power to sharing and mutuality?

Issue 2: Class and Race

Social Class

The most evident economic trend in the United States is that the income and wealth divide between the affluent and the poor is becoming wider. Relatively, the rich are becoming richer and the poor poorer. Further, there has been a persistent 15–20% of the population who are poor, whatever the measure. It is also accurate to add another 15% who are marginal economically (i.e., never in a secure condition). The change is that the once-great "middle class" is shrinking as the service economy provides less security. On the other hand, the "new class" of the skilled, whether in technology or finance, are gaining a larger proportion of the national wealth and income. Those who are costly to replace and important to productivity are moving to levels with considerable discretionary income and power to invest for personal security. Now over 5% of households hold at least a million dollars in assets. They benefit from an economic system that rewards investment before labor and keeps wages low in many economic sectors—especially in the service sector.

On a global level, core economies provide affluence for some and relative security for most, and the peripheral economies in which most are at or near starvation levels. In the peripheral economies, cheap labor costs of a few dollars a week keep all but the elite in poverty. It is no wonder that tourists from the wealthy countries have to be protected from the poor when they visit the periphery.

The general picture in the world, then, is one of division and exploitation. The wealthy, whether the 15–20% in North America or 1–3% in poor economies, control assets, travel, and enjoy cost-intensive leisure. The middle mass has some security and provides markets for mass consumption. The poor are excluded from even the necessities of life and often from any realistic opportunity to improve their lot.

The Future: Will there be an overall rising standard of living or deeper division? In some economies, on the Pacific Rim for example, participation in the world economy has raised overall incomes and the material standard of living. Can even the poorest economies gradually employ their resources to benefit their workers? On the other hand, in capitalist economies such as the United States, the percentage of the poor has changed little for decades. The distribution of income in many less-developed economies remains grossly inequitable. In most, low-wage workers have little power to demand improvement of their conditions. They can always be replaced. After all, the exploitation of such workers benefits corporations that are usually thousands of miles away and whose main aim is to reward their investors.

Leisure: There will continue to be a focus of the leisure industries on the upscale markets, and on those for whom price is secondary in making leisure choices. Perhaps the greatest question concerns the middle masses, those who desire leisure opportunities but with limited resources. Will mass consumption simply produce more accessible mass entertainment, or will it diversify in a recognition of the variety of interests in the population? As for the excluded, are increased programs toward equity likely in a political climate in which most voters want to lower their taxes?

Race

Race may be an arbitrary social construction, but its consequences are real. There may be no defining genetic markers that clearly differentiate racial groups, but in the society customs, norms, and laws take color as a defining factor. Certainly the history of a nation with 200 years of chattel slavery has made race a real factor in its social structure. In the Southwest, some cities will have Latino majorities by 2025. Asian peoples are becoming significant proportions of the population in many areas. High school graduation and higher education rates are increasing for all groups. There is more marriage across racial lines. Nevertheless, disparities persist. Overall, African Americans experience about double the health, employment, and housing problems as European Americans. More profoundly, this remains a society that still makes presumed race a central factor in all kinds of resource allocations and social identifications. It is still a racially divided, not integrated, society.

The Future: Will the improvements in civil rights and educational opportunity in time lower racial barriers and increase economic and social integration? Or, will movements to support diversity keep racial designations central to a divided society? Is it possible for racism and discriminatory racial definitions to gradually become no more than a recognition of ethnic diversity and values? Does the future hold more diversity or integration? conflict or reconciliation? One possibility is that class divisions will continue to accentuate racial divisions. There may be greater economic and educational inclusion for those moving upward and still greater exclusion for people of color caught in the traps of urban and rural poverty.

Leisure: Will leisure be more segregated or more integrated? Racial discrimination may continue to be quietly enforced in leisure settings even when reduced in economic, political, and educational contexts. A stress on the diversity of racial and ethnic cultures may keep leisure more separated than other aspects of the society. On the other hand, it may well be leisure in forms such as sports and music that leads the society toward integration. Is it possible that in leisure cultures quality of performance may erase the divisions of race ahead of economic and social institutions?

Class and Race: In contemporary society, the effects of class and race cannot be separated. Racial designation doubles a child's chances of being poor, living in substandard and segregated housing, and attending inferior schools. The two factors together intensify the divisions of the society and limit the opportunities of the young. There are now more children living in poverty than any other age category with up to twice the percentage African American or Hispanic. The phrase "separate and unequal" continues to characterize American society.

Issue 3: The World Economy and Culture

The World Economy

There is an evident globalization of just about everything. The basis is a world economy in which the former national boundaries have largely disappeared. Global corporations are the foundation for financing business enterprise around the world. Investment markets are closely interrelated. The same corporations market their goods everywhere so that brand names are now worldwide. Technologies and the development of technologies have few national barriers. Banking and communication have become electronically global. In addition, the multinational corporations move their labor-intensive production to wherever costs are lowest and automate the rest. There is a clear centralization of corporate power in the control of capital throughout the world. This control makes it more difficult to develop viable industry in peripheral economies. Participation in the global economy on the terms of the corporate powers may mean the sacrifice of resources and environments in the loss of forests and fossil fuels, and the pollution of water and air—even the endangered health of people becomes a cost of economic growth.

The Future: There seems to be no alternative to such globalized economies. The control of capital permits no insurgent development. North America, Europe, and the Pacific Rim are integrated into an economic system that largely controls the remainder of world economic activity. The issue is whether the rest of the world will, in time, be included or exploited. Or, is a period of exploitation of labor and resources a prerequisite to later inclusion?

Leisure: Global corporations are increasingly controlling the massive tourist industry as well as the culture industries. Airlines, hotel and resort chains, motion pictures, television, and communications are financed and managed by multifaceted corporate giants. Where is there a real opportunity for the local, small, indigenous, and innovative enterprise and production? Anything that attracts a market will just be bought out by the multinationals and incorporated into the system.

Culture

Economic globalization is the base for cultural globalization. Throughout the world, American movies, television programs, music, magazines, and even language are featured in every city. Even the resistance from those who fear the loss of their own culture demonstrates the power of the cultural imperialists. Overseas markets are now a major factor for the marketing and profit structure of every movie, CD, video, and television series. Further, below-cost pricing makes local competition difficult. Again, anything that attracts a market from other sources is just bought up by the major producers.

The Future: Ethnic cultures, including many with a religious base, are resisting such cultural globalization. There is conflict between the global culture and ethnic persistence in many parts of the world. Some such conflicts have produced warfare and even attempts to exterminate other peoples. Nevertheless, the overall trend seems to be toward economic and cultural interdependence. Local businesses distribute more and more products of the world economy. Will there in time come to be some balance between local cultures and their products and the mass markets of the global corporations? In outright conflict, it is clear who has the power. Can a world economy support a cultural diversity of mutual enrichment or will mass culture and mass consumption be overwhelming?

Leisure: International tourism is clearly becoming a world industry with centralized financing and management, and integrated travel, lodging and entertainment sectors. Local ethnicity is becoming packaged for the tourist gaze—whatever the economic level. Consumption of Western culture products is becoming dominate in urban cultures throughout the world. Is there the possibility of resistance, however, as places become more alike? Will there be a revival of local and ethnic cultures to sustain societies? Will tourists become bored with homogenized cultures and artificial show-cultures, and fuel a market for what is authentic, different, and truly ethnic?

Issue 4: Technology

There are many new technologies of leisure. Most evident are consumer electronics with their vast varieties of home entertainment and worldwide communication as digital supersedes analog. While there may still be three times as many homes with televisions as with computers, the union of the two in innovative forms of entertainment and communication is offering more possibilities each year. Computers continue to become more powerful and less costly. The second set of leisure technologies, developing more slowly but still significant, is related to travel. Both short- and long-distance travel is becoming more comfortable, efficient, and affordable. Leisure itself is becoming more global in what is brought into the home daily and for occasional trips to other resources. In general, the trend is for the costs of every technology to fall as the markets widen and improvements make older innovations cheaper.

Most new technologies do not transform patterns of use and behavior. Like videos, they are incorporated into the use of the basic technology—in this particular case television. Other new home electronics may enhance or enlarge what is available as has cable and satellite feeds. Fiber-optic connections promise to add more options and control to what is still an entertainment medium. Computer connections may increase communication options without transforming the nature of the relationships for most. The medium is increasing and diversifying forms of communication and information, but threatens to become one more form of marketing.

Few technologies change basic conditions or orientations of life. In leisure, for example, there remains the core of accessible and low-cost activities—especially informal socializing, watching television, reading, and other daily activities. Such activities persist throughout the life course. No new set of computer games is likely to significantly disrupt those day-to-day patterns except for a few who are already into games. The technologies most likely to be widely adopted are those that fit into and improve what people are already doing. They support and enhance continuity rather than produce dramatic change.

In the larger context of life, technologies are having significant effects. For example, the application of the computer to production through automation has been one factor in structural unemployment that decreased work opportunities in production industries. The computer has also reduced the skills required for most office work and retailing. Computer networks are also transforming the retail economy from one of cash to electronic transfers made by employees with only a few hours training. All this has created an employment structure with most jobs in the services—few of them requiring skills that are costly to acquire, and with a consequent loss of job security and ladders of advancement.

The Future: Some technological developments are predictable extensions of current trends. They include further interconnection through fiber optics, all kinds of financial exchange, communication, records, marketing, and entertainment. One issue is whether life will become less social with less face-to-face exchange, communication, and sharing. Some technologies are so costly that they may be limited to those in the top 15% of incomes and wealth. Others will find adequate markets only in the core economies and even in their cities. What does seem inevitable is that technological developments will be driven by their market potential as investment constantly seeks possibilities for profit. What kinds of technologies will create a demand and command significant markets? Will they increasingly offer production efficiencies and turn more workers to services, consumption, and even entertainment?

Leisure: There will, of course, continue to be new leisure technologies. Most of them will be incorporated into present uses or will attract only limited markets. One possibility is that there will be more diversity in leisure. An expanding industry will offer a wider variety of instruments for activity and for entertainment. The question is "For whom?" Will the markets be divided by cost with high-price resources for the affluent and mass entertainment for the masses? Will they be divided by choice as more individuals choose a lifestyle consistent with who they are and want to be? Will there be technologies that challenge skills and personal development or primarily ones that just increase the possibilities of consumption? Will leisure become more diverse or more standardized?

Issue 5: Urbanization and Suburbanization

The trends in population location have been clear. Cities have grown incrementally at the edges to produce the megalopolis with its rings of suburbs. Despite some renewal in the cities, most growth has been in suburbs that merged to form linked metropolitan regions. Unlike Europe, in the United States the detached home with a yard has remained the standard despite its inefficient use of land and high transportation costs. Central cities have remained the centers of culture and finance, but production, retailing, and services have dispersed with residences. Inner-city areas, especially those identified with racial minorities and poverty, have deteriorated as they have been abandoned by almost all economic opportunity and enterprise. The divisions of class and race are intensified by the geography of the city.

In the process, transportation has become less efficient and more costly in every way. The private car is required for most functions away from the residence. As a result, streets and highways are jammed and the time costs of doing almost anything increased. One response has been to do more in the home—shopping, entertainment, and even work. Attempts to develop more efficient transportation have been blocked by a commitment to the car. Even leisure involves high travel-time costs and coping with the crowding of urban destinations.

The Future: One possibility is there will be more division and decay. The affluent will buy space and privacy. The masses will cope with the crowding. The poor will be increasingly isolated from every kind of resource and opportunity. The other possibility is there will be effective reinvestment in the cities. There could be renewal for the poor as well as the wealthy. Perhaps there could be a recognition that the city and the nation can no longer afford slums with all their economic and social costs. Is there any likelihood of such a reinvestment in the current political climate? If not, what will the future metropolis be like?

Leisure: In the dispersed metropolis, there may be a development of communities of sharing and action around leisure investments. Leisure may become more the action center of small worlds of interaction. In the household, patterns of living may have a succession as people move through the conditions of developing relationships, nurturing children, and later life. The varieties of home entertainment and activities may be balanced by those that offer some social integration. If so, the metropolis will have to be redesigned to provide space for activity-based meeting as well as the multifaceted home. There will be some limit to the dispersal and spreading of the city as the metropolitan area is subdivided into residential enclaves. Such enclaves, based on leisure as well as household composition and wealth, may further divide a society in which people have little sense of commonality and larger community.

Issue 6: Aging and Family

Aging

The "graying" of America is similar to trends in other developed economies. By the year 2030, 20% of the population will be age 65 or over, almost double the 1980 percentage. This aging shift will decrease the ratio of employed workers to those out of the work force and increase the number receiving age-related health and income support. Although a greater proportion of retirees have multiple sources of income and are still consumers and taxpayers, most are heavily dependent on government programs. Further, by living longer, more older adults will receive government and private pension payments.

The other side of the picture is that older adults are healthier for longer, have higher incomes, and are generally more active than previous generations. The "active old" are recognized as important markets for all kinds of goods and services. Many continue to contribute to the society as volunteers and part-time workers. The concern with the frail elderly often fails to recognize that at any given time less than 10% of those over 65 require institutional care.

The Future: The economic issue is between dependency and productive aging. Does having a higher proportion of the population in retirement years necessarily imply costs and dependency? New images of aging are those of years of health, activity, caregiving rather than care-receiving, and economic independence. The problems are more those of social class and persistent poverty than of aging. In the new aging society, the economic and personal independence of most older adults will open new possibilities for communities as well as for markets for goods and services.

Leisure: Older adults are already targeted for many kinds of leisure, especially for off-season tourism when children are in school. Leisure providers will continue to expand their offerings for older adults who have the mental, physical, and financial resources to engage in all sorts of activities. The issue is quality of life. What kinds of leisure contribute most to the quality of life of older adults, especially the "young old" who are the majority and growing in numbers? How will the graying of America transform public and market sector leisure opportunities?

Family

The key concept is diversity. No one family form, certainly not the traditional two-parent one-income with children household, is even close to being a majority. The dissolution rate for marriages continues at about 50%. Most children experience some period of being raised by a single parent. Small families have radically reduced the childrearing and nurturing years. The post-parental period before retirement is now the longest period of the family life cycle for intact marriages. More adults are living alone. Committed residential relationships with and without children are same-sex as well as heterosexual. "Family" now connotes a variety of household compositions including single and same-sex parenting. Further, the same individuals will experience many of those forms of residence and relationship during their lives.

Other changes are that sexual expression is less confined to marriage for both women and men. The former pattern of women's dependence and male power in the family is being transformed by women's increasing economic self-support. Support of traditional norms and structures is being eroded by behaviors that seem to be changing faster than ideologies. Intimacy is developed and expressed in many contexts other than the traditional two-parent family.

The Future: Some support a reinvestment in the family in the face of high rates of divorce. Others believe sequences of relationships are more likely to characterize the emerging society. It remains true, however, that over 80% of adults marry and most have children. One possibility is that there will be an increasing variety of relationships and forms of households. Will this diversity lead to fragmentation and confusion or to greater community and even intimacy? Will there be a reemphasis on traditional forms or on sequences of relationships that are appropriate for that period in life? Is it possible to retain patterns of male dominance in today's world? Which would be better—a return to old forms and ideologies, or the development of new and more diverse kinds of relationships and nurturing contexts?

Leisure: One thing seems sure—leisure is taking an increasingly central place in relationships. The failure to be a satisfying leisure companion may be adequate grounds for divorce. The alternative may be marriages that have greater openness to other relationships in leisure and other contexts. Will leisure become a more important context for building communities and developing relationships? If so, what are the implications for marriage and the family?

Issue 7: Time

Is there a greater abundance of free time, or an increasing scarcity?

One current approach is based on research using diaries in which individuals report what they have been doing every hour or half-hour during the day. A report of trends using this method indicates people are reducing the time spent on household tasks and childcare and devoting much of the gain to watching television and sleep (Robinson & Godbey, 1997). Further, average workweeks have been reduced, dramatically from the 1860s to the 1950s and now leveling off at a little less than 40 hours per week. The finding of slightly increased discretionary time is based on averages and does not distinguish those under greater time pressures. It does take into account, however, longer periods of retirement and shorter periods of childrearing.

The second approach argues there is a greater time crunch for many Americans (Schor, 1992). Admitting the long-term trend toward shorter average workweeks, this approach focuses on those who currently experience more time pressures. They include those whose work is crucial to productivity, including research and development technicians, managers, and many in sales. Workweeks of 50-plus hours are common among such workers. Others are working two or more low-income and low-security jobs to make ends meet. Most mothers with children at home are also in the paid work force with the pressures of the "second shift." Such pressures are intensified for single parents. Reductions in household maintenance time do not fully compensate for the load of multiple roles.

Average workweeks may give some indication of structural changes. However, the more significant figures are those broken down into categories by particular work and family conditions. While one may question the seriousness of a time scarcity for those who watch television an average of 15 hours a week, there are many who have life periods of high demand. This seems to be especially the case for young adults beginning work careers and parenting at the same time.

The Future: With most workers in services such as retailing, healthcare, and household assistance, time schedules will become increasingly variable.

Many such industries operate "24-7" (i.e., 24 hours a day seven days a week). The pressures of the number of hours employed are being intensified by their variety. The productivity demands of the world economy will not lessen time pressures on many workers critical to business success. Further, multiple service sector jobs for many with lower incomes are increasing. There are many indications that time pressure will increase for some at the same time they are lessened for those who are between jobs, work part time, or retire early, voluntarily or involuntarily. Time pressure will be quite uneven. In general, institutional support for both those in conditions of time pressure or of time abundance has been slow to develop. The revolution in time is one of diversity. One problem is that the society is deceived by statistics of average workweeks and has not responded to either those in a time crunch or a time abundance. The real issue is whether that will change. The markets will respond to affluent early retirement, but what about impoverished unemployment? Service industries will respond to clients who can pay, but what about low-income single-parent workers? Is it possible to reconstruct work and family careers so that the highest pressures will not come in early adulthood and increased openness for those with long years of active retirement? Can the workload be redistributed through the life course and a more even work-leisure-family balance be developed?

Leisure: For those with an abundance of time, there is the issue of time-filling versus time-deepening. Can leisure become less devoted to boring entertainment and more to satisfying investment? For those with a scarcity of time, can leisure be more than occasional escape from pressure? There will be longer periods of retirement leisure, but what about earlier years? Can the society and economy be reorganized for flexibility through the life course? If so, what would have to change? Can more freedom be afforded those in the time-crunch periods? How could their roles and supports be reconstituted? Is there more involved than work flex-time and onsite childcare? The current trend is toward role sequences that provide periods of high and low time pressure. Is it possible to have a productive economy with work-family-leisure roles that offer a satisfying rhythm throughout life?

Issue 8: Are People Changing?

Many social changes are going on, but what about people? Are they changing as well in response to social change? This is, of course, a complex question to which there is no simple or complete answer. There are, however, a few critical issues related to life and leisure:

- *Work vs. Leisure ethics:* Are people becoming more leisure-oriented and less centered on work? What are the indications? Or, does the relative importance of work and leisure shift through the life course?

- *Personal development vs. Consumption:* With all the offerings of the market, are people becoming more oriented to what they can purchase and own? Especially for those who can afford the Mercedes and the $500-a-night luxury hotel, has material consumption become more the prime meaning of life? Or, is there evidence that more people recognize the limits of consumption and seek ways in which they can challenge and develop their own lives?

- *Individual vs. Community values:* Are people becoming more preoccupied with themselves or is there a recognition that life is to be shared? What are the indications of concentration on the self to the exclusion of others, and of relationships being evaluated only in terms of what they offer the self? Conversely, is there evidence of a renewed emphasis on life together (i.e., on relationships of commitment and communication)?

The question is whether change is all external. Of course, there are significant economic, social, and political changes. The institutions of any society evolve over time and occasionally change profoundly. Opportunities and resources may be restricted to certain segments of a society or extended more widely. Material standards of living may rise or fall. Cultures may become more inclusive or exclusive. Amid such change, do people change significantly or is "human nature" much the same from culture to culture and era to era?

The premise of education is that we do change. We may enlarge our knowledge and understanding. We may improve our ability to analyze and evaluate. We may become more fully engaged in learning and development. In our relationships, we may learn from experiences in ways that make us better able to understand others and communicate with them. Or we may close in our lives, put up defenses, and fail to develop our human potential.

The kind of society in which we live, our immediate culture, is a powerful force in our development. We are all ethnic, a part of a particular culture. In a culture and among cultures, there are different views of life and leisure. What is the "good life?" Is it free to grow, learn, and develop? Is it deeply related to others in social bonds of community? If both, which is primary? Or are both equally necessary in some balance? In this society at this time, what are we learning about the meanings of life? And, what is the contribution of leisure to this project?

Discussion Questions

1. What elements of society are changing most? Provide evidence.

2. What are the most significant ways in which your lives will be different from that of your parents?

3. How can one best be prepared for social and economic change?

4. Are there some fundamental values that do not change? If so, what are they?

5. How important will leisure be in the 21st century? to individuals? to the society?

6. How, if at all, will the work-leisure relationship change in the coming decades?

7. What is your concept of the "good life?"

References

Robinson, J. and Godbey, G. (1997). *Time for life: The surprising ways Americans use their time*. University Park, PA: Penn State Press.

Schor, J. (1992). *The overworked American: The unexpected decline of leisure*. New York, NY: Basic Books.

Index

The A•B•Cs of Behavior Change: Skills for Working With Behavior Problems in Nursing Homes
by Margaret D. Cohn, Michael A. Smyer, and Ann L. Horgas

Activity Experiences and Programming within Long-Term Care
by Ted Tedrick and Elaine R. Green

The Activity Gourmet
by Peggy Powers

Advanced Concepts for Geriatric Nursing Assistants
by Carolyn A. McDonald

Adventure Programming
edited by John C. Miles and Simon Priest

Assessment: The Cornerstone of Activity Programs
by Ruth Perschbacher

Behavior Modification in Therapeutic Recreation: An Introductory Manual
by John Datillo and William D. Murphy

Benefits of Leisure
edited by B. L. Driver, Perry J. Brown, and George L. Peterson

Benefits of Recreation Research Update
by Judy M. Sefton and W. Kerry Mummery

Beyond Baskets and Beads: Activities for Older Adults With Functional Impairments
by Mary Hart, Karen Primm, and Kathy Cranisky

Beyond Bingo: Innovative Programs for the New Senior
by Sal Arrigo, Jr., Ann Lewis, and Hank Mattimore

Beyond Bingo 2: More Innovative Programs for the New Senior
by Sal Arrigo, Jr.

Both Gains and Gaps: Feminist Perspectives on Women's Leisure
by Karla Henderson, M. Deborah Bialeschki, Susan M. Shaw, and Valeria J. Freysinger

Client Assessment in Therapeutic Recreation Services
by Norma J. Stumbo

Client Outcomes in Therapeutic Recreation Services
by Norma J. Stumbo

Conceptual Foundations for Therapeutic Recreation
edited by David R. Austin, John Dattilo, and Bryan P. McCormick

Dementia Care Programming: An Identity-Focused Approach
by Rosemary Dunne

Dimensions of Choice: A Qualitative Approach to Recreation, Parks, and Leisure Research
by Karla A. Henderson

Diversity and the Recreation Profession: Organizational Perspectives
edited by Maria T. Allison and Ingrid E. Schneider

Effective Management in Therapeutic Recreation Service
by Gerald S. O'Morrow and Marcia Jean Carter

Evaluating Leisure Services: Making Enlightened Decisions, Second Edition
by Karla A. Henderson and M. Deborah Bialeschki

Everything From A to Y: The Zest Is up to You! Older Adult Activities for Every Day of the Year
by Nancy R. Cheshire and Martha L. Kenney

The Evolution of Leisure: Historical and Philosophical Perspectives
by Thomas Goodale and Geoffrey Godbey

Experience Marketing: Strategies for the New Millennium
by Ellen L. O'Sullivan and Kathy J. Spangler

Facilitation Techniques in Therapeutic Recreation
by John Dattilo

File o' Fun: A Recreation Planner for Games & Activities, Third Edition
by Jane Harris Ericson and Diane Ruth Albright

Functional Interdisciplinary-Transdisciplinary Therapy (FITT) Manual
by Deborah M. Schott, Judy D. Burdett, Beverly J. Cook, Karren S. Ford, and Kathleen M. Orban

The Game and Play Leader's Handbook: Facilitating Fun and Positive Interaction, Revised Edition
by Bill Michaelis and John M. O'Connell

The Game Finder—A Leader's Guide to Great Activities
by Annette C. Moore

Getting People Involved in Life and Activities: Effective Motivating Techniques
by Jeanne Adams

Glossary of Recreation Therapy and Occupational Therapy
by David R. Austin

Great Special Events and Activities
by Annie Morton, Angie Prosser, and Sue Spangler

Group Games & Activity Leadership
by Kenneth J. Bulik

Other Books by Venture Publishing, Inc.

Growing With Care: Using Greenery, Gardens, and Nature With Aging and Special Populations
by Betsy Kreidler

Hands On! Children's Activities for Fairs, Festivals, and Special Events
by Karen L. Ramey

In Search of the Starfish: Creating a Caring Environment
by Mary Hart, Karen Primm, and Kathy Cranisky

Inclusion: Including People With Disabilities in Parks and Recreation Opportunities
by Lynn Anderson and Carla Brown Kress

Inclusive Leisure Services: Responding to the Rights of People with Disabilities, Second Edition
by John Dattilo

Innovations: A Recreation Therapy Approach to Restorative Programs
by Dawn R. De Vries and Julie M. Lake

Internships in Recreation and Leisure Services: A Practical Guide for Students, Third Edition
by Edward E. Seagle, Jr. and Ralph W. Smith

Interpretation of Cultural and Natural Resources, Second Edition
by Douglas M. Knudson, Ted T. Cable, and Larry Beck

Intervention Activities for At-Risk Youth
by Norma J. Stumbo

Introduction to Recreation and Leisure Services, Eighth Edition
by Karla A. Henderson, M. Deborah Bialeschki, John L. Hemingway, Jan S. Hodges, Beth D. Kivel, and H. Douglas Sessoms

Introduction to Therapeutic Recreation: U.S. and Canadian Perspectives
by Kenneth Mobily and Lisa Ostiguy

Introduction to Writing Goals and Objectives: A Manual for Recreation Therapy Students and Entry-Level Professionals
by Suzanne Melcher

Leadership and Administration of Outdoor Pursuits, Second Edition
by Phyllis Ford and James Blanchard

Leadership in Leisure Services: Making a Difference, Second Edition
by Debra J. Jordan

Leisure and Leisure Services in the 21st Century
by Geoffrey Godbey

The Leisure Diagnostic Battery: Users Manual and Sample Forms
by Peter A. Witt and Gary Ellis

Leisure Education I: A Manual of Activities and Resources, Second Edition
by Norma J. Stumbo

Leisure Education II: More Activities and Resources, Second Edition
by Norma J. Stumbo

Leisure Education III: More Goal-Oriented Activities
by Norma J. Stumbo

Leisure Education IV: Activities for Individuals with Substance Addictions
by Norma J. Stumbo

Leisure Education Program Planning: A Systematic Approach, Second Edition
by John Dattilo

Leisure Education Specific Programs
by John Dattilo

Leisure in Your Life: An Exploration, Sixth Edition
by Geoffrey Godbey

Leisure Services in Canada: An Introduction, Second Edition
by Mark S. Searle and Russell E. Brayley

Leisure Studies: Prospects for the Twenty-First Century
edited by Edgar L. Jackson and Thomas L. Burton

The Lifestory Re-Play Circle: A Manual of Activities and Techniques
by Rosilyn Wilder

The Melody Lingers On: A Complete Music Activities Program for Older Adults
by Bill Messenger

Models of Change in Municipal Parks and Recreation: A Book of Innovative Case Studies
edited by Mark E. Havitz

More Than a Game: A New Focus on Senior Activity Services
by Brenda Corbett

Nature and the Human Spirit: Toward an Expanded Land Management Ethic
edited by B. L. Driver, Daniel Dustin, Tony Baltic, Gary Elsner, and George Peterson

The Organizational Basis of Leisure Participation: A Motivational Exploration
by Robert A. Stebbins

Outdoor Recreation for 21st Century America
by H. Ken Cordell

Outdoor Recreation Management: Theory and Application, Third Edition
by Alan Jubenville and Ben Twight

Outdoor Recreation: Opportunities for Natural Resources–Based Recreation, Leisure, and Tourism
by B.L. Driver and Roger L. Moore

Planning Parks for People, Second Edition
by John Hultsman, Richard L. Cottrell, and
Wendy Z. Hultsman

*The Process of Recreation Programming
Theory and Technique, Third Edition*
by Patricia Farrell and Herberta M.
Lundegren

*Programming for Parks, Recreation, and
Leisure Services: A Servant Leadership
Approach, Second Edition*
by Debra J. Jordan, Donald G. DeGraaf,
and Kathy H. DeGraaf

Protocols for Recreation Therapy Programs
edited by Jill Kelland, along with the
Recreation Therapy Staff at Alberta
Hospital Edmonton

*Quality Management: Applications for
Therapeutic Recreation*
edited by Bob Riley

*A Recovery Workbook: The Road Back from
Substance Abuse*
by April K. Neal and Michael J. Taleff

*Recreation and Leisure: Issues in an Era of
Change, Third Edition*
edited by Thomas Goodale and Peter A. Witt

*Recreation Economic Decisions: Comparing
Benefits and Costs, Second Edition*
by John B. Loomis and Richard G. Walsh

*Recreation for Older Adults: Individual and
Group Activities*
by Judith A. Elliott and Jerold E. Elliott

*Recreation Programming and Activities for
Older Adults*
by Jerold E. Elliott and Judith A. Sorg-Elliott

*Reference Manual for Writing Rehabilitation
Therapy Treatment Plans*
by Penny Hogberg and Mary Johnson

*Research in Therapeutic Recreation: Concepts
and Methods*
edited by Marjorie J. Malkin and Christine
Z. Howe

*Simple Expressions: Creative and Therapeutic
Arts for the Elderly in Long-Term Care
Facilities*
by Vicki Parsons

A Social History of Leisure Since 1600
by Gary Cross

A Social Psychology of Leisure
by Roger C. Mannell and Douglas A. Kleiber

*Special Events and Festivals: How to Organize,
Plan, and Implement*
by Angie Prosser and Ashli Rutledge

*Steps to Successful Programming: A Student
Handbook to Accompany Programming
for Parks, Recreation, and Leisure Services*
by Donald G. DeGraaf, Debra J. Jordan, and
Kathy H. DeGraaf

*Stretch Your Mind and Body: Tai Chi as an
Adaptive Activity*
by Duane A. Crider and William R. Klinger

*Therapeutic Activity Intervention with the
Elderly: Foundations and Practices*
by Barbara A. Hawkins, Marti E. May, and
Nancy Brattain Rogers

*Therapeutic Recreation and the Nature of
Disabilities*
by Kenneth E. Mobily and Richard D.
MacNeil

*Therapeutic Recreation: Cases and Exercises,
Second Edition*
by Barbara C. Wilhite and M. Jean Keller

*Therapeutic Recreation in Health Promotion
and Rehabilitation*
by John Shank and Catherine Coyle

Therapeutic Recreation in the Nursing Home
by Linda Buettner and Shelley L. Martin

*Therapeutic Recreation Programming: Theory
and Practice*
by Charles Sylvester, Judith E. Voelkl, and
Gary D. Ellis

*Therapeutic Recreation Protocol for Treatment
of Substance Addictions*
by Rozanne W. Faulkner

*The Therapeutic Recreation Stress Management
Primer*
by Cynthia Mascott

*Tourism and Society: A Guide to Problems
and Issues*
by Robert W. Wyllie

*A Training Manual for Americans with
Disabilities Act Compliance in Parks and
Recreation Settings*
by Carol Stensrud

 Venture Publishing, Inc.
1999 Cato Avenue
State College, PA 16801
Phone: (814) 234-4561
Fax: (814) 234-1651